# Vedic
## Love Signs

Komilla Sutton is the co-founder and Chair of the British Association for Vedic Astrology and is also on the board of the American Council of Vedic Astrology. She is an internationally renowned consultant, teacher and lecturer. Indian-born, Komilla Sutton was a Bollywood actress for twelve years, during which time she developed an interest in astrology, which is now her full-time career. Since then she has pioneered making this subject more accessible for Western readers. She is the author of *Vedic Astrology*, *The Essentials of Vedic Astrology* and *Lunar Nodes – Crisis and Redemption*. She divides her time between her home in Hampshire and India.

# Vedic Love Signs

### KOMILLA SUTTON

PAN BOOKS

First published 2003 by Pan Books
an imprint of Pan Macmillan Publishers Ltd
Pan Macmillan, 20 New Wharf Road, London N1 9RR
Basingstoke and Oxford
Associated companies throughout the world
www.panmacmillan.com

ISBN 0 330 49047 8

Copyright © Komilla Sutton 2003

The right of Komilla Sutton to be identified as the
author of this work has been asserted by her in accordance
with the Copyright, Designs and Patents Act 1988.

Illustrations © Raymond Turvey

All rights reserved. No part of this publication may be
reproduced, stored in or introduced into a retrieval system, or
transmitted, in any form, or by any means (electronic, mechanical,
photocopying, recording or otherwise) without the prior written
permission of the publisher. Any person who does any unauthorized
act in relation to this publication may be liable to criminal
prosecution and civil claims for damages.

1 3 5 7 9 8 6 4 2

A CIP catalogue record for this book is available from
the British Library.

Typeset by SetSystems Ltd, Saffron Walden, Essex
Printed and bound in Great Britain by
Mackays of Chatham plc, Chatham, Kent

This book is sold subject to the condition that it shall not,
by way of trade or otherwise, be lent, re-sold, hired out,
or otherwise circulated without the publisher's prior consent
in any form of binding or cover other than that in which
it is published and without a similar condition including this
condition being imposed on the subsequent purchaser.

This book is dedicated to
Krishnan Mavila Nambiar
and Shoma Basu.

# Contents

**Acknowledgements** ix

## Part 1
## Vedic Astrology and Love

How to Use This Book 3
How to Find Your Vedic Star Sign 5
Love 8
About Vedic Astrology 10
Introduction to Vedic Relationships 23

## Part 2
## The Love Signs

Ashwini (13 April–27 April) 41
Bharani (27 April–11 May) 52
Krittika (11 May–25 May) 63
Rohini (25 May–8 June) 73
Mrigasira (8 June–21 June) 84
Ardra (21 June–5 July) 95
Punarvasu (5 July–19 July) 106
Pushya (19 July–2 August) 117

# CONTENTS

Ashlesha (2 *August–16 August*) 128

Magha (*16 August–30 August*) 139

Purva Phalguni (*30 August–13 September*) 150

Uttara Phalguni (*13 September–26 September*) 161

Hasta (*26 September–10 October*) 172

Chitra (*10 October–23 October*) 183

Swati (*23 October–6 November*) 194

Vishakha (*6 November–19 November*) 205

Anuradha (*19 November–2 December*) 216

Jyeshta (*2 December–15 December*) 227

Mula (*15 December–28 December*) 238

Purva Ashadha (*28 December–11 January*) 249

Uttara Ashadha (*11 January–24 January*) 260

Shravana (*24 January–6 February*) 271

Dhanishta (*6 February–19 February*) 282

Shatabhishak (*19 February–4 March*) 293

Purva Bhadra (*4 March–17 March*) 304

Uttara Bhadra (*17 March–31 March*) 315

Revati (*31 March–13 April*) 326

Part 3

# Compatibility Grids and Cusp Charts

Compatibility Grid 338

Sexual Compatibility Grid 340

Spiritual Compatibility Grid 342

The Cusps 345

# Acknowledgements

I'd like to thank the following for their help and support:

Ingrid Connell for being a great editor and going out of her way to make this book special. Jacqui Butler for her help, Liz Davis for caring about the details, Rafaela Romaya for the design.

Chelsey Fox for being an inspired agent. Margie Neal for her help with the manuscript. Margaret and Jim Cahill for the great beginnings.

Kanwal and Sam Panwar, Teena and Ravi Virk for their love.

My brother Kuldip without whose help and support I would not have been where I am today.

Dr Ajit Sinha for being my astrology guru.

And finally, to the embodiment of my positive karma, Nanji, my uncle M. M. Singh and my mum.

# PART 1
# VEDIC ASTROLOGY AND LOVE

# How to Use This Book

If you're new to Vedic Astrology, don't worry. This book is easy to follow and doesn't require any specialist knowledge. Because Vedic Astrology shares the same roots as Western Astrology, some aspects will already be familiar. For instance, the star signs like Leo, Capricorn, and so on, are believed to have an impact on personality and will be mentioned in passing here. But when it comes to relationships, Vedic Astrology uses twenty-seven star signs, giving unique insights that will give you a deeper understanding of love and what it means to you.

## First Find Your Vedic Star Sign . . .

All you need to know, to use this book, is your date of birth. If you turn to the chart on pages 5–7, you'll be able to see instantly which star sign you fall under. If you're born on the cusp of two signs – for example, if your birth date is 27 April you could be either Ashwini or Bharani – then turn to the tables on pages 345–88 to find your sign.

## How Relationships Work

Part 1 of this book explains what Vedic Astrology is, and how it is used to calculate compatibility in relationships. Drawing on the wisdom of ancient Hindu texts, it looks at emotional, sexual and spiritual compatibility. The impact of your ruling sign and your animal sign is explained, as is the importance of karma. You'll find

# VEDIC ASTROLOGY AND LOVE

new ways of thinking about yourself and your partner, what draws you together and what may keep you apart.

## You and Your Relationships

Part 2 is a complete and detailed compatibility guide, sign by sign. Look up your vedic star sign and you'll learn about your own personality and what you seek from relationships, your best and worst sexual partners, and some of the issues you may have to face. You'll also get a breakdown of how you relate to every other sign in the Vedic Zodiac, the strengths and weaknesses of each relationship and what can be done to heal problems.

# How to Find Your Vedic Star Sign

This book is based on the Vedic Zodiac system called the Nakshatras. For every Western star sign, there are three or four Nakshatras or Vedic star signs. Some Nakshatras overlap two star signs. For example, the Ashwini Nakshatra is from 14 to 27 April – therefore you can be Ashwini if you are born under Aries or Taurus.

## Cusps

Two nakshatras rule those days when one star sign ends and the next one starts. If you are born on one of these cusp days, go to pages 345–88 to work our your sign.

## Western Star Signs and Nakshatras

Look up your star sign in the left-hand column and read across to discover your corresponding Nakshatra.

| Western Star Sign | Vedic Nakshatra | |
|---|---|---|
| *Aries* <br> 21 March to 20 April | Uttara Bhadra <br> Revati <br> Ashwini | 21 to 31 Mar <br> 31 Mar to 13 April <br> 13 to 20 April |
| *Taurus* <br> 21 April to 21 May | Ashwini <br> Bharani <br> Krittika | 21 to 27 April <br> 27 April to 11 May <br> 11 to 21 May |

# VEDIC ASTROLOGY AND LOVE

| Western Star Sign | Vedic Nakshatra | |
|---|---|---|
| *Gemini* 22 May to 21 June | Krittika<br>Rohini<br>Mrigasira<br>Ardra | 22 to 25 May<br>25 May to 8 June<br>8 to 21 June<br>21 June |
| *Cancer* 22 June to 23 July | Ardra<br>Punarvasu<br>Pushya | 22 June to 5 July<br>5 to 19 July<br>19 to 23 July |
| *Leo* 24 July to 23 August | Pushya<br>Ashlesha<br>Magha | 24 July to 2 Aug<br>2 to 16 Aug<br>16 to 23 Aug |
| *Virgo* 24 August to 23 September | Magha<br>Purva Phalguni<br>Uttara Phalguni | 24 to 30 Aug<br>30 Aug to 13 Sep<br>13 to 23 Sep |
| *Libra* 24 September to 23 October | Uttara Phalguni<br>Hasta<br>Chitra<br>Swati | 24 to 26 Sep<br>26 Sep to 10 Oct<br>10 to 23 Oct<br>23 October |
| *Scorpio* 24 October to 22 November | Swati<br>Vishakha<br>Anuradha | 24 Oct to 6 Nov<br>6 to 19 Nov<br>19 to 22 Nov |
| *Sagittarius* 23 November to 21 December | Anuradha<br>Jyeshta<br>Mula | 23 Nov to 2 Dec<br>2 to 15 Dec<br>15 to 21 Dec |
| *Capricorn* 22 December to 20 January | Mula<br>Purva Ashadha<br>Uttara Ashadha | 22 to 28 Dec<br>28 Dec to 11 Jan<br>11 to 20 Jan |
| *Aquarius* 21 January to 19 February | Uttara Ashadha<br>Shravana<br>Dhanishta<br>Shatabhishak | 21 to 24 Jan<br>24 Jan to 6 Feb<br>6 to 19 Feb<br>19 February |

# HOW TO FIND YOUR VEDIC STAR SIGN

**Western Star Sign**

*Pisces*
20 February to 20 March

**Vedic Nakshatra**

| | |
|---|---|
| Shatabhishak | 20 Feb to 4 Mar |
| Purva Bhadra | 4 to 17 Mar |
| Uttara Bhadra | 17 to 20 Mar |

# Love

Vedic Astrology teaches that the love of a good partner is necessary for the inner soul. The rich fulfilment that two people in love get from each other is so profound, yet natural and real. Their love if properly expressed brings divine ecstasy and the true merging of two souls into one. The sexual act transcends mere physical pleasure and becomes a powerful spiritual communion. When you are in the embrace of this love, you do not identify yourself as separate personalities but are one with a higher force.

Such sublime love is hard to find. Our soul knows it is possible, so it searches everywhere. This is why we think so much about love, why poets and writers have written countless words describing this intangible emotion. The myth of true love is enduring, yet for most of us it remains elusive.

The wise sages of ancient India wanted us all to experience this sublime love, by understanding that our partner is a reflection of ourselves whom we learn to love spiritually. As long as we feel they are separate, different, we cannot make that link which allows us to experience divine ecstasy. To find true love, we need to stop and think, make the right choices, learn to love properly and make sacrifices. Vedic Astrology was the 'eye' of the Vedas, the Hindu scriptures, and it is through this ancient teaching that we can find the key to life.

## Vedic Astrology and Love

*Vedic Love Signs* uses the wisdom of Vedic Astrology to help you understand love and relationships in a way you never have before.

# LOVE

Vedic Astrology is a power that understands your soul's desires, your karmic needs, your personal blocks on the path of love. We will study the Vedic star signs, known as the Nakshatras, and the insights revealed by their secret language to discover how love works on physical, sexual, karmic and spiritual levels.

The Nakshatras are full of esoteric significance. They bring forth the enchantment, spirit and mythology that underpin the celestial energy. Understanding their language and its influence on our soul helps us to make a real connection to the cosmos and aspire to a love so heavenly that it brings us total happiness. The Nakshatras also make us aware of the restrictions that karma and destiny impose, and the struggles we all go through in our search for that perfect partner.

The Nakshatras can help to refocus the way you think about love. They help you to break your in-built patterns of behaviour and reach for happiness and contentment within relationships; to fulfil the secret desires of your soul; to learn how karma and destiny restrict you but also give you the ability to improve your life.

Your Vedic star sign gives you insight into what your soul needs from love and how you relate to the other Nakshatras. As well as focusing on your sexuality and your best sexual partner, this book will give you a deep insight into your inner struggles, what you want from love emotionally and your weaknesses as well as your strengths.

# About Vedic Astrology

## Vedic Astrology

Vedic Astrology is the traditional astrology of India. It is part of the Vedas, the ancient books of the Hindu scripture, mankind's oldest and most sophisticated body of knowledge. *Veda* means wisdom, the sacred knowledge of truth that we get from direct perception of the world and the study of the scriptures. Their origin is unknown, but they are considered to be around 5,000 years old.

The Sanskrit word for Vedic Astrology is *Jyotish*. The word *'jyoti'* has several meanings. On a practical level, it means 'a candle flame'. Symbolically, it means the light that shines down on us all from the heavens, light that gives us the ability to see through our eyes as well as insight that enables us to look deeper into the subtleties of life. The suffix 'sh' means 'best, wisest'. So in full, *Jyotish* can be translated as 'the science of light' or 'the wisdom of the heavens'. Light banishes darkness; the light of knowledge dispels ignorance.

Vedic Astrology reveals the light of our inner self and helps in our search for eternal happiness and in learning to live life to our fullest potential. One of the key areas Vedic Astrology helps is in understanding relationships. In India it is still used for choosing the perfect partners in arranged marriages. It helps us to live happily within a relationship and learn about the spiritual and material constraints that any long-term relationship has to deal with.

## Vedic and Western Astrology

The roots of Vedic and Western Astrology are the same. They both study the stars, the planets, the Sun and the Moon and their effect on human life. Over the years Western Astrology has moved in different

# ABOUT VEDIC ASTROLOGY

directions incorporating modern ideas and has lost some of its deep philosophical base. It has focused more on the individual. Vedic Astrology retains the deep knowledge of cosmic energy, its spiritual roots and tradition. Vedic Astrology brings with it Eastern mysticism and philosophies, and the understanding of the human spirit through the language of the stars. It places a strong emphasis on the mind and its influence on every aspect of our life. Vedic Astrology believes that we are spiritual beings living in a material world, therefore we always need to be connected to our universal soul. While Western Astrology places power in the individual and our free will, Vedic Astrology wants us to understand the burden of our karma and destiny, so that we can be free from it.

In Western Astrology there are twelve Zodiac signs, from Aries to Pisces, indicating the Sun's apparent journey through the year. In Vedic Astrology we divide the Zodiac into twenty-seven different divisions or Nakshatras, each of thirteen to fourteen days. We study the twelve solar signs as well but in a different way.

## Sidereal Versus Tropical Zodiacs

Vedic Astrology uses a different Zodiac from the one used by most Western astrologers. Western astrologers use the Sayana, or Tropical Zodiac, which shows the Earth's relationship with the Sun. Vedic Astrologers use the Nirayana, or Sidereal Zodiac, which shows the planets' relationship with the stars. Sidereal actually means 'of the stars'. This takes into account the celestial phenomenon known as the 'precession of the equinoxes'.

In this book, I have made the calculation for you and related the Sidereal position of the Nakshatras to the Tropical position of your star sign.

## Nakshatras – The Vedic Zodiac

Nakshatra literally means 'star' in Sanskrit. A star is a point of cosmic light. '*Naksha*' means 'to get closer' and '*Tra*' means 'to preserve'.

# VEDIC ASTROLOGY AND LOVE

And 'nakshatra' also means 'one that never decays': their cosmic remit is to be the guardians of the soul during its journey through many human lifetimes. Nakshatras are full of secret symbolic information we have to learn.

In the Vedic myths, the Nakshatras are the twenty-seven wives of the Moon god, Soma. Nakshatras are *passive*. When the Sun transits the Zodiac, visiting the symbolic wives of Soma, it activates the differing aspects of the human mind, its desires and changing moods. Your birth date shows which aspect of the mind the Sun has activated during his annual journey.

Nakshatras divide the Zodiac into twenty-seven different sections. Each Western Zodiac sign has three or four Nakshatras. The Vedic Zodiac Year begins on 13 or 14 April when the Sun moves into the first Nakshatra of Ashwini. It takes the Sun 13⅓ days to transit one Nakshatra. (See the Nakshatra grid on pages 5–7.) *Nava Grahas* or nine planets rule the twenty-seven Nakshatras. Nakshatras are divided into three cycles of nine, which are always ruled by the planets in the same order. The nine planets are Ketu, Venus, Sun, Moon, Mars, Rahu, Jupiter, Saturn and Mercury.

The twenty-seven Nakshatras are:

1 Ashwini – ruled by Ketu, the South Node – 13 to 27 April
2 Bharani – ruled by Venus – 27 April to 11 May
3 Krittika – ruled by Sun – 11 to 25 May
4 Rohini – ruled by Moon – 25 May to 8 June
5 Mrigasira – ruled by Mars – 8 to 21 June
6 Ardra – ruled by Rahu, the North Node – 21 June to 5 July
7 Punarvasu – ruled by Jupiter – 5 to 19 July
8 Pushya – ruled by Saturn – 19 July to 2 August
9 Ashlesha – ruled by Mercury – 2 to 16 August

10 Magha – ruled by Ketu – 16 to 30 August
11 Purva Phalguni – ruled by Venus – 30 August to 13 September
12 Uttara Phalguni – ruled by Sun – 13 to 26 September
13 Hasta – ruled by Moon – 26 September to 10 October
14 Chitra – ruled by Mars – 10 to 23 October

15 Swati – ruled by Rahu – 23 October to 6 November
16 Vishakha – ruled by Jupiter – 6 to 19 November
17 Anuradha – ruled by Saturn –19 November to 2 December
18 Jyeshta – ruled by Mercury – 2 to 15 December

19 Mula – ruled by Ketu – 15 to 28 December
20 Purva Ashadha – ruled by Venus – 28 December to 11 Jan.
21 Uttara Ashadha – ruled by Sun – 11 to 24 January
22 Shravana – ruled by Moon – 24 January to 6 February
23 Dhanishta – ruled by Mars – 6 to 19 February
24 Shatabhishak – ruled by Rahu – 19 February to 4 March
25 Purva Bhadra – ruled by Jupiter – 4 to 17 March
26 Uttara Bhadra – ruled by Saturn – 17 to 31 March
27 Revati – ruled by Mercury – 31 March to 13 April

## The Planetary Rulers of the Nakshatras

*Grahas*, the Sanskrit word for planets, means 'home'; here it means the homes of celestial power. The planetary energy influences our lives and relationships through the rulership of the Nakshatras and their effect on our birth star.

Vedic Astrology relied on observable astronomy. The Sun and the Moon, Mars, Mercury, Jupiter, Venus, Saturn are observable by the naked eye so were given rulership of the Nakshatras, while Uranus, Neptune and Pluto are not, so, unlike Western Astrology, they are not used. Rahu and Ketu (the north and south nodes of the Moon) are astronomical points where eclipses occur. According to the Vedic seers, Rahu and Ketu were visible during the solar and lunar eclipses so they too rule the Nakshatras.

In Vedic Astrology, these nine planets – the Sun and the Moon, Mars, Mercury, Jupiter, Venus, Saturn, Rahu and Ketu – rule three Nakshatras each.

## Surya – The Sun

*The Sun rules Krittika (11 to 25 May),*
*Uttara Phalguni (13 to 26 September) and*
*Uttara Ashadha (11 to 24 January).*

The Sun is the most important planet in Vedic Astrology. The solar system revolves around it. The Sun represents our soul as well as the soul of the universe. It is the visible form of cosmic intelligence and the pure consciousness. The Sun represents our ability to be enlightened. By studying the position of the Sun in our charts we are identifying with the power of the universe. Our outer Sun deals with how we define ourselves as an individual while our inner Sun recognizes the heart's desires on a sublime level and our search for the inner light. The Sun's position in different Nakshatras shines its divine light and gives us the ability to perceive our differing emotional needs, to awaken from our illusions and embrace reality.

The Sun is fiery and therefore has to be alone. According to the Vedic myths, the brilliance of the Sun god was such that it made it difficult for him to have relationships. His partners found his light too strong to bear. So the Sun god had his effulgence cut off to get close to his wife. Even then he was too hot to enjoy a proper marital relationship.

The Sun Nakshatras sometimes suffer from loneliness because the person they love cannot always get close to them. The warmth they radiate sees a number of people basking in their glory but the closeness of relationship they desire is not always possible. They have to learn to understand and harness their power if they want to relate well.

# ABOUT VEDIC ASTROLOGY

## Soma – The Moon

*The Moon rules Rohini (25 May to 8 June),
Hasta (26 September to 10 October) and
Shravana (24 January to 6 February).*

The Moon is known as *Soma* in Sanskrit. According to Vedic mythology, the Nakshatras are the twenty-seven wives of the Moon god, Soma. The Moon stays one day with each of his wives. Rohini was his favourite wife. The other wives, jealous of the Moon's infatuation with Rohini, complained to Brahma, the creator, who cursed the Moon causing him to lose his power totally. The wives pleaded with Brahma to restore the Moon's strength again. Brahma could not take back his curse but modified it to let him regain his power partially. This became the waxing and waning cycles – the Moon losing his power monthly and then regaining it. The Moon is the symbol of the mind. The myth of the Moon shows the changing nature of the mind, its fickleness, the ability to love, the outward (waxing) and inward (waning) reflections, all within the period of a month – the time taken for the Moon to transit the Zodiac.

The Moon Nakshatras can be restless in their search for love. They can be entangled in many relationships simultaneously or move from one relationship to another, getting bored quickly. They change their minds often and can be moody. They are not choosy about love. They need emotional support from love.

## Mangala or Mars

*Mars rules Mrigasira (8 to 21 June),
Chitra (10 to 23 October) and
Dhanishta (6 to 19 February).*

Mars is known as *Mangala* 'the auspicious one' in Sanskrit and is represented in the Vedas as Kartika, the son of Shiva and Parvati.

## VEDIC ASTROLOGY AND LOVE

According to one of the myths (see also Krittika Nakshatra on page 63), Kartika and his brother Ganesha both vie to be first to marry a bride chosen by their parents. Shiva said the son who would circumvent the world seven times in the quickest time would marry first. Kartika was powerful, strong and fearless; he rushed off to finish his task, confident in his ability to beat his podgy brother, the elephant god Ganesha. Ganesha, aware of his lack of physical prowess, decided to use his mind. He asked his parents to sit down and went around them seven times, then said, 'My revered parents, you are my world, my universe.' The parents were delighted by his ingenuity and married him first.

Kartika was extremely disappointed by his failure to marry first and went into the Himalayas to live an ascetic and harsh life – meditating, fasting and staying in isolation. Kartika remained lonely. The myth explains that Kartika or Mars focuses on physical ability – he is extremely individualistic, self-reliant and does not think about others' needs. This is not always helpful in relationships. The Himalayas are the symbolic representation of going towards higher consciousness. Kartika in his spiritual journey has to be able to travel alone. So while he is living in the world, he can appear too eager for relationships but is able to give them up as well. He wants to have a relationship yet he invariably gets disappointed in love.

Mars is the only planet of action; it needs to be on the go at all times. Mars Nakshatras reflect this quality. They have to be careful, as they do not recognize their strength. Their self-confidence and power can work negatively for them as they can be too domineering. Mars is a dynamic planet and Mars Nakshatras take the initiative in love. They seek passion, excitement and adventure from relationships but are unable to offer commitment and love. Lessons in love can be tough. If disappointed in love, they can choose to be single.

## ABOUT VEDIC ASTROLOGY

# Buddha or Mercury

*Mercury rules Ashlesha (2 to 16 August),
Jyeshta (2 to 15 December) and
Revati (31 March to 13 April).*

Buddha means 'intellect'. Mercury, according to Vedic myths, is the child of the Moon god Soma and Jupiter's wife Tara. Tara lived an isolated and spiritual life with Jupiter who was always involved in rituals and prayer. Her agitation and restlessness led her to experience sensuality and passion. When Soma seduced her, she allowed different energy to enter her life. According to the Vedic philosophy this corrupted her purity (the wife is considered the greatest symbol of purity in India). Out of the relationship of Tara and Soma, Buddha or Mercury was born. The birth of Mercury, or intellect, happens when the pure soul has contact with the material world. Purity, idealism and spirituality meet sensuality, emotions and restlessness. It is Mercury's nature to explore the subtle as well as the material worlds. He represents the polarities of the human mind – the emotions and the intellect.

Mercury Nakshatras end the cycles of Nakshatras: they explore the outer reaches of their intellect but they also learn to let go of their preconceived ideas and go beyond the limitations imposed by their mind. Their psychology changes as a result of their life experiences. This is also very visible in relationships, which they enter with very fixed ideas of what they want from love but, with deeper involvement, their ideas change and they begin to perceive love differently.

Mercury Nakshatras need to be inspired and entertained as they get bored easily. They are forever searching for the inner core of their relationships. They can get dissatisfied very quickly if their relationships are too perfect, they need excitement and tension within the relationship to keep them interested. They tend to analyse, intellectualize and rationalize before they are able to accept. The myth of their birth suggests an inner need for relationships that are different. They can easily get involved in a triangle.

## Brihaspati or Jupiter

*Jupiter rules Punarvasu (5 to 19 July),*
*Vishakha (6 to 19 November) and*
*Purva Bhadra (4 to 17 March).*

Jupiter is known as *Brihaspati* in Sanskrit. *Brihas* means 'to grow and expand', *Pati* means 'the protector'. Jupiter is the most beneficent planet in the Zodiac and is the teacher and adviser of the gods. The mighty Jupiter is invoked in the Vedas for protection and prosperity. Jupiter represents wisdom, expansion, happiness and higher knowledge. Jupiter gives wisdom to do good deeds, to benefit from the fruits of past karma by giving great opportunities and luck. Jupiter also helps to expand your inner world, allowing you to nurture and bring out your latent qualities.

Jupiter Nakshatras have the wisdom to deal with the ups and downs of life but they need to be conscious of their tendency to always be advising their partners. The myth of Tara (see Mercury) shows that the partner of Jupiter needs to experience less hallowed ground. This can be the problem for Jupiter Nakshatras; their partners may find their ideas too high-minded and look for fun elsewhere. Jupiter Nakshatras themselves are seldom happy with one relationship, they want to experience as many as possible and are not averse to extramarital affairs or having two or more relationships going on at the same time. This creates a situation where Jupiter Nakshatras can be good at helping others' relationships to flourish but are not so good at making their own work.

## ABOUT VEDIC ASTROLOGY

# Shukra or Venus

*Venus rules Bharani (27 April to 11 May),
Purva Phalguni (30 August to 13 September) and
Purva Ashadha (28 December to 11 January).*

*Shukra* means 'bright', 'radiant', 'shining' and 'pure'. Shukra also means 'semen', the essence of man that ensures the future of humanity. He is the only deity who has the secret of immortality. Venus, or Shukra, is a male deity in the Vedas. Venus is the adviser of the demons and a spiritual teacher par excellence. He guides the demons towards their lost soul. The story of Venus's daughter illustrates his ability to grant any boon but also his inability to be responsible for her happiness. She wanted to marry a particular king and her father arranged it for her. But the king was in love with another woman and never showed love or affection for his wife. Venus could arrange for his daughter to marry the man of her dreams but he could not give her happiness. Happiness in marriage and the love of this man was not part of his daughter's karma.

Venus stands for refinement, our innermost desires, procreation and life on earth. The Venus Nakshatras will give you pleasure, and fulfil your desires, however outrageous they may be. But even Venus cannot avert your karma or make you happy. This is your own responsibility. Your past actions and present attitudes decide whether you can be happy or not. Spiritually, Venus makes you realize that any amount of material wealth on earth cannot bring true happiness. Venus gives you inner radiance and purity if you so desire.

Venus Nakshatras want beautiful relationships. They are attracted to perfection. They tend to hope that relationships will make their life complete. But remembering the myth of Venus, relationships can add to the quality of your life but it is your own responsibility to be happy within them.

## Shani or Saturn

*Saturn rules Pushya (19 July to 2 August),
Anuradha (19 November to 2 December) and
Uttara Bhadra (17 to 31 March).*

*Shani* means 'black', 'dim', 'slow' and 'little by little'. Saturn is the great teacher of cosmic truths which it does slowly through restrictions, obstructions, frustrations, unhappiness, disillusionments, setbacks, even death. In the Vedas, Saturn is the son of the Sun born of a liaison between the Sun and Chhayya. *Chhayya* means the shadow. The wife of the Sun god had gone away to visit her parents, and she left behind her shadow to look after the Sun in her absence. The Sun mistook Chhayya, the shadow, for the real thing and from this liaison, Shani was born. When the Sun realized his mistake, he rejected Chhayya and her son Shani.

Saturn is the planet of karmic retribution. It keeps an account of all your past acts and releases this karma unexpectedly. It strips away the illusions and detaches you from the pleasures of life. Saturn is also a *Brahmachari* – a bachelor at heart. Relationships do not come easy. Saturn Nakshatras may fear relationships or be cold towards their partners without realizing it.

Saturn Nakshatras are very strong as they face difficulty with calmness and strength. They tend to suffer from poor self-image, not believing that others can love them. Their greatest problem in relationships comes from their negative attitude. They are very conscious of their duty and responsibility towards their loved ones. They are natural workaholics and usually do not pay enough attention to love. They can have difficult relationships with their fathers.

## Rahu Ketu – the Shadow Planets

One of the key features of Vedic Astrology is the importance given to Rahu Ketu. Rahu Ketu is the Sanskrit name given collectively to the

## ABOUT VEDIC ASTROLOGY

Nodes of the Moon: Rahu is the North Node and Ketu is the South Node, but they are often referred to jointly as Rahu Ketu. They are not physical bodies, but the two points ecliptic where the eclipses take place and at which the orbit of the Moon intersects the ecliptic or the apparent path of the Sun around the Earth. They can darken the light from the Sun and the Moon; therefore they control the process of life. The Sun signifies the soul and the Moon the mind; when they are eclipsed they go through regeneration, transformation and change.

They are known as *Chhayya Grahas* (shadow planets). Their impact is mainly psychological. Rahu and Ketu symbolize karma and the past life (Ketu) and its ability to influence present experiences (Rahu). The snake is their symbol. Snakes are given great importance in Vedic mythology and they remind people of their mortality. The main Vedic gods are always pictured with a snake. Lord Shiva has a snake around his neck; Lord Vishnu's throne was *Shesh Naga*, the Eternal Serpent. Shesh Naga represents the cycles of time and space, which seed the cosmic creation. The Naga sheds his skin, symbolizing transformation and rebirth.

# Rahu

*Rahu rules Ardra (21 June to 5 July),*
*Swati (23 October to 6 November) and*
*Shatabhishak (19 February to 4 March).*

Rahu is the projection of past life issues on the present. In keeping with its shadowy nature, this projection is in the mind. Rahu becomes obsessed with externalizing past life wishes through present experiences. Rahu can be fiery and destructive but, when disciplined, it has the capacity to defy convention and make immense changes to the individual psyche. While you are studying Rahu, always remember its negativity as well as its great occult power and the great ability to give you real results in life, both materially and spiritually.

Rahu Nakshatras give a strong sense of your karmic past and future. They long to experience relationships. As the head of the celestial snake, they tend to want intellectual relationships. Their shadowy nature means they are difficult to understand, and you are not always able to trust them. They can be elusive and secretive, not easy partners to relate to. They can enhance fear in their partners and are also afraid to lose out on love.

## Ketu

*Ketu rules Ashwini (13 to 27 April),*
*Magha (16 to 30 August) and*
*Mula (15 to 28 December).*

Ketu is the lower part of the celestial snake. Ketu represents the search for eternal happiness. It is intuitive and feels with the heart. It is the planet of past life. It helps to understand karma and it encourages us to let go of our karmic past and develop into a new person. It can cause pain as we learn to let go of our material attachments and relationships where our karmic debts are over. It directs us towards seeking *Moksha* – the final liberation from the cycle of life and death.

Ketu Nakshatras are idealists and seek liberation. They are acutely aware of past life connections to their present relationships. On a subconscious level they are learning to work through their relationship karma. Ketu have a tendency to reject and they may get involved in a pattern of rejection in their relationships, if they are not too careful.

# Introduction to Vedic Relationships

We all have a relationship that works for us. Whatever you desire from a relationship, there is someone out there who can fulfil your needs. For each Nakshatra there is an almost perfect relationship that works, but there are also several others that may not. There is never 100% compatibility as there are always some aspects of the relationship a couple needs to work out. To find your best relationship you need to look beyond mere physical attraction. Understanding the Nakshatra compatibility allows you to make informed choices about your relationships and guides you in finding the most happiness from them.

Vedic Astrology believes that for a relationship to work well it needs to be compatible on many levels: physical, sexual, spiritual and emotional. The Nakshatras give clues to every aspect of compatibility between a couple. There is a complicated calculation by which relationships are assessed. This is worked out at the end of the book for all relationships.

How one Nakshatra relates to another Nakshatra is fully explained in Part Two. The test of true compatibility is how the relationshop works under pressure. We can love well in perfect conditions but when we face challenges our compatibility ratio comes into play. Good compatibility, above 50 per cent, gives you many strengths on which to build a good relationship, but below 50 per cent can create issues which become stumbling blocks to finding happiness together (see page 38 and individual Nakshatras). The length of a relationship usually has nothing to do with compatibility. Many people choose to live in an unhappy relationship, knowing they have nothing in common.

## Relationships in Mind, Body and Spirit

Relationships and marriages are considered to be a meeting of the mind, body and spirit. A good partnership is good for the soul. The relationship then has a life of its own; two souls are tied together in a spiritual connection. People change their names after marriage symbolizing a rebirth into a new life together.

## The Importance of the Woman's Happiness

Vedic compatibility is always calculated from the woman's point of view. Hindus believe that to achieve a long and happy relationship, the nurturing of the woman is very important as she forms the strength in a relationship. She is *Shakti* or the divine female power. Traditionally women were honoured and looked after to ensure their happiness. Today many relationships are disrupted because women are dissatisfied. The modern man should honour his woman as a partner, mother and lover. Women in the twenty-first century are much more dynamic than their historical counterparts. But some of this ancient wisdom applied to the modern relationship and the honouring of the female instinct by both men and women would go a long way to providing happiness.

## Karma and Relationships

Getting to know about the law of karma is the key to understanding Vedic relationships. The word 'karma' literally means 'action'. Every action we take in this life, our past and future lives is our karma. We choose the fruits of our previous karma that we are going to face in this life, both the negative and the positive. The law of karma says that the ultimate responsibility for our life and happiness rests with us. We cannot blame anyone else for what we are experiencing today.

# INTRODUCTION TO VEDIC RELATIONSHIPS

Our actions past and present create situations that we have to face through the journey of our life.

When we relate to our karma, we realize that this birth is only a small part of the whole, because this life is only one of a multitude of lives. The whole is like a necklace. Each lifetime is one pearl but all the pearls have to be strung together to make the necklace. In different lifetimes we form contacts and relationships. Some relationships get completed but some remain unfinished. These unfinished relationships form part of our relationship karma. The soul remembers. When we meet the soul of loved ones from the past, there is an instant connection. How often have you met someone to whom you are instantly attracted?

## *Rnanu Bandhanas* or Karmic Ties

*Rnanu* means 'debt' and *Bandhanas* means 'ties'. This word is usually used for karmic ties that hold us together. Those ties have an impact on this life if it has some unpaid debts – in this case the word debt is meant as unfinished business. The Vedas teach that before the soul is born it makes a decision on what relationships are going to mature in this lifetime and with whom it is going to pay off its karmic debts. At the time of birth, when the umbilical cord is cut, the mind forgets this but retains it in the subconscious. When we meet someone with whom we have a rnanu bandhana to work out, the interaction begins immediately. But with those with whom we have completed our karma there is an instant recognition but nothing develops from it. It is important to let go of these relationships. They create unnecessary confusion emotionally. Also some relationships are not matured, the time to pay off that debt has not arrived as yet. Again those relationships do not develop.

What type of relationship you experience depends on the karmic equation. When you fall in love, how this relationship works out depends on what your mutual rnanu bandhana is. If you have greater debts to pay, you will be the one who is putting more into the relationship. Sometimes you are stuck in a very one-sided situation and wonder why you stay in it. In an unfinished relationship from a past life where you were the taker, when your souls meet again you need to balance this equation, so this time around it is you who become the giver or vice versa.

In sexual relationships also, the concept of rnanu bandhana is important. If you are in a relationship and your sexual relationship suddenly stops or the sexual attraction suddenly dies, the karma of sex may have been completed. Or if you have a purely sexual relationship, then you had already worked out the other aspects of the relationship.

## The System of Relationship Compatibility

The method by which Vedic compatibility is worked out is called the *kuta* or units of agreement, which evaluates aspects such as love, attraction, sexual orientation, friendship, life direction, spirituality and times of life.

The important areas of compatibility we will be looking at are:

1 Friendships
2 Sustenance
3 Gunas and Temperament: Gods, Humans and Demons
4 Sexual: sex, attraction and passion
5 Doshas and Spiritual: connecting the prana or life force
6 Karmic Connections
7 The Total Compatibility: This synthesizes the factors and gives an indication of how the Nakshatras will interact.

### 1 *Friendships between two Nakshatras*

The friendship between your Nakshatra and your partner's Nakshatra determines whether you are going to like your partner in the long run, have companionship, camaraderie and mutual understanding.

Planets relate to each other like humans. They can feel friendly towards each other or be hostile. If their feelings are mixed, then the relationship is known as neutral. This relationship is expressed by the

# INTRODUCTION TO VEDIC RELATIONSHIPS

Nakshatras through their rulerships. For example, Ketu rules Ashwini Nakshatras; so Ashwini will have full relationship compatibility with Pushya, as its ruler Ketu is a friend of Saturn.

**The Nakshatras rulerships are**
Magha, Mula and Ashwini: **Ketu**
Purva Phalguni, Purva Ashadha and Bharani: **Venus**
Uttara Phalguni, Uttara Ashadha and Krittika: **Sun**
Hasta, Shravana and Rohini: **Moon**
Mrigasira, Chitra and Dhanishta: **Mars**
Ardra, Swati and Shatabhishak: **Rahu**
Punarvasu, Vishakha and Purva Bhadra: **Jupiter**
Pushya, Anuradha and Uttara Bhadra: **Saturn**
Ashlesha, Jyeshta and Revati: **Mercury**

**Natural Planetary Relationships**

| *Planet* | *Friends* | *Neutrals* | *Enemies* |
| --- | --- | --- | --- |
| **Sun** | Moon, Mars, Jupiter | Mercury | Venus, Saturn |
| **Moon** | Sun, Mercury | Mars, Jupiter, Venus, Saturn | |
| **Mars** | Sun, Jupiter | Venus, Saturn | Mercury |
| **Mercury** | Sun, Venus | Mars, Jupiter, Saturn | Moon |
| **Jupiter** | Sun, Moon, Mars | Saturn | Mercury, Venus |
| **Venus** | Mercury, Saturn | Mars, Jupiter | Sun, Moon |
| **Saturn** | Venus, Mercury | Jupiter | Sun, Moon, Mars |
| **Rahu Ketu** | Mercury, Venus, Saturn | Mars | Sun, Moon, Jupiter |

# VEDIC ASTROLOGY AND LOVE

Some planets feel friendly towards others who do not return their feelings. The Moon is friendly to Mercury but Mercury does not like the Moon at all. Therefore if your Nakshatra is Rohini ruled by Mercury and you are in love with Ashlesha ruled by the Moon, you may find your feelings are not reciprocated.

## 2 *Sustenance*

The Nakshatras have a unique way of interrelating with each other. This system is known as the *Nava Tara Bala*. *Nava* means 'nine', *Tara* is another name for the Nakshatras and *Bala* means 'strength'. Together it means the nine strengths your natal Nakshatra can derive from other Nakshatras. This is a very important way of understanding how the Nakshatras sustain each other. At times, due to the position of your partner's Nakshatra from your birth Nakshatra, your relationship can override other planetary indications and give positive results even if they are mutually inimical to each other or vice versa.

**Nava Tara Bala Chart – Personalized**

|   | 1st Cycle | 2nd Cycle | 3rd Cycle |
|---|---|---|---|
| 1 *Similar* | | | |
| 2 *Favourable* | | | |
| 3 *Difficult* | | | |
| 4 *Happy* | | | |
| 5 *Obstructive* | | | |
| 6 *Spiritual* | | | |
| 7 *Complex* | | | |
| 8 *Good* | | | |
| 9 *Best* | | | |

Write your own Nakshatra in Similar under 1st Cycle, then write the

# INTRODUCTION TO VEDIC RELATIONSHIPS

others vertically till you reach the ninth Nakshatra from your birth one. Put the tenth Nakshatra from your birth sign in the column of the 2nd Cycle, then write the others vertically till you reach the eighteenth Nakshatra from your birth one. Finally put the nineteenth Nakshatra from your birth sign in the column of the 3rd Cycle, then write the others vertically till you reach the twenty-seventh Nakshatra from your birth one.

For the Nakshatra Grid see pages 12–13.

The strength you derive from each Nakshatra will be as below.

1 *Similar*. The other Nakshatras in this column are ruled by the same planet and are very similar to you. A relationship between these Nakshatras gives average strength to each other. They will be good friends, not so good for long-term commitment.
2 *Favourable*. These Nakshatras create wealth and prosperity for you. You can have a profitable relationship with them. A long-term relationship based on mutal interests or business will be beneficial.
3 *Difficult*. These Nakshatras are full of challenges for you. They are not able to give support to you at all.
4 *Happy*. These relationships bring warmth and happiness. They will give positive strength to you.
5 *Obstructive*. They impede your personal growth. There can be rivalry and competitiveness. These Nakshatras do not support you.
6 *Spiritual*. These relationships will lead to the realization of ambitions – both spiritual and material. They will give great strength to you.
7 *Complex*. These Nakshatras bring out the negative qualities in you. They do not give you any kind of support. You can get involved in a complicated relationship with them that has the potential to make you unhappy.
8 *Good*. These Nakshatras bring immeasurable support and strength to relationships with you. This relationship has the capacity to override all types of difficulty.
9 *Best*. These Nakshatras are considered excellent relationships for you. There is mutual loving, support and friendship.

## 3 The Gunas or Qualities that Help in Understanding the Temperament

As well as 'quality' *Guna* means 'strand' – the strands of twine that make up a rope. The rope is seen here as an allegory of your personality. The various strands, or gunas, entwine to produce the individuality of a person. The attribute of each guna is usually seen as mental rather than physical, but the mind has a great capacity to affect the physical side of our life.

We all have a balance of the gunas within us. They express themselves as a mental attitude that leads us to see life in a certain way and have particular priorities, and it is vital that we recognize both the gifts and the challenges that they have to offer in our lives. The gunas are very important in relationships. They reflect our psychological qualities, which help or hinder the search for love.

**Sattva** is the attribute of purity. 'Sat' means 'being', 'existing', 'pure', 'true' and 'real'. 'Va' means 'where purity dwells'. A sattvic person believes in purity of being, thought and action. Water is pure sattva. Vegetarianism is sattvic because it rejects killing animals to fulfil the need to eat. Sattvic people have a mental attitude that emphasizes purity.

Sattva works very much on the abstract level and sattvic Nakshatras are usually happy aspiring to their higher self. They will be calm and collected within relationships. They tend to work on a sense of fairness and love. They are godly in temperament.

**Rajas** is the cause of activity in mankind. It is the searching quality that, as humans, we all have. It can be translated as 'pollen of the flowers', 'a particle in the sunbeams' or 'emotional, moral or mental darkness'. 'Pollen of the flowers' indicates the potential of pollen to create new flowers – humans activating more life; experiencing life and birth. 'A particle in the sunbeam' – a sunbeam is pure and the particle introduces a new element in its purity. 'Moral, emotional or mental darkness' is the inability of humans to see the answers within themselves, with the result that they seek fulfilment in the material, illusory world.

Rajas is a mental attitude that emphasizes strong emotional impulses.

# INTRODUCTION TO VEDIC RELATIONSHIPS

Rajasic people are restless and forever seeking answers. They are hardly ever happy within their present relationship. Rajasic Nakshatras have the habit of changing partners, looking for new experiences through each relationship. They forget that the answer to their emotional needs lies within themselves and their present relationship. Rajas reflect the human temperament.

**Tamas** is the attribute of darkness. The Sanskrit word can also be translated as 'ignorance', making it plain that the darkness is a mental one. Tamasic people have a mental attitude that emphasizes sensuality. They can be described as being led by a lack of knowledge or of spiritual insight to a life focusing on human sensual desires. Vedic philosophy encourages tamasic people to dispel their darkness with the light of spiritual insight.

Tamasic people embrace desires. They usually view life in the here and now. These desires keep them tied to the world of happiness and unhappiness – through their own needs they create their own problems. Tamasic Nakshatras can be self-indulgent in their relationships. They tend to choose relationships that fulfil their immediate desires rather than looking at the bigger picture and embracing the desires of the soul. Tamasic people have a demonic temperament.

## GODS, HUMANS AND DEMONS

Nakshatras are classified into three groups of gods, humans and demons. Gods reflect the guna of Sattva, humans of Rajas and demons of Tamas. The gods are steady, humans dynamic and demons sluggish. These qualities are usually said to reflect the nature of an individual. For people to be truly compatible, they should choose a partner who reflects a similar personality as them. So gods must relate to gods, humans to humans and demons to demons.

In today's environment where no one follows rigid rules, these classifications are not necessarily valid.

| Gods (Sattva) | Humans (Rajas) | Demons (Tamas) |
| --- | --- | --- |
| Ashwini | Bharani | Krittika |
| Mrigasira | Rohini | Ashlesha |
| Punarvasu | Ardra | Magha |
| Pushya | Purva Phalguni | Chitra |
| Hasta | Uttara Phalguni | Vishakha |
| Swati | Purva Ashadha | Jyeshta |
| Anuradha | Uttara Ashadha | Mula |
| Shravana | Purva Bhadra | Dhanishta |
| Revati | Uttara Bhadra | Shatabhishak |

## 4 *Animal Signs and Sexual Compatibility*

Each Nakshatra has an animal sign, either male or female. In Vedic Astrology, the male animal is more active and dynamic, while the female is passive, for example, the animal sign of Ashwini and Shatabhishak is the horse; Ashwini being the male horse will be more dynamic and active while Shatabhishak reflects the receptive energy of the female horse.

The animal signs are connected to the animals' characteristics in the wild. They represent the intuitive nature of humans, which if expressed unchecked will reflect their animal qualities. We learn to control and discipline these natural instincts. The impact of the animal signs on the personality and on relationships is explained in more detail in the sections on individual Nakshatras in Part Two.

Sexual compatibility is linked to the animal signs. Ideal sexual compatibility is found between the male and female of the same species, for example between Vishakha and Chitra, the masculine and feminine side of the tiger. If you are seeking sexual happiness, you need to choose a partner who is compatible with your animal sign. Nakshatras whose animal signs are inimical, will not have a good

# INTRODUCTION TO VEDIC RELATIONSHIPS

sexual compatibility. It is important to remember that sexual compatibility does not necessarily suggest that you are in harmony in other areas of your relationship. Two male or female Nakshatras together can be too active or passive regardless of their sex. In such a partnership you would need to emphasize the missing energy to achieve the right balance.

The Nakshatra animal signs and their ideal sexual companions are

| Animal Sign | Male | Female |
| --- | --- | --- |
| Horse | Ashwini | Shatabhishak |
| Elephant | Bharani | Revati |
| Sheep | Pushya | Krittika |
| Serpent | Rohini | Mrigasira |
| Dog | Mula | Ardra |
| Cat | Ashlesha | Punarvasu |
| Rat | Magha | Purva Phalguni |
| Cow/Bull | Uttara Phalguni | Uttara Bhadra |
| Buffalo | Swati | Hasta |
| Tiger | Vishakha | Chitra |
| Deer | Jyeshta | Anuradha |
| Monkey | Purva Ashadha | Shravana |
| Lion | Purva Bhadra | Dhanishta |
| Mongoose | Uttara Ashadha* | |

* The mongoose has no ideal sexual partner. This is a point where the soul realizes that their spiritual journey needs to be completed alone. The mongoose always has to compromise on their sexual happiness. There are partners who will fulfil their sexual needs but never totally satisfy. (More on Uttara Ashadha on page 260.)

## Sexual Adversaries

The sexual relationships of the following pairs do not work, as they are natural enemies in the wild. Relationships between sexual adversaries can make sex a bone of contention with the Nakshatras fighting to establish supremacy through sexual power play.

1. Cow (Uttara Phalguni and Uttara Bhadra) and Tiger (Vishakha and Chitra)
2. Horse (Ashwini and Shatabhishak) and Buffalo (Swati and Hasta)
3. Dog (Mula and Ardra) and Deer (Jyeshta and Anuradha)
4. Serpent (Rohini and Mrigasira) and Mongoose (Uttara Ashada)
5. Monkey (Purva Ashada and Shravana) and Sheep (Pushya and Krittika)
6. Cat (Ashlesha and Punarvasu) and Rat (Magha and Purva Phalguni)

## 5 *Spiritual Compatibility and the Doshas*

The Sanskrit word *dosha* means 'fault' or 'weakness'. This term is used in Ayurveda, the Vedic science of well-being, to find the weakness in the nature of people which when aggravated causes diseases. The weakness represented here is physical as well as spiritual – how nature organizes itself in a physical body. Each person tends to reflect one dosha in dominance. The doshas are very important in spiritual compatibility as your partners have the ability to balance your weaknesses and this allows different souls to merge successfully.

Doshas also reflect the nervous energy within ourselves indicating certain psychological patterns that make up our physical self. The doshas are studied to understand the interplay of your astral body. The astral body plays an important part in merging souls on a deeper level as it connects with *Prana* or the life force. How the life force flows within us and connects to our partner's life force is one of the most important connections for successful relationships.

The three doshas are *Vata*, *Pitta* and *Kapha*.

# INTRODUCTION TO VEDIC RELATIONSHIPS

## VATA – THE AIR QUALITY

The natural qualities of Vata are action, sensation, and enthusiasm. Vata means 'wind'. Perception, enthusiasm, inspiration, communication, exercise, action and dryness are Vata. Vata people tend to be of a nervous disposition. They are extremely active with lots of nervous energy to expend. They have a short attention span and generally live on their nerves. Vata people get stressed out within relationships and they need partners who are Kapha or Pitta. Kapha will calm their nerves and Pitta will help focus them.

## PITTA – THE FIRE QUALITY

Fire is required to digest, eat. Pitta produces heat and controls the digestive system. Hunger, thirst, suppleness of body, cheerfulness, intelligence and vision are pitta. Pitta people are active, motivated and hot-tempered. They tend to be creative, knowledgeable and intelligent. Pitta people can get too dynamic and forceful within relationships and they need Kapha or Vata partners. Kapha help slow them down and do not allow them to burn out. Vata will inspire them.

## KAPHA – THE WATER QUALITY

Water is necessary for sustenance. Stability of the body, potency, strength, suppleness of joints and forbearance are Kapha. Kapha people are philosophical, calm and patient. Laziness can be their problem. Kapha can get too comfortable and dull within relationships and they need Pitta or Vata partners. Vata will activate and inspire them. Pitta will bring passion and ambition into their life.

For the Pranic (astral) body to connect, it is important that your Nakshatra dosha should be different from your partner's. If two partners have the same dosha, they are unable to create harmony with their spirit body and accentuate each other's weaknesses.

# VEDIC ASTROLOGY AND LOVE

## The Nakshatra Doshas

| Vata | Pitta | Kapha |
|---|---|---|
| Ashwini | Bharani | Krittika |
| Ardra | Mrigasira | Rohini |
| Punarvasu | Pushya | Ashlesha |
| U. Phalguni | P. Phalguni | Magha |
| Hasta | Chitra | Swati |
| Jyeshta | Anuradha | Vishakha |
| Mula | P. Ashadha | U. Ashadha |
| Shatabhishak | Dhanishta | Shravana |
| Purva Bhadra | Uttara Bhadra | Revati |

## 6 *Karmic Relationships*

Some Nakshatras have complex relationships with others. They may have good points in all other areas of compatibility but in reality they have to face some karmic restrictions which can create unhappiness. They have soul lessons to teach each other. They may experience karmic situations that test their relationship unexpectedly such as voices from the past that create emotional upheaval, circumstances they have no control over complex situations that create rifts. The most important karmic aspect these relationships face is their feeling of unhappiness and unfinished business from a previous life. Most of us are unaware of our subconscious, but as these relationships come together, those issues come to the fore, and the way they relate to each other is constantly challenged.

**Spiritually Complex Relationships**

Ashwini and Jyeshta

# INTRODUCTION TO VEDIC RELATIONSHIPS

Bharani and Anuradha

Krittika and Vishakha

Rohini and Swati

Ardra and Shravana

Punarvasu and Uttara Ashadha

Pushya and Purva Ashadha

Ashlesha and Mula

Magha and Revati

Purva Phalguni and Uttara Bhadra

Uttara Phalguni and Purva Bhadra

Hasta and Shatabhishak

Mrigasira and Dhanishta

RAHU AND KETU
Rahu and Ketu indicate intense karmic relationships. If you are connecting with any of the Rahu or Ketu Nakshatras, the relationship will have an intangible quality that doesn't make them easy. It can feel as if there are some greater issues being worked out than is immediately obvious. Sometimes emotions can be churned up greatly in order to find the essence of the relationship. Although all relationships are karmic, these relationships have a greater depth and fervour. Rahu and Ketu Nakshatras connecting with each other can feel they are finding partners who were meant to be but at the same time they experience challenging situations in life that complicate the relationship.

**Rahu Nakshatras:** Ardra, Swati and Shatabhishak
**Ketu Nakshatras:** Ashwini, Magha and Mula

## VEDIC ASTROLOGY AND LOVE

### 7 The Total Nakshatra Compatibility

Nakshatra compatibility is a complex way of looking at relationships: you may be very compatible in one area, e.g. sexually, but if other areas are not compatible, you may not get total compatibility. The Nakshatra compatibility grid takes into account all the negative and positive forces affecting Nakshatra relationships and synthesizes it all in a simple to use format.

If your Nakshatra's compatibility with another Nakshatra is:

**75% or above**, this would be an excellent relationship for you. There may be some challenges but you are able to work them out through love and shared goals. Happiness is the result of such partnerships.

**50% to 75%** compatibility still shows a strong connection but the challenges increase. Mutual love will be strong but you are forced to face problems especially if the compatibility is nearer 50%.

**25% to 50%** compatibility shows some areas of your relationship work, but there are many areas that need constant attention. You may find you need to understand the other's need for love and commitment.

**0 to 25%** shows a total lack of understanding. This relationship does not always stand the test of time. When you go through a crisis, your love for each other is tested to the extreme and may not stand the pressure.

Look up the separate grids at the back of this book if you want to check specific areas of compatibility.

Nakshatra Compatibility Grids are on pages 338–43.

# PART 2

# THE LOVE SIGNS

*13 to 27 April*

# Ashwini

Ruled by Ketu
Animal Sign: The Male Horse
Symbol: The Horse's Head

## Meaning and Symbolism

*Ashwin* means a cavalier or a horse-tamer. The symbol of Ashwini is also the horse's head. The horse represents our senses, desires and creative energy. As cavaliers, the Ashwins' ability to ride horses symbolizes their ability to master their desires. The Ashwins are the twin sons of the Sun god. The Sun represents the soul; the soul gives birth to its image through Ashwini.

Ashwins are the harbingers of Usha or dawn. Dawn brings with it a very special energy: the promise of a new tomorrow while we are still attached to the mysterious night. The Ashwins are the link between the darkness of the night and the brightness of the day. Ashwini Nakshatras express this two-fold energy. You are luminous, bright, beautiful and swift. You have an open personality but also a mysterious depth, which makes you hard to understand. The representation of dawn indicates the link of your soul to the past. Hindus believe that past lives fashion your future and you also strongly believe this.

You approach every relationship in a fresh way. You are curiously idealistic about love and emotions. You can be very sensuous; you have the ability to control it as well. You are able to restrain your hopes and desires when you choose to do so.

# The Ashwini Personality

## The Past Life Connection

Ketu rules Ashwini, the first Nakshatra of the Vedic Zodiac. Ketu connects with past lives and aims for spiritual realization. In your relationships you are seeking the answer to a missing part of your inner puzzle, a deeper karmic meaning to it. It does not matter whether the relationships are easy or difficult. You have a strong sense of *rnanu bandhana*, the karmic debts you have carried from past lives. If you feel you owe your loved one something, you will stick with them through thick and thin.

Your soul searches for Moksha, a state of absolute perfection where there is perpetual happiness and the soul is released from the cycles of unhappiness and pain. Very few people reach such a state or find such a perfect world. But you search for it in your relationships, in love and from emotions. You can be disappointed when you do not find it. This can make you reject your partner in the search for your own Utopia.

Ketu is a shadow planet. There are many areas of your nature you like to keep hidden. You are very knowledgeable about the mysteries of life; you have a deeply intuitive nature and are spiritually brave.

## Martian Courage or Venusian Perfection

Ashwini spans the western signs of Aries and Taurus. Aries deals with birth, and freshness of approach, and the start of a new cycle of life. Taurus nurtures our birth potential and allows us to develop our own personalities. Both Mars and Venus can take you towards an openly sexual path; you retain your innocence, idealism and spirituality through Ketu.

# ASHWINI

Ashwini Aries reflects a dual Mars expression. In Aries Ketu acts like Mars but on a psychological level, so the purity of Martian action, courage and protection of humanity is powerfully indicated. You are always protesting about the quality of life, seeking new horizons in the hope of finding a better future.

The other part of Ashwini is in Taurus, ruled by Venus. Venus likes the good things in life but Ketu naturally rejects them. This can create a dilemma whereby you enjoy the pleasures of life yet feel guilty about them. The Venus and Ketu combination emphasizes an overtly sensuous nature tempered by inner asceticism.

## Sexuality – The Male Horse

### The Sexual Warrior

Your sexuality is expressed by your animal sign, the male horse. You can be nervous and highly strung. You are usually very fussy about whom you love and set high standards for your sexual partners. You like finesse from your lovers.

Both male and female Ashwini feel compelled to conquer. If you are attracted to someone, you will take the initiative and enjoy being the hunter. You may have the reputation of a sexual warrior. You are very sensuous, unconventional and natural lovers. Sex should be exciting and adventurous. You enjoy making love outdoors. Sexual independence is the key word. Those who succeed in getting close to you never feel a sense of security with you. You can be selfish in love, not always caring for your partner's pleasure.

### The Best and the Worst Sexual Partners

Your best sexual relationship is with the female horse, Shatabhishak. However, your overall compatibility is not high and sexual compatibility alone is never enough for happiness. Shatabhishak Nakshatras are too independent and never give you enough attention. They are highly strung and need careful wooing, something you are not inclined to do.

Hasta and Swati are the buffalo Nakshatras and your sexual antagonists. The buffalo Nakshatras are practical and earthy. Swati and Hasta may be too unimaginative to satisfy your sexual needs. You get bored with them easily and find it difficult to feel passionate about them. You are fussy and will perpetually remind them of their inadequacies. With Hasta you have very poor compatibility, so you have to tread carefully. You can get on with Swati despite your sexual antagonism and are happy to compromise on the sexual side.

## Relationship Issues

### Adventurous and Independent

You always need new challenges and adventures. Nothing can be more dispiriting for you than not having new areas to conquer. There is never a shortage of admirers but your relationships need to be varied and interesting. You are fiery, passionate and have a wild, untameable quality about you. You are independent and you do not want to be tamed. You are perpetually looking for excitement and fun. Your low boredom threshold and aversion to routine make you a difficult partner.

### Seeking the Soul Mate

You are seeking your soul mate. You will never admit it as it goes against your independent persona. You are looking for a past life connection who will complete you. This feeling is in the subconscious; you can reject love if you feel it does not match up to your karmic imagination. You want to connect deeply to your partners and want a spiritual commitment, not necessarily a physical one.

You are locked into a karmic search for happiness that churns up the life, mind and emotions. Ardra, Swati and Shatabhishak are your spiritual partners. Rahu, the other half of the cosmic serpent rules them. It may not be roses all the way, but you feel invisibly tied to them. The Rahu Nakshatras are karmically programmed to magnify your dissatisfactions. They project your past life inadequacies and make them real. Together you endeavour to untie the knot of emotional problems. Shatabhishak can make you very dissatisfied with the present. Your overall compatibility with Shatabhishak is poor – only 38% – so the karmic entanglement can bring unhappiness with sexual attraction the only fulfilling factor. Ardra's need to analyse you aggravates you intensely. You work on instinct and Ardra on intellect. Swati is more ready to connect with you. Despite all the positive aspects of the relationship, Swati will project and magnify your sexual dissatisfaction with them.

## The Emotional Baggage of Ashwini

You are always active. A part of you feels afraid that if you sit still long enough you may be confronted with emotional issues you are not ready to deal with. Your soul reflects the two polarities of darkness and light. While you are ready to embrace the light of admiration and love, you feel unable to deal with the darker issues of rejection, guilt and accountability for your actions. You never really address relationship issues and over the years you accumulate emotional baggage that becomes a burden for you. This influences the way you act with your partners – always trying to make up for your own guilt over careless actions and casual treatment of your previous partners.

## The Pattern of Rejections and Love

Ketu-dominated people are often afraid to experience life fully in case life rejects them. They tend to reject others, as they fear rejection themselves. The fears of Ketu can be irrational and instinctive.

You are in a hurry to reject your partners as you seek the next new relationship. You may let go of an excellent relationship in the hope that your next love may be even better, may fit your ideal. The question arises: is your ideal too perfect, so that most people cannot live up to it? This cycle of rejection and experience continues till you learn to break it. You must stop rejecting the present for a rosier tomorrow. Once you learn to appreciate love and not link it to rejection and fear, you are on the way to resolving your relationship issues.

## Loving Ashwini

If you love Ashwini, you must understand the extreme idealism and inner purity that makes them so impossible. They need independence, so do not curb their freedom. They are not always able to articulate their love. If you are looking for signs of love and affection from them, watch their actions – they speak louder than words. If they are there for you, this is their way of expressing love.

## Compatibility

**Ideal life partner: Bharani**
**Most challenging life partner: Hasta**

**The full Compatibility Grid is on page 338.**

**Ashwini and Ashwini:** You are very similar; you enjoy the same things and feel comfortable with each other. The love you share is confident, passionate and strong. You instinctively fulfil each other's desires. Learn to curb your independent and dominant nature or there can be frequent clashes. **77% compatible**

**Ashwini and Bharani:** Your best partnership, passionate, exciting and sexy. Bharani exude a sensuous energy and luminosity that keeps you interested. Your sensuality blooms. They know how to deal with your fears of rejection and lack of love. You will feel emotionally supported and loved. **91% compatible**

**Ashwini and Krittika:** Instant attraction can die out quickly if you do not stoke the passion with love. Only then will you enjoy Krittika's loyalty and warmth. They are shy and diffident; you will need to chase them. Always be the predator – this usually keeps you inter-

# ASHWINI

ested. Krittika are insecure within a confident exterior, so make them feel wanted. **61% compatible**

**Ashwini and Rohini:** Sexy, sensuous and desirable, Rohini fascinates you. You find a karmic link that needs exploring. This will be an exciting journey into secret pleasures and sensuous indulgences. Beware of Rohini's possessive nature. They feel threatened by your independence. You must establish trust between you. **62% compatible**

**Ashwini and Mrigasira:** Mrigasira stimulate and inspire you. You like their mind, their ability to know your needs and talk about them. Love will be passionate, fiery and thrilling. Mrigasira's possessiveness can make you uncomfortable. Their suspicions create barriers that may be insurmountable. **61% compatible**

**Ashwini and Ardra:** Ardra appear to conclude your karmic search for a perfect partner. At first you think you have found your soul mate, but the relationship is not an easy one. You can get caught in an emotional turmoil that can make you experience extreme emotions, being deliriously happy one day and totally disconsolate the next. Ardra can make you feel unsettled. **44% compatible**

**Ashwini and Punarvasu:** Punarvasu are better being your friends and partners in adventure than your lovers. You will hate Punarvasu's need to constantly advise you on how to lead your life. Your relationship can improve if both of you curb your independence and are there for each other. **55% compatible**

**Ashwini and Pushya:** This is not an instant attraction. Your first impressions are that Pushya are boring and unadventurous. But their love, support and encouragement gently warm your heart. They have a dry sense of humour; you are surprised by their passionate nature. An excellent relationship with deep foundations. Good for the long haul. **83% compatible**

**Ashwini and Ashlesha:** Ashlesha are mystical and wise; they can keep you interested in them. They excite you intellectually as well as physically. The only problem with this relationship is the possessiveness of

# THE LOVE SIGNS

Ashlesha. They are extremely independent but cannot tolerate you being the same. **75% compatible**

**Ashwini and Magha:** Usually there is unfinished karmic business between you. This can create many highs and lows. Both of you are idealistic of your expectations from love. You can make each other unhappy if you are unrealistic and forget to enjoy what you have.
**55% compatible**

**Ashwini and Purva Phalguni:** You love Purva Phalguni's exquisite taste and their ability to be charming, chic and cool. They match your sensuality. Love will flourish. Your only problem with Purva Phalguni is that they do not always understand your deeper, more spiritual nature. You can live with that – everything else works. **67% compatible**

**Ashwini and Uttara Phalguni:** The cosmic relationship of your rulers Ketu and the Sun is difficult. You will not trust Uttara Phalguni and the feeling is reciprocated. If you overcome the distrust and allow them to find your emotional light, this relationship can be sublime. The lack of compatibility suggests that most do not even try.
**34% compatible**

**Ashwini and Hasta:** Your most difficult relationship. You find Hasta's emotionalism hard to relate to. You cannot accept their possessiveness. There is no sexual spark and love can be unsatisfactory. They are practical and will always try to be useful to you, but you cannot appreciate their positive qualities. **27% compatible**

**Ashwini and Chitra:** Chitra are never able to give you their full attention. You will try to love Chitra, but they do not always love you back. Passion and sex can be good, friendship will survive, but love may not stand the challenges of time. Chitra's volatile temper and your fiery temperament make your relationship a battlefield.
**47% compatible**

**Ashwini and Swati:** You do not find Swati sexy. But they are mentally stimulating, loving, ambitious and full of new ideas. This relationship works despite the lack of sexual compatibility. Swati are able to fulfil

# ASHWINI

your other dreams. Pay special attention to your sexual intimacy and your relationship will be happier. **70% compatible**

**Ashwini and Vishakha:** Vishakha are sensuous, passionate and potent. A sexually athletic affair usually develops. Lack of sensitivity can make it less than satisfactory. Vishakha's restlessness undermines your confidence. Both of you are wary of long-term relationships. Commitment and faithfulness can be a problem. **55% compatible**

**Ashwini and Anuradha:** You appreciate Anuradha's attractions given time. They are passionate and sensuous under a cool and practical exterior. They will intuitively know what you want. You need to make them feel secure. Commitment does not necessarily mean lack of freedom. **66% compatible**

**Ashwini and Jyeshta:** You are caught up in a spiritually complex relationship. On a subconscious level you know Jyeshta can make you unhappy, yet you are unable to let go. You want to explore the reasons behind the connection. You can hurt each other in the process of understanding. Jyeshta can be both possessive and uncaring; you can be passionate and cold. **36% compatible**

**Ashwini and Mula:** You will have lots in common – active, sporty, adventurous, fun and idealistic. You share the same planetary ruler, Ketu. Can you share your life? Spiritually, you do not bond. The past becomes a big demon, unless you exorcise it, you are not able to move forward and be happy. **33% compatible**

**Ashwini and Purva Ashadha:** Purva Ashadha are charming, sexy, talented and creative. They have an eye for beauty – they chose you, didn't they? It soon leads to love. They are fun to be with and enjoy life. Passion is great, they are playful, their sensuality warms you, and their sense of fun keeps you stimulated. **66% compatible**

**Ashwini and Uttara Ashadha:** Uttara Ashadha appear friendly, but they will not let you into their life. They tend to keep an emotional distance. You will take this as a challenge and try to break down their barriers. You should be understanding about their sense of loneliness. Your love can be unconventional and special. **66% compatible**

# THE LOVE SIGNS

**Ashwini and Shravana:** You could easily think that Shravana are serious workaholics with no time for love or emotions. The twinkle in their eyes, their sense of humour and their sensitivity leads you to believe there is more to their personality. They enjoy sex and will be innovative lovers. You could easily fall in love. **72% compatible**

**Ashwini and Dhanishta:** Your love life with the passionate Dhanishta can be fiery and combative. Try not to make sex an issue of your many fights. It will be frustrating, as both of you love sex and lots of it. They are not possessive and they do not expect commitment from you if you do not want to give it willingly. **53% compatible**

**Ashwini and Shatabhishak:** Good at sex and bad at intimacy. That sums up the relationship between Shatabhishak and you. There is usually a past issue that bothers you, either in your own life or in Shatabhishak's. Shatabhishak are unable to empathize with your emotions or be open about their own. **38% compatible**

**Ashwini and Purva Bhadra:** you will want to protect the dreamy, idealistic Purva Bhadra. But soon you will be desperate to escape. When they desire sex, they will be strongly passionate and then they will go away into their own world, not bothering or caring for you. The dreamer also turns out to be an arrogant lion on closer inspection. **42% compatible**

**Ashwini and Uttara Bhadra:** Uttara Bhadra can be your friend, mate or colleague, but never your lover – or so you think till you discover their hidden sensuality. As a lover they will be generous and loving, and enjoy long, sensual lovemaking. Their love will be committed, steady and unconditional and you can find yourself reeled in. **64% compatible**

**Ashwini and Revati:** You will feel intimate and emotional with Revati. Their love makes you feel strong and powerful. They understand you. Their attitude to sex can be frustrating; they usually want love and not sex. You even commit to them as you feel that Revati inspire your protective instincts. **72% compatible**

ASHWINI

## Cusps

Those born at the end or beginning of Ashwini, should see pages 345-6.

27 April to 11 May

# Bharani

Ruled by Venus
Animal Sign: The Male Elephant
Symbol: Yoni, the female sexual organ

## Meaning and Symbolism

*Bharani* means 'cherishing', 'supporting' and 'nourishing'. The symbol for Bharani is Yoni, the female sexual organ. This establishes Bharani as a channel for creation either physically by a sexual act or metaphorically by nurturing other creative energies. Both sexes of Bharani exude *Shakti*, the female power. Female energy has an important place in Vedic philosophy. It is this energy that incubates the soul and transports it from one level of existence to another – from pure spiril to an earthly body. Bharani cherishes and supports the soul in the womb till it is ready to be born. In a wider sense, Bharani can be an incubator of ideas and thoughts. You nourish creativity in any form – arts, ideas and spirituality. The male Bharani is in touch with his feminine side. In Vedic Astrology female power is essentially passive energy that needs outside forces to activate it. Both sexes of Bharani need someone to focus their mind and identify their ambitions, then their Shakti will come into play and their artistic instincts will be brought to life.

## The Bharani Personality

### The Celebration of Sexuality

Venus rules both the Nakshatra and the Western star sign of Taurus. Bharani celebrate female sexuality as the symbol of fertility and fruitfulness. In India, certain ancient monuments like Khajurao honour female sexuality in their immense sculptures. You personify fertility, harmony and growth. You see your sexuality as an expression of divinity.

Bharani are the sensualists of the zodiac. You are forever searching for your spiritual self but are usually most happy expressing your sensual one. Allow your sexual energy to become your creative channel, whether you express it by having children or through ideas, arts and music. If you misuse your sexuality, promiscuity can become a problem.

You reflect the qualities of Venus: diplomacy, creativity, a love of beauty, music and art, a talent for relating and a charming personality.

### The Magnetic Attraction

Both Bharani men and women fascinate the opposite sex. Your confidence in your ability to attract is usually high: if you want to seduce someone, you have all the subtle artfulness to do so.

When a Bharani woman walks into a room, men admire her and women are jealous. A Bharani woman may not be conventionally beautiful or even dressed in the latest fashion, but her aura of sensuality glows around her, attracting men of all ages and types. Other women naturally hate Bharani because they feel that Bharani are after their man. This may not be true, as they are choosy about their partners. But Bharani women do wear sensuality as part of their aura and prefer the company of men.

Bharani men know what women want. They are in touch with their feminine side, therefore can be excellent lovers. They may not be traditionally good looking but women are drawn to them like bees to honey. They want to create something beautiful with you and if you inspire them enough then they will be with you for a long time. However, as soon as they stop finding you sensually stimulating and a challenge, they can move on.

### Earthy and Passionate

Your nature is earthy and sexual. For a relationship to succeed, you need a partner who can match this earthiness and sensuality. You should stay clear of those offering only intellectual stimulation. You can relentlessly pursue the person who takes your fancy. You enjoy the chase and the subsequent victory. Once you have won, you can become bored easily and take your partners for granted.

## Sexuality – The Male Elephant

### The Sexual Sensualists

Your sexuality is expressed by your animal sign, the male elephant. Male elephants are independent and only join the herd for mating. They fight each other to the death to claim the rights to the whole herd.

Bharani is the Nakshatra of sexuality. One of the conundrums of Bharani is that it is a female Nakshatra but its sexuality is male. The female energy comes from its karma to be the receptacle for the soul. The male Bharani keeps the desires of the soul alive and through his semen will create life, and the women by receiving the semen create new life when it enters the womb. The male sexuality indicates that you will be active in seeking partners to fulfil your divine mission to help creation.

You are aggressive and competitive. In a relationship you like to be the ones making the running and will do anything to win sexual favours. You enjoy sex, lots of it. You will love a partner who panders to your sensuality. Silk sheets, soft music, and fine food produce a sensory overload that you love. In a committed relationship, you can get into a pattern of seeking out your partner only when you are ready for sex. They can feel that you only want them for sex and are not interested in their feelings and emotions.

### The Best and the Worst Sexual Partners

You are most sexually compatible with the female elephant Nakshatra, Revati. (You are also compatible in other areas.) However, Revati see their sexuality as sacred so they want to use it sparingly. They can feel guilty about enjoying sex whereas you see the enjoyment of your sexuality as a divine right. You will need to encourage Revati to overcome their guilt about sexuality.

The Lion Nakshatras, Dhanishta and Purva Bhadra, are sexually incompatible with you as the elephant and the lion are adversaries in the wild. (See below: Learning to Share Your Kingdom.)

## Relationship Issues

### Learning to Share Your Kingdom

You believe you are the king of the jungle and you are possessive of your kingdom. You are dominant and strong. Bharani can be admired and even attain a status among your peers. You appear larger than life but your heart is gentle and kind. The moment someone treads on your territory, you will be fierce and fight off any intruder. You are fiercely protective and possessive of your partner. You are usually happy to share with those who are weaker and do not threaten your power.

But with the lions Dhanishta and Purva Bhadra, you can get extremely aggressive. They also think they are the kings of the jungle. You may fight and argue over every aspect of your relationship, just to assert your power. They will try to show their dominance through sex and sexual power play. Avoid sexual games that may become violent.

You can learn to live with your enemy. In the wild, the lion and the elephant live together, apparently in harmony. The lion rarely enters the elephant's patch and the elephant does not go into the lion's den. A relationship with clearly demarcated areas of operation and power can work. But patience and calmness has to be exercised by all. Take care that the lines of demarcation do not become insurmountable walls in your relationship.

## Ecstasy and Obsession

You are seeking a state of such supreme ecstasy that it makes you forget everything. This ecstasy can come momentarily from sexual satisfaction. But to remain in this state for ever is impossible. In search of this extreme ecstasy, you can get obsessive about some partners, especially after a great sexual encounter. Your animal sign, the elephant, also gets into this state, which is known as *musth*. The elephant destroys whatever stands in its way. Bharani, mirroring the elephant, reach such a state of passion that they lose their rationality and forget what is good or bad for them. You will not bother who you hurt, what you destroy. You must always try to avoid the darkness of sexual obsessions. If you find yourself treading this path, put a stop to it immediately, you too will get hurt by the devastation this behaviour unleashes.

## Lazy Lovers

One of the problems you may face is that once you have found your partner and settled down, you get bored, restless and lazy. This can make you put on weight or be self-indulgent emotionally. This usually makes your partner frustrated and they can lose interest in you. The more distant your partner becomes, the more restless you feel. You react by over-indulging in food or drink; you may become lazy. You may even indulge in secret affairs. To stop this pattern destroying your relationships, you need to embrace discipline. Being active and focused will help you overcome your inertia and create a positive channel for your restlessness. There will still be times when laziness or restlessness takes over, but being aware of your weakness allows you to deal with it.

## Loving Bharani

As Bharani's partner, you should always keep them inspired. Never give in to all their demands. Although they want a steady and secure relationship, they need their partner to keep their sexual life exciting, full of mystery and pleasure. Never let them feel too comfortable with you – they need to feel there is always something more to achieve in your relationship.

## Compatibility

### Ideal life partner: Ashwini
### Most challenging life partner: Uttara Bhadra

**The full Compatibility Grid is on page 338.**

**Bharani and Ashwini:** Your best relationship: dynamic, vital and adventurous. You can soothe their fears of rejection and lack of love. They in turn will love, protect and spoil you. You know how to keep the adventurous Ashwini tethered to your side for ever. Remember not to be too possessive Ashwini need their sense of freedom.
**91% compatible**

**Bharani and Bharani:** Your similar natures bind you together: creative, caring, nurturing and instinctively understanding your partner's needs, revelling in the sensual journey. You will feel secure in their need for you. Too much self-indulgence can make you waste your energies and allow this relationship to get bogged down.
**77% compatible**

**Bharani and Krittika:** Krittika are puritanical, loners and appear shy. They are needy for relationships but will never admit it. You may need to seduce them into being exciting and passionate lovers. They

# THE LOVE SIGNS

will be warm, loving, supportive and ready to commit. But if you make a fool of them or laugh at their insecurities, they can be extremely destructive. **65% compatible**

**Bharani and Rohini:** Rohini can fulfil your need for sex and passion. Give them love, romance and fantasy. Do not go into a relationship with Rohini lightly. They are possessive and may not let you go easily. Jealousy and possessiveness will be the main problems. While you may be willing to be possessed, Rohini like to keep their freedom. **64% compatible**

**Bharani and Mrigasira:** Instant attraction, hot and fiery passion can propel you into an affair. The fire can burn out too quickly; you can be left with the burnt ashes of your spent passions and a relationship where there is nothing else to bind you. Then you may be introduced to another side of Mrigasira – critical, analytical and sharp.
**43% compatible**

**Bharani and Ardra:** You are able to understand the deeper needs of Ardra, their fears and insecurities. You touch their emotions in a way few people can. You find them witty, charming and exciting. If you want your Ardra lover to remain faithful, you will need to let them know the sexual boundaries very clearly. **69% compatible**

**Bharani and Punarvasu:** Great potential. Let your Punarvasu lover know that you need a lover, not a guru. They have many admirers. Tell them you hate to share and they will respect your wishes. Punarvasu are forever searching for new horizons and this keeps you interested in them and on your toes. You hardly ever get bored or lazy around them. **76% compatible**

**Bharani and Pushya:** Disciplined, practical and pragmatic, Pushya are what you really need. They balance your sensuality, indulgences and passions. But it is not something you recognize instantly. Their quiet strength has a strange attraction for you and their well-hidden sense of humour and playfulness keep you firmly at their side.
**61% compatible**

**Bharani and Ashlesha:** An unconventional relationship that works despite being based on different rules of engagement. You love the feline sensuality of Ashlesha, their cutting humour and worldly wise cynicism. You must learn to love them for what they are. Try to change an Ashlesha, they will soon move away. **66% compatible**

**Bharani and Magha:** You are attracted to Magha's power and arrogance – and their unexpected sensitivity. While they present a successful persona to the world, you find them insecure and full of doubts. Your sexual confidence will make them unsure. To cover up their own vulnerabilities they can reject you. **53% compatible**

**Bharani and Purva Phalguni:** Venus rules both your Nakshatras. You enjoy a light flirtation with Purva Phalguni but soon realize how similar you are – the mystique of having a relationship with them is not there. Your sexual needs are different. They need plenty of sex whereas you want sex to be a pleasurable journey full of sensuous delight. **47% compatible**

**Bharani and Uttara Phalguni:** Uttara Phalguni are keen to be helpful and will always be there for you. They can be boring and staid lovers, but there are enough compensations. Anyway, you know how to spice up your love life. Both of you can be very stubborn. You should learn to give in now and then. **60% compatible**

**Bharani and Hasta:** Hasta invite you into their homes and hearts. They will love you without accepting anything in return. Be careful how you treat them. Hasta are insecure within. They constantly need your approval. They live unconventional lives with a yearning to be conventional. Their insecurity makes them jealous and possessive. **50% compatible**

**Bharani and Chitra:** A difficult partnership. Chitra are exotic, adventurous, and sensuous. This can lead to an exciting, on-the-edge experience. You can get emotionally involved with them and they are unable to reciprocate. Become obsessed with them and it will be very destructive. If you enjoy their passion and let go, you come through unscathed. **22% compatible**

**Bharani and Swati:** Swati are charmers. You love their verve, energy, and the interesting way they flirt with you. Swati make you feel loved and sweep into your life full of ideas and in a flurry of activity. You love their earthiness and release them from their sexual complexes. Great sex, good friendship and lots of fun. **78% compatible**

**Bharani and Vishakha:** The sexual excitement that brought you together cannot be sustained at the high note on which it started. Both of you will get restless and stop paying each other attention. Keep your magnetism, confidence, stand up to Vishakha and allow your personality to flourish, then you have a chance to be happy with them. **50% compatible**

**Bharani and Anuradha:** Anuradha is your spiritually complex relationship. Karmic issues from the past can intrude and make this relationship more difficult that your 47% compatibility suggests. Their unrealistic approach to love can mar what you have today. Your inner needs are in disharmony. Look into their soul, understand their angst and let them feel your uncertainty. **47% compatible**

**Bharani and Jyeshta:** You can be tied to Jyeshta's deeply sensual nature. They are mystical and intriguing. They love all the things you like; they offer friendship, excitement and mental challenges. They can play with your emotions, you can get very hurt by their on–off attitude. Avoid getting too emotionally dependent. **53% compatible**

**Bharani and Mula:** You are attracted by their unconventional, daring lifestyle. You use all your wiles and sexual experience to get them interested. But your spiritual paths differ. You are sensuous by nature; Mula may be involved in a sensuous relationship with you, but their soul wants them to give it up. **53% compatible**

**Bharani and Purva Ashadha:** You connect to the Venusian qualities in each other. Your directions in life differ and this creates disagreements. You want sensuality and passion; they want creativity and spirituality. They may compromise for a short while with a sensuous life but in the end it is not for them. You can feel let down by them. **47% compatible**

**Bharani and Uttara Ashadha:** You are drawn to the cool asceticism of Uttara Ashadha. The relationship can only be fulfilling if you take the sensual lead. They may appear confident, but they are full of insecurities about their sexuality and relationships. You can have a loving relationship with them, that few can achieve. Try not to be too possessive. **72% compatible**

**Bharani and Shravana:** Great sexual attraction. Shravana's ability to pick up the vibrations of your senses and fulfil your every demand even before you have articulated it, makes them irresistible. They are happy to explore sex and extend the boundaries of enjoyment.
**77% compatible**

**Bharani and Dhanishta:** You should think carefully before embarking on a relationship where your deeper sexual needs may not be met. Dhanishta are your worst sexual partner. You can feel extremely unsettled and restless. Avoid making this a self-destructive relationship – either through sexual obsession or sexual detachment.
**26% compatible**

**Bharani and Shatabhishak:** Shatabhishak can be your good friends, do not mistake friendship for love. You need warm, passionate partners whom you can possess and love. Shatabhishak run away from possessiveness. They need long and careful loving. You are usually experienced enough to deal with their skittish behaviour, but are you patient enough? **53% compatible**

**Bharani and Purva Bhadra:** Who rules this relationship, the elephant or the lion? Sexually your worst partner but compatible in other areas. Royalty marry other royalty so why shouldn't one king of the jungle get involved with another? You have a slightly upper hand as Purva Bhadra usually let their partners make all the relationship decisions. **62% compatible**

**Bharani and Uttara Bhadra:** Your worst relationship. Uttara Bhadra can be ascetic, rigid and cold. They may not express any of the warmth to you that they seem to show others. They can question your sensuality constantly, making you feel uncomfortable. You can feel very weighed down by their goodness. You just do not know how to deal with each other. **11% compatible**

**Bharani and Revati:** Revati are your perfect sexual partner. Why can't they be open and comfortable about sex like you are? As you get to know of their inner purity and spirituality, this influences you into changing for your Revati lover by learning to treat your sexual relationship as special and they reward you by loving you unconditionally. **69% compatible**

# Cusps

Those born at the end or beginning of Bharani, should see pages 347–8.

11 to 25 May

# Krittika

Ruled by the Sun
Animal: The Female Sheep
Symbol: The Razor

## Meaning and Symbolism

*Krit* means 'to cut' or 'divide' and *tika* means 'to challenge'. Krittika Nakshatras are never afraid to challenge and cut through oppositions. They are considered to be fierce and destructive. The myth of Krittika is connected to the demon Taraka and the birth of Kartika, the warrior Mars. Taraka had got the blessing of Brahma, the creator of the universe, that he could not be killed, except by a seven-day-old son of Shiva. Shiva was an ascetic who was meditating in the Himalayas and had no intention of producing a son. So the gods plotted to get the semen of Shiva and when they got his seed, Krittika incubated it. From that seed Kartika the warrior god was born, who destroyed Taraka when he was seven days old. This myth indicates the immense power of Krittika.

The symbol for Krittika is the razor. The razor or knife can be used constructively and destructively. This again highlights the negative and positive forces within you. Do you use the fierceness to defend against oppression and wrongdoings, or to scare others through dominance? You can become a healer or a warrior, care for people or destroy them, defend evil or incubate it – the choice is always yours. In relationships you can construct a beautiful world or you can be destructive. Krittika's relationships are definitely about making personal choices. Are you going to nurture and be loving or are you going to cut yourself off emotionally, are you going to defend those you love against all the negativity of the world or destroy what you love the most through anger, jealousy and possessiveness?

## The Krittika Personality

### The Fierce Sun

The Sun rules Krittika. The Sun signifies authority, power, vitality and strength. The Sun in Krittika is the first experience of the intense heat of summer in the northern hemisphere. Those who have experienced the intense heat of the Sun understand its fierceness. Krittika is the true expression of the Sun. You are warm, fierce, supportive as well as destructive. The Sun is important for survival but get too close to it and you can get burnt. You can be loving but you can overshadow others with your strong personality. Your power can be too strong for the average person to deal with.

You are fiery. Your fire gives warmth to friends but, if allowed to rage uncontrolled, it could become a destructive force. You learn from an early age to contain and control this fire. This fire can be expressed through your intelligence, ideas, passions, emotions, anger and jealousy. Those who have experienced unchecked Krittika passion will testify to its powerful, sometimes devastating, force. The problem with fire is that whenever you take it out of its container you are not sure which direction it will take.

For all your strength, you are shy and quiet. You have a fear of commitment and an inability to express your need for love. However, you are a sucker for vulnerability and if your partners appear weak and needy, you can forget your shyness and will be ready to defend them against the world.

# KRITTIKA

## Venusian Creativity and Mercurial Intellect

Krittika's Western star signs are Taurus and Gemini. Taurus Krittikas are under the dual influences of Venus and the Sun. There is outer sensuality and inner purity. Taurus is the sign of hard work, and under Krittika's influence there is a passion for power added to it. You are charming, creative and artistic. You are attractive to the opposite sex with lots of friends and admirers. But the inner self feels detached and lonely.

The Mercurial influence on the Gemini Krittika shows a great emphasis on intellect, a passion for learning, a need to analyse. Gemini Krittikas are the planners and executors. You like to analyse your relationships and will be particular about who you go out with.

## Sexuality – The Female Sheep

### The Sexual Pacifists

Your sexualitly is expressed by your animal sign, the female sheep. In Vedic Astrology, a female animal sign indicates a passive side to Krittika. Whether you are male or female, you like to be chased and will not show interest unless you are confident of a positive response. You are highly sexed and passionate but are not always able to express your passion. You may appear timid and diffident till you unleash your sexuality. You need partners who understand your sexual needs. Unfulfilled, you may resort to having affairs or secret flings.

You will not fight for a relationship. You let your sexual partners do all the hard work and initiate a more sensual relationship. This is a side of you that people do not understand. You are leaders in every other aspect of life. But when it comes to expressing your sexuality you become passive spectators. You get intensely passionate only with those you feel relaxed with and in whose loyalty you can trust. With others you tend to be reserved, not showing your true depths.

## The Best and the Worst Sexual Partners

As the female sheep Nakshatra, you enjoy sensual and passionate relationships with the male sheep Nakshatra Pushya. Pushya bring out the best in you, being compatible in most areas of life, and the sexual compatibility adds the extra pizzazz.

The monkey Nakshatras, Purva Ashadha and Shravana, are sexually incompatible with you. Monkey Nakshatras are naughty, manipulative and complicated and they can be at times too devious for the straightforward sheep Nakshatras. Monkeys cannot give the fidelilty that you need and they can make you feel sexually inadequate.

# Relationship Issues

## Lessons in Emotions

Your relationships with the Moon Nakshatras are the toughest. The Moon rules Rohini, Hasta and Shravana. It symbolizes the mind, both the emotional and the intellectual. You are seldom in touch with your emotions. You can be at times so concerned about expressing your power that you forget the sensitivity of emotions and the need to love others. Especially with the Moon Nakshatras, your capacity to love will be tested. They have the ability to cool the Krittika temperament and douse your enthusiasm. They make you angry and unnecessarily jealous and possessive.

Rohini will teach you about jealousies, Hasta about moodiness and Shravana, by blowing hot and cold with your emotions, will teach you that love never runs smoothly. Not being afraid of emotions and recognizing your need for love, can help you in relating to all the other Nakshatras as well.

## The Search for Purity

Your need for a pure and perfect partner makes you set impossible standards that are hard to live up to. If you find your partners are less than perfect you tend to leave them. You are a late developer as far as your sexuality is concerned. You have immense self-control. Your puritan streak makes you fascinated by partners who are more experienced than yourself. But you may use their experience against them at a later date, unable to psychologically accept previous partners or being irrationally jealous of past relationships. This creates situations where partners find it difficult to be truthful about their past and you can get hurt when they get to know the truth. But you have usually set yourself up for this disappointment.

### Loyalty and Unconditional Love

Commitment is difficult for you, yet commitment from your partner is a must. You expect fidelity from your partner. You want closeness but find it difficult to express this need. You need to have a relationship where you are respected and admired. You want unconditional love. You usually keep a part of your true nature hidden, finding it difficult to trust your partner enough to open up completely.

You feel your relationships are destined. Once you get seriously involved you can be fiercely loyal and you are liable to hold on to good as well as relationships. One of the great qualities that you possess is being able to get along with most of the Nakshatras. Your attitude is such that you will try to find compatibility with your worst partners.

## Loving Krittika

Krittika need to be seduced and loved. Among all the Nakshatras, they are the most passive when it comes to relationships. They are needy for relationships but will never admit it. You need their trust; they can test your sincerity. They can be emotionally volatile, but it is better that they express their emotions rather than hide them. Suppressed emotions can erupt suddenly and leave you quite shocked by their depth. Do be open about your feelings and let them know your love often. If you love Krittika, be sure to let them know you admire and respect them. Never give them reason to doubt your loyalty and commitment.

## Compatibility

**Ideal life partner: Bharani**
**Most challenging life partners: Rohini and Uttara Bhadra**

**The full Compatibility Grid is on page 338.**

**Krittika and Ashwini:** You find Ashwini's adventurous spirit exciting. Ashwini enjoy the chase and will cut through your defences easily. If it survives the initial passion, you will enjoy a loving and pleasurable relationship. Both of you are commitment phobic and can't talk about love. You must learn to trust Ashwini. **61% compatible**

**Krittika and Bharani:** Bharani fascinates you. You may be uncertain that such a sensuous person is interested in you. The clever Bharani will break through your barriers and expose your emotions and needs. Sexually you will feel nourished. You hate Bharani's possessiveness but your love for them helps you deal with it.
**65% compatible**

**Krittika and Krittika:** You recognize a soul mate. Commitment, loyalty, identical attitudes to love and sex create a powerful bond. This can also split you apart. Vedic Astrology advises against two of the same Nakshatra getting involved. The high compatibility rating suggests that mostly you can overcome difficulties caused by your similarities. **65% compatible**

**Krittika and Rohini:** You will be attracted to Rohini's vulnerability, ever ready to provide strength and protection. But their unrealistic approach to love can unsettle you. You feel unsure and are unable to trust them fully. This usually makes you seek refuge among your friends. Rohini can become very possessive and emotional.
**30% compatible**

**Krittika and Mrigasira:** You enjoy arguing, debating every aspect of

# KRITTIKA

life. Mrigasira are very fiery and opinionated: pitting your wits against them will be an exhilarating experience. Both of you are passive Nakshatras and may not make any effort to take the relationship any further. One of you needs to be decisive and make the first move. **54% compatible**

**Krittika and Ardra:** This relationship has potential for excitement but gets into a rut of mediocrity as both of you are afraid to trust and express your inner emotions. For this relationship to flourish, you need to be unconventional and ready for a different kind of relationship. Trust each other and reveal your inner self. **49% compatible**

**Krittika and Punarvasu:** Punarvasu's charm and wisdom attract you. They need you to be their rock, someone to come home to between their travels. But are you able to accept such a tenuous relationship? You cover up your feelings by being overly possessive. Punarvasu's need for flexibility and your need for commitment pulls you apart. **56% compatible**

**Krittika and Pushya:** The best sexual partnter for you. Pushya can see through your sexual diffidence. They know just how to make you desire them, and they will work hard to be in touch with your sensuality. Pushya love you through thick and thin, and you will feel secure and comfortable in loving them back. **68% compatible**

**Krittika and Ashlesha:** Mystical, independent, fiery Ashlesha fascinate you. Ashlesha teach you to overcome your diffidence, help you feel comfortable with your sexuality. Then the doubts set in: you can be jealous of the very things that attracted you to them initially. You can make the relationship unnecessarily complicated. **57% compatible**

**Krittika and Magha:** You do not trust each other enough. Magha hide their insecurities behind a façade of confidence and arrogance, and so do you. Magha can make you feel unwanted and rejected. If only Magha recognized your feelings. But they can only do so if you talk about them, connect to the inner being rather than the image they project. **47% compatible**

**Krittika and Purva Phalguni:** You can be too puritanical for the fun-loving and social Purva Phalguni. Neither of you will make the effort to make the first date. A relationship can survive if you come out of your shell and Purva Phalguni stays at home a lot more. If they do so, be sure to appreciate them. **43% compatible**

**Krittika and Uttara Phalguni:** You are both ruled by the Sun: warm, caring and loving. You need to be loved and appreciated but you find yourself forever paying homage to your Uttara Phalguni lover and never receiving enough love from them. **53% compatible**

**Krittika and Hasta:** You find the Hasta emotions hard to deal with. They are needy and the more they cling to you, the more you distance yourself. You do not want to give your emotions a free rein. Being romantic with them, telling them you love them does not take away from your power. Love a little more and Hasta will love you back tenfold. **44% compatible**

**Krittika and Chitra:** Confident Chitra always make the effort to bring you out of yourself. You admire them and love them. The passion is fiery and exciting. Do not try to test their loyalty too much: Chitra do not make the effort to hold on, they may move on, rather than pass your tests. Both of you will be the losers. **61% compatible**

**Krittika and Swati:** Sexual chemistry can bring you together but lack of trust can drive you apart. You may feel critical of the way Swati live their life: you need to realize their way is different from yours, not necessarily less valid. Talk to each other. Do not build up silent barriers and appreciate the differences. **32% compatible**

**Krittika and Vishakha:** You have the ability to hurt each other as yours is a spiritually challenging relationship. Your emotional storms create greater problems than this average compatibility suggests. Jealousy, anger, restlessness can make this relationship a trial you have to go through before you can find happiness. **51% compatible**

**Krittika and Anuradha:** Anuradha are so different from you, seeming to be serious and pragmatic until you discover their inner vulnerability and deep romanticism. Their capacity to love you uncon-

# KRITTIKA

ditionally creates an unbreakable bond. They need love and sometimes you find their need to be perpetually romantic wearing.
**60% compatible**

**Krittika and Jyeshta:** Your best relationship. Jyeshta will inspire you; they bring fun into your life. They appear far more experienced, so they make you come out of your shell. You are happy to fulfil their demands and they do the same. Love, happiness and security are the key to the success of this relationship. **76% compatible**

**Krittika and Mula:** You may distrust each other. But once you get closer, you find great qualities in Mula: their philosophical nature, their ability to be brave, their free-wheeling attitude to sex. Sex and philosophy is a heady mix. You support Mula and help them to be rooted. They will love you back in their own way. **65% compatible**

**Krittika and Purva Ashadha:** Your worst sexual relationship. Sexually Purva Ashadha can be terrible teases; you do not always know how to react to them. You tend to keep your defences up; you can never give them your all, knowing on a subliminal level that they can throw it all back at you. You can cut off from them before they do so.
**47% compatible**

**Krittika and Uttara Ashadha:** The same Nakshatra ruler creates a greater distance rather than closeness between you. Both of you are dominant and strong. You usually hide behind your many friends. If Uttara Ashadha try to get closer, you do not know how to deal with them. You can be lonely together if you are not careful.
**30% compatible**

**Krittika and Shravana:** Your worst sexual partner and low compatibility. While you may find Shravana amusing, you soon tire of Shravana emotionalism and moods. Shravana play hot and cold with your emotions. You never reveal your inner feelings. They confuse you with their contrary signals about how they feel about you.
**32% compatible**

**Krittika and Dhanishta:** Dhanishta want to be in control of the seduction and that suits you fine as you are shy in expressing yourself.

They are caring and loving. They believe in equal rights and make strong partners. This is a good relationship where passion and love flourish. **70% compatible**

**Krittika and Shatabhishak:** There is something about Shatabhishak that you do not understand. They are elusive and hard to fathom. They can rebuff you with their coldness but you recognize their vulnerability. This makes you protective of them. You start seeing them in a new light. A deep and caring relationship develops.
**75% compatible**

**Krittika and Purva Bhadra:** You appreciate Purva Bhadra right from the beginning. You can be good friends as well. But you are unable to talk about love. They hardly ever make the first move, so you will need to get over your shyness to ask for the first date. But you always feel them to be a bit remote. **54% compatible**

**Krittika and Uttara Bhadra:** Uttara Bhadra are forever giving you mixed signals. They can be two people at the same time. Do not be put off by their coolness. Take it as a challenge and try to woo them a bit. They need your appreciation and fondness and will open up their emotions to you. **50% compatible**

**Krittika and Revati:** Revati are too unrealistic for your liking. They can put you on a pedestal and hope you behave like some demigod. They make impossible demands of you. You find their need to analyse everything very off-putting. They let you know your shortcomings. You usually walk away from them or avoid getting in too deep with them. **32% compatible**

# Cusps

Those born at the end or beginning of Krittika, should see pages 348–50.

25 May to 8 June

# Rohini

**Ruled by the Moon**
**Animal: The Male Serpent**
**Symbol: The Chariot**

## Meaning and Symbolism

*Rohini* in Sanskrit means 'red', which relates to passion and sensuality. Rohini is considered to be the favourite wife of the Moon. According to Vedic mythology the twenty-seven Nakshatras are the twenty-seven wives of the male Moon god, Soma. Soma stayed one day a month with each wife. The other wives, jealous of the Moon's infatuation with Rohini, complained to Brahma, the creator, who cursed the Moon, causing him to lose his power totally but then let him regain it. This became the waxing and waning cycles. Rohini represents the first realization of love, possessiveness, passion and ecstasy. The twenty-seven symbolic wives of the Moon reflect your differing moods and your ability to be involved in more than one relationship at a time.

Rohini's symbol is the chariot. Chariots were used as luxury transport. You like to live in style and enjoy the sensual side of your nature. You want to experience love in the lap of luxury and comfort. You enjoy partners who are successful and wealthy and who indulge your love of luxury. You love extravagant presents.

# The Rohini Personality

## The Lunar Restlessness

The Moon rules Rohini. It signifies the mind in Vedic Astrology – both the emotional and the intellectual. The Moon represents the physical embodiment of our soul – the ebb and flow of our feelings, emotions and the need for change on a daily basis. Just as the Moon roams the night skies, so the mind remains unsettled in its restless search for answers. You can be unsettled in relationships, always on the move, searching for a love so complete that will make you understand the deeper meaning of life and calm your restless soul.

## The Marriage of the Moon and Mercury

The Moon rules Rohini which is also in the sign of Gemini and is ruled by Mercury. Rohini represents the union of the Moon and Mercury. Both are charming and beautiful, yet indecisive and changeable. Both symbolize the mind. The Moon represents the complete mind and Mercury the intellectual part of it. This Nakshatra reflects the differing qualities of the mind: its fickleness, its changing moods and its subtlety. The essence of Rohini is that they appear to be very detached and unemotional showing the characteristics of Mercury, but within they are full of emotion, romanticism and love.

# Sexuality – the Male Snake

## Active Sensualists

Rohini's animal sign is the male snake. Snakes find potential mates by sending special 'scent messages' to each other. The male snake will rub the female snake with his head as part of their loving. They like a long mating and generally mate for life.

The male sexuality of your animal sign suggests that you will actively pursue the object of your affections. You only express your interest if you believe your feelings are reciprocated. You are cool with those who are too eager and will freeze out those who try to be too forward. Once you choose your sexual partner, you plan your wooing very meticulously. Your sexual pleasure is enhanced by sensual games.

You often mistake sexual attraction for love. This can lead to disappointments and disillusionment.

You can walk away from a sexual relationship in the early stages. But once you are involved, you can be jealous and possessive. You will not let your lover go easily. Like the snake, you will wrap yourself around your lovers and cling to them. At the same time you like your freedom, as you will not like to feel captive. You should be careful not to let your possessiveness and jealousy get out of control.

### The Best and the Worst Sexual Partners

The female snake Nakshatra Mrigasira sexually fulfils Rohini. You understand each other's sexual needs perfectly. You are compatible in other areas of life as well, so this can be a mutually satisfying relationship all round.

The mongoose Nakshatra Uttara Ashadha is the worst sexual relationship for Rohini. (See the Impossible Partnership below.)

## Relationship Issues

### The Impossible Partnership

Your relationship with Uttara Ashadha is complex. This relationship has a very low compatibility rating, which is further complicated by the inimical relationship with Uttara Ashadha's animal sign, the mongoose. In nature, the mongoose is the deadly enemy of the snake. Whenever they meet they fight to the death. As a snake Nakshatra, you feel subconsciously antagonistic towards Uttara Ashadha. You both find it difficult to make allowances for each other. Your passion can soon turn sour. In extreme cases, sexual competitiveness, irrational jealousies and vindictiveness can come into this sexual relationship unnoticed. Then you may want to destroy each other without thinking of the consequences.

When in a relationship with Uttara Ashadha, avoid using your sexual superiority to settle your fights. Sex should never become an issue. Then you are giving yourself a chance for happiness with your Uttara Ashadha lover. This is a relationship that needs lots of work on your irrational feelings and mental blocks.

## Seeking Enlightenment through Relationships

You find *moksha* or enlightenment through devotion and love – to lover, spouse or your god. You want a partner for life. You need to love completely, wholehearted and unconditionally. Your devotion is such that you break any barriers that stand between you and the object of your love. Your love is pure and idealistic. On the negative side this can lead to you feeling incomplete. You need a husband, partner, lover, or a significant other to make your life whole.

## The Romantics

Sex alone does not satisfy you, you need romance. You will sacrifice anything for love. You want love and adoration from your lovers. You have the ability to delude yourself. You can sometimes get involved with people who are not completely faithful. You crave the complete devotion of your partner, while still retaining the right to your own freedom.

## Coping with Rejection

Rohini must learn to deal with the fear of rejection which makes you extra possessive of your partners. The Nakshatras, Magha and Mula, ruled by Ketu can teach you bitter lessons about love and rejection. Magha will cut themselves off from you dramatically: your brand of possessive love has no place in their life. It can take you a long time to get over your Magha lover. Mula are involved in their spiritual struggles. You are looking for love, Mula for spirituality. Mula have the capacity to destroy your illusions and dreams. They fail to recognize your sensitivities and emotional vulnerability. Their overtly sexual behaviour with others can make you feel insecure and bring out your worst jealousies. You can become locked in a complex situation of karmic ties with Magha and Mula where you find it difficult to live with them and equally hard to let go.

## Sensitive but Fickle

You are loving, emotional and you understand the feelings of others. You are very sensitive and get hurt easily. The Rohini men understand women in a special way while the Rohini women are essentially feminine and their allure hypnotizes their men into thinking that they understand all their problems. But understanding and commitment are two different things. You love and appreciate the opposite sex. You want a partner who will satisfy your inner vision of perfection. In reality, you tend to move from relationship to relationship. Your inability to commit is connected to your search for the ideal partner who will complete your life in every way. You are not willing to compromise. So you explore and people accuse you of being fickle.

## Discontented in Love

You may be involved in a good relationship, yet you feel dissatisfied. You are sometimes unable to recognize the beauty and the love of the present relationship. You can reject these relationships only to pine for them at a later date. Your discontent can lead to you breaking up a good relationship in the illusory search for an even more perfect one. You tend to confuse sex with love. This can only make you unhappy.

## Lessons in Self-Appreciation

Others see you as good looking, sensitive, mysterious and charming. You fail to appreciate yourself. You can suffer from low self-esteem.

You can get involved in complex relationships and love triangles as you do not value yourself enough. You will accept these unsatisfactory situations by deluding yourself that you are doing this for love. If the wrong buttons are pressed, you can be extremely vindictive and jealous.

## Loving Rohini

Rohini need someone who can support them, on whom they can rely to be there for them. They are restless and unsure; they need a partner whom they can lean on, who makes them feel secure and at peace. They can be very unrealistic. As a lover of Rohini it is your task to keep them grounded without stripping away their illusions. Do not make them feel unwanted.

## Compatibility

**Ideal life partner: Anuradha**
**Most challenging life partner: Magha**

The full Compatibility Grid is on page 338.

**Rohini and Ashwini:** Ashwini can be your dream partner – exciting, fiery and passionate. They have a wild untameable quality that you want to possess. Ashwini find you sensuous and desirable. Both of you are restless souls and find this quality in each other keeps you interested and the relationship fresh. Don't be too possessive.
**62% compatible**

**Rohini and Bharani:** A relationship with Bharani can be an exploration of sensuality, fulfilling you sexually. Be willing to be possessed by Bharani. They can take you on a journey of ecstasy and love. You both enjoy the good things in life. Beware of excesses – sexually and financially. **64% compatible**

**Rohini and Krittika:** You will find the warm but diffident Krittika

# ROHINI

hard to resist. You will plan your campaign to seduce them and bring them into your orbit. Their strength and potency can thrill you, but soon you will feel dominated by it. You can seek other relationships and this means that Krittika will find it hard to trust you.
**30% compatible**

**Rohini and Rohini:** You are too alike. Both of you look at life with rose-tinted glasses. Practicality will not be your strength. You can find the realities of the relationship hard to handle. Your search for the perfect partner may not end with each other. Lack of trust, jealousy and possessiveness can mar the relationship. **55% compatible**

**Rohini and Mrigasira:** Good friendship and exciting sex. You want the same things from life. You are ready to talk about love; you will introduce Mrigasira to sensuality and passion. Mrigasira will be dynamic on the outside but you call the shots where intimacy is concerned. Emotionally complete and loving. **77% compatible**

**Rohini and Ardra:** Your ruler the Moon fears and distrusts Rahu, Ardra's ruler. As the compatibility otherwise is high, the fear becomes delicious excitement for you. Ardra's practical responses to your need for romance will irritate and frustrate you. Avoid becoming distrustful and possessive. Teach them about love and express your need for them openly. **64% compatible**

**Rohini and Punarvasu:** You enjoy Punarvasu's wisdom, finding their need to advise you comforting. You love playing sensual games with them; you have enough confidence to wait for them to show their interest. You will need to teach Punarvasu intimacy. Both of you are jealous and possessive lovers, and not too hot on commitment.
**66% compatible**

**Rohini and Pushya:** Do not just look for superficial attraction with Pushya. They can love you in a way few others can. They may not allow you to indulge your romantic nature but they will give you support, make you feel secure and bring peace to your restless mind. Pushya practicality is a perfect foil for your emotionalism.
**75% compatible**

# THE LOVE SIGNS

**Rohini and Ashlesha:** Ashlesha are mystical, secretive and at times manipulative. There will be power play and sensual games; you can be intensely possessive of Ashlesha. Both of you can be venomous, uncaring about the hurt your sharp words inflict. Ashlesha's way out is to become detached, whereas you can feel emotionally messed up. **33% compatible**

**Rohini and Magha:** Your worst relationship. You need romance and Magha want sex. But you find their rejection hard to deal with. They can trample on your feelings and aggravate your lack of self-esteem. Their philandering makes you extremely jealous. With Magha, it appears you can lose your sense of proportion. **28% compatible**

**Rohini and Purva Phalguni:** Purva Phalguni will indulge you and try to fulfil your romantic dreams. They make an excellent foil for you – their practicality gives a good base to your more emotional nature. You enjoy life together, for although you may find them lacking in sensual skills, you can teach them that. **66% compatible**

**Rohini and Uttara Phalguni:** You love the Uttara Phalguni strength – they make you feel secure. They are not the most imaginative lovers but they are there for you. They are happy to be possessed by you. But beware of their jealous temper: if you ever give them reason to express it, it can be very destructive. **72% compatible**

**Rohini and Hasta:** You enjoy Hasta's sophistication but you also like their earthiness. You find it easy to connect to both sides of their personality. Both of you are moody but this does not split you apart as you understand this behaviour. You like Hasta's simple approach to life and enjoy teaching them to overcome their complexes. **69% compatible**

**Rohini and Chitra:** You are attracted to the dynamic, confident and passionate Chitra. You let them dominate this partnership, enjoying the thrill of their power. But you also discover their implacability and selfishness. The more possessive you are, the more distant they become. Try to accept what they are willing to give. **49% compatible**

**Rohini and Swati:** This is a spiritually complex relationship. You can

be irrational in your mistrust of Swati. Your ruling planet the Moon is frightened of Rahu, Swati's ruler. In relationships where compatibility is low, this fear is interpreted as lack of trust, the fear of commitment and uncharacteristic behaviour patterns.
**42% compatible**

**Rohini and Vishakha:** Vishakha seem unable to understand your inner needs. They are happy to be with you as long as you play by their rules. You need them to give you their undivided attention. Maybe you have created unrealistic expectations of each other. You should not put all your emotional expectations on them.
**30% compatible**

**Rohini and Anuradha:** Anuradha understand love and romance in a way no one else does. They also hide their romantic nature behind a worldly-wise exterior. Both of you can share your romantic dreams and become the ultimate lovers. Anuradha are usually financially successful, which gives them an ability to support your love for luxury. **80% compatible**

**Rohini and Jyeshta:** You love the mystical Jyeshta, their charm and intellect. You find their ability to savour sensuality exciting. They love you in style, more than satisfying your need for luxury and comfort. You may not be totally in tune with their spiritual needs but you know when to let them be free. After all, you like a bit of freedom too. **67% compatible**

**Rohini and Mula:** You tend to put the responsibility of your love on Mula's shoulders. Mula are ill equipped to handle this. They aspire to freedom and a break from the burden of mundane responsibilities. They may not want your love, especially as it comes with conditions attached. They can be hurtful and cruel in their rejection.
**36% compatible**

**Rohini and Purva Ashadha:** For a relationship to survive with Purva Ashadha you must be ready to give them some freedom. Then you can have some fun together. They are not able to handle emotions too well and if you dump all your emotional and romantic expectations on them, you are really giving them the perfect excuse to leave you. **53% compatible**

**Rohini and Uttara Ashadha:** You can get involved in such extreme jealousy and sexual rivalry, that you will not rest until you destroy each other. Your mutual attraction can be compulsive but you are very sensuous and Uttara Ashadha's coldness and asceticism can make you lose faith in yourself. You can get hurt and the emotional damage will take a long time to heal (see the Impossible Partnership above). **37% compatible**

**Rohini and Shravana:** You know Shravana can be moody and restless. But they have also learnt to deal with their restlessness; they can become detached and develop a hard surface that you find difficult to break. They are not there when you need them, usually lost in their own world. You can feel neglected and ignored. **50% compatible**

**Rohini and Dhanishta:** Dhanishta are happy to romance you but they do not want commitment. They appear to enjoy luxury and the good life but when you show your preference for it, they suddenly become very austere and high minded. You do not know what to make of them. They confuse you with mixed signals. **53% compatible**

**Rohini and Shatabhishak:** You do not like or trust Shatabhishak at first – they appear cold and unfeeling. You soon throw aside your initial caution and fall in love. Surprisingly they respond and you find a unique way of loving. They open up emotionally to you in a way they seldom do to others. They will try hard to be what you want in a partner. **76% compatible**

**Rohini and Purva Bhadra:** Purva Bhadra can be the lover you were seeking for so long. They are generous, flamboyant and will keep you in luxury and comfort. But they also have a detached side to their nature. They need to do some things alone. Try not to feel too insecure and don't let your jealousy and possessiveness spoil your relationship. **60% compatible**

**Rohini and Uttara Bhadra:** You love the dependability of Uttara Bhadra: they love, nurture and support you. You are privy to their secret sensuality. They may present a cool and ascetic persona to others – you know different. There are times when you want more excitement but usually you will not take the risk of alienating them. **75% compatible**

**Rohini and Revati:** You fall for the idealistic Revati, but you find living up to their image of you hard to do. They do not want to be sensuous, usually living a simple life. You want luxury and sensuality and you cannot cope with their guilt or their criticism of you. So what appears to be a perfect relationship to start with can descend into mediocrity. **53% compatible**

# Cusps

Those born at the end or beginning of Rohini, should see pages 350–1.

8 to 21 June

# Mrigasira

Ruled by Mars
Animal sign: The Female Serpent
Symbol: The Head of the Deer

## Meaning and Symbolism

*Mriga* means 'deer' and *sira* means 'head'. The symbol of Mrigasira is also the head of the deer. In Vedic mythology, the head of the deer represents the Moon. The lunar energy that is expressed in Mrigasira makes you restless, sensitive and emotional. Mrigasira Nakshatras may search for an unobtainable perfection, an illusion. The deer here represents the golden deer that we all search for but can never find. You have the spirit not to accept the status quo and as a result you tend to get pulled more and more into life experiences. You will never accept things without question. This leads to dissatisfaction with the given circumstances. In relationships you search for that special person who may be a figment of your imagination. Your partners never seem to fit the image. You explore love in the hope of finding that elusive quality.

# MRIGASIRA

# The Mrigasira Personality

## Active and Passive

One of the important aspects of Mrigasira is that while you are ruled by the active Mars, your animal sign is the female serpent. In Vedic Astrology female energy is passive. Also Mars as the Vedic god Kartika was born to defend not to attack. While you may fume at the injustices of the world or be dissatisfied with the quality of your life, you will probably not do anything about it. You usually act only when challenged or inspired. At times you may appear to be lazy and inactive, but your mind is usually very active, thinking and planning your next move. You do not believe in wasting your energy. When the time is right you can act decisively. You do not usually initiate relationships. Your energy complements the duality of your western sign Gemini – the twins. So sometimes you are the dynamic Mars while at other times you can be passive and still, like the female snake.

## The Intellectual Warrior

Mrigasira is in Gemini. Mercury rules your Western sign and Mars your Nakshatra. The Mercury–Mars association is considered to be difficult. Mars is the planet for action and Mercury for intellect. You have a very sharp and aggressive intelligence. This Mars and Mercury combination gives great talent for writing. You can use your intellect as a weapon and will not be afraid to use it against people in an argument or to get your point across. In fact, you fight and challenge those you love the most, it is your way of showing love. You analyse, discuss and redefine your relationships. Your partners can develop complexes about their lack of intelligence.

# Sexuality – The Female Snake

## Sexually Possessive

Mrigasira's animal sign is the female snake. In nature, snakes find potential mates by sending special 'scent messages' to each other. The female snake will rub the male snake with her head as part of their loving. They like a long mating and generally mate for life.

Metaphorically, the same can be said of Mrigasira. You will not be the aggressive partner. You need someone else to take the first steps in a sexual relationship. The sexuality of the snake is intensely private and very passionate. You keep your sexuality highly controlled – only a person you really desire would release your passion. With others you play the disinterested intellectual.

You find it difficult to be casual in relationships. You can be jealous and possessive. You will not let go easily. Like the snake, you will wrap yourself around your lovers and cling to them. At the same time you like your freedom, as you will not like to feel captive. You should be careful not to let your possessiveness and jealousy get out of control. You need to bite your tongue in arguments as you can spit venom at your partners. Try to control your vicious streak – this usually comes out when relationships are not going your way and your lovers or partners are being openly defiant and challenging.

## The Best and the Worst Sexual Partners

The male snake Rohini is the best sexual partner for you. You have a lot in common. This allows the relationship to flourish on many levels. Mrigasira are more intellectually dominant while Rohini are sensuously so.

The mongoose Uttara Ashadha is the worst sexual relationship for Mrigasira. (See the Impossible Sexual Partnership below.)

# MRIGASIRA

## Relationship Issues

### The Impossible Sexual Partnership

Mrigasira's animal sign is the snake which has a very inimical relationship with Uttara Ashadha's animal sign, the mongoose. Your relationship with Uttara Ashadha is complex. In nature, the mongoose is the deadly enemy of the snake. Whenever they meet they fight to the death. As a snake Nakshatra, you remain subconsciously antagonistic towards Uttara Ashadha. You both find it very hard to make allowances for each other. Your passion can soon turn sour. In extreme cases, sexual competitiveness, irrational jealousies and vindictiveness can come into this sexual relationship unnoticed. Then you may want to destroy each other without thinking of the consequences.

When in a relationship with Uttara Ashadha, you must always guard against being combative sexually. Avoid using your sexual superiority to settle your fights. You are better equipped to rationalize than the other snake Nakshatra, Rohini. Your will analyse the hidden undercurrents and will not be afraid to cross the barriers that block your relationship – intellectually at least. Your planetary ruler Mars is naturally friendly with Uttara Ashadha's ruler the Sun. You are 55% compatibile with Uttara Ashadha but you should always remember the hidden undercurrents of sexual rivalry, anger and inimical natures.

### Seeking Perfection in the World of Illusions

You aspire towards intellectually satisfying relationships. You need a partner who is cerebral and brainy. Your idea of a perfect partner is hard to live up to. You can analyse and dissect your relationships, looking for the smallest imperfection, and this can create a feeling of dissatisfaction. You need to be careful that in your search for relationship utopia, you are not rejecting a good, happy partnership.

Your analytical brain is always trying to work things out; you may not think you are being critical of your partner, but they will see it that way. You get bored easily. Don't confuse boredom in life with boredom within your relationship – you must learn to separate the two.

## Facing Mars Nakshatras

Your most difficult relationship is with the other Nakshatras ruled by Mars – Chitra and Dhanishta. Mars is the planet of war and as Mrigasira's ruler, it does not equip you to work with relationships and love, especially when you deal with other Mars Nakshatras. You tend to leave your analytical skills behind and become combative. While you understand other Mrigasira and can have good relationships with them, when it comes to bonding with Dhanishta and Chitra, the problems begin. Your relationship with Dhanishta can quickly become a battlefield, both trying to exert power and unable to get in touch with your softer selves. Chitra will charm you initially. Chitra want social superiority and you want intellectual dominance – you clash on everything just to show the other who is more powerful.

## Sporty, Adventurous and Argumentative

You are strong, charismatic, sharp, intelligent and witty. You love pitting your intellect against others and take pleasure in winning debates and arguments. You like sports of all kinds. You enjoy new challenges. You lose your temper easily and anger management is necessary for you. You should channel your surplus energy into positive deeds. If you give in to your lazy, easygoing nature, you can store up too much surplus energy that can explode into temper or unnecessary arguments.

You need excitement all the time and get bored easily. You find it difficult to commit to any one thing or person, as there are always new ideas, hobbies, jobs and relationships to entice you.

## Analysing Relationships

You cannot love instinctively. You need to intellectualize everything, even the validity of life. Once you have rationalized the issue, you are happy. This works for relationships as well. When you are thinking about getting involved in a new relationship, you analyse and try to rationalize how it fits into the scheme of things. Once satisfied, you accept it and make a commitment. But it can be frustrating for your partners while you are trying to make up your mind. Also with too much analysis, sometimes, you forget the importance of natural attraction or intuitive signals. You can lose a good relationship because you are unable to make up your mind whether you want to be involved or not.

## Loving Mrigasira

Mrigasira are difficult to love. One moment they are possessive and passionate, the next they can be detached and intellectual. They can also drive you mad with their need to analyse every aspect of your relationship. They can be overly critical. To love them you need to accept this side of their nature but also let them know from the start that you do not accept their criticism without argument. They like you to stand up to them or they can walk all over you.

## Compatibility

**Ideal life partner: Ardra**
**Most challenging life partners: Chitra and Dhanishta**

The full Compatibility Grid is on page 338.

**Mrigasira and Ashwini:** You are both strong personalities. You love Ashwini's adventurous nature, their free spirit, and unconventional view on love and relationships. Ashwini will always keep you on the

edge, so you do not have time to be bored with them. Do not be too possessive: Ashwini hate complications and tend to walk away.
**61% compatible**

**Mrigasira and Bharani:** You find the Bharani magnetism irresistible. Instant attraction, hot and fiery passion can propel you into an affair. You will thrill at their need to possess you, mind, body and soul. But Bharani are not always interested in intellectual debates, hate analysing and working on the relationship and their dedication to sensuality is off-putting. **43% compatible**

**Mrigasira and Krittika:** You enjoy arguing, debating every aspect of life. Krittika are able to match your every argument and pitting your wits against them will be an exhilarating experience. They will be good friends and lovers. Your jealousy can make them feel insecure. They can take your need to analyse them as a personal criticism.
**54% compatible**

**Mrigasira and Rohini:** Good friendship and exciting sex. You will want to be the strong one, but it is Rohini who calls the shots in the bedroom. With Rohini you learn to appreciate sensuality and passion. Rohini's quiet wisdom will not be deterred by your intellectualism. They represent the perfection you seek in relationships. **77% compatible**

**Mrigasira and Mrigasira:** Loving other Mrigasira can be both stimulating and annoying. You appreciate their minds, the habit of debating every topic and clever sense of humour. You enjoy the same things in life and have fun. Your inability to make up your minds may see no decisions being taken in the Mrigasira household.
**64% compatible**

**Mrigasira and Ardra:** Both of you have equally bright minds that excite and thrill the other. Ardra love analysing. In fact, Ardra is one of the few Nakshatras that do not take offence at your need for analysing relationships. The great compatibility suggests that this realtionship will be exciting and fulfilling. **78% compatible**

**Mrigasira and Punarvasu:** You find their knowledge and wisdom sexy. There is hardly ever time to get bored as you get involved in

## MRIGASIRA

lively debates and intellectual discussions. You can be great friends. Both of you are sensuous and tactile, but you will need to teach Punarvasu that commitment and love go together. **67% compatible**

**Mrigasira and Pushya:** You always think of Pushya as your conscience or someone who is forcing you to confront yourself. This never makes you comfortable with them. You feel a sense of frustration when loving Pushya. You have to learn to appreciate their qualities and encourage them to be open about their feelings. **41% compatible**

**Mrigasira and Ashlesha:** You can be deceptive, keep secrets and give false images to each other. This can make your relationship very exciting, but also gives you many lows. The impulsiveness of your ruler Mars can make you behave childishly and Ashlesha can be extremely cynical. Lack of trust and insecurity can stop you from finding true happiness. **47% compatible**

**Mrigasira and Magha:** You find it difficult to be casual in relationships. Magha are ready to give physical commitment but remain sexually uncommitted. You are private about your sexuality. Be open with Magha about sex: they need sex and want a partner who is not shy about it. Sexual jealousy can be a problem in this partnership. **57% compatible**

**Mrigasira and Purva Phalguni:** This is a Mars–Venus combination. The attraction is usually instant. You love the social, fun-loving Purva Phalguni and their practical and hard-working approach to life. But Purva Phalguni can pay more attention to their family and spend less time on you. You can feel ignored and unloved. **46% compatible**

**Mrigasira and Uttara Phalguni:** You are attracted to Uttara Phalguni's sunny warmth. You enjoy their devotion and thrill at their strong sexuality. You admire their ambitions and feel happy with their support for yours. This is not a relationship where you can get bored. Your ready wit keeps them amused; their loyalty keeps you by their side. **73% compatible**

**Mrigasira and Hasta:** You love the sophistication and charm of Hasta. You are delighted by their earthiness. Hasta open up to you in a way they have never before. You are not fazed by their moodiness. In fact you support them and make them feel confident. They care for you and love you. You find happiness and your doubts go away. **82% compatible**

**Mrigasira and Chitra:** Chitra are too similar and will be very competitive. They are not into commitment and you feel insecure and jealous. You will try to analyse why your relationship with Chitra isn't working well when you have so much in common. Chitra will not take kindly to being analysed and this can create further distance. **37% compatible**

**Mrigasira and Swati:** Swati have a way with words: they can stimulate you with their intelligent discussions but also charm you into going out with them. They will also be very direct about sex and sensuality. Your inability to decide usually irritates Swati. Talk to them or you will develop a distance that can be difficult to bridge. **50% compatible**

**Mrigasira and Vishakha:** You can be great friends but not such good lovers. The moment you make the commitment, your expectations change. As you want to get the best out of the relationship so you try to analyse how you can improve it. Vishakha can view this as nagging. If you settle for a compromise relationship, you may feel very restless. **50% compatible**

**Mrigasira and Anuradha:** You are attracted to the cool, successful and practical Anuradha but find a romantic, sensitive soul within. You try to analyse their need for romance. This makes Anuradha very uncomfortable and they tend to put up the shutters. Then you wonder why they are cold and unresponsive. Try to respect their romanticism. **47% compatible**

**Mrigasira and Jyeshta:** You distrust the mystical side of Jyeshta and your criticisms can make Jyeshta feel threatened. Although you enjoy their mind games, when they get too intense Jyeshta can suddenly change the rules, making you feel cheated. This is an exciting relationship but can have too many ups and downs to be completely happy. **53% compatible**

# MRIGASIRA

**Mrigasira and Mula:** Mula never want to talk about your issues. The more you analyse the reasons for your compatibility, the more Mula can direct their anger towards you. There is no point feeling upset when you are not willing to see the relationship from their point of view. Accept them as they are, then you can be happier.
**51% compatible**

**Mrigasira and Purva Ashadha:** Instant passion but the fires burn out quickly. The baggage of the spent passion is powerful: it stops you from constructing something else. Whatever compromise you finally reach in this partnership, the memory of the early days remains a potent reminder. The more you try to capture it, the more elusive it becomes. **40% compatible**

**Mrigasira and Uttara Ashadha:** Your worst sexual relationship. You need to use your analytical skill to work with the issues. Make friends with Uttara Ashadha before you even think about exploring your sexuality. Then develop trust between the two of you. Do not make sexuality your main anchor for the relationship. Finally talk about your inner feelings. (See The Impossible Sexual Partnership above.)
**55% compatible**

**Mrigasira and Shravana:** You find Shravana alternating between hot and cold. You can never pin down their true personality. When you try to analyse their personality, they take offence. Make Shravana understand that it is part of your nature to analyse, and that you are not trying to put them down. You should never underestimate the Shravana sensitivity. **39% compatible**

**Mrigasira and Dhanishta:** You will be competitive and aggressive and your relationship can soon become a war zone. This partnership is also spiritually complex. Dhanishta can disrupt your emotions. The constant fighting can psychologically burn you out. Their inability to understand and adjust to your demands causes you immense frustration. **35% compatible**

**Mrigasira and Shatabhishak:** You do not always warm to Shatabhishak immediately. They are too inhibited, secretive and do not address their issues. Their way of thinking frustrates you as well as excites you. An unlikely relationship develops that defies conventions. Try not to be too possessive and encourage them to open up their inner world. **65% compatible**

**Mrigasira and Purva Bhadra:** Both of you use your intellect as a weapon but never against each other: you are too good friends ever to do so. Purva Bhadra may be cool in the way they show their affections in public; in private they will be uninhibited lovers. They are generous and caring. **69% compatible**

**Mrigasira and Uttara Bhadra:** Uttara Bhadra can be too spiritual and ascetic for you. Uttara Bhadra are naturally diffident. If you need fun and excitement, you must provide it for both of you. They will be happy to follow you and be adventurous. You can feel restricted by them but they usually act with the best intentions. **49% compatible**

**Mrigasira and Revati:** Revati are so strong in their idealistic beliefs, you feel yourself drawn to them. You want to be protective and loving towards them. You also enjoy discussing why your relationship survives despite both of you disagreeing on most things. They are never squeamish in facing the truth and you admire and love them equally. **74% compatible**

# Cusps

Those born at the end or beginning of Mrigasira, see pages 351–3.

21 June to 5 July

# Ardra

Ruled by Rahu
Animal: The Female Dog
Symbol: The Head

## Meaning and Symbolism

*Ardra* means 'green', 'moist' or 'like a teardrop'. The moistness of the eyes can blur the picture yet we feel renewed and refreshed after the tears have flown. The symbol of Ardra is the head, where the brain or the mind is situated. The brain is influenced by experiences from past karma. How you will react in this life is the sum total of the experiences of these karmas. You can meet partners with whom you have unfinished karmas.

Ardra Nakshatras are connected to intellectual fertility, the ability of the mind to create. They are both enhanced by their sharp thinking but also limited by their intellectual barriers. The limitations of intellect can blur your mind or you can use your intelligence and connect to your subconscious to create fertile grounds for new growth. You are often dissatisfied with your present surroundings, so you start looking for answers. The ability to be both confused and enlightened at the same time is possible. You need a partner who understands your intelligence but also inspires and stimulates you.

# The Ardra Personality

## From the Subconscious to Reality

Ardra is the first Nakshatra in the Vedic Zodiac ruled by Rahu. Rahu is the head of the celestial snake. In Vedic terminology, the lower brain is also known as the serpent brain. The lower brain is the organ of the subconscious mind. Within it are stored the stories of our past lives. Rahu is the projection of our past life issues on the present and is obsessed with externalizing the past life wishes through present experiences. Ardra's life journey is about acting on the subconscious, not losing touch with it. Ardra look beyond the physical world.

Emotions, love, instinct and feelings are buried deep in your subconscious. While you explore realism, you must realize that perceptions of reality can change. What appears real to you now, may not be so at a later date. You do not want cut-and-dried relationships. As Ardra, you learn to make your dreams your reality and vice versa. Let your hidden desires into your relationships – they are an intrinsic part of you.

## Mental Challenges

One day of Ardra falls in the Western sign of Gemini and the rest in the western sign of Cancer. Rahu rules Ardra. Both Mercury's and the Moon's rulership of Gemini and Cancer indicates that the sphere of activity is going to be connected to the mind, the emotional and the intellectual one. Most of Ardra's challenges come from their unique way of thinking.

Those born on the cusp of Ardra can be in the end of the Western sign of Gemini. This is a karmic birth time. There are very few people who are born at the end of Gemini and beginning of Ardra. They are mentally active, they want love and emotions to fit into the correct slots. They are not always ready to explore their emotions.

For Cancer-born Ardra, the Moon rules their Western star sign and Rahu the Nakshatra. Rahu and the Moon have a complex relationship. Rahu eclipses the Moon. This is not a physical eclipse where Rahu darkens the light of the Moon, but an inner eclipse. Cancer Ardra fear their light can be obscured, their emotional needs unfulfilled by their partners. So they hide their inner thoughts, usually dreading rejection and emotional domination.

## Sexuality – The Female Dog

### Sexually Silent

Your sexuality is expressed by your animal sign the female dog. In Vedic Astrology female suggests passivity. You often wait for your partners to make the first move. You are forever seeking approval and appreciation. If you are sexually attracted to someone you will show your affection immediately but keep your sexual needs under wraps, hoping to find a loving partner who will unravel and expose your sensuality, slowly and passionately. You can get involved in practical relationships that do not focus on your sensuality. You should polish up your sexual techniques as you can be a bit unimaginative as lovers.

You have a strong sexual appetite and can take on many partners. You will be faithful if your partners demand it. Otherwise, you enjoy exploring your sexuality with no thought of fidelity or commitment. Being silent about your sensuous needs does not mean you do not have them. This makes you easy prey to someone who knows how to press your sexual buttons.

### The Best and the Worst Sexual Partners

The male dog Nakshatra, Mula, is the best sexual partner for Ardra. The overall relationship between Mula and Ardra is average; indicating that for you to find total compatibility you need to look beyond a purely sexual relationship. Mula can give you an exciting time sexually but their personal journey is complex and in the opposite

# THE LOVE SIGNS

direction to yours. They can mess you up mentally and hurt you. Other Ardra also make good sexual partners.

In nature, the dog chases the deer to its death. Similarly in relationships, the deer Nakshatras Anuradha and Jyeshta bring out the worst in you. You suddenly adopt a different personality and can become ferocious, possessive, jealous and demanding. You can restrict the deer's freedom and independence. They like their sex to be fun and frivolous, but you can become perversely practical and unimaginative with them. With Jyeshta, the relationship is extremely difficult. You can make the relationship with Anuradha work, as they have the capacity to give unrequited love and are willing to work through their differences with you.

## Relationship Issues

### Fear of Emotions

You can be heartless – the thinkers who forget to feel. You hardly ever acknowledge your emotions, even to your nearest partners. Like your namesake the teardrop, you can be involved in relationships that make you shed tears. You choose partners who satisfy your mind, but a part of you remains unfulfilled. You can ignore your partner's emotions as well. By allowing your emotions to come to the fore, letting the tears flow, the picture of your life may blur for a time, but it will also cleanse the way you relate to love and emotions. Be in touch with your hidden emotions. If you allow your fears to overtake you and keep your emotional self under lock and key, you will feel perpetually let down by love and relationships.

### Learning to Love the Mercury Nakshatras

Mercury rules Ashlesha, Jyeshta and Revati. Mercury Nakshatras are at a karmic point of life where they are learning to give up their desires and attachments and move towards a more spiritual self. Ardra is in a totally practical place, where you are learning about attachments and not giving them up. Of the three, you find it easiest to relate to Revati. Revati love you unconditionally. It is with Jyeshta that the most difficult and karmic lessons take place. Jyeshta do not want to be bound by intellectual boundaries any longer and you want to erect intellectual restrictions for yourself. Ashlesha is also tough for you. Ashlesha are mystical and complex, they are learning to give up one cycle of life and move into a new one.

## Ambitious Relationships

You are ambitious and want to get ahead in life. This is your weakness as well as your strength. You can pick partners who are useful, without considering your emotional needs. You can give up a perfectly good relationship if your partner does not agree with your ambitions. Think carefully before you sacrifice your inner needs for the sake of your ambitions.

## Seeking Their Lost Spirituality

You have become disconnected from your spiritual past, thinking and acting only in the rational, practical world. You can only get united with your spiritual roots through a partner. Your partners can awaken your spirituality and introduce you to a fuller life. This puts a strong onus on your partners; they have to be a very advanced and mature soul to recognize your hidden, and frequently disguised, need for spirituality.

## Karmically Dissatisfied

Rahu, the ruler of Ardra makes you dissatisfied. This shows itself strongly in your relationships where you can be dissatisfied with your partners. The feeling that you can do better creates unhappiness. You can give up a good relationship to pursue another one. These can turn out to be a big disappointment, as the happiness offered by the new relationship often turns out to be an illusion created by your expectations and not by the reality of the situation. You need to break this pattern if you are to find true happiness. You should look into the true root of your unhappiness and dissatisfaction and not see your partner as the cause of your restlessness.

# Loving Ardra

Ardra never share their innermost thoughts with others, fearing rejection. Loving Ardra means you recognize their vulnerability and see through the image they project to others. It is not necessary for you to make them confront their emotions but to realize that however much they talk about analysis and practicality, if you touch their emotions, they will love you for it.

# Compatibility

**Ideal life partner: Mrigasira**
**Most challenging life partner: Jyeshta**

**The full Compatibility Grid is on page 338.**

**Ardra and Ashwini:** You can feel rejected by Ashwini. But overcoming the initial hurdles can be extremely rewarding. Ashwini can complete your karmic search for a perfect partner. You can also get caught in an emotional turmoil that can make you experience extremes of emotions, deliriously happy one day and totally disconsolate the next.
**44% compatible**

**Ardra and Bharani:** You love the sensuality of Bharani: they bathe you in their earthy warmth, and you feel secure with them. You will tell them about your emotional needs and trust them with your love. With Bharani you explore deeper emotions and learn to express your sensuality. You must also give them loyalty and sexual fidelity.
**69% compatible**

**Ardra and Krittika:** Both of you are afraid to trust and express your inner emotions. You are extremely unconventional while Krittika like

# ARDRA

to be traditional. You have to make them trust you, then they will reveal their hidden nature. You must avoid being too secretive. Krittika are very vulnerable within and you must try not to be too critical. **49% compatible**

**Ardra and Rohini:** This relationship works despite the initial mistrust. Your ruling planet Rahu creates fear within the Moon, Rohini's ruler. As the compatibility is high, you can convert the fear into delicious excitement – where you explore an unconventional relationship that goes against the grain and still survives. **64% compatible**

**Ardra and Mrigasira:** You are instantly aware of Mrigasira's hidden sensual nature. They find your intelligence exciting and will be happy to teach you to love. Both of you enjoy shifting the goal posts of your relationship, improving its quality as your love grows. Give them your commitment and faith. Mutually fulfilling. **78% compatible**

**Ardra and Ardra:** Only another Ardra can understand you. Your hidden emotions are no secret to them. Both of you understand the need for love but also why you usually camouflage it so successfully. An unconventional relationship, practical on the face of it but deeply loving within. A partnership of equals. Trust is important.
**77% compatible**

**Ardra and Punarvasu:** You can settle into a relationship with Punarvasu for all the wrong reasons. You think they can help you fulfil your ambitions, and you enjoy their wisdom and advice. You find it hard to understand their need to love and mother everyone. A relationship between a dog and a cat Nakshatra leads to frequent fights. **51% compatible**

**Ardra and Pushya:** You may feel you are willing to settle for a practical relationship with Pushya while your soul desires love, emotion, romance and idealism. Pushya are unable to fulfil your desires fully, but they can love you for who you are, support you and be there for you. You can develop intimacy and excitement.
**55% compatible**

**Ardra and Ashlesha:** Ashlesha appear to be mystical, wise and very much in control of their life. But you make a fatal mistake: you let them know you admire them. If you allow your emotions to shine, this makes you an easy conquest for Ashlesha and therefore boring. They will love you and leave you. Ashlesha's animal sign is the cat and as dog, you fight with them. **33% compatible**

**Ardra and Magha:** Rahu rules Ardra and Ketu rules Magha, so you are invisibly tied in an eternal struggle to find happiness. The path of love never runs smooth. Happiness comes after struggle and facing unexpected challenges. Magha help you to understand your inner world and not just be in touch with your outer one. **58% compatible**

**Ardra and Purva Phalguni:** Great relationship. You are drawn to Purva Phalguni for their charm and sophistication, but you love them for their ability to give you strong support and recognize your inner vulnerability. They will be your friend and your lover. You may fight and argue relentlessly but it is your way of showing them you care. **75% compatible**

**Ardra and Uttara Phalguni:** Uttara Phalguni are dynamic, vital and sexy. They drench you with their sunny personality; you find their warmth comforting. Their ambitions and their power act like an aphrodisiac. Unknowingly Uttara Phalguni can make you realize your weakness and through this process you discover your strengths.
**61% compatible**

**Ardra and Hasta:** Both of you believe in free will and personal choices. Hasta love you and care for you but they are also practical and successful. You like their independence and enjoy their sophistication. You love their earthiness. Try not to be too analytical about your relationship: Hasta can take it as a personal criticism and feel hurt. **67% compatible**

**Ardra and Chitra:** Chitra means a reflection and here they reflect your soul's desires. An unlikely attraction binds you together where you gain power through their love and they help to fulfil your ambitions. You show your love too easily to Chitra and they are not always easy

# ARDRA

to please sexually. Be yourself and allow them to take the lead sexually. **65% compatible**

**Ardra and Swati:** Swati are exciting, charming and loving. They are happy with your love and are affectionate and supportive. Love can be wonderful with them. This is a meeting of minds, similar ambitions and the need to be someone. You are emotionally satisfied, you are open about your love for Swati and they warmly reciprocate. **75% compatible**

**Ardra and Vishakha:** Both of you are searching for something indefinable, more sublime. But finding this is not always possible. This creates a sense of expectation from you that Vishakha will fill your inner void and make the nagging discontentment go away. Do not put such a burden on them. Both of you can feel unhappy and disappointed by the result. **46% compatible**

**Ardra and Anuradha:** You do not fully understand the romantic Anuradha. Their sensitivity usually makes you impatient with them. The sexual incompatibility means that there is an underlying frustration in your relationship, which can create problems in other areas as well. Learn to love Anuradha for what they are, and control your aggressiveness. **53% compatible**

**Ardra and Jyeshta:** Jyeshta aggravate your fear of emotions; they can really mess you up emotionally. You find the relationship sexually cold. Jyeshta can control you and if you are too malleable, this makes them even more dominant. You can create emotional upheavals for each other and experience the real disillusionment of love gone wrong. **14% compatible**

**Ardra and Mula:** Mula's ruler Ketu is your other half. This relationship can be intense and karmic. You are strongly attracted to Mula but Mula usually shy away from you since being sexually satisfied with you means that they are failing in their spiritual responsibilities. They can be unkind in the way they reject you. Sex alone is never enough for them. **42% compatible**

**Ardra and Purva Ashadha:** You can be great friends and lovers. You usually have no clear definition of your perfect lover and Purva Ashadha are not sure they want a fixed partnership. Somehow two uncommitted souls find commitment in each other. Both of you take an unusual journey together without worrying too much about convention and society. **77% compatible**

**Ardra and Uttara Ashadha:** Uttara Ashadha can support you and be your lover in the true sense. You enjoy bringing them out of their shell. An unlikely friendship and even more unconventional relationship usually follows. Sexually you have to be aware that they are the mongoose and can take a sudden dislike to your ruler Rahu's snake connections. **67% compatible**

**Ardra and Shravana:** You want what Shravana appear to offer: love, emotion, sentimentality and passion. This relationship brings out all your complexes about emotions and feelings. You can reject Shravana for no apparent reason. You can be running away from your dream of having an emotionally mature and loving relationship.
**61% compatible**

**Ardra and Dhanishta:** Dhanishta will question your actions and fight over your need to be intellectually superior. You never feel totally at ease with Dhanishta, so you keep your vulnerabilities hidden. Dhanishta can be loyal and loving if they feel you are weak, or fight you for every inch if you do insist on being strong and impervious.
**50% compatible**

**Ardra and Shatabhishak:** You are so similar that your relationship lacks balance. Both of you forget to work with the heart and emotions. Shatabhishak have encased their heart in steel, but you do not have the necessary skill to break this barrier. You can talk, socialize or work together but loving each other is a totally different matter. **33% compatible**

**Ardra and Purva Bhadra:** You can be too much in awe of Purva Bhadra. To impress them, you can try to be someone who you think they will appreciate more. You also take a lot of nonsense from them,

## ARDRA

allowing them to take your love casually. Stand up to them and do not allow your relationship to become too one-sided. **48% compatible**

**Ardra and Uttara Bhadra:** Uttara Bhadra are such a comforting presence in your life: loving you, encouraging you and helping you come to terms with the obstacles in life. Remember that Uttara Bhadra put a lot of emphasis on commitment and fidelity, so don't promise it without meaning it. They can get hurt and lose their trust. **72% compatible**

**Ardra and Revati:** Revati look beyond the restrictions that intellect imposes on them; you find their views on life fascinating. This fascination can soon turn to love. You talk endlessly. You take risks emotionally that you never thought you would. Philosophy, love and emotions all make up a very nice package for both of you.
**72% compatible**

## Cusps

Those born at the end or beginning of Ardra, should see pages 353–4.

5 to 19 July

# Punarvasu

Ruled by Jupiter
Animal: The Female Cat
Symbol: The Bow

## Meaning and Symbolism

*Punar* means 'again' and *Vasu* 'brilliant like rays of light'. Vasu can also be translated as 'the home of the soul'. Punarvasu also relates to the Vasus who are solar deities that appear at different stages of the soul's birth to guide it towards its true path. Punarvasu is connected to the transmigration of the soul whereby the soul lives in different bodies in search of it's true home.

Punarvasu Nakshatras enjoy travel, whether it takes place physically or on different levels of consciousness. You also like to change homes. You are searching for the Truth and your true identity through your relationships. Till you find it, you can move into another level of consciousness and stop relating to your partner. You can easily trade one relationship for another.

The symbol of the bow indicates you have the means and the ambition to find the objects of your desire. But without the archer and the arrow, there can be a lack of focus. In relationships, you can desire or love someone, but you will not always have a plan of action when it comes to making that person fall for you. This can lead to

# PUNARVASU

unrequited love simply because you lack the focus or means to let this person know of your feelings.

## The Punarvasu Personality

### The Instinct to Advise

Jupiter, the celestial teacher, rules Punarvasu. You care instinctively. You will express this by teaching, counselling, advising or mentoring. If you are involved in a relationship, you need to be careful that you do not become a guide to your loved ones, taking over their problems. The intimate relationship between man and woman is not one of a student and teacher. Your soul's expression is linked to being the guru (teacher) and you need to learn how to express this within the confines of a modern relationship. Your can attract a circle of admirers who hang on to your every word and your partner may feel jealous of them and unloved by you.

### The Wise Ones

Punarvasu is in the sign of Cancer, which is ruled by the Moon. Jupiter rules the Nakshatra. Punarvasu deals with the transfer of knowledge from the spiritual to the earthly. The rulerships of Jupiter and the Moon bring together wisdom and love. Jupiter guides you towards a new way of life from your spiritual connection to the more material world. The Moon, as the representative of the mother in the Vedic Zodiac, steers you through the difficult part of your life from childhood to adult. You trust your mother implicitly as a child, as your guardian she only has the best in mind for you. You too develop mothering skills and the ability to inspire total trust. You become the guardian of emotions and love for other people.

# Sexuality – The Female Cat

## Sexually Independent

Your sexuality is expressed by your animal sign, the female cat. This is not just the domesticated cat but the cat in the wild, so includes the animals of the cat family such as cheetahs and leopards. You can be instinctively catty, fiercely independent and are not above clawing if anyone dares to invade your space. You only want to be loved when *you* are ready. You hate people being forward – you let them know when you are ready to be loved. Once involved, you are extremely possessive and want your lover's attention all the time.

You are generally surrounded by the opposite sex but still feel lonely. You can be jealous of your partner's relationship with others; you mark your territory. But the same rules do not apply to you – you must keep your independence and freedom. If your partners accept your nature, then you will show them your true side by being loving, sensuous and committed.

## The Best and the Worst Sexual Partners

The male cat Ashlesha is your best sexual partner. This is a sizzling relationship full of passions, sensuality, possessiveness and true independence. You will fight passionately – both of you are strong personalities, unwilling to give an inch. The fireworks this creates can burn the spectators but the pleasure of making up with wild, untamed loving will add to the excitement of your relationship.

The worst sexual partner for the cat Punarvasu is their natural enemy the rat, Magha and Purva Phalguni. Rats like sex unembellished and cats are sensual and passionate. There is no common ground sexually. This is a relationship between a predator and its prey – in the end you can be too strong and sexually powerful.

# PUNARVASU

## Relationship Issues

### Lessons in Commitment

You love to travel. Your partners find it hard to seduce or love you as you are forever on the move. Even if you are physically present, you can be on a different plane mentally. Your mind is usually moving in so many different directions, that you can neglect those you love. You need partners who are flexible, who do not get intimidated by your need for freedom and travel. They need to be willing to conduct the relationship long distance and not always mind your lack of presence. You also must take lessons in commitment. You can feel that no one is committing to you whereas it may be your own behaviour that stops them from doing so.

### Loving the Whole World

You enjoy being the giver. You need to love as much as others need to be loved by you. People can surround you or you may opt for having a large family. One-to-one love is important, but your mothering instinct needs to be fulfilled properly – you may not be happy loving just one person, but need to embrace the whole world. While you are being warm and loving to the world at large, you can be cold and unemotional towards your personal relationships. But your partners must allow you to love the world; this is part of your karmic statement. To connect with people, to love them, nurture them and guide them towards a better future is your spiritual role. You are not being unfaithful.

Your most difficult relationships are with Jyeshta and Shatabhishak. You have an inability to understand Jyeshta's complex needs. Jyeshta want to be loved intensely and Punarvasu cannot deal with such intensity in one-to-one relationships. Shatabhishak are too mysterious; they are never able to let you discover their secret needs and desires. You can love them superficially but a deeper connection is almost impossible to establish. Shatabhishak shun your advice, they distrust your love.

## Walking Away from Complications

Punarvasu's solution to problematic relationships is to walk away from them. Whether you do so physically or mentally, the result is the same. You distance yourself from complications because a) you do not want to deal with them and b) you do not want to face up to the fact that your lack of commitment and insensitivity has created these problems in the first place.

## Coping with Jealousy

You can be jealous of real or imagined relationships, not just sexual, but also with work colleagues, professional relationships and even with your partner's career. You find it hard to tolerate competition of any type. You will be ready to fight, use all means available to oust that person from your life. This behaviour can be acceptable if there are valid reasons. But many times, your jealousy can ruin relationships. Your possessiveness can get obsessive and partners would rather move away than accept this behaviour. You have to learn to break this pattern and learn to control your jealousy. Before you bring your claws out, you should think rationally about the situation and try to see how much damage you can do by allowing your jealousy to rear its ugly head.

# Loving Punarvasu

It is difficult to love Punarvasu as they are forever on the move. Even if they are physically present, their mind can be miles away. Enjoy their unpredictability. Be mentally agile so that you can keep up with their various strands of thought. You need to be willing to conduct your relationship long distance. A surefire way of attracting their attention is to ask them for advice. Then they will be all over you, wanting to improve the quality of your life, connect you to your soul and introduce you to intellectual pursuits. But this is not always what you had in mind, as you were looking for a passionate lover not a

# PUNARVASU

wise counsellor. Part of seducing Punarvasu is letting them feel they are changing your life.

## Compatibility

### Ideal life partners: Bharani and Pushya
### Most challenging life partner: Jyeshta

**The full Compatibility Grid is on page 338.**

**Punarvasu and Ashwini:** You are attracted to the refreshing and zestful Ashwini. They never crowd you or take you for granted. There can be many emotional ups and downs, the joy and excitement of mutual love but the sadness of being lonely when you are apart. Don't put all the blame on them: your need for freedom has created these problems. **55% compatible**

**Punarvasu and Bharani:** Your best relationship. Bharani can teach you about love, commitment and sensuality. Mesmeric and fascinating – this is how you view Bharani. You are willing to make adjustments to suit them, as you desire them so much. You find intimacy and love with Bharani. You become their *lover*, not their guru. **76% compatible**

**Punarvasu and Krittika:** Krittika represent security to you and you want some of their stability and quiet strength. You need them to be your rock, someone to come home to between your travels. Krittika cannot always handle your need for freedom and they can become jealous of your friends. In the long term you may find your rock can become a prison. **56% compatible**

**Punarvasu and Rohini:** You fall for Rohini's magnetism and sensuality. Their romantic nature adds to your love. Once you get involved, you will stay focused on them. Let them know you love them frequently. Do not use your friends or colleagues to make them jealous. If they lose trust in you, the cool, moody and jealous Rohini emerges. **66% compatible**

# THE LOVE SIGNS

**Punarvasu and Mrigasira:** You love the mixture of cool intellect and sizzling sensuality that Mrigasira represent. You never have time to get bored, as there is always another part of their complex personality to explore. Their need for security and their possessiveness is hard to deal with. Compromise. **67% compatible**

**Punarvasu and Ardra:** You find it difficult to trust Ardra completely. You are attracted by their exciting outer persona but can become bored with their more practical side. They need your approval and you may not be there for them. A relationship between a cat and dog Nakshatra can result in frequent fights. Both of you tease and irritate the other purposely. **51% compatible**

**Punarvasu and Punarvasu:** You share a common love of knowledge. At last you meet someone who really understands you. For two Punarvasu to be happy together, they have to make a pact of being together, not making the physical distance an emotional one as well. You need to agree boundaries that both of you adhere to.
**57% compatible**

**Punarvasu and Pushya:** Your best relationship. Pushya are cool but they are amusing and fun, having a great sense of humour. You will bathe Pushya in your warmth. Their support makes you feel secure; you want to commit to them. Even if you go off occasionally you know your Pushya love is there for you – strong, supportive and loyal. **76% compatible**

**Punarvasu and Ashlesha:** A good relationship and great sex. You indulge Ashlesha; you enjoy their bright minds and revel in their sensuality. You can fight with each other but enjoy the passion of making up. You have to control your need to advise them: they do not take that well. Being jealous is not an option. Both of you need your independence. **60% compatible**

**Punarvasu and Magha:** How do you cope with a relationship where there is no sexual compatibility? You can deal with this, but Magha find it almost impossible to do so. Sex is a huge motivating force for them. They will not take kindly to your playing fast and loose. The

# PUNARVASU

cat is far stronger than the rat; you have to control your impulses to tease. **51% compatible**

**Punarvasu and Purva Phalguni:** This relationship can work well despite Purva Phalguni and Punarvasu being inimical sexually. Enhance the areas of compatibility, the fun, the socializing, the thirst for knowledge, the shared interests and play down your differences. Resist the temptation to play sexual games and intimidate.
**62% compatible**

**Punarvasu and Uttara Phalguni:** Uttara Phalguni are steadfast and reliable. If you are open with them about your needs, they will be there for you when you want to come back. Do not give in to their demands: Uttara Phalguni are also intrigued by you as you have a fascinating lifestyle. Give it up for them and they can lose interest and hurt you. **50% compatible**

**Punarvasu and Hasta:** Hasta appear very similar to you and you connect to their lunar energy. They are happy to take your advice and improve their inner self. But you are not at ease with their neediness. They are emotional and need constant attention. You are happy to love many but when you have to focus on one individual, you face problems. **57% compatible**

**Punarvasu and Chitra:** You love Chitra's adventurous spirit and their ability to love you on whatever level you want. Let Chitra know they are special to you and how much you love them, then the bonds remain regardless of your independent lives. Ignore them, and they will happily move into a different sphere of self-discovery where you are not needed. **58% compatible**

**Punarvasu and Swati:** Loving Swati is easy for you: you sense their kindred spirit. You may appear very different and have incompatible ideas but your soul needs the same things – adventure, non-conformity, and freedom. But both of you still need love. You respect Swati's ideas and show them how to get the best out of them.
**74% compatible**

**Punarvasu and Vishakha:** Love makes you think that your needs are

very similar. Vishakha may feel unwilling to share your love with others. You need to consciously make them feel wanted. You can easily choose different goals. If your spiritual paths diverge too far, you may have created emotional distance that is hard to bridge.
**51% compatible**

**Punarvasu and Anuradha:** Anuradha force you to stop and think about love and life. Anuradha's gentle questioning of your ways lights an inner spark within you. Anuradha help you to overcome any lack of intimacy by loving enough for two. Also they are supportive and selfless, so have the comfort of knowing that they will be there for you. **62% compatible**

**Punarvasu and Jyeshta:** The most challenging and painful relationship for you. Mysterious Jyeshta attracts you but the relationship becomes too complex. They try to control your life and if you accept these dictates you can feel too restricted. Both of you are usually not prepared to be sensitive to each other's needs and can easily hurt each other in the process. **22% compatible**

**Punarvasu and Mula:** You can't deal with Mula but you cannot walk away from them as you usually do from other difficult relationships. You fight, become jealous and possessive. Instead of loving them, you can act cold and aggressive. They do not improve the relationship by rejecting you one moment and taking up with you the next.
**29% compatible**

**Punarvasu and Purva Ashadha:** You enjoy Purva Ashadha's company: they are fun, full of life and original. You can also sense their mental confusion. You want to protect them but they do not listen to your advice. At least they are not always trying to make you into a conventional bore. You can love them without making complicated commitments. **65% compatible**

**Punarvasu and Uttara Ashadha:** You can form a mutual appreciation society, loving each other deeply. But this is your spiritually complex relationship bringing unnecessary issues to spoil your love. Develop Uttara Ashadha's trust, as they are sensitive and can be jealous of your many friends. Tell them of your love regularly, so they never feel left out. 58% compatible

**Punarvasu and Shravana:** Shravana listen to you and understand your needs before you have spoken them. They help you understand how to use your restlessness more creatively. You can enjoy a great and loving relationship, but it still remains largely uncommitted. Exploring philosophy and creative ideas gives you a joint focus.
68% compatible

**Punarvasu and Dhanishta:** Dhanishta can be very inflexible about what they want from you. Their inability to feel comfortable with your spiritual independence creates problems. While they are not into commitment, they want your attention all the time. A bit of give and take in a relationship will do no harm to both of you.
46% compatible

**Punarvasu and Shatabhishak:** Your worst relationship. You find it difficult to trust Shatabhishak; they will never open up to you, always being secretive. They can perversely stop telling you even the smallest details just to make you suspicious. You cannot control your jealousy. Both of you acting negatively does not promote love. 25% compatible

**Punarvasu and Purva Bhadra:** Purva Bhadra unrealistically expect you to give up your independent life and concentrate totally on them. You like them and enjoy their company, but your love has to be a distant one. You do not have the time to nourish your relationship, which usually becomes frustrating for the person making the compromise. 41% compatible

**Punarvasu and Uttara Bhadra:** Uttara Bhadra will support and love you. They allow you your freedom yet remind you periodically of your responsibilities. They encourage you in your spiritual search and their love makes you keep coming back to them. Try not to promise them commitment if you are unable to follow through. They will be flexible. 70% compatible

**Punarvasu and Revati:** Revati will charm you into loving them. Revati are insecure and you will be in your element advising and guiding

# THE LOVE SIGNS

them. Revati also have the tendency to be possessive and they can cling emotionally. While you are happy to give them their emotional sustenance, you should let them know of your need for freedom.
**69% compatible**

## Cusps

Those born at the end or beginning of Punarvasu, should see pages 355–6.

19 July to 2 August

# Pushya

Ruled by Saturn
Animal: The Ram
Symbol: Flower

## Meaning and Symbolism

*Pushya* means to 'nourish' or 'thrive'. Pushya work to nourish others and create ideal conditions for the world to thrive. They tend to sacrifice their own needs for others. This is especially true in relationships; you will nourish your partners and give up your own desires so that your partners can be fulfilled. The symbol of Pushya is a flower. A flower is the outward expression of inner ideas. A flower also blooms for others and may not recognize its own beauty, further indicating your ability to be there for others.

Knowledge and its expression is the most important aspect of your personality. You feel the need to teach the world. Yours is not the role of the natural mentor that Punarvasu holds, but of a serious adviser who will only speak if you feel those taking your advice are willing to accept it. You have the ability to make ideas real. A balance between expansion and restriction is achieved under Pushya. The soul's restrictions as well as its responsibility to live a good life are fully recognized by you.

## The Pushya Personality

### The Saturnine Responsibilities

Saturn rules Pushya. Saturn is known as Shani in Sanskrit. Saturn is the great teacher of cosmic truths. His influence is tough to deal with. Saturn teaches you about responsibility, which you take on board from a very young age. You hardly ever make commitments lightly. You will tend to stay in relationships even if you are not totally fulfilled, taking that as your spiritual responsibility.

Saturn is a Brahmachari – a bachelor at heart and an ascetic. This gives Pushya a very ascetic attitude to life. You face difficulty in the give and take of relationships. You may fear relationships or be cold towards your partners without being conscious of it. You may try to control your sexual feelings.

### The Light and the Dark

Pushya is placed at the ending of Cancer and the beginning of Leo. The two luminaries, the Moon and the Sun, rule the Western signs respectively. Saturn's relationship with the luminaries is a difficult one. The luminaries shine brightly whereas Saturn is the dimmest planet visible to the naked eye. So while some of the issues of Pushya Nakshatras are easy to comprehend, many of them take a long time to understand.

Pushya in the Western sign of Cancer brings with it the impact of the Moon and Saturn. The Moon is changeable; Saturn is rigid and restrictive. Here this combination can lead to many emotional struggles till the Moon learns the important lesson of control and Saturn the lesson of change. The Cancer Pushya learn about emotions and how to deal with them.

Pushya in Leo focus on the complicated relationship between the Sun and Saturn. In the Vedas, the Sun and Saturn are father and son; the Sun rejects Saturn, leaving emotional scars in Saturn's psyche. Sun the King represents power and Saturn the worker rejects it. Initially,

## PUSHYA

Leo Pushya experience conflict about how to express power, but life teaches them humility. They also learn about love, rejection and acceptance. Cancer Pushya learn to balance the difficulties of life with happiness. Leo Pushya learn to be more democratic within their relationships.

## Sexuality – The Ram

### Sexually Playful

Pushya sexuality is expressed by your animal sign, the ram. Sheep are not usually recognized for their individuality. They tend to live for others – giving wool for warmth and meat for sustenance. You recognize the need to serve others and are rarely ever aware of your own individuality. Through service to others you can find yourself. In your sexual relationships you will also try to please.

The male sexuality makes you active in seeking your sexual fulfilment. You need to be in control of your sexuality. Both sexes of Pushya like to pursue their partners. The ram is passionate and aggressive. You are serious in all other aspects of your life, but you enjoy frivolous sensuality and light-hearted sex. But sheep hardly ever fight for their mate. So if your partners decide to move on you will not fight for them.

Sheep like to follow the flock; therefore you can be very conscious of what the world is doing and follow others. This can create problems within relationships as you can get involved in new things and, in extreme cases, leave a relationship for a new one if you feel the present one is out of sync with new ideas or fashion.

### The Best and the Worst Sexual Partners

The ewe Krittika is your best sexual partner. Pushya relates harmoniously with Krittika in all areas of life so these are good partnerships – sexually satisfying and emotionally complete.

The monkeys, Purva Ashadha and Shravana, are incompatible with

Pushya sexually. You like to pursue your partners and you are possessive. The monkey Nakshatras do not want to be either captured or possessed. They will tease and manipulate you, never making a commitment and can make you feel sexually inadequate and lacking in finesse.

# Relationship Issues

## Learning to Love the Mars Nakshatras

Pushya's most difficult relationship is with the Mars Nakshatras. Mars rules Mrigasira, Chitra and Dhanishta. Relationships with Chitra (22% compatibility) and Dhanishta (24% compatibility) are the most difficult that you have to deal with. Mrigasira with 44% compatibility is easier. The key to these difficulties lies in the complex cosmic relationship between Mars and Saturn. Mars is impulsive, adventurous and active whereas Saturn is cautious, responsible and patient. When Mars Nakshatras wants to act on impulse, Saturn will block their path – forcing them to think. This makes the Mars Nakshatras feel restricted and frustrated, while you feel you are perpetually living with immaturity and childish behaviour. Their aggression makes you feel unsettled.

Mrigasira's intellectual passion is too unrealistic for you to appreciate. You cannot wait to bring them down to earth. You should stop trying to block their growth and Mrigasira need to stop fighting you all the way. You find Chitra's energy and verve difficult to handle. You will always try to mould them into your own image. Chitra rebel and challenge you at every step. Dhanishta are too idealistic; you can get an inferiority complex trying to live up to their image of perfection.

In fact, appreciating what each of you can bring to the relationship and allowing each other space goes a long way towards defusing any tensions you have with the Mars Nakshatras. When you are involved in a relationship with these Nakshatras, it is better for you to enjoy a bit of the Mars passion for life and impulsiveness and refrain from controlling them too much. In the same way, the Mars Nakshatras would do well to learn a bit of the Pushya caution.

## Fear of Emotions

You are good at commitments and responsibility; it is your emotional self that you are anxious about expressing. You will be faithful and correct in your relationships, but you can be detached and distant. Talking about love, passion and sensuality makes you uncomfortable. You find it difficult to express your love, leading your partners to feel unwanted. You need your loved ones to teach you about love. Unless you are careful, you can get involved in a relationship that is cold and aloof, leaving an inner sense of frustration.

## Being More Flexible and Liberal

On a negative level, you can become too dogmatic, restricted and fundamentalist. Your fear of emotions can make you feel unable to express yourself fully. You lack self-confidence and seldom appreciate your good qualities. You tend to put conditions on your relationships that create problems. You find it difficult to see the other side of the argument. This inflexibility can make relationships very tough. Your insistence on doing the right thing means you will not ignore any wrong actions taken by your partner. You should learn to be sympathetic to normal human weaknesses.

You have such high expectations of your partners, you feel let down by their inability to live up to your ideal. This is your relationship challenge. While you face even the most difficult relationship head on, your partners may not be strong enough to deal with the issues in your way. Being supportive rather than critical, flexible in your outlook will help you find greater happiness. While not all Pushya will take this behaviour to the extreme, you need to be aware of your weaknesses.

## Loving Pushya

The Pushya relationship with their parents directly reflects how they relate today. They are attached to their parents, but their upbringing was detached and they were instilled with a sense of responsibility. They were self-sufficient as children and become more so as adults. You need to crack their veneer of self-sufficiency if you want to get closer to them. They respond to love and affection, slowly thawing to reveal their true self. They are like a delicate flower; they need the food of love and gentle emotional watering often. They wilt easily from lack of affection.

## Compatibility

**Ideal life partner: Ashwini**
**Most challenging life partner: Dhanishta**

The full Compatibility Grid is on page 338.

**Pushya and Ashwini:** Your best relationship. Ashwini are attractive, magnificent and sexy. But Ashwini will take time to recognize you as their potential partner. You are patient and wait for Ashwini. Ashwini will bring enthusiasm and love into your life. You will support and love them through the ups and downs of theirs. **83% compatible**

**Pushya and Bharani:** Bharani stand for everything you disapprove of; they are sensual, indulgent and self-involved. Why are you struggling against this attraction? Their passionate nature will help you come out of your shell. Balance your pragmatic personality with their more exotic one. Your sexuality flowers under their expertise. Avoid trying to control them. **61% compatible**

**Pushya and Krittika:** Krittika is your best sexual partner. They are shy and diffident sexually. You can see through their insecurities and make them comfortable with their passions. Krittika's autocratic behaviour can at times annoy you. Take care you do not dash their

## PUSHYA

emotions with your coldness. They express their love because they trust you. **68% compatible**

**Pushya and Rohini:** You may find Rohini too emotional and fickle. Rohini will find you rigid and inflexible. As you get closer, you discover Rohini's ability to bring laughter and joy. They will lighten your load, romance, seduce and help you express your sensuality. They can be needy for your support and you are there for them.
**75% compatible**

**Pushya and Mrigasira:** This relationship has the ability to generate tension and stress. Have you ever tried to understand their needs and see the world through their eyes? It is so different. At best this relationship can be exciting. At worst you will fight constantly and feel frustrated. Mrigasira's constant criticism can make you cool and self-sufficient. **41% compatible**

**Pushya and Ardra:** Ardra are unconventional, a bit crazy, eccentric. They like to live life in a state of super intensity. You may find their lifestyle too extreme, yet you will find them attractive and fascinating. Work hard at keeping your relationship buzzing and exciting. Fall into a rut, and Ardra can look elsewhere for their excitement.
**55% compatible**

**Pushya and Punarvasu:** You are attracted by Punarvasu's bright personality and their interesting lifestyle, but also by the recognition that they can make you complete. They can give you that for which you have been searching all your life. You flourish in their love. You lose your fear of emotions and are willing to take a chance on love.
**76% compatible**

**Pushya and Pushya:** This is a good relationship based on shared ideals and deep understanding. You instinctively know what the other wants and are able to be open and honest about your feelings to each other. You may appear to be a boring and pragmatic couple, but in truth there is humour, emotional commitment and pure love.
**77% compatible**

**Pushya and Ashlesha:** Ashlesha know how to break down your barriers and speak in your language of love, although initially only to love you and leave you. But the moment they get to know you, they find your warm and loving secret self and your steadiness and loyalty. You love their sensuality. An unconventional relationship with deep emotional ties. **80% compatible**

**Pushya and Magha:** You should stop trying to mould Magha in your own image. The reason you were attracted to them was that they were so different. But now those differences can become bones of contention within you. You are suspicious of their sexual loyalty. Make a special effort to love them. Stop being too critical.
**50% compatible**

**Pushya and Purva Phalguni:** Purva Phalguni will bring you out of your shell – you enjoy the parties and the socializing. But you also start to think about their extravagances and they appear too frivolous and superficial. Are you being too judgemental? Appreciate them. Make an extra effort to be loving or this relationship can become cold and passionless. **39% compatible**

**Pushya and Uttara Phalguni:** The Sun rules Uttara Phalguni and Saturn rules Pushya. The Sun and Saturn are karmically linked and have a challenging relationship. You fight for supremacy. Only one can be in control at a given time. Pushya born under Leo will be able to deal with Uttara Phalguni better than the Cancer Pushya.
**52% compatible**

**Pushya and Hasta:** You love Hasta's ability to feel; they help you overcome your own fear of emotions. They are sophisticated on the outside but will be earthy, sensuous lovers – you like this secret side of their personality. You have strong sexual connections. You like their independence and support them with love, which is reciprocated fully. **69% compatible**

**Pushya and Chitra:** You find the impulsive Chitra hard to handle. They are always searching for the indefinable. Why can't they be realistic? The more you try to make them see reality, the more they try to escape from you. You get involved in a stressful and combative relationship. Chitra can hurt you with their careless disregard. **30% compatible**

**Pushya and Swati:** A good relationship that brings together shared ambitions and great friendship. Swati are unusual and you make a special effort to know them and their views on life. You are much more flexible with Swati than with others. Both of you may struggle with your emotions and need to talk about your fears and uncertainties. **69% compatible**

**Pushya and Vishakha:** You can feel intimidated by Vishakha's overt sexuality, but if you allow them to help you deal with your passions, they can be good sensual partners. Always pay extra attention to keep the sexual vibes alive. That is the area most likely to become a divisive issue. They are generous and caring but also need to feel free. **54% compatible**

**Pushya and Anuradha:** You are similar as Saturn rules you both. You admire Anuradha for being so in touch with their emotions. But you also find their need for romance and love all the time is like chasing illusions. They are not willing to give up their dreams. Try to understand them and be part of their dreams rather than detached from them. **47% compatible**

**Pushya and Jyeshta:** You can be both fascinated and repelled by Jyeshta's extreme sensuality. Your basic ascetic nature does not resonate well with the Jyeshta excesses. But they can charm you and you relax a little. Compromise. Jyeshta will bring fun into your life and you do not have to feel so guilty about enjoying a few of life's pleasures. **55% compatible**

**Pushya and Mula:** You are attracted to Mula's unusual lifestyle and their ability to be free of conventional constraints. You nourish, care for and love them. But they can fail to respond. They seem to be caught up in their own struggles and have nothing to give to you. Though you keep on loving Mula far too long, you feel disillusioned by their disregard. **47% compatible**

# THE LOVE SIGNS

**Pushya and Purva Ashadha:** You are responsible and hardworking but Purva Ashadha appear to enjoy life without a care in the world. They are forever changing jobs, relationships, ambitions and philosophies. You feel very unsettled in this relationship. The monkey Purva Ashadha is your worst sexual partner and a spiritually complex relationship as well. You have the inability to understand each other psychologically. **33% compatible**

**Pushya and Uttara Ashadha:** You love the simplicity and naturalness of Uttara Ashadha. They may be in opulent surroundings but their own tastes are austere. You sense their loneliness and you want to love them. The Leo Pushya have an especially intuitive understanding of Uttara Ashadha as they are ruled by the same Sun–Saturn combination. **63% compatible**

**Pushya and Shravana:** Shravana present the conundrum of being one of the most compatible signs for you but your worst lovers. The sexual difficulty between the monkey Nakshatras and the ram Nakshatras is one of different temperament and not one of total enmity. Your love can be so strong that you work to make your sexual relationship better. **75% compatible**

**Pushya and Dhanishta:** Your worst relationship. You do not want to be totally dominated by Dhanishta; this makes you uncharacteristically aggressive. You find the stress of living with Dhanishta hard to handle. But you never try to understand their free and independent nature. Do not make your relationship a cage for them.
**24% compatible**

**Pushya and Shatabhishak:** Shatabhishak are independent and secretive. When you try to get close to them, they shut their emotional doors. How can you go about making them express their emotions when you do not know how to do so? You can become too cold and haughty with them. You can get stuck in a relationship without warmth and love. **36% compatible**

**Pushya and Purva Bhadra:** You put a lot of effort in to your relationship with Purva Bhadra. You love them unconditionally, try to be

# PUSHYA

the image of their ideal lover, run their home efficiently, and make the relationship strong and successful. Remind your Purva Bhadra lovers about your contribution to their life or they may start taking you for granted. **60% compatible**

**Pushya and Uttara Bhadra:** This relationship has the potential of becoming far too serious. The ascetic Saturn rules you both. You need to remind each other about love. Take time out to party and have some fun, and earmark special quality time to be together or both of you can drift into a relationship where love takes the back seat. **50% compatible**

**Pushya and Revati:** Revati charms you, can be your friend and lover. You have many interests in common. Communicating is easy; they help you overcome your fear of emotions. Revati need your support and you are happy to provide that. They take their commitment to you seriously and work hard to make the relationship special and loving. **72% compatible**

# Cusps

Those born at the end or beginning of Pushya, should see pages 356–8.

2 to 16 August

# Ashlesha

Ruled by Mercury
Animal: The Male Cat
Symbol: The Serpent

## Meaning and Symbolism

*Ashlesha* means to 'embrace' – the soul embracing life so that it can act out its karma. As soon as we embrace life, we are subject to the rules and regulations of the earth. We are involved in the process of life and death, happiness and unhappiness. Destiny, born from our own actions from previous lives, influences our life today. Ashlesha need to move from a state of detachment to attachment.

Ashlesha's symbol is the serpent. Hypnotic, mysterious, exotic and dangerous, snakes like a solitary life. If your partners become like snake charmers and play your special tune, you can be enticed. You will dance to their music and remain enthralled. If your solo state is disturbed without true understanding from your partner, it brings out your darker side – you can be vicious and dangerous.

# ASHLESHA

# The Ashlesha Personality

## Mercurial

Mercury rules Ashlesha. Mercury Nakshatras are at the ending cycles of the Nakshatras, where the psychology of an individual changes. Mercury is the celestial bridge between higher forces and the Earth. Here Mercury helps an individual give up their attachment to the eternal soul and make a life on Earth. Before you are willing to do so, you need to know why. You remain intellectually detached as you search within you to find the answers. What you do not realize is that the more you search and analyse the truth, the more you get sucked into worldliness and lose your free spirit.

## Social yet Detached

Ashlesha is wholly in the Western sign of Leo. You express the Sun–Mercury combination. It is one of power and intellect. The Sun is steady and Mercury is fickle. You appear stable and powerful but your mind can be very indecisive. The Sun is a loner and Mercury enjoys connecting and socializing. Your partners get either enthralled or confused by the paradox you represent. You enjoy the limelight, love people and are charming and talkative; yet you can be cool, detached and impersonal.

You find it impossible to be mentally in the same place for too long. You are on a psychic journey, which reveals many of the mysteries of life. Your nature does not allow you to remain in one relationship for too long as your intellectual needs keep changing. There may be someone you feel was just the right one for you, but on a deeper exploration you find the connection is not there. You want to explore the mystery of the next relationship.

# Sexuality – The Male Cat

## Feline and Arrogant

Your sexuality is expressed by your animal sign – the male cat. This is not just the domesticated cat but the cat in the wild, which includes the animals of the big cat family, such as cheetahs and leopards. You have many feline qualities; instinctively catty, fiercely independent and are not above clawing if someone dares to invade your space. You will only want to be loved when *you* are ready. You hate people being forward, you will let them know when you are ready to be loved. Once involved, you demand loyalty and want your lover's attention all the time.

The male cat is a promiscuous animal, usually roaming afar to find mates. Commitment phobic, you can move from one relationship to another or even be involved in more than one relationship at a time. Both male and female Ashlesha will be hunters and actively seek relationships when they desire someone. You only like to work on those who are not interested in you. If someone piques your interest, you will pursue and seduce them with romance and sensuality till you have imprinted yourself on their consciousness. You can lose interest very quickly if your partners are an easy conquest. You will be possessive, but if your partners quickly allow themselves to be possessed, where is the fun? If your partners try to make you jealous, you will fight viciously to win them back. But you will lose trust in them. For you, there in no love without trust.

## The Best and Worst Sexual Partners

The female cat Punarvasu is your best sexual partner. This is a sizzling relationship full of passion, sensuality, possessiveness and true independence. You will fight passionately. Both of you are strong personalities, unwilling to give an inch. The fireworks this creates can burn the spectators but the pleasure of making up adds to the excitement. The overall relationship with Punarvasu is also good; you can find complete fulfilment from your animal counterpart.

## ASHLESHA

The worst sexual partners are your natural enemy the rats, Magha and Purva Phalguni. You are sexually demanding and though the rat Nakshatras like sex in quantity, they are usually unable to deliver the quality sex you demand. Your sexual needs have no common ground and there is a danger that this relationship can become one between a predator and its prey. You can move from emotional passion to sexual rivalry in an instant.

# Relationship Issues

## The Desire for Uncomplicated Relationships

Your spiritual journey is to move from being a free spirit to experiencing emotional and earthly entanglements. You usually go for relationships that do not demand much from you, where you can remain detached and unemotional. Despite your best intentions to remain cool, the moment you explore a relationship deeper, you tend to get involved in ones that bring upheaval. Do not be too afraid of these upheavals. Being in touch with your emotions also opens your inner world; love will help you overcome your personal blocks. But you need a wise and caring partner who is completely supportive, loving but also allows you time to be yourself.

You shy away from too many demands. Simplicity in relationships is key for you. For all your cynicism, you have an idealistic view of love. Reality never truly lives up to your expectations. You have usually experienced tough relationship issues early in life that have transformed your life and thinking. You are not always ready or willing to trust in love and its ability to make you happy. You find it easier to be alone, than in a relationship that is less than perfect.

## Trusting the Emotional Nakshatras

The Moon rules Hasta, Shravana and Rohini. Mercury rules Ashlesha. The Moon is emotional and Mercury analytical. The Moon Nakshatras find it difficult to understand your analytical mind and detachment. You find these Nakshatras too emotional and moody for your liking. You need to trust your instinct more. Stop being afraid of your feelings and you will find it easier to work with the Moon Nakshatras.

You appreciate the outer detachment of Rohini. It is when you are introduced to Rohini's desperate need for emotional satisfaction, their possessiveness and romanticism that you move away. Rohini love your warmth but can get hurt by your selfishness and power.

You have a better chance with Hasta. You are never able to fully understand Hasta's moods. If you try to analyse them, you can become too critical for the sensitive Hasta. This relationship works as long as you learn to trust your emotions and allow Hasta to accept your detachment.

Shravana appear to be in control of their life. Your relationship with them suffers as you can aggravate Shravana's emotional confusion. You fall for their controlled, practical personality but find them full of churning emotions. You do not know how or want to handle their emotional neediness.

## Checking Your Negativity

On the negative side, you can be vindictive, sarcastic and vicious. When you forget to control what you are saying you can spit out poisonous words that cannot be taken back. This can create rifts in relationships that may never heal. Your symbol is the snake. The snake carries its poison in a pouch but its body is not filled with poison. You have the choice of using this venom positively or negatively. You need to learn to bite your tongue, control the urge to be nasty. Slowly you will learn to master this, then you can stop potential self-made disasters from ruining your love life. Allowing your negativity to go unchecked can lead you down a path that is both self-destructive and unhappy.

# ASHLESHA

## Loving Ashlesha

Allow Ashlesha to seduce you and they will make it a wonderful experience – generous, sensuous and romantic. But do not expect romance all the time, as they are not demonstrative. They can be in denial of their emotions. Experience has made them lose trust and become cynical about love and commitment. They usually take a long time to enter into a serious relationship with you. Be patient. If you hurry them too much, they can become distant and leave you. Let them know that your love will not imprison their free spirit.

## Compatibility

**Ideal life partner: Pushya**
**Most challenging life partner: Dhanishta**

The full Compatibility Grid is on page 338.

**Ashlesha and Ashwini:** You have a unique bond. Ashwini are special to you – exciting, adventurous, you connected instantly. You are attracted by their idealism and they remain in your heart as you recognize them as free spirits like yourself. You trust and feel in tune with Ashwini. They understand your vulnerabilities and tolerate your weaknesses. **75% compatible**

**Ashlesha and Bharani:** A beautiful relationship, friendly and sensuous, yet unconventional. Bharani keep you enthralled. You can remain with them, bound by their sexual aura for longer than you anticipated. Bharani possessiveness can make you retreat. Make Bharani feel secure but also be firm about your need for freedom.
**66% compatible**

**Ashlesha and Krittika:** You are attracted to their strong personality, disarmed by their shyness. Their stubbornness surprises you. You fear that Krittika issues will dominate. Gemini Krittika are very similar to you, reflecting a different aspect of the Mercury–Sun combination. You will bond more closely with them than the Taurus Krittika. **57% compatible**

**Ashlesha and Rohini:** You fall for Rohini's charm and witty intellect, but find them to be romantic, emotional and needy. You can be perverse with them: the more they need you, the less you want to give them what they want. It can become an unhappy situation; you bring the worst out in each other. You need to concentrate on each other's positive traits. **33% compatible**

**Ashlesha and Mrigasira:** Both of you can present images to each other that have no connection to reality. The serpent connection further adds to the secrecy and mystery in your relationship. Mrigasira can behave childishly and you can be uncaring when faced with relationship difficulties. Learn to control your tempers: you can hurt each other and be self-destructive. **47% compatible**

**Ashlesha and Ardra:** The crazy and on-the-edge Ardra excites you. But close up, they can be very practical and boring. Ardra can make the mistake of making their admiration obvious and that is an immediate turn-off. Ardra's animal sign is the dog and, as cat, you can fight with them incessantly. There is hardly a time when peace reigns supreme. **33% compatible**

**Ashlesha and Punarvasu:** A good relationship and great sex. You forgive Punarvasu their need to always advise you, fix your life and try to improve you. You constantly remind them that they are your lover not your guru. You can be jealous of the people who surround them. You hate to share your love, but with Punarvasu you need to learn to do so. **60% compatible**

**Ashlesha and Pushya:** You do not think Pushya are right for you; they appear boring, staid workaholics. But their detachment from your attractions makes you go forward and try to make them interested. When you get to know them, they are witty, warm and sexy. Pushya are patient, they love you but do not have unrealistic expectations of you. **80% compatible**

# ASHLESHA

**Ashlesha and Ashlesha:** This is an excellent relationship: you understand the pain each other has been through. You accept each other's shortcomings, something you are usually unwilling to do with other partners. You will move from detachment to attachment, loving the freedom of shared emotions and passions. **77% compatible**

**Ashlesha and Magha:** Your worst sexual relationship. As Magha are very sexual, it is sometimes easy to have a sexual affair with them, only to realize you do not get along. You do not understand each other's needs. Your relationship goes downhill very quickly. They make you feel rejected and unloved so you are cool, arrogant and intimidating. **41% compatible**

**Ashlesha and Purva Phalguni:** You enjoy Purva Phalguni's practical nature, their attachment to family and their endless socializing but their inability to understand your spiritual needs becomes the first barrier. Then there is the problem of your animal signs being sexually inimical. Do not intimidate them. Do not allow them to tease you. Try to be friends. **41% compatible**

**Ashlesha and Uttara Phalguni:** Uttara Phalguni represent a dilemma to you. Get too close to them and they overpower you with their personality and needs; stay away from them and they complain you do not love them or care for them. You have to get your relationship with Uttara Phalguni just right. Then you revel in their warmth and love. **50% compatible**

**Ashlesha and Hasta:** You are attracted to Hasta's sophistication and their independence. They appear fun-loving and social. But their need for emotional dependence is difficult. You try to analyse them and can criticize their dependence on emotion. Hasta love you too much and that puts you off. Their loving you should be a plus point, not a minus one. **53% compatible**

**Ashlesha and Chitra:** You sense the inner beauty of Chitra and you hardly ever take them at face value. They appreciate it and will let you into their inner world. You like the excitement and adventure of loving Chitra. You love the way they show interest in you, yet let you be independent and never try to question your detachment. Enjoy their love. **67% compatible**

**Ashlesha and Swati:** Swati just do not know what you want. You can be distant friends, but the moment you fall in love, the problems start. You may find them sexually boring and seek your pleasures elsewhere. If they love you, you put them off. If they ignore you, you become jealous and possessive. What about the middle way?
**30% compatible**

**Ashlesha and Vishakha:** You feel their strength instinctively: the tiger Vishakha is far stronger than the cat. You try to use all your wiles to establish your superiority over them. Is it necessary? Your relationship becomes one of power play. They can feel manipulated by your ability to use a charm offensive to get your own way and they lose trust in you. **41% compatible**

**Ashlesha and Anuradha:** Anuradha will want to mould you in their own image. You are independent and dislike constraints of any kind. You can cope with Anuradha's polarities, you are comfortable with their ambitions, and you like their coolness and feel turned on by their passion. But you find it hard to handle their need for romance and love. **53% compatible**

**Ashlesha and Jyeshta:** Jyeshta fascinate you: they represent how you would like to evolve as a person. You empathize with their struggles, and analyse your spiritual choices with them. You find this relationship mentally exhilarating, both of you taking each other to new heights. You love Jyeshta as a part of yourself and they do everything to please you. **69% compatible**

**Ashlesha and Mula:** Your relationship with Mula is a spiritually complex one. This puts lots of pressure on the relationship despite the fact that the compatibility is high. You should not be possessive of Mula and also do not allow them to disregard your feelings. Remind them about your love and their need to conform to certain basic rules, if they want to keep your love. **61% compatible**

**Ashlesha and Purva Ashadha:** You make good friends but bad lovers.

## ASHLESHA

You have experienced unhappiness from a few dramatic changes of life. You cannot understand Purva Ashadha's ability to change their philosophy without any pain or angst. You can be a bit jealous. Allow your bitterness to creep into the relationship and you spoil it.
42% compatible

**Ashlesha and Uttara Ashadha:** This relationship can go wrong so fast that you do not have time to fix things. Your symbol is the serpent and their animal sign is its deadly enemy the mongoose. The sexual compatibility is very low. Their anger burns you and they get the full brunt of your viciousness and sarcasm. Both of you get hurt.
27% compatible

**Ashlesha and Shravana:** You can't relate to the world of Shravana: lovely, wonderful, sentimental and quiet. You have a cynical view of life and your world has never been rosy or colourful. The attraction of opposites is usually bad news. You both may try to be what the other wants but both of you can be wilful and fixed in your thinking.
36% compatible

**Ashlesha and Dhanishta:** You are greatly attracted to the primal quality of Dhanishta, their independence, their loyalty and their fiercely protective nature. You love their unconventional nature and their ability to defy tradition. They are passionate lovers. Just do not be too detached: they need to be reminded they are important and that you love them. 60% compatible

**Ashlesha and Shatabhishak:** You think of Shatabhishak as a challenge: they are cool and distant. Your ego gets hurt, as they do not give you the attention that others do. You enjoy the excitement of reining them in, but emotionally you know they are not being honest and neither are you. Learn to talk about love, don't avoid the difficult emotional issues. 50% compatible

**Ashlesha and Purva Bhadra:** Purva Bhadra can have a real weakness for you. You may explore the relationship superfluously but in the long term you prefer to remain detached. You can be casual with their emotions and flirt with them with no real intention of seriousness. They can hurt by the reality and will not find it easy to forgive and forget. **39% compatible**

**Ashlesha and Uttara Bhadra:** Uttara Bhadra can love you too much. You want to explore a relationship where you experience some surprises. They cannot give you an on-the-edge experience. Why don't you try their brand of loving? You can find them surprisingly sensuous and their loving more satisfying than you thought possible. **55% compatible**

**Ashlesha and Revati:** You can never be the type of lover Revati want you to be. You are both ruled by Mercury but whereas you are just starting to search for answers, working within intellectual boundaries, Revati has moved beyond this and has an intense need for self-realization. Your spiritual paths are so different. You may try to love Revati but you are unable to offer them the complete attention they seek. **33% compatible**

# Cusps

Those born at the end or beginning of Ashlesha, should see pages 358–9.

16 to 30 August

# Magha

Ruled by Ketu
Animal: The Male Rat
Symbol: The Palanquin

## Meaning and Symbolism

*Magha* means 'mighty' or 'great'. People born in this Nakshatra aspire towards eminence and are usually prominent in their chosen field. Magha is the second Nakshatra ruled by Ketu, therefore represents the second cycle of the soul's journey. The Nakshatras Magha to Jyeshta indicate the soul's full involvement in the pleasures and pains of the earthly life through relationships, love, children, family life and emotional involvement.

Magha's symbol is a palanquin. The palanquin was a form of transport – a covered litter – for special people. Partners have to make you feel unique; otherwise you can feel unloved. This creates a complex set of rules for your relationships where you feel that you have special dispensation to act whichever way you want. You can feel you are a cut above the rest and behave arrogantly and egotistically.

## The Magha Personality

### Visionary

The shadow planet Ketu rules Magha. Ketu is the tail of the celestial snake. The tail carries with it the past life karmas or the potential of man. It has no head; therefore it reacts instinctively and emotionally. Ketu's role in a birth chart is to look at the bigger picture. Once you stop being restricted by the conscious mind, you make the fusion between the consciousness and the subconscious; your world is open to all sorts of mysteries. You become a visionary, one who has the ability to change the way the world thinks. Ketu shows that the enjoyment of life is part of the soul's divine mission. Here Ketu encourages you to get involved in family life, relationships and putting the stamp of your soul on this earth.

### Natural Leaders

Magha is partly in the sign of Leo ruled by the Sun and partly in Virgo ruled by Mercury. Depending on your birth date, you receive the intellectual support of Mercury or the power of the Sun. This makes Magha powerful, clever and intelligent. You will be enterprising and a leader of your community. You are either in a position of power or you aspire to it. You can feel frustrated if you are not given due importance. When you are in power, you are a good leader – kind, caring and quietly strong.

In Leo Magha, power, courage, aspiring to limitless success and ambition are even more emphasized. The Sun–Ketu connection indicates power and humility, the ability to be just, kind and sensitive.

In Virgo Magha the intellect dominates. The focus is on the development of intellectual power. You aspire to be successful intellectually. Virgo Magha are more likely to have problems with relationships, as they tend to analyse and hold on to the past life issues.

# MAGHA

## Sexuality – The Male Rat

### Insatiable

Your sexuality is expressed by your animal sign, the male rat. In Vedic Astrology, male sexuality suggests dynamic energy. You develop your sexuality early. You enjoy sex and woo unwilling partners till they are sexually aroused. You want lots of sex and often. You pride yourself on being a good lover, usually have perfect foreplay techniques and spend lots of time in satisfying your partners. Magha is a very virile sign; you should be practising birth control if you do not want unplanned pregnancies.

You are forever ready for sex. You enjoy multiple coupling in a sexual encounter. This voracious sexual appetite can be tiring for those who are not equally sensuous. If your partners are unable to keep up with you sexually, you will look for other lovers. You do not recognize sexual boundaries. Different backgrounds, ethnicity, social unacceptability – these factors do not concern you as long as your partner is sexually attractive. You express your attraction immediately and you want the relationship to develop sexually first. You may pick a fight to stimulate passion.

Magha means 'mighty', but the rat is the smallest in the animal kingdom, therefore you have to be careful of predators. So you can over-express your sexual power, in an effort to make it as strong as your outer power. You can feel inferior sexually; you can develop unnecessary complexes. Beware of those who try to dominate you sexually.

### The Best and the Worst Sexual Partners

Your best lover is the female rat, Purva Phalguni. Both of you understand sex, you do not dress up your needs in fancy romantic words. Enjoying the primal need for sex binds you together. Your compatibility in other areas of life is also excellent, so this has the ability to be a match made in heaven.

The worst sexual partners are your natural enemy, the cats, Ashlesha and Punarvasu. The cats will try to play tricks with you, involve you in sexual games and try to undermine your sexual confidence. You enjoy sex and the cat Nakshatras will question your need for sex – limit the sexual part of the relationship. They tell you they prefer quality to quantity, but this maybe just a way of controlling and dominating you. You feel frustrated at not having your sexual needs met. But your feeling of inadequacy can keep you tied to this deeply unsatisfactory relationship. As natural enemies, your relationship takes a very short time to move from ardour to antagonism.

# Relationship Issues

## Searching for the Soul Connection

Your life, with all its ups and downs, is really about finding your soul mate, who will complete your life and make you eternally happy. This feeling is imbedded in your subconscious. In reality, you keep on rejecting love, as it does not live up to your karmic fantasy. You are seeking a spiritual commitment much deeper than physical ties. The fact that you are powerfully sexual and take great pleasure in your sexual adventures tends to make others doubt your sincerity about finding your soul mate.

You can get involved in karmic relationships that have the potential to churn up your life, mind and emotions. Meeting your soul mate does not always bring eternal happiness. It means that you meet up with a partner with whom you have unfinished business from previous lives. Ardra, Swati and Shatabhishak are your spiritual partners. Rahu, the other half of the cosmic serpent, rules them. The Rahu Nakshatras are karmically programmed to magnify your needs, the dissatisfactions and the strengths. Your best karmic satisfaction comes from Shatabhishak – they play down your emotional inadequacies and help you connect to your power. Ardra can bring emotional highs and lows. Ardra being the dog Nakshatra also is not your sexual friend. Swati is the toughest one. They can crush your hopes, create psychological storms that you find very hard to deal with.

## The Problems with the Moon Nakshatras

The Moon rules Hasta, Shravana and Rohini. You have very difficult relationships with all three Moon Nakshatras. The Moon Nakshatras are sensitive, romantic and possessive. The Moon needs light from their partners to feel fulfilled; you have the ability to block this light. The resulting unhappiness can make you disconsolate as well. You are warm and loving but Rohini, Hasta and Shravana all bring out your uncaring and cold side. You bask in their love but will not give them the security they desire, emotionally or sexually. You have a blind spot about loving the Moon Nakshatras and as your overall compatibility is low, once problems start there is nothing to bind you together.

## Coping with Extremes of Relating

You either relate very well with people or not at all. If you look at your compatibility with other Nakshatras (see Compatibility section), you will see that there are wild discrepancies in your relationships. You are only 11% compatible with Shravana but 88% compatible with Jyeshta. You have to choose your partners well. If you get involved in a negative partnership, it can bring extreme unhappiness.

This is the first Nakshatra in the Vedic Zodiac whose spiritual mission is to enjoy life, loves and relationships. Enjoying life also suggests the shadow side of enjoyment – despair and sadness. The extremes of compatibility mean you are spiritually destined to experience both the agonies and ecstasies of love.

# Loving Magha

Magha have an idealistic vision of their partners. Magha will love you, if you fit their vision, passionately and completely. Be aware of their strong sexual appetites. They need sex and if you hate sex, then they are not for you. If they become dissatisfied, they can search for sex elsewhere. They can be extremely critical and hurt you. You have to learn to stand up to them and not take their criticism to heart. In fact Magha usually criticize those whom they love the most. Magha have faced disappointments in love, so you need to reassure them constantly about your love.

# Compatibility

### Ideal life partner: Jyeshta
### Most challenging life partner: Shravana

**The full Compatibility Grid is on page 338.**

**Magha and Ashwini:** Usually there is unfinished karmic business between you. Instinctively you feel this relationship will not be easy to deal with. There are many areas of your subconscious you do not want to face. Both of you are idealistic; you have similar ideals and ways of thinking. This keeps you together. Be realistic about your love. **55% compatible**

**Magha and Bharani:** You are fascinated by their personality and usually give too much of yourself to Bharani. The elephant and the rat have a special relationship in the Vedic myths. Whereas with others you may seek sex, with Bharani you tend to revere them and feel uncomfortable about sex. Bharani can feel ignored and unwanted sexually. **53% compatible**

**Magha and Krittika:** You do not trust each other enough to share your vulnerabilities. You both try to play the game of 'who's stronger?' The truth is that both of you are ignoring your inner feelings, seeing only the outer persona. Don't they realize the persona you show to the world is your way of covering your insecurities? Neither do you. **47% compatible**

**Magha and Rohini:** You can mock Rohini's romantic nature and

# MAGHA

ignore their possessiveness. Rohini need romance and you want sex. Both of you ignore the other's needs. Rohini appear in control of their life, but when they become demanding and jealous you do not want to deal with it. Rohini need you more than you need them.
**28% compatible**

**Magha and Mrigasira:** Intellectual repartee and casual flirtation begin this relationship. You may feel that they are not interested in sex. You can be pleasantly surprised. Mrigasira keep their sensuality under wraps to be revealed to their lovers. But Mrigasira are also jealous and possessive and want commitment, both sexual and emotional.
**57% compatible**

**Magha and Ardra:** A profound relationship, the karmic aspects of which can involve you in a complex give and take. Always remember that it is not the outer issues that you are dealing with but your inner being. The subtle connections that tie you together can at times bring great ups and downs. Love can be special as well. **58% compatible**

**Magha and Punarvasu:** You find Punarvasu stimulating and the tales of their travels amusing. You usually listen to their advice. You can be great friends but a more intimate relationship is extremely challenging. There is often no sexual compatibility. Punarvasu will play with your sexual needs. For you a relationship without sex is not a good option. **51% compatible**

**Magha and Pushya:** Your ideas about life differ. Pushya are egalitarian and you can be quite bossy and powerful. You hardly ever feel comfortable with them, finding them cool and controlled. You can get involved in a relationship that is not fully satisfactory. If you want more from your relationship, celebrate the differences and do not let it fall into a rut. **50% compatible**

**Magha and Ashlesha:** Sex is the bone of contention between the two of you. As a rat Nakshatra, you remain afraid of cat Ashlesha's sexual power. Your way of coping is to reject them or cut them out of your life. You reason that if you remain distant, you do not have to work out any issues. A sexless relationship will be frustrating and you are not into celibacy. **41% compatible**

**Magha and Magha:** Great sex, love, passion, shared goals and commitment; all the ingredients of a great relationship are present. Instinctive understanding of each other's needs goes a long way towards keeping the love alive. You will fight a lot, but this is your way of lovemaking. Try not to be jealous of each other's successes. Learn to be democratic. **77% compatible**

**Magha and Purva Phalguni:** Purva Phalguni's capacity to enjoy life fills your heart with joy. Creative, perfectionist and devoted, Purva Phalguni represent your dreams of an ideal partner. Being your ideal sexual partner they will match your passion, understand your sensuous needs and satisfy your immense capacity for sex.
**83% compatible**

**Magha and Uttara Phalguni:** Your relationship with Uttara Phalguni has the potential to become complex. Both of you are strong and stubborn and unwilling to give way. Your way of coping with this is by rejecting Uttara Phalguni. Trust them with your inner feelings and care for them and they will show you their warmth and love.
**55% compatible**

**Magha and Hasta:** There appears to be a psychological inability to connect to Hasta's needs. You feel some past life connections but usually in a negative way. Learn to appreciate the good qualities and compromise on the others, then you are giving yourself a chance for happiness. If Hasta are being cold towards you, they are hurting inside. **39% compatible**

**Magha and Chitra:** Chitra are very sensual and match your endless demands for sex. You may feel intimidated by them sexually and this can stop you from pursuing this relationship further. You try to fight for supremacy within the relationship. Be democratic and try to share your power equally. This will benefit you both. **58% compatible**

**Magha and Swati:** You feel uneasy with Swati. There is a stressful karmic bond that ties you together; it usually brings issues that create

# MAGHA

unhappiness before you can find true happiness. Learn to work things through, talk about your fears and inadequacies, and you may be able to overcome your karmic difficulties. **27% compatible**

**Magha and Vishakha:** You are on the defensive with Vishakha, always feeling the need to prove yourself and show them your power. Your way of dealing with it is by rejecting what they have to offer. Vishakha can question the validity of your relationship. You need to connect sexually and stop feeling intimidated by them.
**54% compatible**

**Magha and Anuradha:** Anuradha can challenge your autocratic behaviour and, instead of irritating you, this invigorates you. They are your opposite in every way but this is a powerful attraction. Never let politics and differing attitudes spoil your relationship. They will love you so completely that you become addicted.
**66% compatible**

**Magha and Jyeshta:** Your best partner. The mystical Jyeshta can make you feel complete. Their charm works wonders with you: they have a way of bringing you down to earth without hurting. They inspire you sexually; their blend of passionate sex and flirtatious loving is fantastic. Jyeshta nurture your inner person, never making you feel unloved. **88% compatible**

**Magha and Mula:** Both of you are ruled by the mystical Ketu; you understand each other's needs, motivations and spiritual journey. You admire and love Mula. But sexually there can be complications; as a rat Nakshatra you are forever in awe of the dog Mula. You may be successful and powerful but Mula can always dominate you if they choose. **66% compatible**

**Magha and Purva Ashadha:** Creative and talented, Purva Ashadha are an instant magnet to you. Sexually the relationship is fun. But somewhere along the line you can settle for compromise. You may forget why you were attracted to them in the first place. Their inner search undermines you and their inability to concentrate fully makes you feel unwanted. **53% compatible**

# THE LOVE SIGNS

**Magha and Uttara Ashadha:** You see through Uttara Ashadha, their lack of self-confidence and vulnerability. You play on that. You are sexually very active and you may find Uttara Ashadha's diffidence dull and boring. You cannot be sensitive to their needs. Somehow this relationship brings out the worst in you. Be aware of the negative qualities. **15% compatible**

**Magha and Shravana:** You can lose your sense of right and wrong with Shravana. You find it difficult to deal with their sentimental nature and you can be very critical. This is so unlike you. Where are your warmth and your sense of fair play? You feel frozen by their chilly behaviour. You may hurt them immensely with your rejection and haughtiness. **11% compatible**

**Magha and Dhanishta:** You must overcome your complex about your animal sign, as the lioness Dhanishta is far too powerful for the small rat. Dhanishta can be warm and friendly. They usually do not make enough effort to keep you interested and you can try to pay them back for their laziness by looking at, and even getting involved with others. **55% compatible**

**Magha and Shatabhishak:** You could form very deep and intense relationships with them. Shatabhishak will also endeavour to fulfil all your needs. They feel comfortable with you so they will let you into their innermost secrets; very few people are privy to this, so feel flattered. They open their hearts to you – be careful how you treat them. **66% compatible**

**Magha and Purva Bhadra:** You should not allow Purva Bhadra to put you on a pedestal. However enjoyable it may be to be idolized by the mighty lion, your one moment of glory can create lots of problems later on. You feel inadequate inside, unable to compete with them. You can make them feel unwanted, even when you do care. **47% compatible**

**Magha and Uttara Bhadra:** Uttara Bhadra are too restricted about sex and you want to be free to explore it. They do not want to enjoy life, preferring work and responsibility. Uttara Bhadra can be quietly

# MAGHA

sensuous and you need to access this side of their nature. You will be delighted with what you discover behind their cool exterior.
**50% compatible**

**Magha and Revati:** You try hard to live up to Revati's image of you, but you usually feel inadequate and unsure. Being a spiritually complex relationship, you try to cover up your inadequacies by increasingly contrary behaviour. Sexual issues will usually be contentious. You can end up hurting each other if you are not careful.
**33% compatible**

## Cusps

Those born at the end or beginning of Magha, should see pages 359–61.

30 August to 13 September

# Purva Phalguni

Ruled by Venus
Animal: The Female Rat
Symbol: Fireplace and Bed

## Meaning and Symbolism

*Phal* means 'fruit' and *Guni* 'connected to gunas' (good qualities). Phalguni is the Nakshatra which gives the fruit of our good deeds from our past lives now. *Purva* means 'first', indicating it is the former part of the Phalguni Nakshatras. Purva and Uttara Phalguni are parts of a whole Nakshatra of four stars, which looks like a bed in the sky. They indicate similar purposes with very specific differences. Purva Phalguni are considered the lucky Nakshatra. Their good luck comes from having good relationships and being lucky in love.

The symbols of Purva Phalguni are the fireplace and the bed. We gather around the fire with family and friends to relax and let go of our daily problems. In the Upanishads, a collection of tales, the gurus assembled people around the fireplace to teach them the philosophies of life, to enlighten their thoughts. Higher thoughts and the earthy pleasures of life are all intermingled in Purva Phalguni. The Purva Phalguni soul rests from its purpose of finding moksha: spiritual redemption. Leisure, pleasure and enjoyment of life are Purva Phalguni's guiding principles. Family, love, and relationships are extremely important for you.

## The Purva Phalguni Personality

### Divine Creativity

Venus rules Purva Phalguni. The Sanskrit name for Venus is *Shukra* or semen. Shukra directly relates to procreation. Both sexes of Purva Phalguni are very fond of children and are good parents. Children were considered to represent divine creativity and their birth, the ability for a human to harness this natural power. The establishment of the family unit and perpetuating humanity are important to you. You will also express your creativity in artistic areas like drama, films, TV, music, show business, design and paintings.

### Pleasures of Life

Purva Phalguni is entirely in the sign of Virgo ruled by Mercury. The Mercury and Venus combination together gives wealth and happiness on a large scale. Mercury, the mind and the intellect, takes time out from its search for answers to relax a bit, to get itself distracted by its friend Venus, to enjoy the pleasures of life.

Mercury and Venus relate to each other well. Mercury understands both its spiritual connection and its earthly role. You appreciate your material role and enjoy the best in the world. You aim for excellence and success so that you can live life in comfort, surrounded by family and friends. In fact, when you pursue an obviously spiritual path, you can become very dissatisfied and unhappy. Appreciating your position in life, and being in harmony with it, is your spiritual expression.

## Sexuality – The Female Rat

### Insatiable

Purva Phalguni's animal sign is the female rat. You, like your male counterpart Magha, develop your sexuality early. But unlike Magha you will not be always pursuing sex. You enjoy sex, will be sexually ready if your partners take time to woo you. This is a very virile and fertile sign. Purva Phalguni is specially connected to the birth of children. You should be especially careful and use contraceptives if you do not want unplanned pregnancies.

You enjoy multiple coupling in a sexual encounter. This voracious sexual appetite can be tiring for those who are not equally sensuous. If your partners are unable to keep up with you sexually, you may look for other lovers. You do not recognize sexual boundaries. Different backgrounds, ethnicity, social unacceptability – these factors in a partner do not concern you. If you desire a person, they are right for you. Being a female rat Nakshatra, you allow others to make the first sexual move, but you may pick fights and arguments to make them interested.

You can sacrifice your sexual needs for your family. You may feel frustrated, but your family comes first. One of the things that you should realize is that your animal sign, the rat, is the smallest, therefore you have to be careful of predators. You may meet lovers who will try to dominate you sexually.

### The Best and the Worst Sexual Partners

Your best lover is the male rat Magha. Both of you understand sex, you do not dress up your need in fancy romantic words. This fulfilment leads to you finding love together. Your compatibility in other areas of life is also excellent, so this relationship has the ability to be wonderful.

The worst sexual partners are your natural enemy, the cats, Ashlesha and Punarvasu. The cats will try to play tricks with you, involve you in sexual games and try to undermine your sexual confidence. You enjoy sex and the cat Nakshatras will question your need for sex – limit the sexual part of the relationship. You feel frustrated at not having your sexual needs met. You may compromise for the sake of the children or family. But this may not bring happiness.

# Relationship Issues

## Love and Commitment

You generally have good relationships. You aspire to long-term committed partnerships, giving up a lot to keep your relationships. Children form a very important part of your relationships. When your relationship does go wrong, you will still remain very attached to your children. You are willing to sacrifice a lot for them.

If you do not have children as a common binding force, you need to develop shared interests. Pursuing common creative goals can help to keep your relationship alive.

## The Sizzling Passion of Mars and Venus

Instant love, attraction, sexual fire and unbridled passion is what you feel when you meet the Mars Nakshatras, Mrigasira, Chitra and Dhanishta. But this passion can soon get out of control and burn everything in sight. You do not consider what is good for you when you get involved in a passionate affair with them. You have no idea how to control it, bank the fire to make it last longer. The result is a dramatic relationship burnout. There is not much left to do but to gather the ashes of love from the bitter and acrid smoke of recriminations. Consumed by passion you can become destructive and lose what you valued the most.

Mrigasira is the easiest relationship. They are used to controlling their intellectual fire and can find the balance between passion and reality. Chitra lose their sense of proportion with you. The attraction can be intense and disruptive. Chitra is also a combination of Venus and Mars and become fascinated by your charm but are not able to deal with your need for commitment and may love. You must relate carefully with Dhanishta. They become a slave to your passions but your life paths are very different. When the passion is over, Dhanishta can blame you for corrupting their spiritual path. You will be left carrying the guilty burden from this affair. If you change for them, you will be unhappy and after the initial passion, Dhanishta do not try to look at life from your point of view.

## The Practical Nakshatra

You need to keep your feet firmly on the ground and understand that your spirituality is best expressed by living life well, in a moral and ethical way. It is not your karma to give up on material things but to enjoy them. Your soul needs to be happy with your commitments to life. You are not so concerned with the higher purpose of life. This can create problems in relationships with Nakshatras who are aspiring to spiritual realization. In fact when you aspire towards higher realms, you get very emotionally disturbed as it goes against your soul purpose. You should allow your partners to follow their spiritual inclination without trying to follow them in it or criticizing or analysing their need to do it.

## Chasing Fun and Pleasures

As a Nakshatra that discovers enjoyment and pleasure, you have the potential to be relentlessly pleasure seeking. You love to party and have fun all the time. If you have to work hard or go through a tough period, you complain that life has dealt you a terrible hand. You desire perfection – in love, relationships and children. You will be quick to take offence if any of them do not give you enjoyment or pleasure. This makes you feel that your relationships are less than perfect.

## Loving Purva Phalguni

Purva Phalguni are very sexual. While they are seeking a long-term partner with whom to start a family, they will indulge their appetite for sex through secret flirtations and sexual encounters. This can be the basis of mistrust in the relationship. One of the downsides of loving them is that they can be forever criticizing you – the way you dress, talk, behave, etc. Remember, they have chosen you; their criticism is another way of loving you. But let them know when they go too far or this can become very irritating.

## Compatibility

**Ideal life partner: Jyeshta**
**Most challenging life partner: Dhanishta**

**The full Compatibility Grid is on page 338.**

**Purva Phalguni and Ashwini:** You fall for Ashwini's adventurous ways, their ability to bring freshness into your life and their courage facing difficulties. They are perfectionists just like you. You have an intuitive sensitivity to what they need from you. Ashwini have a deeper side to them that you do not understand and they may keep it hidden from you. **67% compatible**

**Purva Phalguni and Bharani:** You are very similar as Venus rules both of you. Your animal signs, the elephant and the rat, have a sacred relationship in the Vedic myths. You tend to revere Bharani too much and feel uncomfortable about sex with them. Bharani can feel ignored and unwanted. Both of you are sexually active Nakshatras and may seek fulfilment elsewhere. **47% compatible**

**Purva Phalguni and Krittika:** You fall for the strong silent personality of Krittika. But despite your signals, they take a long time to show interest in you. They do not share your interest in socializing and can become quite puritanical about your ideas of fun. Keep your individuality. You can feel frustrated if you follow their ascetic lifestyle. **43% compatible**

**Purva Phalguni and Rohini:** You love the romance and sensitivity of Rohini. You indulge them, sometimes too much. They can be moody and changeable; you may not understand them always. You are practical and you help to keep Rohini grounded. They teach you how to be sensuous. Be careful you do not become too self-indulgent. **66% compatible**

**Purva Phalguni and Mrigasira:** A Mars–Venus relationship. Instant passion, lots of emotional fire which can get out of hand too quickly. Mrigasira can rationalize their feelings but you find it difficult to deal with them. Try to take this relationship slowly, develop friendship first, and get to know each other. **46% compatible**

**Purva Phalguni and Ardra:** A great relationship. You find Ardra exciting and their ambitions sexy. But you also recognize their inner vulnerability. Ardra will romance you, try to live up to your expectations. They adore you, are very supportive and loyal. Both of you can be sexually promiscuous but when you find each other, you are faithful. **75% compatible**

**Purva Phalguni and Punarvasu:** The 62% compatibility does not reflect the true experience of this relationship. You can appreciate each other, love each other, but the inimical relationship of your animal signs will always rear its head. As the other areas are so compatible, shift the emphasis of your relationship from sexual to emotional. **62% compatible**

**Purva Phalguni and Pushya:** The cool Pushya appear solid and reliable, and they know how to have fun. You think you have found someone special. In the long run, you may find their qualities boring and Pushya too involved in their work to appreciate you. Keep your finances apart – frugal Pushya may not appreciate your extravagances. **39% compatible**

**Purva Phalguni and Ashlesha:** Yours is a sexually inimical relation-

## PURVA PHALGUNI

ship. The cat must tease the rat and play a game of dominance. You find Ashlesha strong and intimidating and therefore resort to tricks and underhand methods to scupper their superiority. These behaviour patterns manifest in your relationship without you being aware of it.
**41% compatible**

**Purva Phalguni and Magha:** Love, happiness and sexual bliss. Being your ideal sexual partner, Magha will match your passion, understand your sensuous needs and are able to satisfy your immense capacity for sex. You love their power and revel in their glory. They in turn offer you the security, love and the family you yearn for.
**83% compatible**

**Purva Phalguni and Purva Phalguni:** Two similar people sharing the same vision of love and life. Although the relationship is sexually satisfying and emotionally fulfilling, you must remember that you have the same weaknesses. If you emphasize the hedonistic side of your relationship, your can get lazy and selfish. Don't spoil perfection by criticizing it. **77% compatible**

**Purva Phalguni and Uttara Phalguni:** A great relationship – ardent, devoted, and sensual. Uttara Phalguni are supportive, strong and offer you commitment. They are direct about their needs. They may not be sophisticated like you but they make up for it by appreciating what you are and allowing you to be yourself. You flower under their warm loving. **80% compatible**

**Purva Phalguni and Hasta:** You share a mutual love of fun. Parties, going to the cinema, theatre, love of art and a similar taste in books bind you together. You admire Hasta's strong practical streak and they help you to make the most of your creativity. You do not always appreciate their earthiness and can be very critical about it.
**55% compatible**

**Purva Phalguni and Chitra:** Chitra's Martian personality arouses extreme passion in you. In the aftermath of spent passion, you do not know how to relate to them. They can be selfish and self-involved. They ignore you and are careless with your emotions. They are not into commitment and their inability to love you does not make for happiness. **19% compatible**

**Purva Phalguni and Swati:** Swati are good at relationships and so are you. You flower and prosper under their love. You can feel unhappy when their ambitions intrude on your time. You should be supportive of the Swati ambitions, as they are an intrinsic part of them. Let them know of your dissatisfactions as they usually work hard to make you happy. **66% compatible**

**Purva Phalguni and Vishakha:** The smooth Vishakha steal your heart quickly. You find their brand of sensuality irresistible. But the sexual compatibility that appeared so perfect can seem to be an illusion. Do not give up on it; work towards keeping your attraction alive. Do not feel hurt if they are not as enthusiastic as you are about being sociable. **55% compatible**

**Purva Phalguni and Anuradha:** You love the cool Anuradha – they are hard-working and responsible. They also love you. But they may not always be able to join you in your pursuit of fun and socializing. While Anuradha seek the love connection, they may not be emotional and demonstrative about it. So learn to give them some space. **61% compatible**

**Purva Phalguni and Jyeshta:** Jyeshta can make you fall in love easily. They also know how to fulfil you sexually. You enjoy their pursuit of hedonistic pleasures. But you must be sensitive to their spiritual needs. You may not want to be part of their journey but criticize it and your relationship becomes much worse than the suggested compatibility. **66% compatible**

**Purva Phalguni and Mula:** You are attracted to their spiritual, free and easy lifestyle but you soon want to change it to suit yourself. They need their freedom to explore their higher self. If you control them, they will feel frustrated. They can become more and more distant. Develop an understanding, love them as they are and they will remain with you. **53% compatible**

**Purva Phalguni and Purva Ashadha:** Venus rules you both but its

## PURVA PHALGUNI

influence on you is expressed entirely differently. You want to enjoy life and be in love. Purva Ashadha want to be free and spiritual. This may either create a division between you or it may bring you closer together if you learn to understand your differences. **50% compatible**

**Purva Phalguni and Uttara Ashadha:** Uttara Ashadha are dynamic and will pursue you extravagantly. You are attracted to their coolness but are surprised by their ascetic lifestyle. They are not good at intimacy and they are also not very comfortable with their sexuality. You should teach them about sensuality and take charge of the relationship. **60% compatible**

**Purva Phalguni and Shravana:** You find Shravana sensitive and full of life, with an excellent sense of humour. But as the relationship grows you find they need more and more time alone. You can feel very put off, even rejected. Compromise. Start a give-and-take routine. They enjoy socializing if they are released from the pressure of doing so. **50% compatible**

**Purva Phalguni and Dhanishta:** You never know how Dhanishta can be loving and caring to all those less fortunate than them but when it comes to you, they become cold and uncaring. You feel you are living next to a volcano, you never know when they can burst out. Why can't they make a little effort to understand you? **19% compatible**

**Purva Phalguni and Shatabhishak:** Shatabhishak are mysterious and exciting: you feel you are flirting with danger and this excites you. While they may start off being indulgent with you, they can become restless and unhappy. They may want time away and do not fit into your image of an ideal partner, who makes commitments and keeps to them. **50% compatible**

**Purva Phalguni and Purva Bhadra:** You fall for Purva Bhadra quickly – they are warm, generous, and loving. They are happy for you to take charge of your relationship. You try to live up to their idealistic vision of you. Disagreements happen when they are not always willing to socialize with you; you cannot understand their need to be alone. **64% compatible**

**Purva Phalguni and Uttara Bhadra:** Both of you want commitment. Uttara Bhadra can be too cool and ascetic; their love can become a burden when it does not allow you to be the way you like to be. A more sympathetic attitude and willingness to compromise on the disagreements can make your relationship a lot better. Show them your love. **44% compatible**

**Purva Phalguni and Revati:** You love the way Revati make you feel. They never put themselves first. But you also love them in return. You never try to take what they are not willing to give. This can be a happy, contented and committed partnership. Try to understand Revati's spiritual needs – do not feel insecure about their need to be alone. **67% compatible**

## Cusps

Those born at the end or beginning of Purva Phalguni, should see pages 361–2.

13 to 26 September

# Uttara Phalguni

Ruled by the Sun
Animal sign: The Bull
Symbol: The Four Legs of the Bed

## Meaning and Symbolism

Uttara Phalguni is the continuation of Purva Phalguni, the male energy to Purva's female. It represents the other half of the picture. *Phal* means 'fruit' and *Guni* is 'connected to gunas' (good qualities). Phalguni is the Nakshatra which gives the fruit of our good deeds from our past lives now. *Uttara* means 'higher' indicating it is the latter part of the Phalguni Nakshatras. Purva and Uttara Phalguni are two parts of a whole Nakshatra of four stars, which looks like a bed in the sky. They indicate similar purposes with very specific differences. Your soul is starting to question the need for your involvement in the material side of life.

The four legs of the bed represent the sexual energy of the soul, the downward flow of the power. Each of the legs represents the sheaths in which the soul becomes entangled – the physical, the ethereal, the astral and the mental. The number four also represents the four heads of Brahma, the four points of the compass and the four Vedas. Your soul is involved in the magic of earthly life. You want love, commitment and relationships but you have an awareness that you should aspire to more.

## The Uttara Phalguni Personality

### Sunny Disposition

The Sun rules Uttara Phalguni. The Sun signifies creation and carries within it the knowledge of individual karma. The Sun also signifies authority, power, vitality and strength. The Uttara Phalguni Sun is autumn sun of the Northern Hemisphere when it is losing its intense heat and becoming easier for people to tolerate. This solar energy encourages relationships and allows people to bask in the warmth of Uttara Phalguni love and care. You can feel isolated at times as people still feel overshadowed by your warmth. They do not see your need for love.

### Caring and Impartial

Uttara Phalguni is mostly in Virgo and the rest in Libra. Virgo is the sign for service and Libra for justice. The Virgo Uttara Phalguni expresses the solar power added to the mercurial desire to be of service to the world. You are active intellectually and physically, and can be very agitated if your life pattern gets disrupted. You are responsible, idealistic and hard working. You seek perfection and can feel very dissatisfied if you do not achieve it. In relationships you want to care for your partners, but also want them to fall into your life patterns and not disrupt your life in any way.

Libra is about balancing the spiritual and the material and Uttara Phalguni is about ambitions, power and justice. The Libra Phalgunis learn to bring some kind of balance. You are idealistic but realists as well. You are more able to understand your restrictions and find it easier to deal with their material life. Libra brings about an appreciation of the finer arts and Venus concentrates this area of the Nakshatras on relating and relationships.

# UTTARA PHALGUNI

## Sexuality – The Bull

### Virile

Your sexuality is expressed by your animal sign, the bull. Shiva's Nandi bull is the symbol of divine virility. Indian women pray to the bull to give them the ability to bear children. This makes Uttara Phalguni symbolic of fertility, creativity and the power to create the next generation. Both the sexes will have powerful sexual drive. It can become a divine mission to experience sex.

You have lots of love to give, you will chase those you desire but once they succumb, you can become disinterested. You will work hard to make sexual conquests but when you are sexually content, you forget to please. This causes huge problems for you as your lovers do not take kindly to this type of behaviour and can move on. You then feel hurt and let down. But think of how your own behaviour influenced their actions.

You also believe that sexuality is a commitment and should bear positive results. Your vitality can lead to easy pregnancy. Be careful and use contraception if you do not want children.

You have a slow burning temper. You usually remain placid but when annoyed you can be destructive. You are possessive and jealous – making you jealous is one way of making you angry.

### The Best and the Worst Sexual Partners

Your best sexual partner the cow Nakshatra, Uttara Bhadra. Uttara Bhadra knows how to satisfy the deepest desires of Uttara Phalguni. You are very compatible in other areas of life as well, making this a relationship that is happy and long lasting. Both of you view your sexual relationship as sacred and will honour the other with your loyalty and commitment.

Your worst sexual partners are the tigers Chitra and Vishakha. In the wild the tiger kills the bull and is one of the few animals who is not in awe of the bull's strength. In life, they will try to control you by showing their power and making you feel inadequate. This is an unusual position for you to be in – you do not take kindly to being dominated. The sexual power struggles can mar your relationship. As the compatibility is average with both the tigers, these relationships do not always bring much into your life.

# Relationship Issues

## The Frustrations of Being Lucky

While Purva Phalguni are happy to enjoy the fruits of their past karma, you get frustrated by it. You feel restricted by the conditions of your life, always wanting to break away and experience spirituality. You can be disapproving or negative about your relationships and create problems. You should appreciate your good luck rather than always focusing on the challenging aspects.

## Working out the Karma with Ketu Nakshatras

Magha, Mula and Ashwini are the Ketu-ruled Nakshatras. You are enjoying the fruits of past life karma today, but you are also carrying the burden of your past karma, especially in relationships. The Ketu Nakshatras bring forth the past life connection. Whatever type of relationship you enjoy with these Ketu Nakshatras – emotional, spiritual or business – you feel strongly that you have found the person who will complete you. But this initial instinct belies the reality. In the sky, Ketu has the ability to eclipse the Sun. In relationships they have the ability to block your path. You should not give up these relationships – working out the issues allows you to find their hidden treasures. Both of you have something precious to give each other but you have to fight to clear the initial hurdles.

The Ketu Nakshatras can reject you and bring out feelings of inadequacy. Ashwini make you feel staid and boring, Magha vie with you for power and Mula ignore your needs and concentrate on their own desires.

# UTTARA PHALGUNI

## The Practical Nakshatra

You are practical but unlike Purva Phalguni you are extremely idealistic as well. You need to keep your feet firmly rooted to the ground and understand that your spirituality is best expressed by living life well, in a moral and ethical way. You can opt for a practical long-term relationship, but you still desire a perfect one. You can be hard on yourself and your partner.

## Divine Dissatisfaction

Uttara Phalguni is the Nakshatra of divine dissatisfaction. You love and enjoy life yet feel guilty that you are not demanding more from it. You forever live in the future feeling dissatisfied with today. This puts lots of pressure on your relationships. You make your partners aware of your sense of dissatisfaction. They can feel that they are the reason for your lack of happiness. You can be miserable with your present situation, regardless of its quality. If you are extremely successful, then you'll want to lead a simple life. If you were leading a simple life, then you would want the trappings of success. You must realize the present situation is not as negative as you imagine. Learn to enjoy life for what it has to offer. If you stop looking for an alternative way of life and learn to appreciate your blessings, you will stop spoiling the quality of your life. Then you will give yourself a true chance of happiness.

# Loving Uttara Phalguni

The key to Uttara Phalguni seduction is to allow them to think that they are seducing you, not the other way round. The greatest challenge is to keep them interested sexually. Do not give in to them too easily. They like commitment but commitment itself can make them bored and lose interest in you. The tightrope you have to walk with them is to keep them committed and attracted. Let them be strong while keeping your own individuality. They can be super-critical.

Loving them means accepting their criticism without letting it hurt you. They have a volatile temper and they need you to calm them.

## Compatibility

### Ideal life partners: Purva Phalguni and Anuradha
### Most challenging life partner: Shravana

**The full Compatibility Grid is on page 338.**

**Uttara Phalguni and Ashwini:** The Sun and Ketu have a difficult cosmic relationship and this creates weak foundations for your relationship. You may find it difficult to trust each other. You are attracted by Ashwini's sense of adventure, their unusual lifestyle and individualism. Ashwini can highlight your own insecurities, making you feel unwanted and unloved. You struggle to be happy with them. **34% compatible**

**Uttara Phalguni and Bharani:** You love the exotic and sensuous Bharani. They know how to get your passions flowing. You hardly ever get bored with Bharani. In fact you should not give in to them too easily. Just like you, they can become complacent and ignore your needs if they become too comfortable with you. **60% compatible**

**Uttara Phalguni and Krittika:** You are attracted to Krittika as they appear to be hewn in your own image. You need love and attention from them and they want the same from you. But they may be too self-involved to provide you with the love and attention you need. Learn to appreciate their individuality, consider their needs, and make them aware of your love. **53% compatible**

**Uttara Phalguni and Rohini:** Rohini are happy to bask in your warmth and reflect your love back to you. They are emotional and romantic. You are never bored with them. You are always trying to please them and be there for them. Rohini bring out the romantic in you. They wrap their love around you. You feel secure and happy within their aura. **72% compatible**

# UTTARA PHALGUNI

**Uttara Phalguni and Mrigasira:** Great friendship, similar life directions, and shared passions. Mrigasira's sharp intellect is a perfect foil for your practical nature. While Mrigasira do not usually like to make commitments, with you they make an exception. They help you find the courage to deal with your inner guilt. Great relationship.
73% compatible

**Uttara Phalguni and Ardra:** You do not trust Ardra fully but you find them irresistible. Ardra appear to be very analytical and unromantic but when you discover their emotional nature you are hooked. Ardra can make the mistake of loving you too much. Don't break their heart by losing interest in them just because they love you.
61% compatible

**Uttara Phalguni and Punarvasu:** Punarvasu can never commit to you and make you feel totally secure. They need to be free and explore life. If you love Punarvasu, let them have this freedom, then they will come back to you. If you try to control them too much, become too demanding, they can leave you or make you feel very unhappy.
50% compatible

**Uttara Phalguni and Pushya:** The Sun and Saturn have a challenging cosmic relationship. In real life, you are not always warm and caring towards Pushya and they are the same. You find Pushya too involved in their responsibilities to pay attention to you. What about your attitude to them? Did the cold war begin because you made them feel undesirable? 52% compatible

**Uttara Phalguni and Ashlesha:** While you can spend lots of time at first wooing them and trying to keep them interested, when the relationship gets serious you may start taking them for granted. Ashlesha take refuge in detachment. You feel hurt by their lack of appreciation. Stop taking them for granted and develop trust. See how your relationship improves. 50% compatible

**Uttara Phalguni and Magha:** Both of you are strong and stubborn. You try to dominate Magha sexually and make them aware of your strengths. Magha make you feel unwanted. You have to stop impressing the other with your power but start trusting them with your vulnerabilities. Show your caring side and there will be greater harmony. **55% compatible**

**Uttara Phalguni and Purva Phalguni:** Your best relationship: warm, loving and partner. Purva Phalguni are your ideal partner. They touch the inner you; you feel love for them as they brighten up your life. Try not to feel too guilty about enjoying your happiness. This is as perfect as relationships can get. Don't spoil it by hoping for even more. **80% compatible**

**Uttara Phalguni and Uttara Phalguni:** Both of you present a powerful persona to the world and find satisfaction in your careers, social position and success. The downside is that you may ignore your emotional needs. You both need to appreciate the other's strength without trying to grasp all the power for yourself. **61% compatible**

**Uttara Phalguni and Hasta:** You love the sophisticated and independent Hasta, but are equally comfortable when you discover their earthy sensuality. You are happy to deal with their moodiness and support their emotionalism. Learn to bring excitement into your life and avoid being overtly critical of Hasta – they can take your criticisms personally. **58% compatible**

**Uttara Phalguni and Chitra:** Your worst sexual partner. You have strong sexual needs and this creates an immediate barrier. You can find Chitra's domineering behaviour difficult to deal with. Do not allow your dissatisfaction to show too often. Chitra can move on without a backward glance and you can feel hurt and rejected. **47% compatible**

**Uttara Phalguni and Swati:** There is a fascination that transcends initial distrust. You start knowing the real Swati, their inner sensitivity and vulnerabilities. This relationship works because Swati always appear slightly mysterious to you. You never feel you know them fully and this keeps you interested, as you are always hoping to unravel their mystique. **69% compatible**

**Uttara Phalguni and Vishakha:** The Nakshatra rulers the Sun and

# UTTARA PHALGUNI

Jupiter are good friends and your friendship is the lifeblood of this relationship. There are many challenges – lack of sexual compatibility (Vishakha is your worst sexual partner) and your differing spiritual needs. Vishakha's spiritual quest can churn up your inner self and make you unsettled. **50% compatible**

**Uttara Phalguni and Anuradha:** Anuradha love you selflessly and completely. You find this intensely fulfilling. You support them and love them back. You are not always demonstrative but your love for them is real. With them you are no longer unhappy with the burden of material expectations and recognize it as a part of your karmic process. **80% compatible**

**Uttara Phalguni and Jyeshta:** Jyeshta baffle you. They never give you a straight answer and enjoy confusing you with their word play and emotional games. You are straightforward; you say what you feel. Jyeshta make you feel insecure; they can play with your feelings. Once you lose your trust in them, you find it difficult to build it back. **39% compatible**

**Uttara Phalguni and Mula:** Your relationship with Mula usually begins with many highs. Mula make you see the world, love and emotions in a completely different way. But they are unable to sustain love on such a high level. They disrupt your life; they can reject you or completely block you out. You can feel agitated and dissatisfied. **32% compatible**

**Uttara Phalguni and Purva Ashadha:** You instantly touch the soul of Purva Ashadha. You are happy for them to be free to explore their spirituality. You can love them for who they are. But they love you back in a way they can love few others. You both add colour to each other's unfinished picture and make your lives complete.
**75% compatible**

**Uttara Phalguni and Uttara Ashadha:** You recognize the loneliness of Uttara Ashadha and try to support them through your love. As a Nakshatra who is totally involved in material pursuits, you appreciate

the difficulties of the spiritual journey of Uttara Ashadha. You try to encourage them to be comfortable with their soul's desires.
**68% compatible**

**Uttara Phalguni and Shravana:** You are drawn to the high-minded Shravana. You appreciate their need for emotional support and will be there for them. You have to be careful that you do not create too much distance between you by being too accepting of their need to do their own thing. Your goals can get polarized and your love suffers. **61% compatible**

**Uttara Phalguni and Dhanishta:** You can be good friends but not such great lovers. You demand too much from each other, you expect the other to be perfect while you do not adhere to the same rules. Dhanishta love a fight and you do not shy away from confrontation. Rivalry, competition, fighting and aggression can mar your relationship. **40% compatible**

**Uttara Phalguni and Shatabhishak:** The more you try to get to know Shatabhishak, the greater the distance they put between you. Maybe you should stop trying so hard. Let them get to know you and trust you. They may open up and show their feelings for you. Always try to make an extra effort to look good and well-groomed: they like chic partners. **37% compatible**

**Uttara Phalguni and Purva Bhadra:** You try to be supportive and caring, they can become aggressive when they find they are not getting it all their way, you yearn for the soft and tender Purva Bhadra. They can be quite destructive and cutting when they decide to move on. You are left quite shattered and unhappy.
**39% compatible**

**Uttara Phalguni and Uttara Bhadra:** Uttara Bhadra is the best sexual partner for you but also your most spiritually complex relationship. You can be faced with situations that test your love. You can act perversely and hurt each other even if it means hurting yourself more. Do not let your inner dissatisfactions spoil this wonderful relationship. **75% compatible**

## UTTARA PHALGUNI

**Uttara Phalguni and Revati:** You love the charm and quick intellect of Revati. Revati have deep spiritual roots. You appreciate and aspire towards spirituality but you are blocked by a life more rooted in reality. But Revati needs your reality and practicality while you can do with a bit of their mystic spirituality. Both of you benefit.
**69% compatible**

## Cusps

Those born at the end or beginning of Uttara Phalguni, should see pages 363–4.

*26 September to 10 October*

# Hasta

Ruled by the Moon
Animal: The Female Buffalo
Symbol: The Hand

## Meaning and Symbolism

*Hasta* means 'the hand'. Its symbol is also the hand. The hand reflects the destiny of an individual and the individual effort. The right and the left hands are positive and negative, male and female energies, past and future lives. The four fingers of the hand show the four motivations – *Artha*, *Kama*, *Dharma* and *Moksha*, the three joints on the fingers are the three gunas or psychological qualities – *Rajas*, *Tamas* and *Sattva*; and the three Ayurvedic doshas – *Vata*, *Pitta* and *Kapha*. The four fingers are also the four directions – North, South, East and West. The fingers and the thumbs represent the five senses (sight, hearing, taste, smell and touch) and the five elements (water, earth, sky, air and fire). The joints on the four fingers represent the twelve Zodiac signs; the joints of the thumbs and fingers are the thirty days of the solar month. The hand also reflects the solar system and its planets. The hand symbolizes a large field of knowledge – this all reflects the Hasta Nakshatra.

You feel that you can change the face of your destiny by harnessing your own power and directing it towards your life ambition.

# HASTA

You use this energy to improve and at times control your relationships. You believe that you can change your relationship to your way of thinking, which can lead you into partnerships that are inherently flawed.

## The Hasta Personality

### Moody

The Moon rulership of this Nakshatra makes for changing perspectives and moving realities. You can be very moody. Your moods reflect the waxing and waning phases of the Moon. You should recognize the rhythms of the lunar phases and learn to relate to them. This helps you by bringing you in tune with your planetary ruler and understanding its impact. Your lunar moodiness makes it difficult for your partners to understand you; they never know what mood you are going to be in on any given day. You need emotional support. Although you appear confident and in control, your inner self is vulnerable, insecure and in conflict.

### Intuitive and Inspirational

Hasta is placed entirely in the sign of Libra, which is ruled by Venus. The ruler of Hasta is the Moon. The Moon controls the mind and Venus inspiration. This Nakshatra connects the mind to inspiration – you use your emotional inspirations to establish relationships with individuals and the world. You are practical yet intuitive. Emotional yet detached. You appreciate arts and music with the finesse of a true connoisseur.

Libra balances opposing forces of negative and positive, spiritual and material, day and night. Libra learns stillness on the physical level but the mind, represented by the Hasta ruler Moon, is active and searching. Involvement in relationships and material values can make your life static, but the inner self never stops its search. To find true happiness you must learn to calm your mind, achieve a dynamic balance between your opposing desires. Both are important. You will be unhappy if you choose one over the other.

## Sexuality – The Female Buffalo

### Earthy

Your sexuality is expressed by your animal sign, the female buffalo. Buffaloes are wild animals who live near swampland and grass jungles. They are earthy, powerful and wild. Their appearance can instill fear in others. You can be wild and untamed. You tend to keep this part of your nature under wraps and appear refined but will enjoy the rough and tumble of life. But buffaloes are also domesticated in India. You have the ability to control your nature.

You can be very sensuous and earthy. On the negative side, you could be aggressive and crude. You keep a tight control over your baser instincts, afraid of unleashing the animal within you. You show a homely, domesticated side to the world by being shy, charming and pleasant.

You do not place too much emphasis on your sexuality. You wait till you know you are desired and prefer that your mate make all the effort for you. You can wait to satisfy your sexual desires. You have a very fragile ego. You hardly ever forget a sexual slight. You hold grudges for a long time. You can be vindictive and obsessive.

### The Best and the Worst Sexual Partners

You find sexual happiness with your male counterpart Swati. They help release your sensual nature. You usually keep your sexuality under wraps and never express your more earthy nature. With Swati there is no need for subterfuge, as they instinctively connect to your earthy self.

You are hostile to the horses Ashwini and Shatabhishak. They cannot appreciate you. There is low compatibility in other areas of life, so you can be very unhappy with them. (See below – The Pain of Loving the Horse Nakshatras.)

# HASTA

## Relationship Issues

### The Desire for Free and Open Relationships

You are independent. You keep your own independence, even if you are in a serious relationship. You are open about your desires and needs. You can create problems for yourself by being too open.

You fight against following rules. You feel trapped within relationships, but once you are committed, you will be caring and giving. You have many and varied relationships. You feel you are fulfilling an important task by loving your partner. You look after them without expecting any rewards. You are generous to a fault – that is why you feel hurt when sometimes people label you as selfish.

You are very insecure about your attractions and need constant approval from your partner. You are not overly confident about your relationships. You tend to cloak your emotional needs in a hard exterior, ignoring them rather than getting hurt by them. You need a partner who appreciates your good qualities.

### The Pain of Loving the Horse Nakshatras

You have a difficult relationship with the horse Nakshatras, Ashwini and Shatabhishak. They are the worst sexual partners for you as well as the worst overall compatibility. The horse Nakshatras appear to be exotic, sleek and beautiful. You are fascinated and attracted to them. But this is where your greatest lessons come from. The earthy buffalo does not attract the horse. They are fussy and will perpetually remind you of your inadequacies.

You have a blind spot regarding your relationship with Ashwini and Shatabhishak. You usually feel that you are able to overcome the restrictions posed by destiny. Here the frustrating part is that you cannot do that without distress to your self-esteem. You bear the pain of loving Ashwini or Shatabhishak and are reluctant to let go. There are no sexual sparks and hardly any emotional ones. If you can accept the constant battering your self-esteem takes, you can make this relationship work. Being philosophical helps you deal with your emotions.

When the relationship is over, you pine for your lost love even though the pain of loving them can at times be unbearable.

## Lack of Self-Belief

You appear to be in control of your destiny but you hide a secret. You are unable to appreciate yourself. You can create huge problems if you allow your psychological complexes to rule you. You strongly identify with your animal sign, the buffalo – an animal not known for its beauty. You feel you lack beauty within. You struggle to overcome this complex throughout your life. You feel you are rough, inferior and unsubtle. You must realize you are beautiful and special. Poor self-image leads you to overcompensate in relationships. For that reason alone, you accept less than satisfactory relationships and allow negative partnerships to flourish as you feel that this is all you deserve. You should avoid relationships that reinforce your lack of self-esteem and go for partners that empower, love and support you.

This pattern of self-doubt, which is like self-abuse, has to be stopped. You, more than most Nakshatras, can be in charge of your destiny and not let destiny rule you.

## Loving Hasta

If you desire Hasta, you will need to make all the effort. Hasta may not realize that you find them attractive as they usually have a poor self-image. They can give a lot materially but emotionally they are very unsettled. They can drive you mad with their moods and their need for support. To make Hasta happy, you need to give them emotional support. You must realize that they appear confident and in control of their life, but their inner self is vulnerable, insecure and in conflict.

# HASTA

## Compatibility

**Ideal life partner: Mrigasira**
**Most challenging life partners: Ashwini and Shatabhishak**

The full Compatibility Grid is on page 338.

**Hasta and Ashwini:** Your most difficult relationship. You may be successful and attractive, but Ashwini will find faults in you and fail to appreciate your positive points. However hard you try to be what they want you to be, you fail to live up to their high expectations. You have to learn to be more philosophical, detached and less needy. **27% compatible**

**Hasta and Bharani:** You are fascinated by Bharani's sexual confidence. This is the area where you are the least confident. You will love them without expecting anything in return. But they may not always be so careful with your feelings. Both of you are stubborn and possessive. You can feel insecure, always suspicious of Bharani's friends. **50% compatible**

**Hasta and Krittika:** Both of you appear confident but are insecure within. You lean on Krittika for strength and they are usually happy to give you this support. You should not dump your emotions on Krittika. They are afraid of letting emotions control their life. You have to gain their trust and introduce them to love. **44% compatible**

**Hasta and Rohini:** This is a good partnership. Rohini like the sophisticated you but they also give you confidence in your sexuality. Both of you are moody but at least you understand these moods and do not let them come between you. Rohini's need for independence jars, as you can be jealous and insecure. Trust them. **69% compatible**

**Hasta and Mrigasira:** Your best relationship. Mrigasira are bright, confident and passionate. They support you and teach you to be confident. You are able to talk to them without being afraid of exposing yourself. They stop you from being too emotional and know how to cope with your moods. You remain true, supportive and loving. **82% compatible**

**Hasta and Ardra:** Mutual distrust at the beginning develops into deep love later. You find Ardra's persona daunting, their lifestyle too different. But Ardra are strongly influenced by the Moon and they understand you a lot better than you thought possible. Their devotion and unquestioning support help you overcome your insecurities. **67% compatible**

**Hasta and Punarvasu:** Punarvasu have a strong lunar influence and they have many similarities to you, so you can connect with them very well. You must let Punarvasu have their freedom and not make it an issue. You find Punarvasu's inability to love on a one-to-one basis hard to accept. **57% compatible**

**Hasta and Pushya:** Pushya are very responsible about their commitments. You find their strength great to lean on. They don't want more than you are willing to give. You in turn give them all your love. They may not be demonstrative in love publicly but they more than make up for it in private. You teach them to get in touch with their emotions. **69% compatible**

**Hasta and Ashlesha:** Ashlesha analyses, Hasta feels. Ashlesha will have a tendency to criticize your dependence on emotions and you feel Ashlesha do not understand you. You will always try to love Ashlesha, but you find it difficult to cross the barriers set up by their cynical attitude. In fact you make the mistake of loving them too much. **53% compatible**

**Hasta and Magha:** Magha and Hasta have a karmic relationship, where past life issues were not easy, and this conflict creates problems now. You are a generous lover but why do you not show this generosity to Magha? You can be cold and uncaring and they react by being selfish and critical. Be normal, show them you care. **39% compatible**

**Hasta and Purva Phalguni:** Purva Phalguni are social, practical and fun-loving – very similar to you. They may think of your indepen-

# HASTA

dence as a threat. But you are happy to commit to them. Your greatest problem with them is their tendency to criticize you; you are always trying to justify your behaviour and trying to live up to their expectations. **55% compatible**

**Hasta and Uttara Phalguni:** You may choose a practical relationship with Uttara Phalguni. They support you, love your sophisticated personality but are equally comfortable with your earthiness. They are good lovers; sexually you find lots of passion and pleasure. Do not get bogged down in routine or your relationship can become boring. **58% compatible**

**Hasta and Hasta:** You understand and accept each other's qualities, especially the insecurities that underpin your lives. You give love and support through thick and thin, deal with the ever-changing moods and together you are able to defy destiny. Don't aggravate your Hasta partner's emotional crisis by feeling emotionally unsettled yourself. **77% compatible**

**Hasta and Chitra:** A great relationship. Chitra love you for what you are and that is their greatest gift to you. They teach you about self-sufficiency and confidence. They support your insecurities. You love their passion, courage and exciting life. You wonder why they love you. But they do. Try not to let your insecurities come in the way of happiness. **79% compatible**

**Hasta and Swati:** Swati are your best sexual partner – you do not need to hide your sexuality from them. They love the contrast between your earthy sexuality and your sophisticated outer personality. They are one of the few Nakshatras that make you feel totally at ease with them, so you can be natural and carefree.
**72% compatible**

**Hasta and Vishakha:** Do not fall for Vishakha in the hope you can change them to be what you want. Vishakha will be happy to be your mentor, teacher and even lover but they cannot love you as completely as you wish them to. This does not mean that they do not love you at all. Just not the way you want them to. Stop trying to control the relationship. **53% compatible**

**Hasta and Anuradha:** Anuradha seek idealistic love and their brand of unconditional love helps you overcome your insecurities. Anuradha have the ability to make you face realities without making it too difficult for you. While you are emotionally very vulnerable, they can be emotionally strong. Their vulnerability is their need for love, which you can supply. **72% compatible**

**Hasta and Jyeshta:** You are never too confident with Jyeshta. They appear so bright, charming and intellectual and you fear you will never match up to them. Jyeshta can turn their passion on and off and this confuses you further. You have to learn to be strong with your Jyeshta partner. If you allow them to take control you may pay a high price emotionally. **36% compatible**

**Hasta and Mula:** Sexual versus emotional, this is the conflict. You are full of sexual insecurities. You want to change the emphasis of your relationship from sexual to emotional. This can make you moody and cool. Mula do not understand your sexual distance. Both of you want something from the other that they cannot freely give.
**42% compatible**

**Hasta and Purva Ashadha:** Purva Ashadha presents a clean slate to you, pure and clear. Together you can create a different palette of colour that is your relationship. Your ruler the moon makes you the perfect chameleon, adapting to their new ideas fluidly and seamlessly, keeping love and commitment alive through their many changes.
**75% compatible**

**Hasta and Uttara Ashadha:** Mentally, emotionally and spiritually, Uttara Ashadha brings strength and calmness to you. You are happy to shine in their reflected warmth. Both of you suffer from lack of self-belief. Your animal signs are the cause of your grief. When you meet someone experiencing similar pain, you feel healed by it.
**64% compatible**

**Hasta and Shravana:** Shravana are unconventional and philosophical.

# HASTA

But they are also very sentimental and romantic. You cut through their coolness to find their warm inner core. You never feel inadequate with them. Love is strong. Being too similar can be a drawback as you react to situations in a similar way. **66% compatible**

**Hasta and Dhanishta:** Dhanishta give you courage and confidence. They run away from emotionalism and romantic constraints. You have to be careful you do not have too many expectations of them. They will remain loyal to you as long as you do not become too possessive. Develop your own emotional support system and they will love you for it. **51% compatible**

**Hasta and Shatabhishak:** Shatabhishak fascinate you, but the more you try to know them, the more mysterious they become. They do not live up to their promise: it is like catching an elusive shadow, and you never can. They are your spiritually complex partners as well as your worst sexual ones. Sexual experiences with them may not be pleasurable; you can become afraid of expressing your personality, fearing criticism and rejection. **27% compatible**

**Hasta and Purva Bhadra:** You never quite believe your luck in being involved with the magnificent Purva Bhadra. They usually have unrealistic expectations: the more you try to live up to them, the more you fail. Appreciate yourself more and be assertive or this can become a one-sided relationship – you giving and they taking.
**38% compatible**

**Hasta and Uttara Bhadra:** You feel Uttara Bhadra are unable to understand your emotional nature. Their inflexibility is blocking your self-expression. You feel unsure and insecure. As you get to know them you realize they want to be supportive and loving, you were just misreading the signals. This leads to a strong bond and warm love.
**72% compatible**

**Hasta and Revati:** You can become very attached to Revati. You vibrate well with each other and develop spiritually through your contact. You should not allow your lack of confidence to make you feel you are of no use to them. They need your love, your practical support keeps them grounded and they are unconcerned about your earthiness. **66% compatible**

## Cusps

Those born at the end or beginning of Hasta, should see pages 364–6.

10 to 23 October

# Chitra

Ruled by Mars
Animal sign: The Female Tiger
Symbol: The Pearl

## Meaning and Symbolism

*Chitra* means 'image', 'reflection' or 'beautiful picture'. You connect to illusions, rather than reality. You can have a habit of living a life of illusions, not being in touch with the reality of the soul. You embrace illusions as reality; this makes you immerse yourself in materialistic life. Materialism is considered the greatest illusion according to Vedic philosophy. The beautiful picture is the revelation of the soul. The soul within you is beautiful and pure regardless of the illusion you have embraced. The story of your life is strongly connected to the revelation of your true personality.

The symbol of Chitra is the pearl. The pearl is found in a hard shell. Till that shell is broken, the lustrous pearl cannot emerge. The process of finding your hidden self is extremely painful. You have to go through great unhappiness, usually connected to your relationships, in this process. You are ambitious as you know of your hidden talents, but others may not see you in the same way. You work hard to externalize your talents, therefore you can leave behind partners who did not move with your vision.

# The Chitra Personality

## Courageous

Mars rules Chitra. Mars is a dynamic planet which imparts plenty of courage. You need plenty of it as you search for your true personality. Your personality depends on whether you have discovered your potential or not. You begin life with your inner pearl well hidden; you are controlled by your desires and can be lazy and selfish. But from an early stage, you are aware there is more to you than meets the eye. Mars gives you the courage and confidence to externalize your potential regardless of the personal cost. You are not fearful of what the next part of your life will bring or the obstacles you have to face. As you externalize your latent talents, the second type of Chitra emerges who is selfless and truly beautiful.

## Confident and Talented

Chitra is placed in Libra ruled by Venus. Mars rules Chitra. Venus is the planet of love, romance, commitment, marriage and the luxuries of life; Mars the planet of action, leadership and courage. Mars is tough and independent and Venus is refined and cultured. You combine the polarities well. Mars gives you the confidence to unfold your hidden gifts; Venus gives you the ability to appreciate them and use them properly. Libra symbolizes the scales of justice, the true balance of life. Mars knows about defending life and working for justice and peace. Venus gives you the ability to enjoy the fine things in life – you have a good eye, you are creative and much of your life is spent externalizing your creativity. The creativity here is not expressed physically in the form of children, but by ideas and inspiration. You can become involved in the arts as actors, writers, painters, etc.

You are intuitive and inspirational. You have many ideas and the ability to make the ideas become reality. You should not reject any idea out of hand, however outlandish it may seem at first. Your powers of intuition allows you to see into the future and understand

# CHITRA

trends much before their time. This search for your hidden capabilities does not leave you much time for emotions, relationships and love, and people can accuse you of being self-involved. You have to make time for relationships and love.

## Sexuality – The Female Tiger

### Powerful

Chitra's animal sign is the female tiger. The tiger is exotic, lively and beautiful. They have the ability to hide but also to be the most attractive animal of the jungle. Chitra make a great impact. Tiger sexuality is supposed to be the strongest amongst the animal kingdom. Parts of the tiger's body are used to make aphrodisiacs and sexual potions in Chinese medicine.

You are virile and sensuous. You have powerful sexual needs. Being the female sign, you need partners to stimulate and interest you. You are sexual by nature. You need partners who can match your strong sexuality. This is an area where you should never compromise. You are passionate. But your passion is the slow-burning type. You need long periods of foreplay before you are ready for sex. You need to be wooed in good surroundings. You hate to be hemmed in. Both male and female Chitra need to be free.

You are possessive and you will fight to establish your rights. At the same time if you decide to detach yourself from the sexual race, you can be celibate and withdrawn. You can hide yourself in the sea of humanity and suppress your sexual desires. You can make yourself available and move out of your camouflage when you are ready for sex and relationships.

### The Best and the Worst Sexual Partners

The male tiger Vishakha is able to fulfil your every desire. You are very compatible in other areas of life, so this makes your relationship sexually satisfying and emotionally fulfilling.

Your worst sexual partners are the bull Uttara Phalguni and the cow Uttara Bhadra. In the wild tigers kill bulls and cows, and the tiger is one of the few animals who is not in awe of their strength. You will subconsciously try to exercise your power. They are strong lovers, but are boring and staid to you. Your relationship goes downhill too fast. Compromise is never an option. You have the strongest sexual desires among the Nakshatras and for you to have a relationship that is not sexually exciting is not an option. You can still have a go at a relationship with Uttara Phalguni, but with Uttara Bhadra your overall compatibility is so poor that both of you may be extremely unhappy and frustrated.

# Relationship Issues

## Emotional Disappointments with Venus and Saturn Nakshatras

Two groups of Nakshatras have difficult relationship issues and very low compatibility with Chitra. The development of Chitra is connected to having tough relationship choices. Chitra needs to experience some kind of pain and disappointment in relationships to allow the other side of their nature to develop. The Saturn Nakshatras are first to shatter your illusions. Pushya, Anuradha and Uttara Bhadra are the Saturn Nakshatras. Saturn is naturally a difficult energy for you as Saturn deals with reality and discipline. The Saturn Nakshatras question your independence, your need for action and your creativity. They bring you down to earth, which is not a pleasant experience. You struggle against the restrictions imposed by them in the name of love and at the first opportunity, you leave.

Purva Phalguni, Purva Ashadha and Bharani are the Venus Nakshatras. You should be able to deal with the Venus Nakshatras as you are in the sign of Libra which is ruled by Venus. But Chitra strive to achieve a fine balance in their life. The Venus Nakshatras create difficulties as they encourage complete concentration on desire and sensuality at the cost of other, more spiritual aspects of life.

## Living on the Edge of Excitement

You are looking for excitement, intellectual stimulation and sexual fulfilment. You do not recognize boundaries and happily experiment with sex and with sexual partners. You are passionate and have a great sexual drive so are searching for partners who fulfil you sexually. You also like partners who are powerful and successful. Ideally, you want to be involved in an exciting, on-the-edge relationship with another notable person. You may compromise on other qualities if your partner is an important entity.

On the negative side you can be fickle, search for excitement all the time and get bored easily. You find it difficult to commit to any one thing, as there are always new ideas, hobbies, jobs, and relationships to entice you.

## Inability to Share

You learn to be alone at a very young age. You want to share yet you are unable to give a hundred per cent of yourself. You keep a bit of it back. You always want others to commit, but are unable to do so yourself. One of the reasons your relationships do not work is that you do not give them enough time and you do not commit yourself to them fully.

# Loving Chitra

Chitra hate it if people take liberties with them or get too familiar. Chitra will let you know with subtle hints about their interest in you. You should learn to look beyond the façade they present to the world. Challenge them to reveal their true self. There is usually more to them than they present to the world. Love them without trying to control them. Always make them feel special.

# Compatibility

**Ideal life partner: Hasta**
**Most challenging life partner: Uttara Bhadra**

**The full Compatibility Grid is on page 338.**

**Chitra and Ashwini:** Ashwini is exactly the opposite Nakshatra to Chitra. In theory they should be the best partners for you. The reality is different. You need to look beyond your personal needs and understand what Ashwini want from you. Ashwini's habit of rejecting does not make you happy. You should nurture Ashwini and do not lash out at them. **47% compatible**

**Chitra and Bharani:** A challenging relationship. You can fall for Bharani swiftly. It is an exciting, fun and sensual experience. The cold reality in the aftermath of spent passion is that there are hardly any interests that keep you together. Bharani's possessiveness is impossible to handle. You want out and you may not be very kind with their emotions. **22% compatible**

**Chitra and Krittika:** You can be great friends with Krittika. You love them and indulge their passions. You can fight with each other, but you know how to make up. You introduce Krittika to a more exotic life. They can be disapproving of your more adventurous exploits but they will stick by you. Be appreciative and stop being competitive. **61% compatible**

**Chitra and Rohini:** You love Rohini's sensuality, romanticism and ability to love you so completely. But you hate their jealousies, their tantrums and their possessiveness. These usually cause a rift between you. You are unable to give your soul to them but they want it all. Find a middle ground so that you enjoy the pleasure while minimizing the pain. **49% compatible**

**Chitra and Mrigasira:** You are too similar – aggressive, combative and fiery. This relationship may become a competition. You will try to compete with each other for everything – career, success and

# CHITRA

appreciation. Mrigasira's analysis of your feelings does not go down well. Your dominance is not acceptable to them. Stop fighting and start loving. **37% compatible**

**Chitra and Ardra:** Ardra are so different from you. But an unlikely attraction flourishes. They love you unconditionally and you enjoy their love. You find their brightness exhilarating and life with them is an adventure. They can show their love too readily and this is boring, but their brand of simple love can soon be just as palatable and enjoyable as the rest of the relationship. **65% compatible**

**Chitra and Punarvasu:** You appreciate the Punarvasu wisdom. You are happy to relate to Punarvasu on whatever level they want to connect. You are happy with Punarvasu's flexible attitude to love; you are also not into commitment and appreciate someone who does not make this a priority. You are willing to commit to non-commitment. **58% compatible**

**Chitra and Pushya:** Pushya are tough to deal with. While you know they have a lot to teach you, you are not sure you want to listen or want a relationship where you are always reminded of reality. What's wrong with chasing your dream? You rebel against Pushya; this will set the tone of the relationship. There is mutual lack of understanding. **30% compatible**

**Chitra and Ashlesha:** You fall for Ashlesha's charm, but also enjoy their wisdom and deep knowledge. You are intrigued by their air of detachment and love the way their mind works. Ashlesha explore the relationship with you, as if it is a deep mystery and as you can always surprise them with your depth, they remain interested.
**67% compatible**

**Chitra and Magha:** You find the Magha status, power and ambitions sexy. Just make sure you are not falling for them for the wrong reasons. There are many similarities that tie you together. Both love and sex are powerful and you enjoy the idealism of Magha. You connect to their vision. Magha can be in awe of you sexually and you can intimidate. **58% compatible**

# THE LOVE SIGNS

**Chitra and Purva Phalguni:** This is a Mars and Venus relationship – volatile, intense and passionate. But when the passion has died down, you find nothing in common with Purva Phalguni. You find their sensuality unbalancing. You block their every effort get to know you; you can ignore them and make no effort to appreciate them.
**19% compatible**

**Chitra and Uttara Phalguni:** You can be good friends but Uttara Phalguni are the worst sexual partner for you. Sexual frustration can bring out a tendency to fight and a struggle for supremacy. Uttara Phalguni can be too practical and boring. You may also stop making the effort to woo them or care for their needs. **47% compatible**

**Chitra and Hasta:** Your best relationship. You love Hasta's sophistication and their ability to care for you. You are unfazed by their moodiness, enjoying the various strands that make up their personality. Their earthiness, their generosity and their ability to inspire you to love; all are potent attractions that survive the test of time.
**79% compatible**

**Chitra and Chitra:** You find other Chitra good companions and excellent lovers. Both of you are strong personalities so you can fight, disagree and argue, but you will also love each other. Being too similar, you can forever be seeking excitement, thrills and stimulation and may not know how to deal with the boring bits like responsibility. **66% compatible**

**Chitra and Swati:** Both of you appear hard and uncaring, your symbols, pearl and coral, are found in the deep seas. Esoterically sea reflects emotions; both of you are connected by emotions. If you learn to love each other and show your emotions, you become tied in a wonderful bond. You share something precious and special.
**65% compatible**

**Chitra and Vishakha:** Vishakha is your best sexual partner and its ruler Jupiter your best friend. Exciting and sensual, this relationship helps both of you find happiness and love. You learn to share with

# CHITRA

Vishakha. Love between you is great, sex even better. You are usually happy to sacrifice your independence for them. **74% compatible**

**Chitra and Anuradha:** You find Anuradha's brand of love stifling and inhibiting. But you never really try to understand Anuradha's emotional needs. Initial attraction will quickly die off, leaving you finding ways to get out of this relationship. In the long term this relationship is about differing ideologies and stressed relationships. **23% compatible**

**Chitra and Jyeshta:** You always disagree with them, you do not always see eye to eye. But you allow Jyeshta to charm you. Jyeshta are great lovers: sensuous, hedonistic and pleasure seeking. You can love them easily. You are also amused at their attempts to control you. Their psychological games can irritate and you may choose not to play them. **62% compatible**

**Chitra and Mula:** You know you could love Mula the moment you meet them. They connect to you and cut through the façade you present to the world. They recognize your deep spirituality and your beauty. They also never ask for more than you are willing to give. You love their lifestyle; your relationship with them can be one long adventure. **75% compatible**

**Chitra and Purva Ashadha:** Purva Ashadha are creative, unconventional, sexy and totally wrong for you. But the attraction flares and passion explodes. This is a Mars–Venus fascination – uncontrollable, unreliable and ultimately unsatisfying. You never tried to get to know each other. Neither of you know how to handle the aftermath. **36% compatible**

**Chitra and Uttara Ashadha:** Uttara Ashadha's lack of confidence in your relationship can spoil it all. You are with them because you like their cool strength. Your sensuous nature is attracted to their stark simplicity even though they may live in most plush and rich surroundings. You can be good friends. Sexually you need to take the initiative. **55% compatible**

**Chitra and Shravana:** You will always be friends with Shravana even

after your relationship is over. They bring out the protective streak within you. You want to care for them. Sexually you can have exciting times. They know how to keep you interested. You love it when they are cool, as you know how to change their attitude.
**58% compatible**

**Chitra and Dhanishta:** Your similar natures become a huge stumbling block to this relationship. You both want to win every fight and have the last word. You should recognize each other's strengths and not challenge them at every step. Be democratic, consult, and not argue. Keep quality time aside for love and tenderness.
**50% compatible**

**Chitra and Shatabhishak:** Shatabhishak appear so remote, so difficult to know that you take them on as a challenge. They can be very attracted to you and they break their personal rules in getting to know you more intimately. They tell you their secrets and open their soul to you. It takes time but love and strong commitment is the outcome. **69% compatible**

**Chitra and Purva Bhadra:** You like Purva Bhadra, you can enjoy an affair, even love them in your own way. But your way is not their way. You want too much from life to settle. You are no good at domestic responsibility. You need to be admired and loved always. Purva Bhadra can ignore your needs; they can also be too lazy.
**45% compatible**

**Chitra and Uttara Bhadra:** Your worst relationship. The buffalo Uttara Bhadra can be unexciting lovers, but they also try to shape you in their own image. They challenge you at every step, making you doubt yourself totally. You fight back, being merciless in your condemnation and rejection. You can be very unhappy with them.
**18% compatible**

**Chitra and Revati:** You find Revati hard to handle. It begins as profound love; you feel you have met your soul mate. Then you are constantly under pressure trying to live up to their demands for

# CHITRA

perfection. You are not into commitment, and sex for you should be fun and passionate. You are not able to revere Revati enough.
**43% compatible**

## Cusps

Those born at the end or beginning of Chitra, should see pages 366–7.

23 October to 6 November

# Swati

Ruled by Rahu
Animal: The Male Buffalo
Symbol: Coral

## Meaning and Symbolism

*Swati* means 'sword'. Swati carry the sword as a tool for self-advancement, cutting through competition, obstacles in their path. In Vedic mythology Swati is also the name of the Sun wife. In Swati, the Sun forgets its spiritual purpose and becomes involved in the pleasures and pains of relationships. Relationships are very important to you, but you can forget about them in your relentless pursuit of success.

Your symbol is coral, which has a hard outer sheath but is self-propagating. It lives in a marine environment that it both affects and is affected by. This symbolizes the human being; we live in the world which influences our life but we in turn make an impact on the world around us. You influence those around you, in turn you use the influence of your society to improve yourself. You can develop a hard surface and appear insensitive to your partner's needs. But usually this hardness is your reaction to your experiences in life.

# SWATI

# The Swati Personality

## The Ambitions of Rahu

Rahu, the shadow planet rules Swati. Rahu forms just the head of the celestial snake; therefore it has no body. It thinks and forgets to feel. In Vedic terminology, the lower brain is also known as the serpent brain. The lower brain is the organ of the subconscious mind. An individual initially projects the subconscious through the strong identification with their personality. You choose to project your personality by becoming someone of influence. You start believing in your ability to achieve whatever you put your mind to. You are ambitious and aspire towards reaching the pinnacle of commercial and creative success where you make an impact on the life of others. There is so much to do and achieve that you usually are unable to decide which ambition you need to fulfil first.

You are an 'ideas' person, disciplined with the ability to turn your ideas into good commercial and profitable realities. Your ideas do not remain in the fantasy realm. Once you have decided what to do with them, you can change the course of history. Many of your ideas are new or undiscovered. Rahu, your ruler gives you the ability to go where others have not been. Your partners should learn to be supportive of your ideas. You have a tendency to ignore your partners when you are working on a hot new idea.

Politics is another of your ambitions. Swati are good strategists. You can see them involved in politics at some time. They know how to plan, manoeuvre, beguile and play power games.

## The Stresses of Being Swati

The first day of Swati can be in the sign of Libra ruled by Venus and the rest is in Scorpio ruled by Mars (Vedic Astrology uses traditional rulerships, therefore does not use Pluto as the ruler of Scorpio).

Being born at the end of Libra and beginning of Swati is a karmic birth time. There are very few Swati who are born at this time as

Swati is seldom in Libra. The location of this Nakshatra at the end of Libra indicates that those born here will need to be fully involved in earthy, materialistic pleasures. This brings with it dissatisfaction because the Libra scales will be weighted too heavily to one side. Business, politics and creativity are all Swati Libra's forte.

Scorpio Swati feel dissatisfied. They try to sort out their dissatisfaction with more material achievement. This brings with it emptiness and lack of pleasure with their accomplishments. Rahu and Mars are a difficult combination. Rahu gives ambitious ideas and Mars the physical capacity to fulfil them. But they are two polarities; pulling in different directions and creating stress and tension in the life of Scorpio Swati. Swati desires to make an impact in life, but they also desire spiritual satisfaction. They are not willing to give up one for the other; this keeps pulling them in different directions. They should pursue and fulfil both their inner needs and not make them areas of anxiety and stress. Partners feel the fall-out from Scorpio Swati's inner war and they have to learn to deal with the anxieties and try to calm their struggle.

## Sexuality – The Male Buffalo

### Untamed

Your sexuality is expressed by your animal sign, the male buffalo. Buffaloes are wild animals who live near swampland and grass jungles. They are earthy, powerful and wild. Their appearance can instil fear in others. But they are also domesticated in India, where they are used on farms and for food.

The wildness and the domesticity are reflected in the Swati sexuality. You have a wild, untamed side but you can also harness these qualities and be restrained and civilized. You try to keep a tight control over your baser instincts, afraid of unleashing the animal within you, but you do not always succeed. You take an active interest in your sexuality and are quick in expressing your interest. Your planetary ruler is the passionate Mars and the elusive Rahu. Both the planets have great interest in experiencing life. You are

# SWATI

unlike your female counterpart Hasta who have the finesse of Venus as part of their personality. What you desire, you go for. You can be aggressive and dynamic in your pursuit of sexual gratification and passion. You can be very sensuous and earthy. On the negative side, you could be aggressive and crude.

Sex can take a back seat to your other ambitions. You also have the ability to control your ardour. You can wait to satisfy your desires. You are possessive and if your partners try to make you sexually jealous, you never forget. You can be vindictive and obsessive. If your partners stir up your inner beast, you can hurt back regardless of the cost to your self.

## The Best and the Worst Sexual Partners

You find sexual happiness with your female counterpart Hasta. You can be yourself with them, with a passionate, earthy sex life with no need for control and sophisticated imagery.

The horses Ashwini and Shatabhishak are your worst partners. You are one of the few Nakshatras that has very good relations with both your sexual antagonists. You know how to give prominence to other human needs such as love, emotions and happiness. Ashwini and Shatabhishak are not always able to appreciate your more earthy nature and you find it hard to understand their highly strung and finicky attitude. Your sexual relationship with Ashwini and Shatabhishak may not be totally fulfilling, but the important thing is that you try to override the issues that usually split others apart. You work to make your relationship more exciting by caring for your partner's needs.

# Relationship Issues

## Understanding Relationships

The Sun in Swati is in its natural Nakshatra for relationships. Swati is the name of the Sun's wife. Therefore long-term committed relationships form a very important part of your agenda. You have a vision of an ideal partner and when you find them, you can be very possessive. You do not trust easily and your suspicious mind can create problems in relationships where there were none.

You try to get on with most of the other Nakshatras. But some experiences baffle you, especially with the Mercury Nakshatras. Their criticism, their cynicism, and their changeable personality confuse you. You are able to work out your differences with Jyeshta and be happy with them, but you are never able to understand Ashlesha and Revati however hard you try. Revati is your worst relationship – their idealistic dreaming does not make you happy.

## Inability to Recognize True Love

The perfection you demand from your partners may be something they cannot realistically live up to. This can make you dissatisfied. You can spoil a great relationship by being critical and fault-finding. In your unhappy state of mind, you think that another relationship may bring greater love. But that may not always be the case. This dissatisfaction in your life does not really come from your relationships but from lack of fulfilment within. If you understand this, you find happiness. If you don't, changing relationships is not going to help. The sense of dissatisfaction remains. You must learn to work with your present relationship and recognize the happiness it brings. Multiple relationships can unsettle you and aggravate your inner soul.

# Loving Swati

It is complicated seducing Swati as they do not play by conventional rules. They love to go against tradition. Do not show interest in others: Swati can be aggressive in getting the better of any opposition. They want an exciting and thrilling relationship, and need a partner who can bring passion into their life and become a source of inspiration for their ideas. The problem arises when the initial excitement dies down and they forget all the good points of your relation-

# SWATI

ship. As a Swati partner you need to keep reminding them of the reasons your relationship works.

## Compatibility

**Ideal life partner: Bharani**
**Most challenging life partner: Revati**

**The full Compatibility Grid is on page 338.**

**Swati and Ashwini:** Ashwini will fascinate you and you can fall in love with them easily. But they can reject you sexually. Ashwini have a karmic lesson to teach Swati about sensuality. Once you look beyond the initial sexual rejection and work with the relationship, this will help you find a love that completes you; Ashwini may be your soul mate. **70% compatible**

**Swati and Bharani:** Best relationship. Great sex, good friendship and lots of fun. Bharani bring out your sensual nature, make you feel wanted and love you passionately. You are hypnotized by their magnetism. They empower you, make you feel sexually confident. They enjoy your earthiness and release you from your sexual complexes. **78% compatible**

**Swati and Krittika:** You do not trust Krittika and they return the compliment. You feel Krittika are selfish and they do not pay enough attention to you. If you try and overcome the distrust and give them a chance to prove themselves, you will find them warm and friendly. Talk to each other. What has remained unsaid can become a barrier in love. **32% compatible**

**Swati and Rohini:** You fall for the romantic and sensuous Rohini. Yet their romantic nature, their inability to be realistic drives you apart. This is your spiritually complex relationship; the Moon–Rahu combination is tough, where the Moon fears Rahu's ability to eclipse it. This translates to a lack of trust and the fear of commitment. **42% compatible**

# THE LOVE SIGNS

**Swati and Mrigasira:** A relationship that starts well but which can get into a rut. You like Mrigasira; they are bright, intelligent and fun. Their sense of adventure and free spirit attracts you very much. But their inability to make up their mind and their ability to analyse you and your relationship to death, both create conflict and tension. **50% compatible**

**Swati and Ardra:** Love can be wonderful with Ardra. You understand each other completely: your ambitions, your emotional needs are entwined. Both of you have a down to earth sexuality. Ardra can be very devoted to you and you open your feelings to them. When you pool your resources, you are able to fulfil each other's wildest dreams. **75% compatible**

**Swati and Punarvasu:** Punarvasu are both wise and fun. You are both adventurers in different ways and you create a relationship that can be unconventional and loving. They usually help you with your ambitions – this is important for you. Punarvasu are usually not good at commitments but somehow you know how to make them change their mind. **74% compatible**

**Swati and Pushya:** Your love usually starts as a practical friendship. You are similar, being ambitious, hard-working and focused. You have a fund of ideas, but may have impractical ways of expressing them. Pushya give you strength to flourish in the competitive world. You also find love, and they love selflessly in return. **69% compatible**

**Swati and Ashlesha:** A tough relationship. Ashlesha may be your friend and lover, if you only give them a chance. But somehow your love can deteriorate quickly and your relationship become one of distrust and secrecy. Try to learn what Ashlesha want and see the relationship in a positive light. Do not always think about what is wrong with your relationship but what is right. **30% compatible**

**Swati and Magha:** Magha and you are tied in a karmic bond, both searching for happiness. Can you transcend your subconscious feelings that block this relationship from developing fully and create new bonds? You have to overcome your lack of trust and work through

# SWATI

many layers of distrust and suspicion to be able to love again successfully. **27% compatible**

**Swati and Purva Phalguni:** Purva Phalguni help you with your ideas, adding new life into them. They are fun to be with, social and sophisticated. You love their ability to be elegant, aesthetic and poetic. You are both into commitment and will try to establish a good relationship. Be careful that your ambitions do not overshadow your family life. **66% compatible**

**Swati and Uttara Phalguni:** You take time falling in love. You are not sure that you trust Uttara Phalguni. But you soon find that they are solid, caring and extremely supportive. They are usually influential and powerful and you like that. You bask in their warmth and loving; their love helps you to come out of your shell. **69% compatible**

**Swati and Hasta:** Your best sexual partner. Hasta are ideal for you sexy, fun and sophisticated. They help you to get in touch with your emotions. You are both hard-working and ambitious. You use your creative intelligence to profit and Hasta are financially astute. You make financially sound partnerships where love also flourishes. **72% compatible**

**Swati and Chitra:** You love the exotic Chitra. They excite you and make you feel sexy and loved. They are extremely creative and lead interesting lives, and you fit into their world easily. It is a scintillating relationship as long as you work on keeping the sexual frisson alive. You have to learn to tolerate their independence and show your love to them. **65% compatible**

**Swati and Swati:** Relationships with your own Nakshatra work well, as you understand each other instinctively. This is the reason so many people choose partners from the same Nakshatra. Problems happen when you face difficulties and you are unable to find a different way of dealing with them. Love and affection overcomes many hurdles. **77% compatible**

**Swati and Vishakha:** You try hard to live up to Vishakha's sexual fantasies and feel unable to satisfy them. This aggravates your sense of dissatisfaction and makes you very unsettled. Talk about your feelings and vulnerabilities. Do not pressurize Vishakha for commitment. They may not be willing to make it and then you feel disappointed. **40% compatible**

**Swati and Anuradha:** You are attracted to Anuradha's strong and ambitious personality but you can then find them vulnerable and needy. If you pay attention to their dreams, they will love you back tenfold. Learn to be happy with what you have with them and your relationship goes from good to better. Let them trust you and make them feel secure. **58% compatible**

**Swati and Jyeshta:** You are never comfortable with Jyeshta: you feel their power and know you are unequal to their sexual prowess. You also try to play games with them, but they are past masters at this and you can get easily hurt. Avoid lashing out at them – it can only be destructive. Be their equal and do not show them your inadequacies. **41% compatible**

**Swati and Mula:** This relationship can be intense and karmic. Mula appear to be your ideal partner, yet there is a distance you cannot fathom or bridge. You try to hold on to them by being possessive but that makes them even more distant. Allow your inner feelings to show and appreciate the relationship for what it is. It can be blissful and joyous. **63% compatible**

**Swati and Purva Ashadha:** Creative, talented, bright – and intelligent Purva Ashadha has the ability to be your special friend. You should recognize deep bonds. Purva Ashadha will tame your wildness but encourage you with your originality and creativity. This can be a thrilling relationship where you can make lack of commitment an art form. **75% compatible**

**Swati and Uttara Ashadha:** You are not sure you trust Uttara Ashadha, so you never really open up for them fully. Polite, tactful, civilized and refined can be the words to describe your relationship. Both of you can disguise your earthiness, passion and true feelings

## SWATI

from each other. The relationship between animal signs the snake and mongoose makes loving them tough. **55% compatible**

**Swati and Shravana:** You fall for Shravana very quickly but they keep on putting up invisible barriers. They will be warm one moment and cold the next. You are not sure whether they are teasing you. They may be protecting themselves from future hurt. Show them that they can trust you and they will start to bare their soul to you. **61% compatible**

**Swati and Dhanishta:** You desire Dhanishta's strength and courage. You feel they have reached the place where you would like to be, spiritually at least. You are always self-critical and do not recognize your good qualities. Putting yourself down in front of Dhanishta is not such a good idea. They need you to be confident and assured. **65% compatible**

**Swati and Shatabhishak:** This is a relationship that defies convention: you have no obvious sexual compatibility yet you can be happy and compatible in all other areas of life. You may have a complex about whether you can ever satisfy the fussy and exotic horse Nakshatra. Talk about your sexual incompatibility and try to work something out. **61% compatible**

**Swati and Purva Bhadra:** When Purva Bhadra show an interest in you, you make every effort to keep their attention. You use strategy unashamedly to keep them by your side. You know how to fight for their causes. There are times when you feel that you are making all the effort, but their love is usually enough for you. **60% compatible**

**Swati and Uttara Bhadra:** You love Uttara Bhadra for the support they give you but you forget to appreciate them. Your problem is that you never think they are your ideal partner. Usually you can be quite selfish, taking and not giving. But you will feel the loss if they decide to take their support away or stop loving you. **53% compatible**

**Swati and Revati:** Your worst relationship. Revati can put you on a pedestal and you know that you cannot live up to their ideal. Your mistake can be to perpetuate their myth but the reality is unpleasant.

# THE LOVE SIGNS

You find the gentle Revati has a much tougher and unforgiving side. Both of you get hurt. It is best to be open and up-front from the start. **24% compatible**

## Cusps

Those born at the end or beginning of Swati, should see pages 367–9.

6 to 19 November

# Vishakha

Ruled by Jupiter
Animal: The Male Tiger
Symbol: The Archway

## Meaning and Symbolism

*Visha* means 'to enter' and *Kha* means 'heaven'. In Vedic mythology Vishakha is portrayed standing on the gates, aspiring to cross the threshold into heaven. Vishakha stands for transformation. You are at a stage where the soul is standing on the threshold of higher experiences, willing and able to take on board new lessons that change your outlook. This change does not take place without a great churning of emotions. The price you pay is in relationships. By being dissatisfied and feeling that the heaven is somewhere else, you neglect the present and feel unloved. You need to change your perspective of reality. You can feel fulfilled and happy if you accept the quality of life today instead of always hankering for the future.

The archway symbol represents the threshold of a new life. The change is yet to take place, as this is the soul looking in from the outside. You have reached that place in life where you are drawn on a spiritual search, to uncover the great unknown. There is no guarantee of the experience. When you begin to look inwards, your partner may not understand or follow your journey. This can be a crucial time, where your relationship remains either supportive or it breaks.

## The Vishakha Personality

### Heavenly Aspirations

Jupiter rules Vishakha. Jupiter is the largest planet in the cosmos and its effect brings joy and happiness. Jupiter's Sanskrit name is Guru or the adviser. Vishakha are always advising, guiding and nurturing.

You aspire to touch the heavens. You want to make this life special and work towards it. Jupiter gives you the ability to expand your horizons. It also bestows the wisdom to be able to think beyond limitations that usually restrict humans.

You are very interested in unraveling deep mysteries of nature. You should definitely try yoga, as your Nakshatra is so closely connected with it. This will help to calm you. You embrace both sensuality and, when you are ready for it, austerity and hardship. Your relationships work if you make them important. But you can get bogged down in unsatisfactory relationships. You can be unfaithful rather than change your status quo. But once you understand what is required to find happiness, you will completely transform your life.

### The Strength to Embrace Happiness

Vishakha is placed entirely in the sign of Scorpio ruled by Mars. Scorpio creates the desire to unveil the original soul and represents hidden power which, when properly harnessed, can give tremendous ability. Jupiter bestows knowledge and wisdom. Mars gives you power and courage. Jupiter teaches you to use your courage and inherent strength. Scorpio Vishakha energy has immense capabilities, which can be externalized spiritually and materially or wasted away. You have the strength to make real changes to your life, happiness and inner being, to transcend any restrictions destiny has presented you. You are standing at the threshold of happiness; you can either go for it or reject it. To embrace happiness, you need to use your courage and confidence and grab it with both hands.

## Sexuality – The Male Tiger

### Virile and Potent

Vishakha's animal sign is the male tiger. The tiger is exotic, elemental and unspoilt. Tiger sexuality is supposed to be the strongest amongst the animal kingdom. Parts of the tiger's body are used to make aphrodisiacs and sexual potions in Chinese medicine. Tigers need equally strong sexual partners.

You are virile and potent. Being the male sign, you are the sexual predators of the Zodiac. You have strong sexual appetites and will hunt out your partners. You need partners who can match your strong sexuality. This is an area where you should never compromise. If your partners do not match your sexual needs, you look elsewhere. Sexual frustration can only lead to unhappiness and sorrow.

You are a smooth operator; you do not wait for others to make up their minds. If you fancy someone, you will make a play for them. You know how to charm and make your seduction exciting and fun. But if your sensual victory is too easy, you lose interest quickly. You do not get into commitments easily but once you do so, you stick with the relationship. You are possessive and do not like others encroaching on your territory, but you hate your partners being possessive. You need solitude and independence.

You struggle with your intense sexual needs. You may learn to conquer them and move towards celibacy and temperance. But your sexuality smoulders below the surface and given the right conditions can come back to its full force instantly.

## The Best and the Worst Sexual Partners

The female tiger Chitra is the best partner for you. With Chitra there can be a sizzling relationship that is full of sensuous promise and exciting sex. Tigers are considered to have the strongest sexuality in the animal kingdom. Chitra fulfils this need completely.

The worst sexual partners are the bull Uttara Phalguni and the cow Uttara Bhadra. In the wild, tigers kill bulls and cows, and the tiger is one of the few animals who is not in awe of their strength. You will subconsciously try to exercise your power. Your relationship goes downhill too fast. You have the strongest sexual desires among the Nakshatras and for you to have a relationship that is not sexually exciting is not an option. Uttara Phalguni and Uttara Bhadra are diametrically opposite to you – pragmatic, industrious and (to you) boring. The hidden sexual issues will make you frustrated and you can take it out on them emotionally.

# Relationship Issues

## The Difficulty of Trading Independence for Love

You become very uncomfortable with Nakshatras that demand unconditional love. You like your freedom too much and are unwilling to trade one for the other. While you can be a good partner and parent, you are not willing to give your all. Rohini, Shravana, Revati, Purva Ashadha and Uttara Ashadha all demand more than you are willing to give. Rohini will cling to you, hoping you will become their emotional support. Shravana want you to settle their restlessness – how can you do that, when you do not know the answers to your own restlessness? Purva Ashadha are not necessarily looking for commitment but they still want your love. Uttara Ashadha is a loner and they take pleasure in criticizing you. They will express their coldness to you but want you to give them love. Revati is the worst partnership for you. At the first hint of trouble, you can become intolerant of each other's qualities.

# VISHAKHA

## Restless Relationships

The special restlessness in your personal life creates immense dissatisfaction and can lead you to keep changing partners or to be untrue to your present one. You must understand your restlessness. You need to look within for answers and not without. Unless you do this, you may remain deeply unhappy.

You can have a difficult childhood and as a result may experience problems in your adult relationships. You need unselfish love and affection that will calm you down. You have a lot to give in return. You find it difficult to be faithful however. This Nakshatra is most at risk from divorce or separation.

## The Inner Calmness and the Outer Conflict

Life revolves so fast for you that you may never stop to think. You are always on the go – partying, enjoying life and working all hours. Your relationships also involve a very hectic schedule. It appears that you make yourself so active that you forget what your life issues are or perhaps hope that these issues will go away in a whirlwind of activity.

## Fear of Change

You find it very hard to change and any change is brought about through great turmoil and personal cost. Your inability to change keeps you in situations and relationships that are no longer valid. Mediocre relationships or boring careers can bog you down because you are afraid to make a move. Your unhappiness with life can lead you to having affairs and being unfaithful. This can create unhappiness for you and your partners.

# Loving Vishakha

Vishakha knew how to seduce you. Your main difficulty with Vishakha will be to keep their interest after the initial seduction. You

# THE LOVE SIGNS

must not give in too easily. Vishakha can relate to you on a purely sexual way or a deeply spiritual one. They are happy if you understand their spiritual path while you satisfy their sensual one. You soon realize the restlessness of Vishakha and this can make you feel very unsettled with them. Let them know how insecure you feel. Your love for them should not be too demanding or possessive. They need warmth and inspiration from their partner, not criticism and possessiveness.

## Compatibility

**Ideal life partner: Chitra**
**Most challenging life partner: Revati**

**The full Compatibility Grid is on page 338.**

**Vishakha and Ashwini:** At first Ashwini appear to fulfil your needs. Ashwini are seeking adventure in the outer world, you are in the inner world. You admire Ashwini yet you come to feel they are ignoring your needs. This starts creating rifts. Work hard to keep loving each other or you will make Ashwini very insecure and they will make you feel unloved. **55% compatible**

**Vishakha and Bharani:** A great affair. Sensuous, passionate Bharani can hypnotize you into their love. But their stubbornness and inability to understand your deeper needs is what drives you apart. You want different things from life. Unless you can agree to disagree and love unconditionally, harmony will be hard to find. **50% compatible**

**Vishakha and Krittika:** This is spiritually challenging for you. Emotionally very stressful, this relationship needs deep understanding and unselfish love to keep it going. You need to recognize your vulnerabilities and care for each other. Fighting and discord will create greater havoc than this average compatibility suggests. **51% compatible**

**Vishakha and Rohini:** Rohini have no understanding of your spiritual needs. You enjoy the romance, but love and commitment are not for

# VISHAKHA

you. You find their type of emotional possessiveness trying. If you ignore them and they amuse themselves elsewhere, you can find it difficult to forgive. Not a relationship to explore in depth.
**30% compatible**

**Vishakha and Mrigasira:** An average relationship that usually lacks that special spark. Both of you can compromise too much. Mrigasira's perpetual analysis of your life restricts you. If you work at the emotional and instinctive connection you feel, you can make this relationship a lot better. If not, you can get stuck in a routine relationship with little happiness. **50% compatible**

**Vishakha and Ardra:** Both of you feel a sense of dissatisfaction regardless of the true circumstances. By understanding that your soul needs to overcome discontent from within and not blame others, especially your partners, you will remove the added burden from your relationship. Learn to appreciate your Ardra partners more.
**46% compatible**

**Vishakha and Punarvasu:** Both of you are on a journey to seek your true identity, standing at a junction where you can choose any direction. If you share your spiritual travels, choose similar paths, you can find love along the way. If you go separate ways, then you forget to care about Punarvasu's issues and emotionally disconnect as well.
**51% compatible**

**Vishakha and Pushya:** Pushya can be too restrictive and cool. You do not find them sexy to start with but then you discover their hidden passions. You have to let them know of your need for freedom. They will compromise as long as they are confident of your love. Your restlessness can make them feel insecure. **54% compatible**

**Vishakha and Ashlesha:** The tiger Vishakha is far stronger than the cat Ashlesha. As your animal signs are both from the cat family, there is an uncomfortable relationship between you. Ashlesha try to wage, usually losing, battles to establish their superiority over you. Your relationship can get involved in unnecessary fights and power play.
**41% compatible**

# THE LOVE SIGNS

**Vishakha and Magha:** You want to be Magha's lover but you cannot help wanting to teach them how to make the best of themselves. Magha can reject you and what you have to offer. You do not trust them enough to express your true feelings. Love them and they will be yours. Sexually, both of you have to try to be faithful.
**54% compatible**

**Vishakha and Purva Phalguni:** Purva Phalguni are chic, perfectionist and creative. You warm to them immensely and can fall in love easily. Sexually, you have to work hard to find compatibility. They like sex too much but when you try to introduce them to your brand of sensuality they can feel intimidated. Their endless socializing can be a bore. **55% compatible**

**Vishakha and Uttara Phalguni:** The Nakshatra rulers the Sun and Jupiter have a good planetary relationship but you cannot always translate it into a great personal one. Your inimical sexuality poses the greatest problem. Use your friendship to work through the difficulties and you may reach a level of contentment.
**50% compatible**

**Vishakha and Hasta:** Hasta need someone to guide them. You try to calm Hasta emotionally and teach them how to deal with their earthy nature. Both of you can mistake this teacher–pupil relationship for love. Hasta feel unsettled by your inability to love them more, but you may not find them sexy. This love needs time and effort.
**53% compatible**

**Vishakha and Chitra:** Exciting, sexy and passionate. After compromising on your sexual happiness for so long, you find a partner who can match your desires. Chitra calm your restlessness and you are ready to give up your prized freedom. Both your emotional histories make you vulnerable. Share your thoughts and work to build a strong relationship. **74% compatible**

**Vishakha and Swati:** You are never sure what to make of Swati. You explore emotions and love. You are attracted to their mental agility and their knowledge but you are also wary of them. They can be

# VISHAKHA

secretive and manipulative. Sexually this relationship is a compromise – Swati may lack the sexual finesse you want in your lovers. **40% compatible**

**Vishakha and Vishakha:** You share a common love of knowledge, you complement each other intellectually and are united by your search for answers. Fear of change can make you both accept less than perfect situations and compromise, not with each other, but with other things like your job or home, and this creates disturbances in your relationships as well. **60% compatible**

**Vishakha and Anuradha:** When you meet the inspirational and spiritual Anuradha, they light a spark within you with their ability to love you and support you unconditionally. At times, you may find their love claustrophobic and their neediness too much. But they usually calm your restlessness. You counteract each other's negativity. **59% compatible**

**Vishakha and Jyeshta:** With Jyeshta you feel you are at the gates of heaven; their sensuous approach to life touches you. Their deep knowledge of the mysteries of life helps you to understand your inner angst a bit better. They also teach you to embrace happiness. They help you to break the bonds of tradition and really aspire towards ecstasy. **72% compatible**

**Vishakha and Mula:** You find Mula to be stimulating and exciting companions. They have learnt not to compromise with life. Your relationship develops deeply because Mula can understand your spiritual quest. They can introduce you to a world where philosophy, knowledge, and the study of higher truth are important. Both of you gain a lot. **66% compatible**

**Vishakha and Purva Ashadha:** Purva Ashadha's sensuality attracts you. Getting entangled in a purely sensual relationship blocks you from following your spiritual path. This creates a restlessness within you that is hard to calm. The relationship can die due to lack of attention from both of you. You must also try to be a lover to them, not just their mentor. **38% compatible**

**Vishakha and Uttara Ashadha:** Uttara Ashadha need constant reassurance. You are perpetually satisfying their emotional needs. You may do so willingly at the start of your relationship but your inner restlessness means that you are soon searching for more. They want to live their life one way and you another; both of you are unwilling to compromise. **32% compatible**

**Vishakha and Shravana:** Shravana are too emotional, fickle and possessive. You cannot be bothered with their emotional agenda. You may have a short fling with them but tend to shy away from long-term commitment. They tend to aggravate your discontentment and make you feel even more unsettled. Instead of trying to be there for them, you do the opposite. **36% compatible**

**Vishakha and Dhanishta:** Dhanishta have a strong personality and will not give in to your demands. They want your full attention but do not get fazed by your independence. They love you through your difficult periods and care for your inner battles. A sensually satisfying relationship, as long as you accept Dhanishta's occasional selfishness. **70% compatible**

**Vishakha and Shatabhishak:** Shatabhishak are elusive like a shadow and they cast a spell over you. Your fascination with them can turn to love. You like their intelligence and you can understand their fears. You try not to demand what they cannot give. They learn to love you and you reciprocate. You have something special – work to keep it that way. **70% compatible**

**Vishakha and Purva Bhadra:** Purva Bhadra are very similar to you as they too are ruled by Jupiter. You find it difficult to be totally focused on one person, one relationship. You need something more. This creates a barrier between you. You are willing to help their causes, but you have your own life to live. Don't always think of your own agenda. **49% compatible**

**Vishakha and Uttara Bhadra:** Your worst sexual relationship. While Uttara Bhadra can understand your spiritual needs, they cannot satisfy your sexual ones. You may feel deeply frustrated by the control

# VISHAKHA

Uttara Bhadra exercise on their sexuality. They appear cold and frigid and you struggle with the barriers they erect around their emotions. **41% compatible**

**Vishakha and Revati:** Your worst relationship. Revati can go from being charming to critical in a short time. You do not know how to relate to them and nothing you do seems to please them. They are also very strong and stubborn. You can act contrary to your true nature with them. They aggravate your restlessness and you may seek others to love. **18% compatible**

## Cusps

Those born at the end or beginning of Vishakha, should see pages 369–70.

19 November to 2 December

# Anuradha

Ruled by Saturn
Animal: The Female Deer
Symbol: The Lotus

## Meaning and Symbolism

Anuradha has several meanings. It means a 'small flash of lightning' or 'a tiny spark'. Here it suggests that it takes only a small flash of intuition or a tiny spark of consciousness to make us aware of what we really want from life. This opens our mind to our path to happiness. Also *Anu* means 'small' and *Radha* is the name of the beloved of Lord Krishna, the important Vedic god. Radha was a separate entity to Krishna, but desired to merge with him. Radha's love of Krishna was unrequited. Similarly you fall in love with someone with all your heart and will not care whether it is reciprocated or not. For this divine love, you can give up everything: family, country and wealth.

The symbol of Anuradha is the lotus. The lotus seeds in the mud and as it flowers, it appears to reach towards the Sun. Once it has flowered, it withers away and goes back to the mud, where it will root again to repeat the whole process. The lotus is said to flower so that it can be laid at the feet of the gods; the soul is born to experience life and death so that it can break away from it to find enlightenment.

This shows the evolutionary aspect of the Soul. It reaches to the Sun (universal consciousness) from the Mud (ignorance and soul concealed in matter) and its withering away shows death, and its rebirth is the process of rerooting and flowering. You flower for each new love but also wither away when faced with rejection or disappointment. This does not stop you from aspiring to great love or falling in love again.

# The Anuradha Personality

### Saturn's Lessons in Love

Saturn rules Anuradha. Saturn is known as Shani in Sanskrit. Saturn is the great teacher of cosmic truths. His influence is tough to deal with. Saturn teaches you about responsibility and you learn about restrictions early on. Saturn gives you the ability to endure what life has to offer in the hope of finding the love that will transform your life and bring happiness beyond your imagination. You have tremendous ability to face pain. You can stay in an unhappy situation far longer than seems possible. You feel you are experiencing this for some karmic reason. Your search for divine love sometimes spoils the relationship you are in at present, as you do not connect the great love you expect to the mundane reality of the experience. When you learn to love those who you are with at present and stop thinking that the future will bring your true love, you find yourself and happiness.

### Knowing their Hidden Strengths

Anuradha is placed partly in Scorpio ruled by Mars and partly in Sagittarius ruled by Jupiter. Mars gives the courage and confidence to face the spiritual trials and tribulations created by the Nakshatra's ruler, Saturn. Jupiter provides the balance to Saturn's restrictions.

The Scorpio Anuradha represents hidden power and the need to access it. Anuradha is the divine spark that can illuminate this power. This creates frustrations as Mars wants to act and Saturn keeps restricting. This causes a great deal of trauma until these contrary energies are harnessed and used properly. In relationships they feel blocked at every stage of love and they learn to restrain their natural desires. But once they learn patience, become realistic about their expectations of love (very difficult for Anuradha), they start taking the first steps towards finding true love.

Sagittarius Anuradha bring in the dawn of new consciousness. Jupiter provides wisdom to Saturn and balances its restrictive energy with its expansive one. They begin to find their links with the divine consciousness and, with it, the key to divine relationships.

## Sexuality – The Female Deer

### Love, Sex and Lust

Your sexuality is expressed by your animal sign, the female deer. In Vedic Astrology female energy is passive, allowing others to take the initiative in sexual relationships. The deer is also considered to represent the Moon: both love passionately and emotionally. You need loving sexual relationships and should avoid purely sexual ones because you can get involved in superficial sexual relationships, mistaking lust for love.

In the wild, deer can get into a state of musth, where ecstasy of passion takes them over completely. You can express this when you get involved so intensely that you lose all comprehension of what is good or bad for you. You then get carried away in such a state of ecstasy that you lose your sense of reality. In this state you can get obsessive about your lovers or become involved in self-destructive relationships.

The deer, according to Vedic myth, is vain. He loves the beauty of his antlers and hates his ugly feet. But his antlers get tangled in the branches making him vulnerable to his predators and it is his ugly feet that help him survive. This myth explains your tendency to fall for a pretty face and put more importance on outer beauty rather than a person's inner qualities.

# ANURADHA

## The Best and the Worst Sexual Partners

The male deer Jyeshta is the best sexual partner for you. Jyeshta know how to woo you with love, as purely sexual relationships do not make you happy.

The dog Nakshatras Mula and Ardra are your worst sexual partners. In the wild, dogs corner deer and will kill them. So the deer Nakshatras Jyeshta and Ardra are usually afraid of the ferocious side of the dog Nakshatras. This ferocity is usually expressed in their sexuality: Mula and Ardra can be controlling and scare you with their extreme demands. They can be selfish too. Being practical and unimaginative, they ignore your need for romance and love.

# Relationship Issues

## The Fear of Losing Control

You are a workaholic and can become caught in the rat race. You appear practical and ambitious and do not have time for love or romance. But this is a façade that you cling to for safety as the other side of your nature frightens you. You feel it is too dangerous to follow the path of love. Unreliable passions can make you lose control of your carefully planned life. You keep your emotions tightly under control but the aspiration towards love remains. You are not comfortable with emotions.

## Loving the Mars Nakshatras

Anuradha's most difficult relationship is with the Mars Nakshatras. Mars rules Mrigasira, Chitra and Dhanishta. Relationships with Chitra (23% compatibility) and Dhanishta (32% compatibility) are the most difficult. Mrigasira, with 47% compatibility, is easier. The key to these difficulties lies in the complex cosmic relationship between Mars and Saturn. Mars is impulsive, adventurous and active whereas Saturn is cautious, responsible and patient. The Scorpio Anuradha should find it easier to deal with the Mars Nakshatras. Also the deer Anuradha is the preferred food for the tigress Chitra and the lioness Dhanishta. When you fall in love with them, they proverbially eat you for breakfast. They can ruin your dreams and cause pain. You have learnt instinctively never to trust them but love usually takes all caution away from you.

## Coping with the Polarities

Your life and emotions are polarized. You can be spiritual yet extremely materialistic, kind yet cruel, sparkling company one minute and depressed the next. At times there is no happy medium. In this search for the meaning of life, you can experience many ups and downs. Suddenly the mist clears and you become aware of how to deal with the conundrum of your life – then you can find success, happiness, peace and love. Your polarized personality is hard for your partners to understand; they do not know which Anuradha to relate to. However, there are some who understand your angst and respect your inner struggles.

## In Love with Love

You have the ability to love unwisely, as you tend to invest your fantasies in the lover of your choice. You are realistic about all other aspects of your life. But in love, you have no sense of proportion. You are in love with love.

You can fall prey to unscrupulous people who can use this vulnerability. While your friends and family may recognize the unsuitability of some of your relationships, you tend to look at them through rose-tinted glasses, hoping against hope that your love will change your nightmare lover into a dream one. You are willing to take the pain of love rather than not experience it at all.

## Loving Anuradha

Anuradha want love so much that they will fall for you quickly. This is why you need to think carefully about whether or not you want to seduce Anuradha. It is never easy to leave them. They are good at one-sided love; a love that, while flattering to start with, can become a burden if you want to move on. They appear to live in a dream world and they tend to put all their romantic hopes on your shoulders. So your job in loving Anuradha is to forever remind them of the reality of your relationship while not dashing their romantic dreams.

## Compatibility

**Ideal life partner: Jyeshta**
**Most challenging life partner: Chitra**

The full Compatibility Grid is on page 338.

**Anuradha and Ashwini:** Ashwini make good partners for you as long as you do not make the mistake of clinging to them too much. They need to feel free, and this does not mean they do not love. They are passionate and carefree, so different from you. They are not romantic with words but by being with you, they are showing their love.
**66% compatible**

**Bharani and Anuradha:** This is your spiritually complex relationship. Bharani want sex and you want love, both of you can mistake one for the other. You feel insecure with them and this makes you restless. Talk to them about your feelings and how they can appear to be uncaring when they do not want to talk love and romance.
**47% compatible**

**Anuradha and Krittika:** Powerful and dynamic, Krittika have a strong pull for you. They are the strong and silent type – their ability to protect you makes you love them even more. They envelop you in their warmth and you feel your defences melting. Be careful you are not building up too many expectations. **60% compatible**

**Anuradha and Rohini:** You aspire to divine love and Rohini seek self-realization through love – a perfect combination. Both can fulfil each other's need for romance and a love so sublime that others can only fantasize about it. Rohini's passionate love brings out the best in you. Just remember to come back to earth from time to time.
**80% compatible**

**Anuradha and Mrigasira:** Your relationship with Mrigasira can be frustrating. They refuse to accept your love without questioning it at every stage. They make you put up your defences fast. You usually live in hope that your Mrigasira lover will change and become more like the love you want. Never mistake their need for sex as a need for love. **47% compatible**

**Anuradha and Ardra:** Your attraction to Ardra is usually a slightly fearful fascination, but the romantic in you thinks it will turn out right in the end. Ardra's inability to combine sex with softly spoken words of love makes you feel unloved. They may try to dominate or control you and can dash your hopes. **53% compatible**

**Anuradha and Punarvasu:** You enjoy Punarvasu's ability to be everywhere all the time, and mostly you are happy to wait for them. In a way, both of you have something vital to give each other: Punarvasu expand your horizons far beyond where you usually venture and you give them stability in their life by loving them selflessly.
**62% compatible**

**Anuradha and Pushya:** Saturn rules both Pushya and Anuradha. You can be inflexible about your search for divine love. Pushya are afraid to be enveloped so completely by emotions and will keep a strict control over their feelings. Teach them about love and help them deal with their emotions, then you can hope to make this relationship better. **47% compatible**

**Anuradha and Ashlesha:** Ashlesha hate complications and, of course, love usually involves passion, possessiveness and complex emotions.

# ANURADHA

They shy away from this. Your lifeblood is love. How do you overcome this? By keeping the relationship simple and uncomplicated to start with. Do not put the burden of your emotional expectations on their shoulders. **53% compatible**

**Anuradha and Magha:** You have different outlooks on life, work ethics and romantic needs. You can be cool and Magha warm, but together there is an alchemy that defies convention. You care for Magha, love them, cherish them and their warmth adds sparkle to your life. Be more generous sexually, as Magha need that just like you need love. **66% compatible**

**Anuradha and Purva Phalguni:** Purva Phalguni are fun, social, witty, charming and creative; loving them is a wonderful experience. Your main challenge is dealing with your expectations of each other. You want them to forget everyone else and focus on your needs and they want you to go out a bit more, be social and forget about your work. **61% compatible**

**Anuradha and Uttara Phalguni:** Although you have different priorities in life, together you make something beautiful. Uttara Phalguni return your love so completely that you feel fulfilled. They support your dreams and ambitions. Although they may not be talkative and demonstrative, you are confident of their love. **80% compatible**

**Anuradha and Hasta:** Hasta are good partners for you – attractive, sophisticated but also very emotional and intuitive. Both of you are practical and ambitious. Your unconditional love helps Hasta overcome their insecurities and they love you back in return. You can become their anchor. **72% compatible**

**Anuradha and Chitra:** This relationship is tough, challenging and frustrating. Chitra may appear glamourous and different to start with but their habit of challenging you at every step and fighting to establish their every point becomes very troublesome. You usually do not give up easily but with Chitra the lessons are complex.
**23% compatible**

**Anuradha and Swati:** Swati are pragmatists; they are never able to become what you desire and love you in the way you want. You should not expect all your fantasies to become reality in this relationship. Love Swati for what they are – this is something you do very well – and they will work hard to make you happy. **58% compatible**

**Anuradha and Vishakha:** This is the meeting of two opposing forces; you are cautious and Vishakha are expansive. Together you can make a splendid partnership. Love should not put barriers in life, never think your love gives you the right to dictate what your partner wants. It should be free and giving, then Vishakha will love you even more. **59% compatible**

**Anuradha and Anuradha:** Both of you want the same things: solid, successful lives for the world to see, and emotional, spiritual and idealistic love to complete the inner you. Who better to understand than another Anuradha? No words are necessary – when you meet they know what you desire. Sex is wonderful, and the love divine. Great. **77% compatible**

**Anuradha and Jyeshta:** Sexy, passionate, sensual, Jyeshta are your best partner. They fulfil all your desires for love and emotional satisfaction. Although Jyeshta usually do not have time for emotions, with you they can be patient and loving. You find your ideal. Love is divine and flourishes under mutual nourishment. **86% compatible**

**Anuradha and Mula:** Mula can destroy your illusions. You think they offer true love, but they are unable to fulfil your desires. Are you reading too much into a light-hearted flirtation? They are also your worst sexual relationship and they can be very aggressive towards you. They can dump their anger on you and make you extremely unhappy. **41% compatible**

**Anuradha and Purva Ashadha:** You fall for their charm, creativity and their ability to enjoy life and be unconventional. But you may be falling for an image. Be realistic and develop a friendship first. They may never be what you want to be. They need to be free and while they may love you for a while, long-term commitment is not their scene. **36% compatible**

# ANURADHA

**Anuradha and Uttara Ashadha:** You know you love Uttara Ashadha more than they do you. But you sense their loneliness and you understand their need for love and emotional security. You wish they could be more demonstrative. You aspire to their spiritual wisdom and their ability to be there for you even when the going gets tough. **64% compatible**

**Anuradha and Shravana:** You love the lunar radiance of Shravana. You endeavour to find realization through them. Shravana are usually happy to respond. You meld on spiritual, emotional and physical levels. Shravana feed your love and they will care for you. You trust them with you deepest thoughts and they try not to let you down. **72% compatible**

**Anuradha and Dhanishta:** Dhanishta represent your spiritual longings as their Nakshatra is connected to Krishna. You can fall in musth with them, a state of divine ecstasy where you do not think about reality. You start living in an imaginary world. Dhanishta may not be able to deal with your needs sensitively – you can get hurt, and your illusions shattered. **32% compatible**

**Anuradha and Shatabhishak:** Shatabhishak can be elusive, never there when you want them, making promises that they are not always able to keep and keeping secrets. You have to encourage them to talk about love and feelings as you try to cross the hard barriers they have put in front of their heart. Love them and cherish them but be realistic. **61% compatible**

**Anuradha and Purva Bhadra:** You fall for the generous and warm Purva Bhadra. They are very different from you, confident and strong. They allow you to be in charge of the relationship. Sometimes it can weigh too heavily in favour of Purva Bhadra, or so your friends tell you. But you remain happy as long as you know they love you. **66% compatible**

**Anuradha and Uttara Bhadra:** Both of you hide your emotional needs behind a mask of practicality. Saturn gives you both the ability to bear pain. Do not just accept the difficulties, work to improve them.

While Uttara Bhadra will move or live alone if the relationship does not work, you find it hard to give up on their love. **47% compatible**

**Anuradha and Revati:** Revati make you feel whole again. You no longer have to live your life in polarities. They are the divine love you were seeking and they want to be as much part of you as you want to be part of them. Together you can live in a cocoon of love and happiness. You can be their support while they are your vision of true love. **72% compatible**

## Cusps

Those born at the end or beginning of Anuradha, should see pages 371–2.

2 to 15 December

# Jyeshta

Ruled by Mercury
Animal: The Male Deer
Symbol: The Earring

## Meaning and Symbolism

*Jyeshta* means 'elder sister', 'middle finger' or 'holy river Ganges'. In India, the elder sister is looked upon with great respect as she is like one's mother. The river Ganges is said to wash away all our negative karma. The middle finger is the finger of destiny. It is used in yoga during pranayama to control the flow of breath. The disciplining of breath allows us to control our mind.

Jyeshta's symbol is the earring, which signifies occult status. In Vedic mythology the earring was given to the divine kings who had mastered their lower nature and gained magical powers that allowed them to rule the world, communicate with the spirits, and have knowledge of past and future lives. This is the potential contained within Jyeshta.

You enjoy the sensuality and pleasures of life to the full, as you think you know how to master them. This can make you arrogant. The reality comes as a rude shock to you as not everyone has the power to give up their desires as and when they chose. The potential ability to give them up is within Jyeshta – whether you realize this power is another matter. In relationships, you want to control your partner's life.

## The Jyeshta Personality

### The Intellectual Struggles

The ruler of Jyeshta is Mercury. Jyeshta represent the struggle of the mind. You are extremely bright and intellectually gifted. Your mental superiority makes you one step ahead of the rest of the world. But your intellect can limit your perception when you want to widen the scope of your spiritual understanding. You need to be careful not to become involved in using mind-enhancing drugs or dabbling in occult rituals that you are not mentally equipped to deal with.

You may find that your relationships limit your progress along your chosen path and this makes you careless of others' emotions. You should see your relationships as helpers in your path to self-realization. A loving partner can be supportive and ease your way. You should choose partners who are not conventional and constraining but thoughtful and liberating.

### The Mastery of the Kundalini

Jyeshta is placed entirely in the sign of Sagittarius ruled by Jupiter. The ruler of Jyeshta is Mercury. Jyeshta gives you a strong sense of destiny as you learn to master your desires through the knowledge of the *kundalini*. The kundalini is the human link to the pure consciousness and is latent within us. As kundalini changes from static to dynamic, it opens a whole new inner world to us: our hidden power, individual consciousness, and links to the past, present and future lives. As you access your kundalini power you learn to control your desires rather than be controlled by them.

Kundalini brings with it a changed perception of reality and you understand this new reality fast. You can transform your frailty into accomplishments, weakness into strength and sexual love into spiritual love. A shift in consciousness can make you regard your relationship as an organic part of you and not as a separate entity to be controlled and dominated. Your kundalini recognition can either make you comfortable with love or you can pay a high price emotionally and intellectually by leaving your partner completely.

## Sexuality – The Male Deer

### The Joys of Sexual Ecstasy

Your sexuality is expressed by your animal sign, the male deer. The male is aggressive sexually. The sanskrit word for 'deer' is also considered to be another name for the Moon, which represents passionate and emotion. The Moon, as a male god, enjoys relationships with twenty-seven Nakshatras (symbolically his wives). You can get involved in multiple relationships and sexual intrigues.

In the wild, deer can get into a state of musth – where passion takes over. Jyeshta, expressing this same emotion, can get involved so intensely they lose all comprehension of what is good or bad for them. You get in such a state of ecstasy you can get into self-destructive relationships and allow passion to control all your actions.

The deer according to Vedic myths is vain. He loves the beauty of his antlers and hates his ugly feet. But his antlers get caught up among the branches making him vulnerable to predators and it is his ugly feet that help him survive. This myth explains your tendency to fall for a pretty face and put more importance on outer beauty rather than a person's inner qualities.

### The Best and the Worst Sexual Partners

The female deer Anuradha is your best sexual partner. Anuradha will love Jyeshta with their heart and soul. You fulfil Anuradha's sexual passions while being sensitive to their emotional needs. Together you can enjoy the joys of sexual ecstasy to the full.

The dog Nakshatras Mula and Ardra are the worst sexual partners for Jyeshta. You try to be dominant and controlling but it is never as simple as that. Your relationship with Mula and Ardra can be exciting but also destructive. In the wild, dogs corner deer and will kill them. Sexually you are subconsciously afraid of releasing the ferocious side of the dog Nakshatras, but are unable to help yourself provoking them to express it. This can lead to a relationship that varies between dominance and aggression. In extreme cases, it can take you over the edge and create extreme unhappiness.

# Relationship Issues

## The Chameleons

You are usually torn between two sides of your nature: your sensuality and your spirituality. This can create problems in your relationships because you will go from loving intensely to feeling guilty about love to exploring your spirituality. It makes you hard to define. One moment you are completely enthralled by your senses, the next you start feeling that you are neglecting your spiritual progress and therefore give up your passions and desires. When you choose to concentrate fully on spirituality, you find that does not satisfy you fully. What you need to do is to build a bridge between your sensual desires and your spiritual ones. Learn to make them co-exist rather than think that you have to make stark choices.

## Dealing with Poor Compatibility

You have extremely complex issues to resolve through relationships. What you need from love is not easy to fathom. You are seeking more than others dare to dream about. This makes you very idealistic and always seeking the impossible from partners. This is expressed by the extremely low compatibility you have with certain Nakshatras like Ashwini, Punarvasu, Ardra, Uttara Phalguni, Hasta, Mula and Purva Bhadra. If you get involved in these relationships, then the issues they deal with are karmic in nature and have the potential to give great sorrow. You need to tread carefully. Ardra is the worst with only 14% compatibility. Nothing works with them. Ardra are struggling to accept life and enjoy the interplay, the social side, whereas you are learning to give it up. You find it difficult to trust Ardra. Ardra–Jyeshta relationships can deteriorate very quickly, but you are unable to give up on the relationship or find pleasure in it.

## Spiritual Arrogance

You can get involved in psychological games with your partners to test your spiritual strengths. This may be entirely subconscious but it can lead to extreme unhappiness if you do not learn to control it. You can be intensely and intimately involved with someone and suddenly, to test your resolve, you can give up the relationship, not worrying about the hurt or upset you cause.

These are dangerous games for you – while you may be strong mentally, your partners may not be able to cope with the sudden rejection. You should respect your partner's emotional vulnerabilities. The cycle of experience and rejection, involvement and asceticism can in the end pull you apart. You need to break this pattern which can only make your partners miserable.

# Loving Jyeshta

Jyeshta are masters of seduction. While you may feel you are seducing them, they can turn the tables very quickly and become the seducer. They have extremely complex issues to resolve through relationships. Their mind games and their ability to love you to death one moment and ignore you the next can create lots of emotional turmoil. Jyeshta respond to tough love; being soft with them can encourage them to behave badly.

THE LOVE SIGNS

# Compatibility

### Ideal life partner: Magha
### Most challenging life partner: Ardra

The full Compatibility Grid is on page 338.

**Jyeshta and Ashwini:** You are caught up in a spiritually complex relationship. Ashwini have a cavalier attitude to your passions, which is exciting to start with. You also express yourself negatively – loving them, leaving them, emotionally messing them about. You need to love Ashwini on a spiritual level and let Ashwini into your spiritual search. **36% compatible**

**Jyeshta and Bharani:** Your relationship with Bharani can bring excessive sensuality as you try to fulfil your greatest desires. You are hypnotized by the Bharani allure, but you soon start feeling guilty about ignoring your spirituality. Let Bharani know of your spiritual needs – they may not understand them but will appreciate your openness. **53% compatible**

**Jyeshta and Krittika:** You will feel invigorated by Krittika's warmth, their love, and their straightforward approach to life. They are strong so you can never manipulate them, but they love you and try to adjust to your needs and demands. You feel secure and loved, and their love is a balm to your restless spirit. Great. **76% compatible**

**Jyeshta and Rohini:** Rohini stretch you mentally and emotionally. They are exciting, romantic and sensuous. You satisfy their love for luxury and their need to wallow in sybaritic pleasures. Mentally exhilarating and emotionally satisfying, this relationship makes you feel complete. You may become too tied to your desires and this makes you frustrated. **67% compatible**

**Jyeshta and Mrigasira:** You constantly challenge Mrigasira and they usually rise to your provocation, making this a passionate relationship. You find their criticism and ability to rationalize everything irritating. This usually stands in the way of your relationship. They do not always understand your spiritual path. You can get along in the practical areas. **53% compatible**

**Jyeshta and Ardra:** You bring the worst out in each other. You become dominant and aggressive, thinking you can deal with the aftermath. Ardra can react ferociously to your machinations. You can both press the self-destruct button. Be very careful. Keep extremes of behaviour tightly under control. **14% compatible**

**Jyeshta and Punarvasu:** The attraction you feel for Punarvasu is on the surface. Punarvasu are not into complicated relationships, but you enjoy them. You find their inability to love you exclusively difficult to handle. You try to control them, to manipulate the relationship. Punarvasu may then leave you, without any consideration for your feelings. **22% compatible**

**Jyeshta and Pushya:** You find Pushya too disciplined and rigid in their views. They are not into any kind of mind game and appear too ascetic to be totally comfortable in your sensuous world. But give them a chance and they may be your best friend. They can also be surprisingly good lovers and warm behind their coldness. For this relationship to work you need to make some compromises.
**55% compatible**

**Jyeshta and Ashlesha:** You both have to learn to look beyond the intellectual restrictions of your ruler Mercury and connect with a higher way of thinking. You understand each other's life path. Love and friendship hold you together. Ashlesha are not into uncomplicated relationships but with you, they take a risk. **69% compatible**

**Jyeshta and Magha:** Your best partner. Magha are everything you want: confident, dynamic, sexy, passionate, soulful and loving. They envelop you in their warmth, and their loving brings security to your restless mind. You have often both suffered some poor relationships and that becomes an added bond. Best of friends and happy lovers. **88% compatible**

**Jyeshta and Purva Phalguni:** Purva Phalguni endeavour to satisfy your senses in every way as lovers, partners and friends. They are creative, sophisticated and exciting. Your sexual life is full and your social life entertaining. Purva Phalguni cannot always support you when you start moving away from pure sensual pleasures to spiritual ones. **66% compatible**

**Jyeshta and Uttara Phalguni:** Stop playing mind games with Uttara Phalguni. You can make them emotionally unsettled by loving them passionately one moment and transferring your interests elsewhere the next. You are often unable to appreciate the good qualities of Uttara Phalguni. Don't start an affair if you are uncertain about how you feel. **39% compatible**

**Jyeshta and Hasta:** The sophisticated Hasta fascinate you but you react too instinctively to their animal sign the buffalo, which can be seen as rough and ugly. You may overlook all their good points and concentrate on their negative ones. You do not always understand emotions and with Hasta you don't even try. You can be too critical, reinforcing their poor self-image. **36% compatible**

**Jyeshta and Chitra:** You can take an instant dislike to Chitra and argue incessantly, but there is a strong underlying attraction. You overcome your initial antipathy to find passion and love. You will have to agree to disagree. Both of you have unresolved complex spiritual issues but this gives you an instinctive understanding of each other. **62% compatible**

**Jyeshta and Swati:** Swati have a way with words, which can be very exhilarating, and you feel you have found your true partner. Their ambitions take precedence over you. If you try to play mind games with them, they can give as good as they get. They can be too possessive. Avoid creating turmoil within them: they can hurt you back regardless of the cost to your relationship. **41% compatible**

**Jyeshta and Vishakha:** Love, sex, desire, philosophy, mysticism and esoteric knowledge – all the things that interest you, interest Vishakha. You both share the ability to enjoy sensuality but know when to control your senses. Your relationship can be sensual heaven till

# JYESHTA

the spiritual self calls. You both aspire towards spirituality and adjust your needs accordingly. **72% compatible**

**Jyeshta and Anuradha:** Anuradha love you unconditionally and you flourish under their love. They are also your best lovers and best friends. They are supportive when you want to explore your spiritual self. They understand pain and asceticism, so they empathize with your inner turmoil. They care for you emotionally, loving and soothing you. **86% compatible**

**Jyeshta and Jyeshta:** As you are both at the same junction of life you share a subtle understanding of love, sex and sensuality. However, in Vedic tradition two Jyeshtas should not marry. The reason being, Jyeshta has a complex spiritual remit and together they can create painful turmoil, despite this great compatibility. **77% compatible**

**Jyeshta and Mula:** Mula can teach you about rejection and love. You feel this rejection acutely, as you usually want to be in charge of your relationships. You are the one who plays the sexual games. When the tables are turned, it creates huge emotional distress in you. There is no sexual compatibility, the dog Mula being aggressive to the deer Jyeshta. **39% compatible**

**Jyeshta and Purva Ashadha:** Purva Ashadha flexibility is hard for you to handle. You want them to concentrate fully on you but their outside interests keep interfering. Your paths may be different but appreciating them is a better basis for a relationship than forever fighting about them. Try to be friends. Keep communicating about your feelings. **44% compatible**

**Jyeshta and Uttara Ashadha:** Your spiritual side relates to the austere and cool Uttara Ashadha but your sensuous one remains unfulfilled by their diffident approach to love and sex. You need to teach them about intimacy. This is not a relationship with which you should experiment; if they lose trust in you, you will never be able to win them back. **50% compatible**

**Jyeshta and Shravana:** Shravana appear to be like you, thinking and philosophizing about life, love and the universe. But as you get closer you realize there is an important difference. You think and they feel. They can get very emotional and sentimental. They are not always rational, and can't change easily as they can be very fixed in their ideas. **55% compatible**

**Jyeshta and Dhanishta:** You admire Dhanishta's courage and forbearance in dealing with life's challenges. This admiration translates into a strong and loving relationship. You will bask in their warmth. They teach you to face life's harsh realities with poise and equanimity. You learn not to hide from your emotional issues.
**68% compatible**

**Jyeshta and Shatabhishak:** As Shatabhishak try to control their inner demons, you may not be willing to stand by. You understand their spiritual struggle more than they understand it themselves. This relationship works if you celebrate the compatible aspects but try not to worry about the incompatible ones. Don't try to control and allow them to have their own space. **47% compatible**

**Jyeshta and Purva Bhadra:** You show Purva Bhadra a new sensual world, where they become bewitched and enchanted, and you use the words of love without meaning to, weaving a web of illusions. You can feel disdainful when they give in to you so easily. Be careful, it is not just they who are getting hurt. You can pay a heavy price emotionally and spiritually. **26% compatible**

**Jyeshta and Uttara Bhadra:** Uttara Bhadra can teach you about discipline. The bonds between you are not those on which a relationship develops initially. They have no time for sensuality and are good at controlling their senses. In fact, you can learn from them. Their ascetic nature does not always please you, but their ability to love you for what you are does. **55% compatible**

**Jyeshta and Revati:** You are similar, but with different agendas. You want to explore sensuality and Revati want to explore love. You can get along, even love each other, but both of you have the tendency to be super critical. When you put your relationship under the micro-

JYESHTA

scope many things are less than perfect, and you each blame the other. **55% compatible**

## Cusps

Those born at the end or beginning of Jyeshta, should see pages 372–4.

15 to 28 December

# Mula

Ruled by Ketu
Animal: The Male Dog
Symbol: The Elephant's Goad

## Meaning and Symbolism

The Mula Nakshatra represents the start of the final part of the soul's mission towards finding eternal happiness or moksha. *Mula* means 'root' and it is connected to the *Muladhara Chakra* (the repository of latent spiritual energy). Mula suggests that we are the root of all our problems as well as the blessings of all our good fortunes. You are rooted in the physical, the objective and the material but your aspirations may be for the subtle and psychic. Your dissatisfaction with life will lessen if you realize that a tree needs strong roots to grow upwards. You need to be practical and build strong foundations for your life before you can move towards your higher aspirations. The most important of these roots are a loving and stable relationship. While you tend to reject this, accepting it would give you immense rewards.

The symbol of Mula is the elephant's goad. The elephant's goad is used to guide the elephant in the correct direction. In people this symbol represents the constant prodding or pain we have to suffer in search of happiness. You can experience the pain from unhappy relationships or disappointments in love.

# MULA

# The Mula Personality

## The Need for Moksha

Mula is the final Nakshatra of the Vedic Zodiac ruled by Ketu. Ketu symbolizes for Moksha or self-realization. According to Indian philosophy a soul is born to earth to enjoy life but not get attached to it. Its ultimate aim is Moksha, the final liberation from the cycles of life and death. You aspire to freedom, release and the break from the burden of responsibilities. This usually makes you careless about your responsibilities to your partners and family.

You connect with past lives. You seek the answer to a missing part of your inner puzzle from your relationships. It does not matter whether the relationships are easy or difficult. You connect to Rnanu bandhana – the karmic debts you have carried from past lives. You can look beyond the purely illusory nature of most relationships. You also accept that your relationships are part of your past-life baggage; that you are in a cycle you started before in a previous life, which must be either completed now or progressed on to the next level.

## Learning to Renounce

Mula is placed half in the Western sign of Sagittarius, which is ruled by Jupiter, and half in the Western sign of Capricorn ruled by Saturn. Jupiter represents wisdom, Saturn renunciation and Ketu is the past karmas.

Sagittarius expresses the point at which the animal turns into man, and symbolizes the striving to control the baser impulses so that the soul can move towards its final journey. Mula Sagittarius moves towards the path of self-discovery, and the conflict with the sexual and spiritual self emerges. Mula Sagittarius can become overtly sexual or totally spiritual, struggling to settle in one direction.

The Capricorn symbol in Vedic Astrology is the crocodile. In the wild, crocodiles live on the banks of the sea or rivers (earth) and swim occasionally in water (the universal soul). Similarly in Capricorn, man still living in the practical world is moving towards spirituality. In Capricorn Mula, the past karmas begin to activate, many unexpected events happen, some connected to challenging relationships, so that the burden of the karma is lessened.

## Sexuality – The Male Dog

### Sexual Freedom

Your sexuality is expressed by your animal sign, the male dog. Dogs in the wild are fierce and aggressive. They are very dangerous animals. However, dogs can be trained and become the working dog or the household pet. Similarly, if Mula allow their natural instinct to take over, they can be wild and aggressive. But if they become disciplined, they can be hard working, charming, loyal and loving. Dogs give unconditional love and support to their masters. You can be forever seeking approval. If you are sexually attracted to someone you tend to show your love immediately. This can cause you to be treated shabbily by your partners who do not appreciate love so readily given.

You will actively pursue those that you love. You can get involved in sexual relationships easily and give them up equally easily. Your strong sexuality worries you. This is the part of your nature that you want to transform. You want to be in control of your sexuality rather than be controlled by it. You can be faithful if your partners demand it. Otherwise, you enjoy exploring your sexuality with no thought to fidelity or commitment.

### The Best and the Worst Sexual Partners

Your best sexual relationship is with the female dog, Ardra. The overall relationship between Mula and Ardra is average; Mula needs more than just sexual compatibility in their true partner. Ardra can thrill you sexually but they remind you too much of your animal instincts – the instincts you are trying to control in your mission to embrace spirituality.

# MULA

Your worst sexual relationship is with the deer Nakshatras, Anuradha and Jyeshta. In the wild, dogs corner deer and will kill them. You can become very hostile to these Nakshatras once the initial glow of the relationship has faded. You can try to restrict Anuradha's and Jyeshta's freedom and independence. They like to their sex to be fun and frivolous, but you can become perversely practical and unimaginative with them. You are better at handling these tough relationships than the female dog Ardra because of your greater spiritual awareness. Anuradha have the capacity to love you, warts and all. Both of you will try to balance the negativity and work through the differences. Jyeshta can make you feel cornered by their constant manipulations and you can be goaded into attacking them – not so much physically but emotionally and mentally.

## Relationship Issues

### The Painful Relationships

Pain is part of the Mula spiritual process. Some Nakshatra relationships bring pain and disillusionment into your life but they are the ones who also teach you profound lessons about loving. Punarvasu usually find it easy to love others, but not you. They will fight with you, refuse to commit but also may become jealous and possessive. They may not want to love you but they will not let you go. Your spiritual path is different from Uttara Phalguni. You need to move towards a higher path and Uttara Phalguni need to stay in the material world.

The Moon Nakshatras are Hasta, Shravana and Rohini. This Ketu–Moon relationship is karmic but it can never be completely without problems. The Moon Nakshatras are changeable and fickle like you. Your habit of rejecting them creates emotional turmoil. If you set aside preconceived ideas about each other, you can connect very deeply and change your inherent attitude to each other.

## Unconventional Attitude

You find it difficult to conform to traditional norms of behaviour in relationships. You are not too hot on commitment and can tend to keep moving on to a newer relationship, a newer experience. If you remain with one partner throughout your various adventures and experiences, you are giving them a strong message that they are special, since the saying 'if you love somebody, let them go' appears to be made for you. You hardly ever verbally commit – if you give them your physical commitment, then they should be happy with that.

## Avoiding Self-Destruction

You have self-destructive tendencies, destroying what you love the most. You can ruin your love, relationships and happiness. Sometimes the price you pay may be too high, but you are unable to help yourself. This is your karmic weakness. You feel both anger and pain in your heart, and when you try to express these you create problems. You can lash out at your partners for no obvious reason. This creates unhappiness for your partner while your own pain remains unnoticed as you hide it well. Working out your anger and pain through philosophy, meditation and yoga will help you to stop from touching the self-destruct button.

# Loving Mula

Mula enjoy life on the edge and their seduction has to take in the element of excitement. They can make you experience heaven and hell in a matter of seconds. Loving Mula is tough. They hardly ever appreciate you, take you for granted and are uncaring of your emotional needs. They can be indecisive and fickle. If you are seeking a partner who will be responsible and stable, Mula are not for you. It is a mistake to be too understanding. Being firm with Mula without being possessive and restrictive can make them change their habits.

# MULA

## Compatibility

**Ideal life partners: Mula and Purva Ashadha**
**Most challenging life partner: Punarvasu**

**The full Compatibility Grid is on page 338.**

**Mula and Ashwini:** Your subconscious tells you not to trust. It could be your past that is not allowing you to be happy in the present with Ashwini. They understand you better than you think. For this relationship to develop, you have to let them in. If you continue to hold them at a distance and direct your anger towards them, how can they love you? **33% compatible**

**Mula and Bharani:** You embark on an affair with the sensuous, hypnotic Bharani. But the moment you get entangled with them, you try to extricate yourself. Bharani's possessiveness can be very constricting. You need to be honest with them about your feelings and work out a compromise between total freedom and complete possession. **53% compatible**

**Mula and Krittika:** You are attracted to the fiery warmth of Krittika. Their diffidence and lack of confidence charm you. You help them to open up. Your attitude to sex helps them overcome their inhibitions. Krittika help you understand that you need to be rooted and this security supports your spiritual quest. Be faithful and let them know you care. **65% compatible**

**Mula and Rohini:** You are attracted to the cool and unemotional Rohini: you think they are not going to demand more than you can give. When you discover they are emotional, romantic and possessive, you may try to get out of this relationship. The lack of compatibility suggests that you may not be nice about it. Be careful, you can break their heart. **36% compatible**

**Mula and Mrigasira:** Everything works but only just. You take relationships as they are, being willing to experience the ups and downs as and when they come. You intuitively understand what works and what doesn't but Mrigasira need everything in its fixed compartments. You can fight and argue, but usually muddle through the relationship. **51% compatible**

**Mula and Ardra:** Ardra's ruler Rahu is your other half metaphorically. Ardra is also your best sexual relationship. But 42% compatibility suggests that mere sexual pleasures will never be enough for you. Ardra's ambitions for the mundane are of no interest to you. An affair to remember, but long term you will have to work hard to make the relationship successful. **42% compatible**

**Mula and Punarvasu:** Mula in Sanskrit means root; Punarvasu is rootlessness. You need wisdom and care while working out the issues. Your rejections can have a profound effect on Punarvasu. They can be jealous and possessive whereas you can be destructive, uncaring of the cost. They feel insecure and you feel aggravated. **29% compatible**

**Mula and Pushya:** Pushya will try to nourish you and love you; they can sacrifice their own needs for you. If you fail to appreciate their efforts, Pushya feel left out and unloved. Get to know Pushya better and you will find their warmth and compassion. They help to steady you and are there for you. They can be your strong roots so do not take them for granted. **47% compatible**

**Mula and Ashlesha:** Ashlesha are in total harmony with your spiritual desires, but sexually you can be aggressive. This is a spiritually complex relationship. Despite the 61% compatibility, you react to each other negatively even when you want each other. Keep your love strong as circumstances may test your relationship and your feelings. **61% compatible**

**Mula and Magha:** Magha know and understand your spiritual path. You love their idealism and vision. They are there for you and they can love you intensely. Sexually the dog Mula is always in control of the rat Magha. This can lead to frustrations and mental struggles. Be more supportive of Magha and ignore your need to dominate them. **66% compatible**

# MULA

**Mula and Purva Phalguni:** Creative, fun and party-loving Purva Phalguni are so different from you, not bothering about their spiritual self, happy to enjoy what life has to offer. Purva Phalguni's lack of understanding of your spiritual needs makes it difficult to sustain a relationship. As a dog Nakshatra, you can easily intimidate the rat Purva Phalguni and they can tease you. **53% compatible**

**Mula and Uttara Phalguni:** The conventional Uttara Phalguni attracts you very much. You are drawn to their ordered life and their high-profile, usually successful, careers. You enjoy basking in their warmth and love. However, too much conventionality soon bores you and your soul feels restricted by their love. You can hurt them by suddenly giving up on the relationship. **32% compatible**

**Mula and Hasta:** You embark on a relationship with them, thinking that Hasta are worldly wise and can deal with love and sex in a detached way. But you find them full of insecurities, especially about their sexuality, and they need your emotional support. You must be careful that you do not hurt them unnecessarily. It can leave them emotionally scarred. **42% compatible**

**Mula and Chitra:** You can love Chitra easily. They fulfil your desire for adventure and thrills. They are also brave and strong; they give you real support, as and when you need it. They do not want you to conform to rigid and traditional ideas. Love can be unconventional and sex fun. They love you passionately without being possessive. **75% compatible**

**Mula and Swati:** You know Swati can make you complete yet there is an invisible barrier that you cannot quite overcome. You can also be fearful of loving so completely. What happens to your spiritual life? If you stop trying to work out the reasons but go with the flow, you will find karmic love. Both of you can love each other in a special way. **63% compatible**

**Mula and Vishakha:** You link to Vishakha very strongly. They are wise and strong. They too are restless in relationships. Vishakha want to unveil the mysteries of the world and together you can explore this. They teach you to turn anger into love. But your relationship endures; it is loving and emotional, despite any problems you face. **66% compatible**

**Mula and Anuradha:** You do not always appreciate Anuradha's good qualities, finding them too unrealistic and emotional. You usually have nothing to offer Anuradha except a short-term affair. But Anuradha can cling on. As your worst sexual partner, the more they want you, the more you feel the need to dominate and aggravate them. **41% compatible**

**Mula and Jyeshta:** Jyeshta charm you but you soon find their brand of mystical knowledge is of no interest to you. You can be restless, angry and irritated with them. Jyeshta are your worst sexual partner. Sexually you feel so aggressive towards them; you have to really try to control yourself. Learn to stay calm, temperate and philosophical. **39% compatible**

**Mula and Mula:** The relationship with other Mula is excellent but Vedic Astrology cautions against two Mula being involved. Your similar personalities leave no place for balance if the situation becomes difficult or out of control. If you hit troubled waters, you must seek outside mediators, as you may not be able to judge your problems rationally. **77% compatible**

**Mula and Purva Ashadha:** Your love for each other may be expressed in unconventional terms. You may not opt for a committed marriage, but you need each other and can be very happy. Purva Ashadha knows how to calm your anger and encourage you to direct it positively. They also help your spiritual journey. **77% compatible**

**Mula and Uttara Ashadha:** Uttara Ashadha can be icy one minute and aggressive another. Both of you can get involved in proving who is stronger and therefore your relationship can become a war zone. You need to control your extreme reactions to each other, talk about them and never underestimate their ability to create problems for you. **36% compatible**

# MULA

**Mula and Shravana:** Shravana are in denial of their emotional nature. They can send out conflicting signals – warm and passionate one moment and totally detached the next. You are not always willing to explore their needs. You have to learn to discriminate between your spiritual and your relationships issues. **39% compatible**

**Mula and Dhanishta:** Dhanishta are genuine. They can become your roots and security, and this frees you to express yourself spiritually. They help you find direction in life and you love them for it. Although Dhanishta don't demand love from you, you must keep letting them know you care for them or they can feel lonely and neglected.
**65% compatible**

**Mula and Shatabhishak:** You are drawn to Shatabhishak but you are wary of them. You think they want to take over your life and that your needs will play no part in this relationship. Try to give in to your true emotions and express love, not rejection. Shatabhishak will try to fill the empty areas of your life. Both of you can feel complete and spiritually at peace. **58% compatible**

**Mula and Purva Bhadra:** Purva Bhadra's world seems to be full of illusions; they expect you to be what you are not. While Purva Bhadra need their own independence, they are never as understanding about yours. You want to love them, but cannot give them your full attention. This usually makes your relationship difficult to sustain.
**41% compatible**

**Mula and Uttara Bhadra:** Uttara Bhadra can create a favourable environment for you. They love you for who you are. They make you stop and think, and help you to understand the importance of your inner search. You can at times take your Uttara Bhadra partner for granted. They do not always ask for anything in return.
**66% compatible**

**Mula and Revati:** Revati appear wise and caring. They love you without expecting anything in return. You are usually willing to change for your Revati love. They understand your inner dilemma

# THE LOVE SIGNS

and their instinctive knowledge of your spiritual search calms your inner agitation. They are strong for you when you need them.
**72% compatible**

# Cusps

Those born at the end or beginning of Mula should see pages 374–5.

28 December to 11 January

# Purva Ashadha

Ruled by Venus
Animal: The Male Monkey
Symbol: The Elephant's Tusk

## Meaning and Symbolism

*Purva* means 'first', indicating it is the former part of the Ashadha Nakshatras. *Ashadha* means 'unsubdued'. It indicates what we cannot suppress. True human nature comes out, regardless of how we try to conceal it. It links to the following Nakshatra Uttara Ashadha; together they represent the common principle of unfolding new talents. Purva Ashadha still face some blocks to expressing their nature fully while Uttara Ashadha embraces the changes.

The symbol of the elephant's tusk further symbolizes the revelation of the inner qualities. The tusk is the most expensive part of the elephant. It is valued for its beauty and others kill the elephant to try and own it. The tusk, if cut off, will grow again; similarly if you create something innately valuable, however much others like to destroy it, it remains part of your treasure – wisdom once gained cannot be taken away.

Your search to externalize your inner talents can lead to difficulties in relating properly. You can never fully concentrate on your relationships. You have a clearly defined but forever changing spiritual path. How can you be in a fixed or permanent relationship?

## The Purva Ashadha Personality

### Venusian Talent

You are creative, talented, bright and intelligent. If you work with your talents, you can create something wonderful and long-lasting. Venus, the planetary ruler, gives you talent for the arts, crafts, music and drama. Many creative geniuses are born under this sign. However successful you may be in your chosen career, you will always feel humble and self-effacing. I am not talking about the outward image you project but how you feel inside. You prefer partners who appreciate beauty and understand art. You like to have relationships with other beautiful people.

### Creative and Productive

The Purva Ashadha is in the Western sign of Capricorn. Saturn rules Capricorn and the Nakshatra ruler is Venus. Capricorn are practical, determined and disciplined, Purva Ashadha are fluid and capricious. You try to work hard, to conform and take your responsibilities seriously. You have strong creative urges, the need for constant change, but Saturn forces you to be realistic, to use your creative ability and hone it into something special. Use the creative directions that are offered by Venus and the practical ones by Saturn, to make a real impression on the world around you.

Again this journey leaves little time for relationships. You do not have a natural talent for them. As the Nakshatras move towards the ending of the Zodiac, the spiritual needs become more pronounced and the material ones less so. Ask your partners to respect the needs of your soul. You cannot take responsibility for their happiness, neither can they for yours.

## Sexuality – The Male Monkey

### Serial Monogamists

Purva Ashadha's animal sign is the male monkey. Monkeys live in communities in the deepest jungles as well as in urban areas. Monkeys jump from one tree to another to escape retribution for their naughty acts. Similarly, you develop instinctive self-defence skills. You can cause trouble and allow others to take the blame. With all the other animal signs, you will avoid the issue of relationships, proverbially jump from one tree to another to avoid being caught.

You are serial monogamists. You want your love life to be full of fun and the joys of the world. You are sociable and like having a family, but you are never ready to commit. You will lead your partner a merry dance before you allow yourself to be caught. You can be charming, playful and impish. You like sex to be enjoyable. You rarely show your lighter side to their world; this is reserved for those you love. You can stay uncommitted and if you do not find a true partner, you can be promiscuous as sexual commitment is not very important to you.

### The Best and the Worst Sexual Partners

Your best sexual relationship is with the female monkey Shravana. They understand your sexual needs; they make sex fun, light-hearted and exciting. Both of you are commitment phobic and your relationship remains based on loose ties rather than intense closeness.

Your worst sexual relationships are with the sheep, Krittika and Pushya. The shy sheep Nakshatras do not enjoy being made fun of by the monkey Nakshatras. They are unadventurous by nature and will not be able to deal with the boldness of Shravana and Purva Ashadha. Both Krittika and Pushya need loyalty and commitment and they do not enjoy your free-wheeling attitude to sex.

## Relationship Issues

### Changing Colours

You have the ability to reinvent yourself periodically. You can completely change your ideas, personality and characteristics from time to time. You are like water, pure and clear to start with, but if you mix any colour with it, you become that colour. You have to be careful that you do not allow your life to be tinted by negativity.

The issues of your partner also influence you. Your personality changes to become more like your partner's. But as this process never stops, you can take in as much as you want from one partner and then move on to experience some new colour from others.

### Facing Jealousy and Envy

Purva Ashadha may face extreme forms of jealousy. Others will desire your talents, success and partners. You should take precautions against this. The jealous meddling of others can ruin your relationships.

### Flexible Attitude to Relationships

You are in a perpetual state of flux. You can be deeply involved one moment, even living in domestic harmony, then you discover a new ideology and completely change your philosophy of life. After this metamorphosis, if your partner is unwilling to accept the new you, you may move on. You don't always care about the feelings of those you have left behind. You are capable of emailing or faxing your partners with the message that your relationship is no longer on. This creates lots of heartache. You can feel lonely and bereft. But you should understand that your behaviour is often to blame.

## PURVA ASHADHA

### Burning Desires and the Mars Nakshatras

The Mars Nakshatras are Mrigasira, Chitra and Dhanishta. The Venusian in you can get into a serious passionate relationship with them. When you fall in lust with the Mars Nakshatras the passion is so hot and fiery that it soon rages out of control. But as suddenly as the passion erupts, it can burn out. When the passion dies down you may realize you have nothing in common with Mars Nakshatras to keep you together. The passions of a Mars and Venus relationship always come with a warning – be careful and take things slowly.

### Confused Mind

You adapt to change so easily that you are often accused of liking change for change's sake. But the reality is that you are in turmoil. Your questions throw up new answers daily, influencing and changing your views. You then feel that adopting this new reality is the right way forward. But this only adds to your confusion and bewilderment. You can leave behind a chaotic life of broken promises and disharmonious relationships. You feel that your relationships, career, family or friends restrict your personal growth and that by changing these, you are going to reach new spiritual highs. But what you must understand is that the changes you make are only cosmetic – to truly find your spiritual essence you must alter your inner consciousness, not just your physical reality. You do not need to move on to a new relationship to find yourself: the real you was always there, inside. If you accept this, then you will find harmony instead of chaos; happiness instead of pain and you will slowly start realizing your real potential.

## Loving Purva Ashadha

The first rule of loving Purva Ashadha is: adapt to their fluid nature – do not try to restrict them, now or later. The second rule is: develop a defence mechanism that allows you to deal with their sudden rejection or change. You need to have a philosophical attitude and lots of tolerance. Not all Purva Ashadha will up and leave but that is their extreme potential. Don't get heavy – go along with them, enjoying the seduction and let the future take care of itself. Be realistic about your relationship with Purva Ashadha; putting all your emotional investment in them is never a good idea.

# Compatibility

### Ideal life partner: Revati
### Most challenging life partner: Dhanishta

**The full Compatibility Grid is on page 338.**

**Purva Ashadha and Ashwini:** You are drawn to the bright and beautiful Ashwini. Their approach to you is so innovative and different that you are charmed. You connect to their idealistic and spiritual self. Their adventurous spirit is in total harmony with you. There may be hidden shadows, but it doesn't bother you: mostly you bask in their love. **66% compatible**

**Purva Ashadha and Bharani:** You find harmony in your shared Venusian qualities, your similar tastes and shared sensuality. Sex is great. But Bharani are possessive, dominant and jealous; things you find hard to deal with. If you find some middle ground, you give this relationship a chance. Because you have different goals in life, you may make choices that create distances between you. **47% compatible**

**Purva Ashadha and Krittika:** Krittika are strong and powerful but you find their diffidence enchanting. Sexually dissatisfaction may cloud the happiness. Don't play with their feelings and love: they may cut you off before you decide to move on. You can find this emotionally unpalatable. Don't you usually do the leaving?
**47% compatible**

**Purva Ashadha and Rohini:** The mystical quality of Rohini attracts you but their possessiveness and jealousy can strangle you. Even if

## PURVA ASHADHA

you move on, they remind you of their presence. You need to be cautious before you start to get involved: afterwards it is usually too late. Compromise with your individual needs without hurting the other. **53% compatible**

**Purva Ashadha and Mrigasira:** A Mars–Venus combination. The passion is instant but so is the burnout. Both of you miss the passion but do not know how to rekindle it. Get to know each other properly before giving in to your passions. Then you can develop some common links and not have to search for them at a later, more complex time. **40% compatible**

**Purva Ashadha and Ardra:** Ardra have a wonderful imagination and they keep you enchanted with their mental agility and creativity. You bond powerfully and it leads to an excellent relationship. You discover many new things, your perception of love also changes through life and both of you can explore the changing reality of love together. **77% compatible**

**Purva Ashadha and Punarvasu:** Both of you enjoy change and adventure. You appreciate Punarvasu's ability to be on many different levels at one time. It can be fun; they care for you just enough without it being cloying or too emotional. However, you get annoyed about their constant advice. You want them as a lover not a teacher and you prefer to make your own decisions. **65% compatible**

**Purva Ashadha and Pushya:** Pushya are so steeped in responsibility and work that they have no time for fun and enjoyment. When you try to make them see the lighter side of life, they are not too amused as they feel you undermine them. The sheep Pushya is also your worst sexual partner and to top it all this is a spiritually complex relationship. Not a lot to base a relationship on. **33% compatible**

**Purva Ashadha and Ashlesha:** You can be friends with Ashlesha but as soon as you become lovers, your attitude changes. You can find Ashlesha too intense and analytical, always talking about their transformations. You have also had to face many changes but you take them in your stride. Learn to love them as they are and be more tolerant. **42% compatible**

**Purva Ashadha and Magha:** You are drawn to the Magha power. You like to bask in their warmth and passion. Sexually it seems to be going well. Then they ignore your needs and are arrogant and selfish. Your relationship varies between wonderful and dire. After all, you did not promise each other complete bliss. Mutual love would help. **53% compatible**

**Purva Ashadha and Purva Phalguni:** Leisure, pleasure and enjoyment of life are Purva Phalguni's guiding principles whereas spirituality and inner search are yours. Purva Phalguni needs family, love and relationships whereas you don't want the commitment. You have to create a bridge between your polarized directions if you want to be together. **50% compatible**

**Purva Ashadha and Uttara Phalguni:** You recognize the inner loneliness of Uttara Phalguni and connect directly to their soul. They love your creativity and understand your spirituality. They are happy for you to make your inner journey, discover new and wonderful worlds, but they will be there for you, supportive, loving and caring. **75% compatible**

**Purva Ashadha and Hasta:** You love the many moods of Hasta, their ability to be emotional one minute and detached the next, practical yet intuitive. You feel inspired by their love and their ability to appreciate your creativity with the eye of a true connoisseur. They can be your best critics, while being impartial; they inspire you to scale new heights. **75% compatible**

**Purva Ashadha and Chitra:** Chitra spark unbridled passion. Their Martian personality is just the type you fall in lust with. They are stunning, provocative and independent. You go down this route at extreme cost to yourself. They inspire you to love but the love may turn out to be just an illusion: you have not prepared for the fall-out. **36% compatible**

**Purva Ashadha and Swati:** Swati are a fund of ideas, which they use

## PURVA ASHADHA

in an innovative and unusual way. However extravagant your idea, whatever your path to your inner creativity, they will encourage you to take it to the limit and fulfil your true potential. This creates powerful ties. You can love each other and have a good relationship. **75% compatible**

**Purva Ashadha and Vishakha:** Your restlessness means you may not be there for each other. You also feel Vishakha live on the threshold of life, never taking the plunge to experience the new and the unconventional. You often cannot empathize with Vishakha, as you have very different ideas about life and love. Neither of you are too hot on commitment. **38% compatible**

**Purva Ashadha and Anuradha:** Behind the cool and detached demeanour of Anuradha, there is insecurity and emotional neediness. You can never be the type of lover they want. If you get involved, they find it hard to let go and you can feel blocked and imprisoned. Tread carefully at the start and you will not have so many regrets later on. **36% compatible**

**Purva Ashadha and Jyeshta:** You can be drawn into Jyeshta's sensuous world. It can be a fun and light-hearted affair but Jyeshta can take it too seriously. You resist their attempts to control you. They can be jealous, possessive and demanding. You have a different route to travel in life and you have no time for their criticism or analysis. **44% compatible**

**Purva Ashadha and Mula:** You are not hot on commitment but, when you are with Mula exploring your spiritual, emotional and physical connections, you remain interested in each other. You accept that you may never be able to commit fully to each other. This brings a huge release from conventional restrictions but it also helps you stay together. **77% compatible**

**Purva Ashadha and Purva Ashadha:** Two Purva Ashadha together have the capacity to draw the best out of each other. You look beyond the façade and see the potential. You know your creative powers and both of you work hard and responsibly to bring out the best. You spend quality time together that is loving, emotionally fulfilling and productive. **77% compatible**

**Purva Ashadha and Uttara Ashadha:** Great relationship. You admire Uttara Ashadha's ability to take your spiritual quest a bit further. You encourage them to be more sociable and help them with their lack of self-confidence. Your contact with them is profound, so you do not mind the difficulties created by their rather cool attitude to life. **77% compatible**

**Purva Ashadha and Shravana:** Remember when you fall for Shravana that they are looking for stability and dependability. Be honest and open with them right from the beginning. Your casual attitude to relationships can hurt them. They are your best sexual partner, so sensually this will be a great partnership. Try your best to be romantic. **61% compatible**

**Purva Ashadha and Dhanishta:** Passion in a Mars–Venus relationship burn out too quickly, then you wonder what drew you to Dhanishta. They appeared to be kind, warm and caring. Now you only see their arrogance and argumentative nature. You can accuse them of attracting you under false pretences. But you did not think about the future while passions ran high. **26% compatible**

**Purva Ashadha and Shatabhishak:** An easy-going and flexible relationship. Shatabhishak are in their own world and never try to control you. You enjoy their company, their unconventional thinking and their interest in spirituality. You know them better than they think you do. You let them believe that they have secrets from you. **64% compatible**

**Purva Ashadha and Purva Bhadra:** You are both on a journey of self-discovery; if you make each other your destination you keep the relationship alive. Both have the wisdom to accept the boring bits of your relationship. You love Purva Bhadra even when they are being selfish. You never have time to pay them your full attention; this keeps them keen and interested. **66% compatible**

**Purva Ashadha and Uttara Bhadra:** Uttara Bhadra are good for you:

## PURVA ASHADHA

they love you for who you are but they also know when to remind you to be responsible and caring. While they may not change with you, they remain a constant in your life to whom you can turn for support and guidance. They may love you more than you do them, but they do not complain. **61% compatible**

**Purva Ashadha and Revati:** Revati will love you so much that you can get addicted. You stay around much longer than usual, forgetting to leave. Revati communicates with both sides of your nature – the serious and the fey. Revati do not try to hold on, and you are happy to be there for them. An excellent relationship. **83% compatible**

# Cusps

Those born at the end or beginning of Purva Ashadha, should see pages 375–7.

*11 to 24 January*

# Uttara Ashadha

Ruled by The Sun
Animal: The Mongoose
Symbol: The Planks of the Bed

## Meaning and Symbolism

*Uttara* means 'higher' and *Ashadha* means 'unrestrained'. It indicates what cannot be suppressed. The true nature of man comes out however much we try to conceal it. Uttara Ashadha links to the previous Nakshatra Purva Ashadha; together they represent the unfolding of new talents. Purva Ashadha experience a dawning of these new realities, which affect them psychologically, but the assimilation into the psyche takes place in Uttara Ashadha. Uttara Ashadha are creative and talented like their cosmic half, Purva Ashadha, but they have moved on spiritually so their journey is more internal. Their creativity is not always expressed through artistic expression but may take a more philosophical route.

The planks of the bed are the symbol of Uttara Ashadha. This is an austere bed, not made for comfort. The hard bed reflects your austere attitude to relationships. You are moving away from sensuality and comfort and adopting a simple life even when involved in materialistic pursuits. You like to keep control of your life and slowly move your attention to the inward flowering of your personality. This can make your partners feel left out.

## The Uttara Ashadha Personality

### The Cool Sun

The Sun rules Uttara Ashadha. The Sun signifies authority, power, vitality and strength. The Sun rulership is about influence and power in the community. You are dynamic and intellectually gifted. You can be a leader and can doggedly pursue your ambitions. The Uttara Ashadha Sun is the winter sun of the Northern Hemisphere and that cool sunshine is expressed in your personality. You can be composed and stoical. You tend to keep an emotional distance from others. You can have difficulty expressing warmth and love. You can have a difficult relationship with your father and this colours how you view love.

If you are involved in something that bores you or you are stressed, you can become dull and lazy. There is a self-indulgent streak within you that defies your otherwise austere nature.

### The Influence of Ascetic Saturn

The first part of Uttara Ashadha is in Capricorn and the rest in Aquarius. Saturn rules both. Vedic Astrology uses traditional rulerships and does not give the planetary rulership of Aquarius to Uranus. Saturn is ascetic, hard-working and realistic. He teaches knowledge through experience of life and facing up to karma.

Uttara Ashadha in Capricorn are aware of their spiritual responsibilities and choose to pay the price of their previous karma now. Saturn restricts the Sun's glory. Saturn is dark and the Sun bright. Practical and pragmatic becomes the Capricorn Uttara Ashadha approach. They take on the obligations of the soul and will never shirk from the responsibilities their relationships put on them, however difficult or unpleasant they may seem.

Uttara Ashadha in Aquarius signifies psychological changes. Aquarius detaches from traditional ideas and worldly attachments. They find happiness through selfless work and will remain intellectually distanced from partnership issues.

## Sexuality – The Male Mongoose

### Complex Sexuality

The animal symbol of Uttara Ashadha is the mongoose. There is no female mongoose in the Nakshatra animal signs. For you, there are no ideal partners; you have no instinctive understanding of your sexuality. To fulfil your spiritual path, you have to learn to compromise on your sexuality.

To hide your lack of sexual confidence and low self-esteem, you appear active and bold. If you fancy someone you make a play for them. You are a fast worker and you can get involved very quickly. But once you are involved, you do not know what to do with your lovers. Not having an ideal mate in the Nakshatra system hinders your sexual knowledge. You can be passionate yet cold, self-indulgent yet ascetic. The right partner is one who accepts your intrinsic spirituality and makes you comfortable with your sexuality.

You hate secrecy or deception so you set high standards for your partners and if they fail, you can be very aggressive and will not wait till you have rooted out their dishonesty. Avoid becoming suspicious for the sake of it. As you are plain-speaking and direct, you may not understand harmless wiles and sexual play from others. Try to work on this aspect. Many of you can't be bothered and choose to lead the life of an ascetic.

### The Best and the Worst Sexual Partners

Uttara Ashadha is the only Nakshatra that does not have a best lover. The mongoose has no female partnership in the nakshatra system, suggesting a life where perfect sexuality and emotional partnership

# UTTARA ASHADHA

are not available for Uttara Ashadha. Yours is a highly spiritual sign where the mind is being guided to focus on matters beyond sex. This aspect does create difficulty in finding your ideal sexual partner, but there are many Nakshatras that have 75% sexual compatibility with you, such as Krittika, Pushya, Purva Ashadha and Shravana.

The snakes, Rohini and Mrigasira, are your worst sexual partners. In nature, the mongoose is the deadly enemy of the snake. Whenever they meet they fight to the death. In the psychological make-up of both Rohini and Mrigasira and yourself, adjusting to the needs of the other is a major obstacle. Your passion can turn sour quickly. In extreme cases, sexual competitiveness, irrational jealousies and vindictiveness can come into this sexual relationship unnoticed. Then you may want to destroy each other without thinking of the consequences.

With Rohini all the compatibility percentages are low so this is a relationship best avoided. Mrigasira is better equipped to rationalize than Rohini. They will analyse the hidden undercurrents and will not be afraid to cross the barriers that block your relationship, intellectually at least. Meet them halfway. Mrigasira's ruler Mars is the friend of your ruler the Sun. Use this friendship to settle the differences.

## Relationship Issues

### The Lonely Nakshatra

You have very complicated relationship needs. All the symbolism connected to your Nakshatra stands for being alone: your Nakshatra ruler is the Sun, who stands alone; Saturn your Western sign ruler favours abstinence and asceticism; the animal sign is the mongoose, which does not have any companion among the other Nakshatras. This gives you a very difficult remit regarding your relationships. How are you going to work this one out? Does this suggest that all Uttara Ashadha are incapable of having relationships?

My Uttara Ashadha clients enjoy the usual ups and downs in relationships – some happy and some unhappy experiences. I have a close friend who is Uttara Ashadha; she has been happily married for twenty-five years. The issue is that relationships alone cannot fulfil your soul. You must spend more quality time pursuing spirituality. Your emotional requirements are different. Your definition of happiness is unconventional. You mustn't reject relationships completely, but learn to relate on a new level of consciousness and with a new set of rules.

## Adjusting to the Snake Nakshatras

You have a blind spot for the snake Nakshatras; the deadly enemies of your animal sign the mongoose. There are nine Nakshatras – one-third of the Zodiac – which are in some ways connected to a snake, and they can be potentially tough relationships for you. The two snake signs are Rohini and Mrigasira. The snake symbolism also dominates the Rahu-ruled Nakshatras (Ardra, Swati and Shatabhishak) and Ketu-ruled Nakshatras (Ashwini, Magha and Mula). Rahu Ketu are the halves of the celestial snake. Ashlesha's symbol is the snake. With the snake animal signs the issues will be primarily sexual, but with the snake-dominated signs your issues of contention can be personal and emotional. Bitterness, hatred, anger, vindictiveness and jealousy can rear its ugly head and spoil it all.

## The Need for Love

You need constant assurances of love from your partners. You lack confidence but hardly ever speak of your vulnerabilities. You must learn to talk about yourself and your needs. Your partners are not telepathic – how can they learn your needs if you do not tell them? They are usually so used to leaning on you for support that they can fail to recognize that you also crave their love and support.

Your neediness can make you susceptible to flattery and insincere praise from others. You can fall for someone who professes to love you without actually doing so. You want love and you can mistake talk of love for real true love.

## Loving Uttara Ashadha

Being involved with Uttara Ashadha is never easy: they play by different rules. They can be oddly clumsy or diffident lovers unless they have worked hard on developing their sensual skills. There is an underlying asceticism about them such as you might see in yogis or sages. If you are one of the snake Nakshatras, take the relationship carefully. Talk about your feelings. Do not let them fester. By doing so you can deal with even the most difficult issues that could otherwise spoil your love. Loving Uttara Ashadha means you have to establish a strong trust. Also give them enough space but without creating so much distance that it cannot be bridged.

## Compatibility

**Ideal life partner: Uttara Bhadra**
**Most challenging life partner: Magha**

**The full Compatibility Grid is on page 338.**

**Uttara Ashadha and Ashwini:** Ashwini are vital, strong and passionate. They disarm you but you can feel inadequate. How can such a dynamic person love you? But they do. They are strong enough to bring you out of your coolness and make you feel alive again. Learn to trust them or your suspicions can spoil an otherwise good relationship. **66% compatible**

**Uttara Ashadha and Bharani:** Bharani is the sensualist of the Zodiac and one of your good relationships. Learn the art of sensuality from the masters. They are consummate at relating and you must take the lead and learn from them. Meet them halfway and you will find yourself daring to hope and love. **72% compatible**

**Uttara Ashadha and Krittika:** You are both loners, ruled by the Sun. The Krittika Sun is warm, and yours is cool. Both of you are afraid of your emotions. You can be apprehensive about taking the first steps towards establishing a relationship. If you do get together, you can create emotional distances, living together but unable to relate to each other. **30% compatible**

**Uttara Ashadha and Rohini:** Your animal sign the mongoose and Rohini's the snake are deadly enemies. Never underestimate the potential of this relationship to spiral into self-destructive behaviour. Jealousy, rivalry, viciousness – you can bring out the worst qualities in each other. Distance yourself if you can or love cautiously.
**37% compatible**

**Uttara Ashadha and Mrigasira:** Mrigasira, the thinker, will try to find the psychological reasons for this incompatibility. They will work with you to find a way to love and be together. Be ready to meet them halfway. You know this relationship needs patience and perseverance. Be constantly aware of the destructive possibilities.
**55% compatible**

**Uttara Ashadha and Ardra:** This is a relationship between darkness and light. Like day and night you are both connected. One needs the other. Through your struggles, you will find light and the ability to bond in a way which is full of karmic possibilities. Be alert to Ardra's snake connections through its ruler Rahu and avoid jealousy and rivalry. **67% compatible**

**Uttara Ashadha and Punarvasu:** You can aggravate Punarvasu by being unduly suspicious and untrusting. Punarvasu have a freewheeling lifestyle and their friendship with others does not mean that they are emotionally involved with them. This is a spiritually complex relationship. Talk to them or you can end up feeling unnecessarily unloved and lonely. **58% compatible**

**Uttara Ashadha and Pushya:** You are both loners, distant and cool. But you can have such deep understanding of each other's needs that you become warm and supportive to each other. Pushya usually yearns for your approval and love. They are happy for you to pursue your spirituality but do so in a way that also makes them feel secure and loved. **63% compatible**

# UTTARA ASHADHA

**Uttara Ashadha and Ashlesha:** Ashlesha's symbol is the snake; as a mongoose you are their deadly enemy. Your relationship can move from fascination to war in a very short time. Ashlesha can be vindictive, sarcastic and vicious towards you for no reason at all and you retaliate immediately. Both of you are unable to control your temper. **27% compatible**

**Uttara Ashadha and Magha:** The snake-like Ketu rules Magha. This makes you act extremely aggressively towards them. If you decide to pursue this relationship go in with your eyes open and watch for the negative side of this partnership. If already in it, you have to make the best of your situation. Work to be positive and suppress the negative. **15% compatible**

**Uttara Ashadha and Purva Phalguni:** You love the sense of perfection and creativity of Purva Phalguni. They need and enjoy sex. If dissatisfied, they are likely to look elsewhere. You may feel unsure about your ability to fulfil them and this makes you distrust them. Talk about your fears and they will respond. They will not knowingly hurt you. **60% compatible**

**Uttara Ashadha and Uttara Phalguni:** Both of you are ruled by the Sun; you understand each other perfectly. Uttara Phalguni are warm and caring, they love you and support you. You feel you can trust them and this makes you relax in their company. Uttara Phalguni are realistic about sex and will not pressurize you to be what you are not. **68% compatible**

**Uttara Ashadha and Hasta:** The Sun rules you and the Moon rules Hasta. The Moon loves to reflect the glory of the Sun, similarly Hasta like to bask in your warmth. Hasta recognizes your loneliness and, through love, they help eleviate it. Sexually Hasta also has many complexes and they recognize you as a soul mate struggling with similar feelings. **64% compatible**

**Uttara Ashadha and Chitra:** Tough, independent, refined and cultured; Chitra are full of attractive contradictions. Can the exotic tiger be totally happy with the plain mongoose? You can make it worse by

# THE LOVE SIGNS

being jealous of Chitra's friends. Loving them also means letting them have some freedom. They bring colour and fun into your life.
**55% compatible**

**Uttara Ashadha and Swati:** Swati are happy with your material successes; they are not always able to connect to your spiritual ones. Why do you need them to understand your soul's journey? By now you must realize that this is essentially a lonely one, your partners can only block its progress. So love Swati and compromise on the rest. **55% compatible**

**Uttara Ashadha and Vishakha:** Vishakha and Uttara Ashadha have a friendship that does not translate well into intimacy. Vishakha can be too fixed in their ideas to understand your complicated emotional needs. You relate their restlessness to the fact that you are unable to live up to their expectations. You can feel unhappy and lonely.
**32% compatible**

**Uttara Ashadha and Anuradha:** Anuradha's love can penetrate your loneliness. But you may find that they love you a bit more than you can love them. Their love makes you feel secure and wanted and you try very hard to offer them security and stability. Remember to let them know of your love: they can be hurt by your aloofness.
**64% compatible**

**Uttara Ashadha and Jyeshta:** Your austere nature does not enjoy Jyeshta's conspicuous addiction to sensuality and passion. The spiritual part of your relationship works wonderfully but the sensuous part is often distant. The success of your relationship depends on how well you can bridge the polarities and learn to appreciate their sensual nature as much as their spiritual one. **50% compatible**

**Uttara Ashadha and Mula:** You are drawn to the unconventional Mula but soon realize that this relationship may not work. Ketu, the tail half of the celestial snake, rules them. This brings out unnecessary aggression within you. Mula can also make you the butt of their anger. Love finds it hard to flourish under these conditions.
**36% compatible**

## UTTARA ASHADHA

**Uttara Ashadha and Purva Ashadha:** Purva Ashadha and Uttara Ashadha are two halves of the same principle. Purva Ashadha's creativity amazes you, as does their ability to bring sensuality and love into your life without demanding the sacrifice of your spirituality. You go beyond mere physical love; you experience spiritual togetherness. **77% compatible**

**Uttara Ashadha and Uttara Ashadha:** Other Uttara Ashadha are the only ones who fully understood your sexuality so potentially this relationship may be sensuous and fulfilling. If you put two relationship misfits together it will take some trial and error before you are comfortable together. The high compatibility suggests the ability to bridge the difficult communication barriers. **68% compatible**

**Uttara Ashadha and Shravana:** Do not keep pushing Shravana away. They are one of the few who can understand your emotional loneliness. They can be moody and distracted at times but they know how to deal with your complex emotions. Sometimes you can get too comfortable with them and become lazy. That does not help you spiritually. **58% compatible**

**Uttara Ashadha and Dhanishta:** You must not try to compete with Dhanishta for everything. Just enjoy their friendship and see how the relationship develops. If you try to fight with Dhanishta to establish your superiority, they will fight back. Dhanishta need to know of your love and if you express that from time to time, they will be less inclined to fight you. **52% compatible**

**Uttara Ashadha and Shatabhishak:** Shatabhishak is ruled by Rahu, the celestial snake, and any relationship with a snake sign must have very clear personal boundaries. Despite this negative factor, you can actually overcome your instinctive distrust to take the next step with them. You can learn to love their detachment from sexual passions and the unconventional approach to you. **63% compatible**

**Uttara Ashadha and Purva Bhadra:** You find their warmth comforting and sexy. You enjoy exploring your sensuality with them. They are strong but do not crowd you; they allow you to explore your relationship at your own pace. Their positive attitude gives you confidence. Their way of being your friend, lover and mentor makes them special indeed. **66% compatible**

**Uttara Ashadha and Uttara Bhadra:** Your best relationship. They will try to fulfil all your desires and love you completely and deeply. You must not take Uttara Bhadra for granted. They understand your vulnerabilities and help you overcome your emotional barriers. You need to honour and love them; they make you feel happy and complete. **83% compatible**

**Uttara Ashadha and Revati:** Revati have the ability to charm and attract you. They hover around you, showering you with their affection and love. You can't resist them even when you try. Revati are good for you as they have a philosophical attitude to love and sex. But they can be critical and living up to their ideals is not always easy. **55% compatible**

# Cusps

Those born at the end or beginning of Uttara Ashadha, should see pages 377–8.

24 January to 6 February

# Shravana

Ruled by the Moon
Animal: The Female Monkey
Symbol: The Ear

## Meaning and Symbolism

*Shravana* means 'listening specially to the scriptures'. To listen to the sound of silence can only be done through self-discipline and meditation. We can hear the true meaning of the scriptures when there is silence of the mind, then we begin to hear new sounds that we were not aware of before. To sit in silence we have to like ourselves; it forces us to recognize the truth about ourselves and not hide within the cacophony of life.

The symbol assigned to Shravana of the ear further enhances your listening quality. In the collection of tales called the Upanishads there is a prayer to grant the capacity to listen properly. When you learn to listen properly, you learn to hear the meaning behind the spoken word. In relationships, you learn to hear what your partners are really saying.

## The Shravana Personality

### The Lunar Mind

The Moon rules Shravana. The Moon symbolizes the mind in Vedic Astrology – both the emotional and the intellectual. The Moon is the physical embodiment of your soul, the ebb and flow of your feelings, emotions and your need for change on a daily basis. The Moon is the controller of life on earth where nothing is certain. As Shravana, your mind has to learn the lesson of equilibrium and to be at peace.

The mind dominates every aspect of your life. Your thinking is very unconventional. In relationships you worry about every aspect, think about what your partner said and what they left unsaid. You can develop an instinctive understanding of your partner's emotions.

### The Balancing Act of the Moon and Saturn

The Moon rules Shravana and the Nakshatra is placed in Aquarius which has the rulership of Saturn (Vedic Astrology uses traditional rulerships and does not take Uranus as the ruler of Aquarius). This Saturn–Moon combination makes for a difficult situation. The Moon waxes and wanes, is emotional and changeable; Saturn is disciplined, rigid and inflexible. Saturn will teach you to control your emotions, be detached from the ups and downs of life. Shravana forces you to take more responsibility for yourself as you experience inner growth and move towards higher spiritual knowledge.

Aquarius is called *Kumbha* in Sanskrit. Kumbha is a pitcher or water carrier. Water is synonymous with the mind and emotions. As pitcher contains water so Aquarius has the ability to contain the wavering mind. Kumbhaka is the practice of controlling the breath in yoga that helps us control the mind. As Shravana you learn to still the mind so that you can master your emotions. You try to develop the capability to control the mind and stop being controlled by it. Spending so much time in trying to control your mind can make you into a control freak. You can try to control every aspect of your life including your relationships.

## Sexuality – The Female Monkey

### The Fun Lovers

Shravana's animal sign is the female monkey. In Vedic Astrology, female sexuality indicates passive energy and shows a strong mothering instinct. Monkeys live in communities in the deepest jungles as well as in urban areas. Monkeys jump from one tree to another to escape retribution for their naughty acts. You develop instinctive self-defence skills. You can cause trouble and allow others to take the blame. With all the other animal signs, you skirt around the issue of relationships, proverbially jump from one tree to another and avoid being caught.

You want your love life to be full of fun and joys of the world. You are social and want to have a family. Unlike your male counterpart, you do seek to make a long-term commitment and enjoy having the security of family around you. Still you will lead your partner a merry dance before you allow yourself to be caught. You like sex to be enjoyable. You fool around, are playful and do not take sex too seriously. You rarely show your lighter side to the world; this is reserved for those you love. If you do not find a true partner, you can be promiscuous.

### The Best and the Worst Sexual Partners

Your best relationship is with the male monkey Purva Ashadha. This relationship brings fun and joy into your sexual life. They make you feel wanted and will play all the sexual games you want as they know instinctively that you will allow yourself to be caught eventually, when you are ready. The sex is lively and fun. Commitment comes with time. You know Purva Ashadha are not the best at commitment and, as long as they are there for you, you are not bothered by the lack of conventional ties.

Your worst sexual relationships are with the sheep, Krittika and Pushya. The shy sheep Nakshatras do not enjoy being made fun of by the monkeys. They are unadventurous by nature and will not be able to deal with your boldness. Krittika object to your free-wheeling attitude to sex and feel insecure; your compatibility in other areas is also poor. With Pushya, you are able to override the sexual incompatibility to have a loving and fulfilling relationship.

# Relationship Issues

## The Emotional Struggles

You are very emotional, although you may not show it. You need love and protection from your partners. Your parents probably taught you to control your emotions from a very young age. You may appear calm on the outside but you can be a mass of seething emotions within.

You find it difficult to say what you really feel. You may appear hard but you are really as soft as marshmallow. Emotional, tender, sentimental, sensitive and loving – you can develop a shell to hide your real self. You need someone who can discover your true nature.

You must recognize that you are sending out signals that conflict with what you desire. You may have disciplined yourself to control your mind and you think you can be detached. But you are fooling yourself by denying your need for love. Admit your needs; only then will you be ready to receive love.

## Blowing Hot and Cold

You can be very passionate, committed and possessive. Even though you may be totally in love, you can suddenly end the relationship without explanation. You can blow hot and cold with your emotions,

# SHRAVANA

being passionate one moment, cool and distant the next. Before you accuse your partners of not loving you enough, you must recognize that your behaviour confuses and puts them off.

The truth is you are struggling to control your sexual nature, which makes you feel guilty about your passionate needs and emotional nature, so you can suddenly become cold and uncaring. In reality, few Shravana are on such a deeply spiritual path that they can exercise complete control of their sexuality. You, like the other Nakshastras need love, relationships and sex. You should recognize your need for a commitment to a more spiritual path but that should not mean you shy away from relationships.

## Dealing with Rejection and Fear

Your usual response to rejection or lack of appreciation is to move on and start another relationship. Your relationship with two Nakshatras is worth a special mention. With Magha, you have a very low compatibility of 11%. Magha are at a crucial junction in life and when they meet you, many karmic issues come forth. They fear your emotionalism and may be quick to reject you. Sexual infidelity can be the big issue. Your involvement with Magha is a huge learning curve. Do not be quick to opt out of this relationship. Recognize the need for effort to make it work.

Although your compatibility with Ardra is strong at 61%, this relationship is spiritually complex. You fear Ardra's ability to see right into your soul. You feel exposed and vulnerable to such sharp scrutiny. Ardra will be secretive and arouse feelings of jealousy and inadequacy. They can make you unhappy. You usually freeze them out but your heart hurts for a long time.

The relationships with Ardra and Magha, ruled respectively by the shadow planets Rahu and Ketu, gives a clue to your vulnerability. You fear rejection and loss, and develop a shell to hide your fear appearing to be uncaring. You must not take rejection at face value. You should discuss your fears and talk about your relationship issues as they arise. If you fear losing your partner, let them know that their attitude is aggravating your fears and that your irrational behaviour is due to this, then you are taking positive steps in making your relationship better.

## Loving Shravana

When you love Shravana, you have to recognize that the sensible and practical persona is an image they show to the world to protect their inner sentimental nature. Because they try so hard to control their emotions, they sometimes lose the ability to express them. As their partner, you have to make them feel comfortable with their emotions. They also need time alone, to be in silence.

## Compatibility

**Ideal life partner: Uttara Bhadra**
**Most challenging life partner: Magha**

The full Compatibility Grid is on page 338.

**Shravana and Ashwini:** You are attracted to the verve and energy of Ashwini. In relationships they are adventurous and fun, they do not want to tie you down to a boring conventional life. You can love them too easily. Don't try to control your emotions too much or you will miss out on the spontaneity that Ashwini are so good with.
**72% compatible**

**Shravana and Bharani:** Emotional, fun and loving – good relationship and great sexual chemistry. Bharani know how to be intimate. They are tactile and awaken your latent desires with their slightest touch. This is very enticing, as you also pick up their silent messages – your senses can get highly attuned to their every gesture and touch.
**77% compatible**

**Shravana and Krittika:** Your worst sexual partners with low compatibility. The fact is you just do not understand each other's needs. You think Krittika will support you and care for you whereas they can be

# SHRAVANA

withdrawn and unfeeling. They do not react to your romantic overtures and you cannot appreciate them in the way they get accustomed to. **32% compatible**

**Shravana and Rohini:** You can enjoy the romanticism of Rohini but their brand of possessive love may become too intense. They are restless, unsettled, moody, fickle and emotional – so like you. You don't know how to deal with their love. You want them but they make your mind even more unsettled and sometimes you long for peace and quiet. **50% compatible**

**Shravana and Mrigasira:** You are emotional and Mrigasira rational. They cannot love instinctively. They try to analyse every bit of your relationship and you want to hide from their inquisition. They never fully understand your sentimentality and question your emotionalism. You may never be comfortable enough with Mrigasira to love them completely. **39% compatible**

**Shravana and Ardra:** A spiritually complex relationship. While Ardra may be willing to love you completely, they can treat your emotions carelessly. You can be irrationally possessive and untrusting. Learn to talk about your love and keep communicating, then you give happiness a chance. Bury your emotions and you may both feel dissatisfied. **61% compatible**

**Shravana and Punarvasu:** Punarvasu have a knack of being supportive even if they are not there. You are happy to have them to love you in whichever way they want. Both of you need to be free to pursue your spiritual interests. Punarvasu never question this need and you try to help them to use their restless mind more creatively. **68% compatible**

**Shravana and Pushya:** This is a good relationship that transcends poor sexual compatibility. Pushya are your worst sexual partner yet they are compatible in all other ways. Pushya will nourish and love you in a way no one else can. You can lean on them for support. Sexually you compromise and learn about real spiritual love as a result. **75% compatible**

**Shravana and Ashlesha:** Ashlesha never try to understand your

emotional needs. You might pretend to be cool and rational like them but their cynical attitude to love and life is opposite to your more romantic one. Can you ever understand where the other is coming from? If you do, then you have hope for happiness.
36% compatible

**Shravana and Magha:** Initially you feel that Magha will fulfil your emotional needs. But they are unable to give you the security you desire: they will always rubbish your emotions and continuously reject you. They can also be sexually promiscuous and openly capricious. Slowly you can lose all your joie de vivre and emotional friendliness. 11% compatible

**Shravana and Purva Phalguni:** Sophisticated, creative and fun Purva Phalguni appears just your type of partner. But they only complete half of your picture. You aspire to silence, whereas they favour activity and noise. You have to appreciate their qualities since they cannot change, compromise on your needs, if you want to find more harmony and love. 50% compatible

**Shravana and Uttara Phalguni:** You need Uttara Phalguni's love to sustain you. You need to let them know this. Secure in your love, they will care for you, support you, love you and wait for you. Uttara Phalguni are frustrated at not being able to be more spiritual so they are happy that you improve yourself spiritually and strive for higher knowledge. 61% compatible

**Shravana and Hasta:** Hasta are emotionally needy. They can be very insecure and hide their sensitivity behind a hard and strong exterior. You can empathize with them. For so long you have covered up your real feelings as well. At last, a partner who intuitively understands you. This is the secret of the success of your relationship.
66% compatible

**Shravana and Chitra:** You are attracted to Chitra's larger-than-life persona. You enjoy playing sexual games with them with the exciting prospect of being caught and thoroughly loved by them. They will

# SHRAVANA

care for you and look after you. Your problems occur with their inability to commit – you want their undivided love and attention. **58% compatible**

**Shravana and Swati:** You are wary of Swati, afraid of allowing them into your life. Your attitude to them remains ambivalent for a long time, unsure whether to trust them or not. Swati are unable to understand why you would not open up and care for them. They sense your insecurity and try to be patient. Swati will work hard to make you happy. **61% compatible**

**Shravana and Vishakha:** You have a complicated relationship. Vishakha like their independence too much and you can never feel totally comfortable about that. If you let them know of your love then they tend to distance themselves. You may not be emotionally strong enough to deal with Vishakha's restlessness and dissatisfaction. **36% compatible**

**Shravana and Anuradha:** Your Moon rulership has sacred significance for Anuradha. The Moon reflects Krishna, the god of love to whom the Anuradha soul is devoted. You can be their divine inspiration. They will love you unconditionally. You enjoy basking in their love. Anuradha's love inspires you spiritually as well. **72% compatible**

**Shravana and Jyeshta:** Jyeshta can be very passionate but also become suddenly critical and detached. While you enjoy Jyeshta's extravagances, your austere side does not like it. Jyeshta can try to intellectualize too much and in your opinion they miss the point. This relationship needs both of you to make an effort, and then you can make it quite good. **55% compatible**

**Shravana and Mula:** Mula's spiritual frustrations can mar your relationship. They can aggravate your personal fear of partners loving you and leaving you. You need to talk with Mula about your feelings and how their attitude affects you. If you allow them to take out their disappointments on you, you set a pattern of behaviour that can be hard to break. **39% compatible**

**Shravana and Purva Ashadha:** Your best sexual partnership. Purva

Ashadha will be great lovers, good friends and wonderful companions but if you need them to be forever by your side you are choosing the wrong partner. You have to accept their nonconformist attitude to relationships, and then you can enjoy what they have to offer. **61% compatible**

**Shravana and Uttara Ashadha:** Uttara Ashadha can have quite an austere attitude to love and relationships. They remain detached and seem to prefer their own company. So you have quite a mountain to climb if you want to reach them emotionally. They will be strong for you. Win their trust and let them know often how much you care. **58% compatible**

**Shravana and Shravana:** You connect well with other Shravana. Instinctive understanding of each other helps in establishing this relationship but your similarities can create problems for long-term happiness. Be conscious that your best points of compatibility can become your worst, especially your moodiness and your need to be alone. **77% compatible**

**Shravana and Dhanishta:** Dhanishta make you feel complete. You are happy to bask in their warmth. They support and love you. Emotionally this is very satisfying. Just be careful that you are not too possessive. Also, let them fight their inner battle themselves. You must be conscious of not shutting Dhanishta out. They need your warmth and love. **61% compatible**

**Shravana and Shatabhishak:** You do not understand or trust Shatabhishak, yet you are drawn to their wisdom and knowledge. Shatabhishak usually give you mixed signals: they say they love you, but they also break their promises and are generally unreliable. You have to decide not to take them at face value and not create emotional expectations. **47% compatible**

**Shravana and Purva Bhadra:** Purva Bhadra can soon become essential to you. You love their strength and the way they care for you. You can burden them with your emotional expectations and they will

# SHRAVANA

cheerfully bear them. You agree with their idealistic visions. They can be cool and distant, but you feel secure in their love. **66% compatible**

**Shravana and Uttara Bhadra:** Saturn, the ruler of Uttara Bhadra, is the most difficult teacher for you so you go into this relationship reluctantly. But once you become involved, you find Uttara Bhadra loving and supportive. They also help you to find peace and to balance your emotional and practical needs. Together you find real happiness. **80% compatible**

**Shravana and Revati:** You show the world you are strong, but you are vulnerable within. Revati instinctively know that. You do not need to pretend to be what you are not. Revati love you deeply and emotionally. Your relationship may not have any defences against difficult times. So be prepared and do not blame each other if things go wrong. **64% compatible**

## Cusps

Those born at the end or beginning of Shravana, should see pages 379–80.

6 to 19 February

# Dhanishta

Ruled by Mars
Animal: The Lioness
Symbol: The Drum or the Flute

## Meaning and Symbolism

*Dhani* means 'wealthy' and *Ishta* means 'complete'. Together *Dhanishta* means 'complete wealth'. Dhanishta is wealthy in mind and spirit. In the Vedic texts when the sages alluded to a person being wealthy, they meant that they had the wealth of good character, thoughts and actions. This was considered far superior to mere material wealth. Your nature is more spiritually inclined and therefore you are not always good at relationships, preferring to go it alone.

Dhanishta is connected to the symbols of the drum and the flute – Shiva's drum or Krishna's flute. The drum or the flute are beating to the rhythm of someone else – others are to play their song through you. Both the drum and the flute are hollow from within; this means emptiness within you unless something or someone can fill it. You try to find a person who can fill your life with their music but you can also get involved in other people's dreams and feel unfulfilled as you are not pursuing your own goals.

You must learn to write your own music, create your own life and fill it with love and joy. Or you can feel very empty within.

## The Dhanishta Personality

### Life is a Battlefield

Life, for Dhanishta, is a battlefield. They learn early in life to defend their corner. The prime motivation for Dhanishta is *dharma* – it is at its most potent. Dharma is your moral responsibility to life. Krishna, the Vedic god, taught dharma to Arjuna, the reluctant warrior in the *Bhagavad Gita*. The *Bhagavad Gita* is the 'Divine song', an epic that is the essence of the Vedas. The setting of the *Bhagavad Gita* is a battlefield and Arjuna does not want to fight this war as it means killing those he loves the most. Krishna teaches him the knowledge of the Immortal Self. As a warrior Arjuna's dharma is to fight a righteous war regardless of the personal cost. Arjuna's war is a metaphor for the inner war we fight every day when we are trying to conquer our senses, desires, feelings and temptations.

Your ruling planet Mars is the planet of courage and action. Mars allows you to be single-minded in the pursuit of dharmic responsibility. You have to conquer your inner demons and outer enemies. In relationships you can get very combative if challenged. The tension of your various battles create discord, as you do not always consider others when you think you are fighting a righteous war.

### War between Mars and Saturn

Dhanishta is placed in Aquarius, ruled by Saturn (Vedic Astrology uses traditional rulerships and does not take Uranus as the ruler of Aquarius). Mars rules Dhanishta. Mars and Saturn are opposing energies, one standing for bravery and action and the other for caution and restrictions. When Mars and Saturn conjunct, it is usually considered a warlike formation, again emphasizing your inner and outer struggles. Saturn does not allow you to avoid responsibilities. You are immensely stressed and frustrated by the restrictions life places on you. Saturn forces you to harness the powerful Mars energy. This can make you great achievers but also extremely tough to live with.

# Sexuality – The Lioness

## The Strong Lovers

Your sexuality is expressed by your animal sign, the lioness. In the wild, lionesses hunt side by side with lions. They are strong and powerful. They live in wild open places and are masters of all they survey. They exemplify female power. Dhanishta, male or female, will defend their cubs. There is no passivity, unlike the other female animal signs. You are in charge of your sexuality. If you desire someone, you will make it very obvious. You have a strong and insatiable sexual appetite. You like plenty of sex, but once satiated you may not look for another sexual encounter till you are ready for it. You stay true to your partners as long as they are true to you. If your partners stray, so will you. You do not believe in double standards at all.

You are not possessive. You are not willing to commit and do not expect commitment from your lovers. You love to be competitive and enjoy the thrill of a fight to win their affections. But you do not hold on if your partners deliberately try to make you jealous. You can be slow developers; your sexuality flowers later in life and you feel more comfortable with your sensual needs as you mature.

## The Best and the Worst Sexual Partners

You need the lion Purva Bhadra to satisfy your sexual needs. Both of you are powerful and strong and can commit sexually to each other. Exciting and sensual, you find happiness together.

Dhanishta are sexually incompatible with the elephants Bharani and Revati. Both elephants and lions are powerful in the animal kingdom and naturally inimical. Both of you jealously guard your terrain and will not allow the other to dictate what you do or not do. You can learn to live with your enemy. In the wild, lions and elephants live together apparently in harmony. Lions rarely enter the elephant's patch and the elephant does not go into the lion's den.

A relationship with clearly demarcated areas of operation and power can work. With Revati there is still a possibility of having a relationship. Bharani is incompatible in every other area of life as well, so the relationship is tough.

## Relationship Issues

### The Passion Burnout of Mars and Venus

Instant love, attraction, sexual fire and unbridled passion are what you feel with the Venus Nakshatras. The fire has the capacity to rage uncontrolled, both parties giving in to your passion with no idea how to control it. If you don't bank the fires to make them last longer, there can be a dramatic relationship burnout. There is not much left to do but to gather the ashes of love from the bitter and acrid smoke of recriminations. In the aftermath of spent passion, you can become destructive and lose what you valued most.

Purva Phalguni, Purva Ashadha and Bharani are the Venus Nakshatras. You must relate to them with care. Passion is your weakness; the Venusian ardour will also block your spiritual growth. While you may enjoy a dalliance with passion, your soul needs more in order to fulfil your karmic purpose. The Venus Nakshatras can frustrate you, as you need to keep your spiritual options open.

### Karmic Vulnerability

You unload your karmic burden through your relationships. You can get involved in relationships that weigh you down with responsibility. You do not turn your back on uncomfortable situations, tending to face up to your obligations and work through them. The weight of these responsibilities can create a crisis within you, which teaches you a lot about life, love and karma. You cleanse some of your difficult karma but the price you pay can be high in terms of emotions and heartbreak. It is like living on a volcano – when the eruption occurs, it is like an emotional explosion.

## Coping with Stress

Your life can be full of stress. You want to shoulder everyone's burdens. Internally you are forever involved in your personal wars. You are not shy of taking on contentious issues. This can make you very stressed and explosive. You need to follow exercise routines that burn up all your excessive energy and relax you to calm your stress. Your relationships can benefit enormously from the new, calmer you. Your partner can heave a sigh of relief, as they no longer have to deal with your volatility.

## The Many Masks

Will the real Dhanishta please stand up? You have many different personalities. Different people will see different sides of your personality. You can be arrogant and humble, extremely materialistic and charitable, a warrior and a peace lover. You are a born idealist and, whatever path you undertake, you are always doing it for the right reasons. Others may take you the wrong way. You do not hide yourself deliberately. Wearing your different masks is natural to you; you take on whatever persona is suitable for the task in hand.

# Loving Dhanishta

When you live with Dhanishta, you can feel the tension within them and it can soon permeate into your relationship. It is like living on the edge of a volcano – you do not know when they are going to erupt or how you are going to deal with the fall out. One of the keys to loving Dhanishta is to learn to keep their personal inner battles separate from your relationship issues.

# DHANISHTA

## Compatibility

### Ideal life partner: Shatabhishak
### Most challenging life partner: Uttara Bhadra

**The full Compatibility Grid is on page 338.**

**Dhanishta and Ashwini:** When you meet Ashwini, there is an instant sexual frisson, but the sparks can fizzle out just as quickly. They can give you lots of excitement and fun. You do not ask for commitments but this can be a mistake as you may be leaving loopholes to allow either of you to get out quickly of the relationship. **53% compatible**

**Dhanishta and Bharani:** Sexual joy can be very limited, as this is your sexually incompatible relationship. Both of your animal signs, the lioness and the elephant, want to dominate. While your spiritual side can keep you fulfilled, Bharani can become restless and unhappy without sensual fulfilment. This can lead to affairs or lack of love.
**26% compatible**

**Dhanishta and Krittika:** You fall for the shy warmth of Krittika. You can be good friends, share lots of passion and be happy together as your relationship balances your mutual strengths and weaknesses. You instinctively respond to Krittika's needs. They remain loyal, loving you through the different phases of life, even the difficult ones.
**70% compatible**

**Dhanishta and Rohini:** You are entranced by the charming and beautiful Rohini but their indecisive and changeable nature does not appeal to you one bit. Rohini are romantic and possessive. You enjoy the romance but hate the constraints of possession. You are not usually indulgent of Rohini's moods and will forever question their emotionalism. **53% compatible**

**Dhanishta and Mrigasira:** Your relationship can be a perpetual battlefield with both of you sporting emotional scars from your no-holds-barred fights. Mrigasira try to dominate you intellectually, criticizing you often. You are not willing to take such criticism; you tend to lash out in return. Your relationship is also spiritually complex so give peace a chance. **35% compatible**

**Dhanishta and Ardra:** Your relationship suffers from lack of trust. You never try to understand Ardra's emotional vulnerability, seeing them as strong, analytical and unnecessarily dissatisfied with life. While you get along well with them, your relationship can remain superficial. Their need for secrecy can spark off your fights.
**50% compatible**

**Dhanishta and Punarvasu:** You can be good friends but the moment you get serious, your expectations of each other can weigh the relationship down. You have to stop expecting the world from them and love them like you did when you were just friends. The moment this pressure lifts, Punarvasu start being natural, free and loving.
**46% compatible**

**Dhanishta and Pushya:** Challenging. Pushya can be too dogmatic and inflexible. They tend to expect you to follow their agenda alone. They put conditions on love that are impossible to fulfil; you can feel locked in a cage, frustrated and angry. You can lock into the downward spiral of extremely negative behaviour towards each other.
**24% compatible**

**Dhanishta and Ashlesha:** You want to experience the excitement of hypnotic, mysterious and dangerous Ashlesha. You are very different personalities but you are attracted to the differences. Ashlesha are quite idealistic about love and you can fulfil their needs in many ways. Be careful that your independent natures do not make you drift apart. **60% compatible**

**Dhanishta and Magha:** Learn about the Magha insecurities and complexes. They can appear haughty and self-important. Remember that Magha's sign the rat is the smallest animal in the Nakshatras; they can feel powerless in front of the mighty lioness. Treat them kindly; allow them their occasional arrogance because you know who is powerful regardless of appearances. **55% compatible**

**Dhanishta and Purva Phalguni:** When you meet Purva Phalguni there

# DHANISHTA

is instant attraction. When passion fizzles out, there may be nothing left to hold you together. You hate Purva Phalguni's incessant need for socializing. Bad behaviour, inability to compromise and pining for lost passions can create huge problems: all are a result of your rulers, Mars and Venus, causing dissatisfaction with each other.
19% compatible

**Dhanishta and Uttara Phalguni:** Uttara Phalguni cause you stress by being dissatisfied. You are not the cause of their dissatisfaction: it is just the way they are. Even if you build them a Taj Mahal, they will find reasons for being discontented. If you can love this quality and take it with a pinch of salt and dollops of friendship, this relationship survives. **40% compatible**

**Dhanishta and Hasta:** You fall for Hasta's sophistication and admire their independence. You woo them. Hasta will love and care for you deeply. But when you discover their poor self-image you are not always able to be supportive. You do not want to give up your independence to cater for their emotionalism. **51% compatible**

**Dhanishta and Chitra:** You are too similar: dominant, controlling and strong. Your relationship is always passionate and exciting but the passions burn out quickly. Then you become competitive, leaving no room for tenderness and love. You do not have to win every argument. Learning to give in gracefully promotes happiness.
**50% compatible**

**Dhanishta and Swati:** Swati are different, they thrill at challenging mediocrity and going against the grain. You love their volatile and unconventional personality. Others can never understand the attraction. They are earthy lovers, and you like the contrast between their sophisticated and worldly-wise persona and raw primal sexuality.
**65% compatible**

**Dhanishta and Vishakha:** Vishakha can be your great friend. They understand your angst and support you through your crises. They have the knack to calm you and make you feel loved. You do not try to battle with them as is your usual habit because they wisely refuse to be drawn into your personal wars. You develop a lasting bond. **70% compatible**

**Dhanishta and Anuradha:** Anuradha's expectations from you can be unrealistic and full of illusions. They can get obsessive about you and just want to be part of your life. Take care you do not hurt them. Keep them distant from the start. Anuradha can fall for you so completely that you will find it difficult to detach yourself from them. **32% compatible**

**Dhanishta and Jyeshta:** You fall for the fast-thinking, quick-witted Jyeshta. You love the way they can be different people at different times. You do not feel threatened by their independent nature. You also connect strongly to their spiritual journey, being able to support them through their difficulties as you have already made this journey yourself. **68% compatible**

**Dhanishta and Mula:** Yours can be a volatile relationship but when the going gets tough, you will support and love each other. Mula are complex, restless and unsure of their spiritual direction. You understand their search; you help them find their roots so that they can be secure. You are usually willing to sacrifice a lot to make Mula happy. **65% compatible**

**Dhanishta and Purva Ashadha:** A Mars–Venus relationship. The strong passions are short lived. Without the intense sexual energy, your relationship seems passé and boring. There are hardly any mutual interests to bind you. You think of Purva Ashadha as confused and unable to live up to their promises. You lose trust in them quickly. **26% compatible**

**Dhanishta and Uttara Ashadha:** Uttara Ashadha are unconventional. They can be detached and lonely. Uttara Ashadha's inability to understand the subtleties of love tends to rub you up the wrong way. You can be too competitive and contrary, passionate one moment and at war the next. If you find a happy balance, the relationship can flourish. **52% compatible**

# DHANISHTA

**Dhanishta and Shravana:** You love the way Shravana think about every aspect of your relationship and how to make it work. They hang on to your every word, thinking about what was said and what remained unsaid. They can develop an instinctive understanding of your emotions. You make good partners; you will always be protective of your Shravana love. **61% compatible**

**Dhanishta and Dhanishta:** These relationships can be ardent and exhilarating. Your passions will be strong and demanding: there is never a middle ground in your relationship with another Dhanishta. You want everything. Your fights will be legendary, but the making up can be wonderful. Talk about your feelings; stop demanding the impossible. **63% compatible**

**Dhanishta and Shatabhishak:** You are very attracted to the mysticism and shadows that surround Shatabhishak. You are happy to be in love with them. You need your independence and you are happy for them to have theirs. If they hurt you, you will hurt them back. But generally Shatabhishak are careful with you because they care so much. **77% compatible**

**Dhanishta and Purva Bhadra:** Purva Bhadra is your ideal sexual partner. You demand respect and will fight with them if you do not get it. Whatever the rules are for them apply to you as well. If they want to be independent, so will you. You do not give any quarter or expect any. This is an equal partnership. You keep Purva Bhadra on their toes. **58% compatible**

**Dhanishta and Uttara Bhadra:** Uttara Bhadra does not always take notice of what you want. They are happy in their own world and will not bow to your superiority. You may feel they cramp your style; they do not give you the excitement you seek and they never appreciate you enough. Both of you are acting contrarily as this is your worst relationship. **17% compatible**

**Dhanishta and Revati:** Your worst sexual partner. The instinctive barriers that you set up become areas of discord. Both of you have a powerful need for sex, but Revati can demand you respect them and honour their sexuality. You are not so willing to comply. You can be arrogant and they can be fussy; both of you may not find a common ground. **36% compatible**

# Cusps

Those born at the end or beginning of Dhanishta, should see pages 380–2.

19 February to 4 March

# Shatabhishak

Ruled by Rahu
Animal: The Female Horse
Symbol: A Hundred Stars

## Meaning and Symbolism

Shatabhishak can have many meanings. *Shat* means 'hundred' and *Bhishak* means 'demons'. *Abhishak* means is 'healers'. This Nakshatra can be both demonic and godly. Shatabhishak highlights the good and evil, the two sides of humanity. You are perpetually fighting with the negative forces within you, trying to control your inner demons so that you can aspire towards the divine.

Your symbol, the hundred stars, show your deep connection with the cosmos and past karma. The stars are the silent watchers of the play of life and the transmigration of the soul. The hundred stars are said to resemble the lotus of a thousand petals, which is the *Sahasara Chakra*. Sahasara Chakra, or the Crown Chakra, Lotus represents the highest power within our astral body. When you reach the highest understanding of your spiritual path, the lotus flowers and gives you the ability to transcend the restrictions that destiny and past karma have imposed on you.

You seek divine guidance to lead you from the darkness to the light. Your aspirations are idealistic and great. But not all of you can achieve such lofty goals. Most struggle to control their inner demons. You try to hide these from your partners and lovers. You feel that if they really knew your true nature, they would not love you. Let your partners into your world. Let them be the judge of whether they love you or not. Humankind has struggled with good and evil from time immemorial and your partners will be much more understanding than you think. It is your secrecy and attempts to hide part of your true nature that they will find harder to come to terms with.

## The Shatabhishak Personality

### Shadows of the Mind

Rahu is the mental projection of the past life issues into the present. Rahu becomes obsessed with externalizing the unfulfilled past life wishes through present experiences. Your subconscious memory carries both positive and negative force; you try to dampen the demonic and expose the godly. You want to create something positive from the shadows within, but both coexist however much you try to shut them the negative out.

Most interpretations only focus on the negative side of Rahu and Shatabhishak, the Nakshatra linked to the demonic personality. This is only seeing half the picture. For example, when the dormant kundalini (your latent power) rises, it is fiery and destructive; without true knowledge of your higher self, you can be self-destructive to start with. Once you train your energy to become a positive force, you learn to heal your inner poisons, and you awaken to a glorious new world where you have the capacity to defy convention and make immense changes to your way of thinking. More than most Nakshatras, you can learn to control the demon within and become masters of your destiny.

You can also be like a shadow. You can be elusive and unreliable. No one can catch you. As people try to chase the shadow, they realize you are so intangible that they may not ever really know you. You can give shade from the intense sunlight or obscure the light completely. Those who take refuge in the coolness of your shade feel grateful but those who feel obscured by your shadowy presence can feel only fear. You inspire both these emotions in your partners.

Your inner struggles create great challenges in relationships. You have to cope with most of your inner struggles alone. You can feel lonely and isolated. Your partners can only be a loving stand-by, being there for you and supportive. They cannot take your burden away from you.

## Restrictions and Expansion

The first day of Shatabhishak is in the Western sign of Aquarius. Saturn rules Aquarius and Rahu has a similar effect. This double saturnine influence is difficult to handle unless your activities are directed towards service to humanity. Very few people are born in Shatabhishak and Aquarius, here the struggle with the restrictions is immense but the reward can be the opening of the doorway to the cosmic connection and true understanding of your relationship with it.

The rest of Shatabhishak is in the Western sign of Pisces ruled by Jupiter. (Vedic Astrology uses traditional rulerships therefore it does not use Neptune as ruler here.) Jupiter helps and guides through his wisdom. The Shatabhishak Pisces impulse is to expand beyond traditional limits and experience true freedom from the restrictions of life.

# Sexuality – The Female Horse

## The Fussy Lovers

Shatabhishak sexuality is linked to the female horse. In Vedic Astrology female energy is passive. You rarely make the first move to initiate a sexual relationship. You can be nervous and highly-strung. You are usually very fussy about whom you love and set high standards for your sexual partners. You like finesse from your lovers and enjoy love in special surroundings. You need partners who are very sophisticated and cultured.

You can find it difficult to trust others with your sexual desires. You have a strong sex drive but keep it firmly under control. You trust very few with your sexual secrets, not always sure that your partners will be comfortable with your unconventional approach to sex.

## The Best and the Worst Sexual Partners

You find sexual happiness with the male horse Ashwini. Your overall compatibility is not high, showing that sexual compatibility alone is not enough for you. Sex with Ashwini may be fun and adventurous. You rarely try to connect to them in other areas of life, preferring to keep your independence.

The buffaloes Hasta and Swati are never fully sexually confident and therefore they do not project the sexual aura necessary to keep you interested for long. The earthy buffalo does not attract the horse. You are fastidious and will perpetually remind them of their inadequacies. With Hasta you may experiment sexually, but you will hate yourself for giving in to your weakness. You can get on with Swati despite your sexual antagonism. You get along in all areas of life and you are happy to compromise on the sexual one.

# Relationship Issues

## In Denial of Your Emotions

Rahu, as the head part of the celestial snake identifies with the mind and the intellect and forgets to work with the heart and emotions. You usually allow your heart to be encased in steel, not allowing yourself to feel or care. The Shatabhishak soul needs to be free flowing.

Your relationships with other Nakshatras show how some of them have the ability to block your path emotionally while others allow you to go that extra distance. One of your best relationships is with Rohini, a Nakshatra ruled by the Moon. Rohini is about romance, passion and feeling from the heart. Rohini encourage you to overcome your self-imposed barriers and experience happiness beyond your intellectual expectations. Whereas Hasta, another lunar Nakshatra completely blocks you and makes you question the validity of love and happiness. The karmic lessons you learn from Hasta make you wary of emotions and send you back in denial. Both relationships are important for you, even if one of the experiences is uncomfortable, as they force you to break the barriers around your emotions and explore what you think is forbidden.

## Searching for the Soul Mate

Rahu has a celestial soul mate in Ketu. They form two parts of a whole. The Ketu Nakshatras are Ashwini, Magha and Mula. Meeting your soul mate does not guarantee happiness: it means you have a mutual need for it. The love that ties these Nakshatras to you carries with it the karmic memory of many unfinished matters – guilt from the past which has to be dealt with now. Ashwini do not usually allow you to develop a deep relationship with them despite all the sensual ties. Magha and Mula are more readily willing to work at a relationship with you. You must learn to trust and expose your secret desires and passions to them. The Ketu Nakshatras are karmically programmed to reject you. You must look beyond these physical rejections and learn about the invisible bonds that tie you together.

## The Unconventional Approach to Relationships

Shatabhishak are a real contradiction: they can appear to be traditional, yet their relationships need to be unconventional and exciting. In the traditional society of ancient India, this created many difficulties for Shatabhishak. Usually the relationship of their choice and the relationship of tradition were diametrically opposed. In present-day society where we can experience various relationships, these problems are not so common. Your only problem arises when you still feel the obsessive need to not be open about your desires and build a network of secret relationships.

## Loving Shatabhishak

Loving Shatabhishak is not for the faint-hearted. It can be like loving a shadow. They are evasive, difficult to pin down and mysterious. They can also be undependable and capricious. Be prepared to discover some dark secret you knew nothing about. Do not talk about your sexual needs openly or about your mutual relationship: they would usually hate it.

## Compatibility

**Ideal life partners: Dhanishta and Rohini**
**Most challenging life partner: Punarvasu**

**The full Compatibility Grid is on page 338.**

**Shatabhishak and Ashwini:** Sexually great but emotionally indifferent. You can trust Ashwini sexually but never allow them access to your intimate thoughts. You put your emotional barriers up so fast with Ashwini that they do not know where it all went wrong. Past life memories spoil what you have today. Learn to live in the present.
**38% compatible**

**Shatabhishak and Bharani:** Good friends, great sex, but differing spiritual direction can create a feeling of dissatisfaction. You are secretive and Bharani are open. They want a partner who can give them long-term commitment – you shy away from that. Bharani's strong sensuality attracts you but it also makes you afraid of losing control. **53% compatible**

**Shatabhishak and Krittika:** Krittika represent the light to your darkness. You like being close to such light. Krittika appear strong and powerful but they are also shy and do not try to overpower you. In

## SHATABHISHAK

fact you have the ability to influence them more. You open your heart for Krittika. Krittika will lighten your fears and protect your vulnerabilities. **75% compatible**

**Shatabhishak and Rohini:** Why you fall in love with Rohini is one of life's mysteries. They are romantic, emotional, believing in illusions and love – all the things that you usually run away from. With Rohini you enjoy the very things you avoided. The steel around your heart melts and you learn to be in touch with your emotions. Love thrives. **76% compatible**

**Shatabhishak and Mrigasira:** You love the way Mrigasira think and their habit of challenging you to change your thinking helps you to overcome many of your preconceived ideas and fears. They analyse your relationship. You usually hide from any potential problems. By confronting them head on, you learn to deal with them.
**65% compatible**

**Shatabhishak and Ardra:** Two people, both uncomfortable with their emotions, find it hard to establish a love connection. Ardra are the thinkers who forget to feel and you hardly ever acknowledge your emotional nature. If you have similar ambitions, then you can follow them together, but this relationship can remain emotionally barren.
**33% compatible**

**Shatabhishak and Punarvasu:** Your worst relationship. Punarvasu are either too caring or completely unconcerned. They can be irrationally jealous and suspicious or totally apathetic. You are also not too reliable where they are concerned. Missed appointments, differing agendas, and secret lives – all make it difficult for love to survive.
**25% compatible**

**Shatabhishak and Pushya:** Both of you find it difficult to recognize your emotions. Pushya have a very ascetic attitude to life. They have difficulty acting spontaneously and with you this gets exaggerated. You can also be cold, closing your heart to emotions. So you end up in a relationship which can become emotionally bankrupt if you are not careful. **36% compatible**

# THE LOVE SIGNS

**Shatabhishak and Ashlesha:** You are drawn to Ashlesha's unusual personality. They are different somehow. You try to keep your relationship simple but it soon becomes complex. Ashlesha slowly start keeping a part of themselves away from you. You also never let them totally into your heart. Let them into your world and you have a chance. **50% compatible**

**Shatabhishak and Magha:** Magha is ruled by Ketu, the other half of the celestial snake. They are really your soulmate; a partner with whom you stay despite the difficulties you face. You may have different ambitions, ideas, life directions, but Magha truly understand you. You can be yourself and do not need to make difficult promises. **66% compatible**

**Shatabhishak and Purva Phalguni:** Purva Phalguni are fun, amusing, sophisticated and sociable. This relationship is the attraction of opposites, and can only last if you recognize areas of difficulty. You will hate their social engagements, feeling exposed and uncomfortable. They can never understand your spiritual needs, as they are a very materialistic sign. **50% compatible**

**Shatabhishak and Uttara Phalguni:** You are private and naturally secretive and think that Uttara Phalguni do not appreciate your needs. They can carelessly expose your secrets and you will feel vulnerable with them. This usually makes you very fearful and distrustful of Uttara Phalguni. You shy away from developing a relationship.
**37% compatible**

**Shatabhishak and Hasta:** A spiritually complex relationship and your worst sexual partner. Hasta appear sophisticated but you soon discover their self-doubting and unconfident self. Sexually they may appear too earthy and rough for you. In trying to distance yourself from them, you can be extremely critical. You can also make promises which you cannot keep. **27% compatible**

**Shatabhishak and Chitra:** You adore the way Chitra combine their need for love and romance with their feisty and independent nature. In fact you do not realize that they want commitment as well till you are far too involved with them to easily escape. Exciting and sensual, intimate and emotional – this relationship works out very well once you start trusting them. **69% compatible**

**Shatabhishak and Swati:** Yours is an unconventional relationship where sexuality doesn't always work but intimacy does. Swati are your worst sexual partners but both of you transcend this problem to create a wonderful and happy partnership. You have to be extra careful you do not criticise or hurt Swati about the lack of sexual attraction. **61% compatible**

**Shatabhishak and Vishakha:** Vishakha will seduce you before you have had the chance to have any doubts. They are charming, wise and intelligent and you quite like their way of wooing. The more you try to get away from them the more interested they become. You should allow them into your heart: they are wise enough to treat it with love. **70% compatible**

**Shatabhishak and Anuradha:** You learn to like Anuradha's dual personality; cool and controlled on the outside and romantic inside. Anuradha's key role in loving you is to teach you about love and emotion. They can take pain and they do not run away from love just because it causes unhappiness. Remember not to make them false promises. **61% compatible**

**Shatabhishak and Jyeshta:** You know that Jyeshta are not sharing everything with you, but how can they if you do not do so either? You have to understand the complexities of the Jyeshta dilemma. You can certainly be friends and if you accept that, you develop a relationship where you keep your individualities clearly defined. You can find some happiness. **47% compatible**

**Shatabhishak and Mula:** You connect deeply. Mula carry some unresolved past life issues. When you meet them, you realize they are the missing part of your inner puzzle and can make you complete. This does not mean that your relationship is easy. Mula may feel overpowered by your influence and they keep rejecting your love.
**58% compatible**

**Shatabhishak and Purva Ashadha:** You will always like Purva Ashadha and be happy to take their advice. As lovers, they charm you and you easily fall in love. Purva Ashadha accept you and are not too bothered about your secrets and hidden personality. They are very changeable and you can be hurt when they no longer want to be your lover. **64% compatible**

**Shatabhishak and Uttara Ashadha:** You are one of the difficult relationships for Uttara Ashadha. Here your relationship is not necessarily inimical sexually, but jealousy, anger and control can become issues. Be careful not to let negative emotions take root. Learn to trust them. Your relationship is unconventional but can be exciting for both. **63% compatible**

**Shatabhishak and Shravana:** Shravana's special quality is the ability to listen – when they listen intently to your every word you feel flattered and loved. But when they also try to hear what you are saying by your silences, you feel cornered and besieged. You want to be with them but you also want to keep your distance. You cannot have it both ways. **47% compatible**

**Shatabhishak and Dhanishta:** You combat Dhanishta's dominantion with skill and intelligence. You feel excited to be involved with them. They seduce you, make all the effort but they do not want to own every part of your soul. They do not even try to know your secrets. They appear to be secure in their own power and that attracts you strongly. **77% compatible**

**Shatabhishak and Shatabhishak:** Can one Shatabhishak ever trust another? You can be jealous and untrusting, but in extreme situations only. Mostly you feel comfortable in the knowledge that at last someone truly knows and understands you. While you can be negative with others, with a Shatabhishak partner you strive to be positive. **77% compatible**

**Shatabhishak and Purva Bhadra:** Purva Bhadra want to be your lover. They also want to advise you spiritually. You explore, even try intimacy and closeness. But you do not want to open your soul to

# SHATABHISHAK

them just because they ask you. They do not feel totally at ease with you. Your relationship suffers because neither of you tries hard enough to love. **51% compatible**

**Shatabhishak and Uttara Bhadra:** You need Uttara Bhadra's love and support to keep you grounded and realistic. You do not always appreciate yourself; their love makes you feel happy and at peace. You love their philosophical nature and their ability to stay calm in all types of crisis. Remind yourself of their good qualities when you feel bored. **66% compatible**

**Shatabhishak and Revati:** You can be friends with Revati. Do not make them fall in love with you if you are not serious about them. They will trust you and feel very disappointed if you destroy their belief in you. If you are in a relationship, love them and appreciate them and do not try to aggravate their lack of self-confidence. **42% compatible**

# Cusps

Those born at the end or beginning of Shatabhishak, should see pages 382–3.

4 to 17 March

# Purva Bhadra

Ruled by Jupiter
Animal: The Lion
Symbol: The Sword

## Meaning and Symbolism

Purva Bhadra is connected to Uttara Bhadra. While having distinct personalities, they form a singular principle that is split into two opposing forces. Jupiter rules Purva and Saturn rules Uttara. Together they represent the Sun and Moon, darkness and light, fire and water, heat and cold, masculine and feminine, the lion and the cow.

*Purva* means 'first' and *Bhadra* has many meanings: beautiful, auspicious, blessed, gracious and happy. The blessings usually come from good deeds from past lives, which are now being experienced as good luck. In Vedic literature good luck is not connected to financial wealth alone. Good fortune means having good family, excellent relationships, wonderful children and a good life, where knowledge and wisdom guide you to find your true beauty. This is not physical beauty, but the loveliness of a good soul and spiritual inner being. You place a lot of emphasis on the quality of your relationships and are always conscious of doing the right thing by your partners and loved ones.

Your symbol is the sword, an instrument that can be used to attack as well as to defend. The pen has been considered a verbal sword. The sword cuts through any restrictions to further an ideal. The quality of the ideal, whether it is positive or negative, is in the hands of the users. You are very idealistic but your relationships can get neglected when you decide to fight a righteous war. You expect your partners to be supportive, whether they believe in your causes or not.

# The Purva Bhadra Personality

## The Blessings of Jupiter

Purva Bhadra is in the Western sign of Pisces. Jupiter rules both the sign and the Nakshatra. (Vedic Astrology uses traditional rulerships therefore it does not use Neptune as ruler here.) Jupiter is the auspicious planet in Vedic Astrology. Jupiter is known as Brihaspati in Sanskrit. Brihaspati is the teacher of the gods in the Vedas.

Jupiter stands for expansion, happiness and higher knowledge. Jupiter represents the positive fruits of past karma, which bring forth conditions in this life of affluence, comfort and happiness. Jupiter's main concern is to give you a good material life so that you can concentrate on the essential spiritual development.

Pisces is the stage of merging individual consciousness with the universal one, where you forget your personal needs to fulfil your responsibility to the universe. You are generous and usually lucky in your relationships. You live life without worrying about what you will get in return; hence success or failure do not bother you. Unscrupulous partners can take advantage of your idealism and good nature. You tend to see only good in others so fail to recognize the negative qualities of your partners.

# Sexuality – The Lion

## The Arrogant Lovers

The Purva Bhadra animal sign is the lion. Lions live in wild open places and are masters of all they survey. They dominate the animal kingdom, are proud and beautiful.

You can be arrogant; you feel you only have to show an interest in a member of the opposite sex and you will get them. This can be true. You have a strong and insatiable sexual appetite. You like lots of sex and once satiated you may not look for another sexual encounter till you are ready for it.

You are not possessive. If you are not willing to commit you do not expect commitment from your partners. You fight for your partners if you are interested in them. But if you find that they are trying to manipulate you, you will first see off your competition and then drop your partners.

## The Best and the Worst Sexual Partners

The lionesses, Dhanishta, are your best sexual partners. Exciting and sensual, you find happiness together.

You are sexually incompatible with the elephant Nakshatras, Bharani and Revati. Elephants and lions are powerful in the animal kingdom and naturally inimical. Both of you jealously guard your terrain and will not allow the other to dictate what you can or can't do. You can learn to live with your enemy. In the wild, lions and elephants live together apparently in harmony. Lions rarely enter the elephants' territory and the elephant does not go into the lion's den. A relationship with clearly demarcated areas of operation and power can work. Surprisingly, you get along well with both Bharani and Revati, showing the ability to overcome sexual enmity through diplomacy and careful sharing of power.

## Relationship Issues

### The Urge to Advise

You love to give advice. The double influence of Jupiter in both your Western star sign and Nakshatra makes you ready to help out with time, money and ideas. Your friends, relatives and acquaintances can draw out energy from you with their constant demands and need for support. You do not mind as you feel that advising and helping people is part of your spiritual destiny.

If you are not careful, you can feel extremely depleted with nothing left over to give to your relationships. Your partners can feel left out by the constant demands of others. Also be sure to establish intimate love relationships and not ones where you are forever in the role of the adviser.

### Complex Love Lessons from Mercury Nakshatras

Ashlesha, Jyeshta and Revati are the Mercury Nakshatras. They have the ability to force you to face reality. The worst lesson comes from Jyeshta. The Jyeshta's animal sign is the deer. In the wild, the lion is perpetually trying to catch the deer and they seldom succeed. In life Jyeshta can arouse wild desires in you. Their mercurial quality can make them transform themselves into the type of person you desire, thus creating an illusion. You can easily get obsessed by Jyeshta – loving them, desiring them but unable to really make them your own. Ashlesha will entice you into their world but again what you expect them to be and what the reality is are two different things. Here there is not deliberate manipulation by any of the Nakshatras but a karmic situation that makes the relationships develop in a strange fashion. Revati, the final Mercury Nakshatra, has a good relationship with you except when it comes to sexuality. You have to compromise. The great compatibility between you two means that you usually do find common ground and can live a life of comparative harmony while occasionally pining for sexual highs.

## Cool and Majestic

Yours is the royal sign of the Nakshatra system, powerful and strong. You draw an invisible line between you and your relationships, both intimate and impersonal. When royalty go on a walkabout and meet with their public, they may be charming, warm and friendly, but they know that they belong to a different world and there can never be any real closeness. This can also be your attitude – a feeling of detachment and separation.

Does this create problems for you or can you have good relationships? You are usually detached from family life, if not physically, then mentally. Your partners have full control of how your relationship is run. You tend to make occasional forays into the real world and make your presence felt. You need a partner who can understand your coolness and is not intimidated by your majesty. Your ability to have happy and normal relationships depends on your choice of partner. They have a vital part to play in your life and will wield great influence over your happiness. Choose wisely.

## The Romantic Dreamers

You love to be in love. You are seeking a relationship that will complete you, but usually your expectations are so unrealistic that people find it difficult to live up to them. You have the ability to see the world through rose-tinted glasses, usually only seeing the positive in any relationship. Your generousity, your positive attitude to love and your willingness to make even the most difficult relationship work makes you a good partner. You are usually lucky in love; your ability to see the best in others encourages them to be like that too.

You have to be wary of making the wrong choices. You can be disappointed or feel cheated when partners do not live up to your rosy picture of them. People can try to be what they are not in order to woo you and it can take a long time for you to see the truth.

## Loving Purva Bhadra

Loving them can be a huge responsibility. Purva Bhadra needs a strong and independent partner willing to shoulder the entire burden of your relationship. Also they expect you to love them and love their cause. They do not make an effort for you and can be selfish sensuously. Once they are sexually fulfilled, they can ignore you. If you let them be, they are back whenever they are ready. If you deal with their arrogance and sensual laziness, their generosity and warmth reward you.

## Compatibility

**Ideal life partner: Uttara Bhadra**
**Most challenging life partner: Jyeshta**

The full Compatibility Grid is on page 338.

**Purva Bhadra and Ashwini:** Both of you can be selfish and independent – no one is there to be at home to make it cosy and comfortable. It is better to introduce them to your dominant side early on or Ashwini will think you are a dreamer and pliable to their every wish. They can be unpleasantly surprised when they meet the roaring lion.
**42% compatible**

**Purva Bhadra and Bharani:** The lion and the elephant: who will be the king of the jungle? Bharani are your worst sexual partner but tend to be compatible in other areas. Allow them to be strong while retaining your own power. Respect them and they will reciprocate. In other areas of life also establish a democracy, not dictatorship.
**62% compatible**

**Purva Bhadra and Krittika:** Krittika are shy and quiet, being unable to express their need for love. You will naturally like Krittika, you can even advise them how to make the most of their life. But moving from adviser to lover is the difficult step. Your relationship can be good but suffers from selfishness and the inability to talk about love. **54% compatible**

**Purva Bhadra and Rohini:** You click with the romantic Rohini, you love the way they make you feel special and focus their entire emotional attention on you. Their possessiveness can make you feel claustrophobic. You should warn them that if they impose too many conditions, you might leave. Remember to love Rohini; they will compromise on the rest. **60% compatible**

**Purva Bhadra and Mrigasira:** Mrigasira look up to you, ask your advice, look upon you as a friend and a mentor. They will also love you passionately and completely. You know your relationship is in good hands. If you need their support for any of your causes, they will give their unquestioning support, emotionally and intellectually. **69% compatible**

**Purva Bhadra and Ardra:** You find them intellectually stimulating and you enjoy their company. But Ardra can hide part of the truth. As long as you remain unaware, your Ardra lover can do no wrong. But once you get to know, you find it hard to forgive and can be detached and cool. You can treat your Ardra lover casually. Watch out for negativity. **48% compatible**

**Purva Bhadra and Punarvasu:** Punarvasu are always on the move, never in one place to appreciate what you have together. They share your temperament but not much else. They usually are unable to take charge of your relationship and you do not bother as well. So this makes for a good affair. In the long-term this relationship can die of neglect. **41% compatible**

**Purva Bhadra and Pushya:** They will cosset, love and care for you. They will work hard to make the relationship a happy one, establish a happy home life for you to saunter in whenever you choose to. They will not ask too many questions. When you want their support they will be there for you. In this relationship, you are the taker and Pushya the giver. **60% compatible**

## PURVA BHADRA

**Purva Bhadra and Ashlesha:** You find Ashlesha sexy, vibrant and stimulating. You fall for them and feel you are finding a beautiful soul there. But they remain inwardly detached even if they pretend to be exploring the mystery of your attractions together. You feel extremely let down once you realize the pretence. Ashlesha can hurt you. **39% compatible**

**Purva Bhadra and Magha:** Magha is connected to the royal star Regulus. You can idolize Magha too much. You are sure to be disappointed as Magha, despite their grand presence, are the rat, the smallest animal in the Nakshatras. They cannot stand against the might of the lion. Magha appear grand and powerful, but the real power rests with you. **47% compatible**

**Purva Bhadra and Purva Phalguni:** Purva Phalguni are creative, interesting and sophisticated. They enjoy life but they are also committed to having a home and family, something you desire. They are happy to take charge of the domestic affairs and do so magnificently. You will invest a lot of energy in caring for them in return.
**64% compatible**

**Purva Bhadra and Uttara Phalguni:** You are drawn to the warmth of Uttara Phalguni, but when you get to know them better you find them stubborn and inflexible. They can become very dissatisfied, being pessimistic about the prospects for your relationship. They can also try to be too controlling. When you show your power, the problems really begin. **39% compatible**

**Purva Bhadra and Hasta:** You fall for the image they present and you feel quite let down when you find the reality different from your expectations. Hasta try very hard to please you but once you decide that they are not up to your standard, you don't wait around. Hasta will keep on investing in the relationship. Give them another chance. **38% compatible**

**Purva Bhadra and Chitra:** Mars and Jupiter, the Nakshatra rulers, are good friends, but it is not enough. Chitra want excitement and fun all the time whereas you may want quiet periods as well. They do not bother about the daily grind of domesticity. You can feel unloved and unappreciated by them. A good love affair but not always for the long term. **45% compatible**

**Purva Bhadra and Swati:** You are not always sure of Swati but they make lots of effort to woo you and make you happy. They are great at managing your relationship. They will stand up to you when you know you are being unfair. But they are supportive of your causes, giving you lots of ideas on how to fight them. Be appreciative often.
**60% compatible**

**Purva Bhadra and Vishakha:** Vishakha seduce you successfully; you find them potent and exciting. Their restlessness makes you unsettled. You step back. Both of you appear to need your independence too much and love suffers as a result. Learn to spend quality time together and use your Jupitarian wisdom to resolve your differences.
**49% compatible**

**Purva Bhadra and Anuradha:** Workaholic and practical Anuradha are surprisingly romantic at heart. You love these contradictions. When they make you the focus of their love, you know you have their full attention. You love them back as well. They are supportive and understanding. Remember to appreciate them and their love.
**66% compatible**

**Purva Bhadra and Jyeshta:** Your worst relationship. Tread carefully. You are too charmed by the illusion of Jyeshta. They appear to love you, become very serious and then they suddenly dump you. You can feel very hurt, enraged and destructive when you meet the real Jyeshta. You may not like your behaviour afterwards but you just cannot help it. **26% compatible**

**Purva Bhadra and Mula:** Purva Bhadra's ruler Jupiter is the guru or teacher, while Mula's ruler Ketu has collective wisdom from past life. Mula Sagittarius is able to get along with you better than Mula Capricorn. They can reject whatever you have to offer. You usually withdraw, unsure how to deal with them. Learn to be more tolerant of your differences. **41% compatible**

## PURVA BHADRA

**Purva Bhadra and Purva Ashadha:** You can be detached with others, but with Purva Ashadha you make a special effort to make them love you. They represent so much of what you want in a partner that you tolerate their careless attitude. You support them through their difficult times. They start to love you back and make you feel special. **66% compatible**

**Purva Bhadra and Uttara Ashadha:** You can see how troubled they are by their inability to love properly. While you do not always try very hard with relationships, with your friend Uttara Ashadha you make a special effort to love them and make them feel secure, and slowly they warm towards you. They love you, are loyal to you and support you. **66% compatible**

**Purva Bhadra and Shravana:** A relationship between the emotional and the idealist. You want to fulfil the dreams of Shravana ande them feel secure so that they can love you properly. You recognize their emotional struggles and endeavour to support them. Your philosophies on love coincide. You don't even mind their possessiveness. **66% compatible**

**Purva Bhadra and Dhanishta:** Dhanishta are your ideal sexual partner. They believe in equality and if you try to impose your superiority, they will not tolerate it. This is the war of the sexes as old as time itself, it does not matter which Nakshatra is male or female. Usually Dhanishta can control your relationship; they let you think you are in charge. **58% compatible**

**Purva Bhadra and Shatabhishak:** You can never trust Shatabhishak fully. Even when you try to be positive, your instinct advises caution. You remain detached, exploring a relationship with them without making a commitment. You may enjoy a dalliance, but a long-term relationship only works if they pay more attention and open up emotionally. **51% compatible**

**Purva Bhadra and Purva Bhadra:** You are very similar, both dreamers and idealists. If both of you want to be king, who is going to do the mundane work? Also be careful with your finances: you are both unwise investors and extravagant spenders. Your understanding of each other usually keeps you together and generally happy. **60% compatible**

**Purva Bhadra and Uttara Bhadra:** You are idealistic, Uttara Bhadra are practical. They keep this relationship strong and thriving. They will love you sensibly. As with the other Saturn Nakshatras, the scales are weighed slightly in your favour. Uttara Bhadra doesn't complain so why should you. This is a specially blessed relationship. Be happy. **76% compatible**

**Purva Bhadra and Revati:** Revati is your worst sexual partner but with good overall compatibility. You can establish a satisfactory relationship with them because you believe in dividing responsibilities. Revati are in charge of the relationship and you bow to their demands there. Revati know how to use charm on you. Sexually you compromise. **68% compatible**

# Cusps

Those born at the end or beginning of Purva Bhadra, should see pages 383-5.

17 to 31 March

# Uttara Bhadra

Ruled by Saturn
Animal: The Cow
Symbol: The Twins

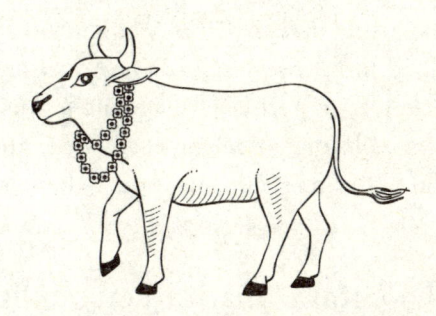

## Meaning and Symbolism

Uttara Bhadra is an extension of the previous Nakshatra, Purva Bhadra. While having distinct personalities, they form a singular principle that is split into two opposing forces. Jupiter rules Purva and Saturn rules Uttara; together they represent Sun and Moon, light and darkness, fire and water, heat and cold, masculine and feminine, the lion and the cow. While Jupiter bestows wisdom in Purva Bhadra, Saturn rewards all of life's trials and tribulations in Uttara Bhadra.

*Uttara* means 'higher' and *Bhadra* has many meanings: beautiful, auspicious, blessed, gracious and happy. All aspects highlight positive qualities that Uttara Bhadra are blessed with. The blessings usually come from good deeds in past lives, which are now being experienced as good luck. You understand about your blessings on a higher, a more subtle plane. Your soul wants more than just the ordinary. You can remain passive and non-active, till an event or happening makes you change your perception of life altogether. You begin looking beyond your immediate consciousness and this allows you to grow spiritually. Your need to transcend ordinary life makes it difficult for you to have traditional relationships. You need partners who understand the essence of your spirit. This is why you can have either superb relationships or face real difficulty from love.

Your symbol is that of the Twin. You represent duality in every form. You are one of the Bhadras, you have found inner light so you must experience the darkness, you are sattvic (pure) therefore you also understand tamas (darkness, impurity), you are ascetic and sensuous, you want to shun relationships yet you also know how to relate properly. These polarities that are Uttara Phalguni make you extremely complex and full of intuitive energies. Your dual nature makes you hard to fathom and your partners never know which part of your personality you are reflecting. You can easily lose interest in relationships but your real test is in learning to cope with them successfully.

## The Uttara Bhadra Personality

### The Blessings of Saturn

Saturn rules Uttara Bhadra. Saturn is the great teacher of cosmic truths. His influence is tough to deal with. Uttara Bhadra has the blessing to use the lessons of Saturn in the best possible way.

Saturn is the planet of karmic retribution. It keeps an account of all the past acts and releases this karma unexpectedly. Faced with such powerful karmic forces you have to dig deep into your inner resources. In childhood, teens and young adulthood, this causes misery and frustration as Saturn restricts your natural energy from expanding. With maturity you learn to use the Saturn forces properly, you start on the path towards self-realization.

Saturn is a Brahmachari – a bachelor at heart – therefore you prefer a solitary life. Relationships do not come easy. You may fear relationships or be cold towards your partners without realizing it. Childhood experiences usually make you hold back from freely expressing love.

# UTTARA BHADRA

## The End and the New Beginnings

Uttara Bhadra spans the Western signs of Pisces (17 to 20 March) and Aries (21 to 31 March). Jupiter and Mars are the rulers. Pisces is the end of the spiritual journey and Aries the beginning. Uttara Bhadra has the capability to transcend consciousness. Saturn who rules Uttara Bhadra gives you the durability and patience, Jupiter the wisdom to face adversity philosophically and Mars brings courage. These three powerful forces complete the spiritual journey that ties the beginning to the end, completing the cycle. You can forever be ending relationship or starting new ones. Your main aim should be in starting over within existing relationships, allowing them to evolve with time so that you rise above the problems and issues that restrict your growth. New seeds of love can be sown even in the most difficult partnerships.

## Sexuality – The Cow

### Sacred Sexuality

Uttara Bhadra's animal sign is the cow. The cow is sacred in India and the sexual act was traditionally considered a sacred expression of love for your partner, fulfilled through committed relationships. This sacred aspect of sexuality is seen as anachronistic in today's world, where sexual desire is used freely to satisfy us. The rewards of sacred sexuality are profound: peace, happiness, sublime love and complete fulfilment of passions.

You seek a partner who can fulfil this aspect of your sexual need. You seem out of place in the modern world of free and easy sex. You experiment with sex but you feel a misfit. You do not care whether you are sexually active or not. You want love, relationships and sex like the rest of us, but you would also like to have commitment and one partner for life if that is possible.

You do not base your relationships purely on sexuality. Therefore with other Nakshatras, such as Uttara Ashadha who have complex sexual issues, you form wonderful relationships. Like the *Kamdhenu*, a special holy cow that had the ability to fulfil all desires, you try to fulfil others' desires, however difficult and impossible they may be. If someone is in need, you will try to help. People can take advantage of your giving nature, but you do not usually care as this forms an important part of how your soul expresses itself.

## The Best and the Worst Sexual Partners

You connect well with the bull, Uttara Phalguni. Both of you view your sexual relationship as sacred and will honour the other with your loyalty and commitment. Love will be deep and spiritual.

Your worst sexual partners are the tigers, Chitra and Vishakha. In the wild, tigers kill cows and are not in awe of their strength. In life, Chitra and Vishakha will try to control you by showing their power and making you feel inadequate. They seek excitement from sex and you seek divinity. Their lack of commitment and their philandering nature makes it a painful partnership for you. Chitra are sexually demanding and adventurous. Vishakha are easier to deal with. They may try to value you more but their lack of commitment can be hurtful.

# Relationship Issues

## Detached

You have a strong sense of detachment – if your relationship does not prosper you will move on or live alone. You can face impossible emotional situations and are forever trying to work out difficult relationships. You are a loner and therefore there will always be a part that you withhold from those who love you. If you find your spiritual direction, you are likely to give up on love and personal relationships.

## The Pain of Loving the Elephant, the Tigress and the Lioness Nakshatras

The male elephant Bharani, the tigress Chitra and lioness Dhanishta are the worst relationships for Uttara Bhadra. Mars rules Chitra and Dhanishta. Mars's impulsive nature is totally at odds with the studied patience of Saturn. Venus rules Bharani. Saturn and Venus are good friends but in the Uttara Bhadra and Bharani relationship it appears that good friends becoming intimate brings out all your weaknesses and encourages you in the wrong directions.

The real key to understanding the pain of these relationships is to look at the animal signs. Uttara Bhadra is the cow and in the wild both the tigress and the lioness hunt the cow and love its meat. In life, the fear and the dominance of Chitra and Dhanishta spoil the relationship. They can completely take over your life and create a one-way street in this relationship. For any relationship to work there has to be give and take. The elephant and the cow relationship between Bharani and you, shows no mutual understanding. You tend to have different agendas. Both of you are dominant in your own way and can be either aggressive or cold towards each other – there is no middle way.

## The Hidden Sensualist

You love the good things in life – luxury food, fine wines, beautiful clothes, long sensual lovemaking, etc. But you keep this firmly under control. You feel if you allow your sensual nature to express itself, you can become dull and lazy and lose your spiritual edge.

You can put on weight by bingeing. You usually hide your sensuality from the world, being secretly self-indulgent. Your partners may be delighted to be introduced to your sensuality but they find it hard to deal with your need to suppress it and the guilt you may feel about it.

# THE LOVE SIGNS

## Loving Uttara Bhadra

Uttara Bhadra feel only they can truly love, so loving them will be not so easy. They hardly ever acknowledge their own need to be loved in return. You first need to seduce them slowly and make them comfortable about being loved. Also let them know of your own needs: this usually makes them caring. You can feel overwhelmed by their love.

## Compatibility

**Ideal life partner: Revati**
**Most challenging life partners: Bharani, Chitra and Dhanishta**

The full Compatibility Grid is on page 338.

**Uttara Bhadra and Ashwini:** You fall for the unconventional Ashwini but you can spoil it by making conventional demands. Your expectations of Ashwini are not what they are happy to fulfil. Don't be shy to expose your sensuality to them. They will love it. They are also hiding their spiritual self. Revealing these hidden facets can create a strong bond. **64% compatible**

**Uttara Bhadra and Bharani:** Your most difficult relationship. Bharani's life appears to be dedicated to sensuality and you do not want to go down that path. Bharani can be as stubborn as you, creating situatioins where neither of you give way. They can also be takers and will be happy as long as you are the giver. This one-sided relationship can be painful and unhappy. **11% compatible**

**Uttara Bhadra and Krittika:** You struggle to come to terms with your feelings for Krittika. You want them to love you but you always feel that they reject you. Give them a fair chance. You think of their efforts at being warm and friendly as trying to overpower you or oppress you. Learn to accept their love and not back off from it.
**50% compatible**

# UTTARA BHADRA

**Uttara Bhadra and Rohini:** You will love the exotic and wonderful Rohini, their emotionalism and their ability to make you the focus of their love. You are happy to be supportive and loving. Nothing is too much for your Rohini lover. They teach you to be comfortable with your sensuality. You love the way they sparkle in your company.
**75% compatible**

**Uttara Bhadra and Mrigasira:** You find Mrigasira too critical, always questioning everything. You want them to look beyond the small issues of your relationship. They want you to stop glossing over the immediate problems. Try to see Mrigasira's point of view and don't ignore their need for excitement or they may seek it elsewhere.
**49% compatible**

**Uttara Bhadra and Ardra:** Ardra are intelligent, unusual and creative; you love all their qualities. You understand their restlessness, learn to trust their intuitiveness and help them come to terms with their dissatisfactions. Ardra love you back with total faith. You need to let them know that fidelity is important to you and they are usually happy to please. **72% compatible**

**Uttara Bhadra and Punarvasu:** Punarvasu are not always able to give you the total commitment you desire, but you are usually willing to compromise. They can be your great friends. You value their advice and you love their bright and spiritual minds. You are happy to be supportive and Punarvasu make you feel loved and wanted.
**70% compatible**

**Uttara Bhadra and Pushya:** You are both ruled by Saturn whose actions restricts individual growth to a slow and steady pace and does not allow relationships to flourish. Both of you know all about duty and responsibility, but not a lot about love and tenderness. You are restrained by Saturn on some level and may be too self-reliant to enjoy a close relationship. You may forget to love. **50% compatible**

**Uttara Bhadra and Ashlesha:** You get enthralled by Ashlesha, mesmerized by their magnetism. But you do not always know how to deal with them. They give you mixed signals, being either greatly loving or totally detached. You can love them too much. While they lap up your love, they are not always able to love you in return in the way you like. **55% compatible**

**Uttara Bhadra and Magha:** Your different attitudes to sexuality play an important part in whether you find happiness and contentment with each other. While Magha want lots of sex, you regard it as a sacred expression of your love. Magha may spoil it all for you by rejecting you sensually, thinking you to be frigid and cool. Let them know your views. **50% compatible**

**Uttara Bhadra and Purva Phalguni:** You can enjoy a great friendship, even a short affair, but when the relationship becomes serious you start finding fault. Fun-loving Purva Phalguni do not always understand your spiritual needs but neither do you understand their need to enjoy life. To sustain your love, you need to compromise.
**44% compatible**

**Uttara Bhadra and Uttara Phalguni:** Your best sexual relationship but also a spiritually complex one. You appear highly compatible, but on a psychological level this partnership can cause sorrow and unhappiness by your inability to appreciate each other. Forget about responsibility and duty and concentrate on love and happiness.
**75% compatible**

**Uttara Bhadra and Hasta:** You love Hasta's sophisticated persona but you also recognize their insecurities. At first they appear to shun all your efforts to support them. Your patience wins out; they warm to you and lean on you for love and support. You learn to express your emotions to Hasta. Together you can create a special bond.
**72% compatible**

**Uttara Bhadra and Chitra:** Your worst sexual relationship, which is aggravated by very poor compatibility. Chitra can fascinate you. They can be beautiful but also merciless where you are concerned. They can take, take and take but when it is their turn they cannot give anything back. They can be cruel and reject everything you stand for.
**18% compatible**

## UTTARA BHADRA

**Uttara Bhadra and Swati:** Swati will look to you for support and love when they are working on a new project but can become uninterested and elusive when they do not need you. You love them, and some love and appreciation in return would not go amiss. Swati usually make you feel that you are blocking their ambitions whereas the opposite is true. **53% compatible**

**Uttara Bhadra and Vishakha:** Your worst sexual relationship. Whereas lack of sexual compatibility does not bother you, you mustn't forget that it bothers the highly sexed Vishakha. They will feel hemmed in by your ascetic views on sex. Allow your spiritual relationship to develop and encourage them to change the emphasis of your relationship. **41% compatible**

**Uttara Bhadra and Anuradha:** You are both realistic, practical and hardworking. This can make you detached and impersonal at times. You care for Anuradha, so try to be supportive. You do not always understand their romanticism but will bear this burden stoically. Even so, you are not always able to talk romantic nonsense to them. **47% compatible**

**Uttara Bhadra and Jyeshta:** Jyeshta's intellect stimulates you and their angst touches you. But you are usually wise enough to understand that it is their personal journey. You support and love them. They can charm you into doing anything for them. But they can also be deceptive and try to play games with you; a part of their nature you do not like. **55% compatible**

**Uttara Bhadra and Mula:** You love the spirituality of Mula and the way they deal with their challenges. You are willing to be their root. Mula love you back but can never give you their all. You understand their pain and their dilemmas at times better than they do themselves. Mula can hurt you by rejecting you but they also know you are just the partner they need. **66% compatible**

**Uttara Bhadra and Purva Ashadha:** Loving Purva Ashadha is hard for you, as you never know what to expect. You need to have a philosophical attitude to them and lots of tolerance. You develop an easy relationship: you love their creativity and you are not fazed by their sudden changes of direction. You try to keep their feet on the ground. **61% compatible**

**Uttara Bhadra and Uttara Ashadha:** Uttara Ashadha are so grateful for your love and unconditional support that they want to fulfil all your desires. You appreciate their emotional control but also understand their angst. You are never happier than when you are caring for them. For all their complexities, they have the capacity to love you very deeply. **83% compatible**

**Uttara Bhadra and Shravana:** Shravana instinctively understand your needs – something few others are able to do. They care for you and love you. Their emotional neediness makes you feel wanted. You help them find balance and equilibrium. Shravana make you feel comfortable with your emotions. You express your love to them without hesitation. **80% compatible**

**Uttara Bhadra and Dhanishta:** In nature, the lioness eats the cow. In life, the lioness Dhanishta will always be a dominating presence for you. You are naturally giving. But Dhanishta can hurt you, always trying to undermine your generosity. You are unnecessarily appeasing. Do not allow them to ride roughshod over your emotions.
**17% compatible**

**Uttara Bhadra and Shatabhishak:** If you want to keep your Shatabhishak partner in love, you need to pay attention to your style, the way you dress and general sensuality. These are important to them and can create problems. They do love you. Your relationship works well so maybe you should make this extra effort for them.
**66% compatible**

**Uttara Bhadra and Purva Bhadra** You are cosmic twins: both very different, yet you express the other's unspoken needs. You love Purva Bhadra's idealism and adore the way they encourage you to open up and be more adventurous. You are happy to be supportive; you do not expect anything in return for your efforts. You feel life has rewarded you with their love. **76% compatible**

# UTTARA BHADRA

**Uttara Bhadra and Uttara Bhadra:** Both of you are dutiful and hardworking. You can form a spiritually powerful relationship. You must not forget to have fun and enjoy life. Both of you find it hard to express your emotions. Remember to talk about love and take time out from caring for the world to care for each other. **77% compatible**

**Uttara Bhadra and Revati:** Revati love you unconditionally. They understand your spiritual complexities and introduce you to spiritual love. You overcome your fears and embrace this special feeling. You make your relationship sacred. When faced with difficulties, you are strong together and your love deepens and flourishes with time. **91% compatible**

## Cusps

Those born at the end or beginning of Uttara Bhadra, should see pages 385–6.

31 March to 13 April

# Revati

Ruled by Mercury
Animal: The Female Elephant
Symbol: The Fish

## Meaning and Symbolism

Revati means 'abundant' or 'wealthy'. Revati's wealth is connected to spiritual wealth. In India, crops are usually harvested at the time when the Sun transits the Revati Nakshatra and seeds are sown for the next harvest.

Being the last Nakshatra of the Zodiac, Revati has the power to realize the ultimate truths about life, love, relationships, transformation, change and death. The planet Venus is exalted in the last part of Revati. As Venus always orbits close to the Sun, this indicates a strong Venus in your chart. Venus symbolizes sex and procreation and Venus being at its most powerful here means that this Nakshatra is not all about endings, there is a strong element of future growth. You plan for a future which is different from the one you live in today. Revati should think of all their actions as seeds for harvesting at a later date. This does not mean in a different lifetime but even in this lifetime. This is especially true for relationships and love; you can decide to take positive action now and see the reward almost immediately.

# REVATI

Revati's symbol is the fish. Fish can only live in water. Water here symbolizes spirituality. You need to be totally involved in spiritual goals. Even your relationships have to be secondary to your spiritual quest.

## The Revati Personality

### Analysing Relationships

Mercury rules Revati. According to the Vedic myths, Mercury is the son of the Moon. The Moon is the subconscious mind and Mercury is the rational, practical conscious mind but it is still only a fragment of total consciousness. What Mercury perceives as reality, is only a small part of the ultimate reality. Mercury Nakshatras rule the ending cycles of the Nakshatras, where the change of individual consciousness takes place through understanding and going beyond the limitations of intellect. Revati ends a major cycle of life where the consciousness meets the intellect to form new realities for the future.

You like to analyse every aspect of your relationships so that you can judge their merits and demerits. The standards you set are very high and your analytical skills are used in defining and achieving perfection. This creates problems as you can refuse relationships because your analysis tells you that they are not good enough. As soon as you stop analysing and start enjoying the state of being in love and accepting the relationships for what they are, you start changing your sense of perception. Love and emotions can never be quantified. The sooner you accept it, the quicker you can move towards happiness and true love.

One of the qualities of Revati is that although you spend a lot of time analysing all aspects of love and relationships, when you fall in love, you lose all sense of perspective and allow your fantasy to cloud your judgement.

## The Courage of Mars

Revati is entirely in the Western sign of Aries. Aries is where the seed is sown for future harvest. What this seed grows into, no one knows. Mars gives you the courage and fortitude to go into this new dimension. Aries and Mars have the ability to sacrifice themselves so that others can live; this impulse is at its strongest at Revati. As a warrior fights the enemy so that others can live safely, the Mars–Mercury combination gives you both the intellectual and physical strength to go into the unknown, to make extreme sacrifices to gestate the seed for future growth. In relationships you may sacrifice your love for the security of your partner.

# Sexuality – The Female Elephant

## Sacred Sexuality

Like Uttara Bhadra, you are seeking a relationship that is sacred. Uttara Bhadra is also your best relationship, scoring 91% compatibility. The main connection between these two Nakshatras is that you are no longer looking to the past life but hoping to create something beautiful and abundant for future generations to enjoy. Therefore just sexual enjoyment or sexual contact is not enough. Uttara Bhadra's sexuality is linked to the sacred cow and yours is linked to the elephant or Ganesha – the most sacred Hindu god. Ganesha combines the elephant head with a human body. At Revati's state of consciousness, the body of the present life is soon to meet a new head and a new life. You want to create a new order or a new generation for tomorrow, therefore your sexuality is sacred and not to be misused. According to the Vedas, sexual power should be conserved. Only then does it become *Ojas*, an inner radiance that glows from those who are at peace.

You have a strong and healthy sexual appetite. Your animal sign is female which suggests passivity. You will rarely go out seeking a partner and can be very puritanical in your sexual habits. You mature late sexually but you also remain sexually active till a late age. You are disinterested in sex just for the sake of it.

## The Best and the Worst Sexual Partners

The female elephant Revati is passionate towards the male elephant Bharani. You can fall madly in lust with Bharani. But this can also make you feel guilty about such strong sensual feelings. You are compatible in other areas with Bharani, so you can have a good relationship.

The lion Nakshatras Dhanishta and Purva Bhadra are your worst sexual partners. Dhanishta and Purva Bhadra will try to dominate you. While you may appear soft and spiritual, you can also be strong and stubborn. You do not take easily to bullying. Mostly you play out your enmity through sexual power play. The lion and the elephant live peacefully in the jungle, each respecting the other. Maybe you should try that.

# Relationship Issues

## The Supreme Idealist

You are idealistic and you look for the good in everyone. Such purity and belief in truth can make you see others in your own reflection, giving you an idealised picture of the world. This can create unhappiness as your relationships hardly ever live up to your high expectations. You should consider being more realistic and less sentimental in your choices. You tend to put your partners on a pedestal. They are not always able to live up to your rosy image of them. You should try to see the faults as well as good qualities and be more critical in your evaluations.

## Self-Realization through Love

Moksha, or the need for self-realization, becomes intense for you and you learn to let go of your ego. This usually creates low self-esteem, as you do not rate yourself as an individual. You only feel worthy when you are involved with someone special. You seek intense relationships that help you to reach spiritual heights. But not all your partners are able to offer that. You may feel disappointed by life, by the lack of truth and morals especially in your partners. You connect to Sattva, the inner quality that promotes purity of thought, purpose and feeling. You mustn't allow this disappointment to change you – what you have is so beautiful and sacred. You should live your life and set your standards of idealism and purity without trying to influence your partners. Also do not reject what they offer you. Your Sattva will inevitably affect them and you will find their behaviour changes.

## The Aptitude for Complicated Relationships

You can get involved in complicated relationships. This stems from your lack of confidence in your abilities. You can allow yourself to be persuaded into relationships that are complex and unworthy.

You do not value yourself and therefore you overcompensate and love too much. Your partners can take advantage of your love. You stay in difficult relationships because you feel they are all you deserve. You can become unnecessarily jealous and lack trust in your ability to attract. You have to learn to trust more and not let your jealousies spoil relationships for you.

In extreme cases, you can change partners in your perpetual search for love. But you can fail to recognize true love when you find it. You must guard against your tendency to lose interest in your partners very quickly, forgetting to love them and care for them. If you want perfect love, as you profess to, you must make an effort to seek this in your present partner rather than perpetually chase an illusion.

## Loving Revati

When was the last time you appreciated or thanked your Revati lover? You can get so used to your Revati being there for you, loving you and caring for you that you forget to appreciate them. Revati can love you quietly. You do not realize their impact till they have moved on. It is like living in paradise, after some time you stop looking at the beauty of the surroundings, taking the stunning attractions of the place for granted, looking yet not seeing. It can take an outsider to appreciate their beauty and they can get taken away from you. So loving Revati means you need to appreciate them unless you want to lose them.

## Compatibility

**Ideal life partner: Uttara Bhadra**
**Most challenging life partner: Vishakha**

**The full Compatibility Grid is on page 338.**

**Revati and Ashwini:** Ashwini are fiery and passionate and special to you. You can love them too much. They are not into commitment and can treat you in a cavalier fashion. You find them sexy and exciting and usually accept whatever type of relationship they want. Ashwini usually treat you well as you bring out their protective instincts. **72% compatible**

**Revati and Bharani:** Bharani sensuality fascinates you but you can also feel unsure about using your sexuality the way they do. They are involved more in the material world and you in the spiritual. By following your separate paths in the right manner, you fulfil something important. Love them without guilt and they will respect your spirituality. **69% compatible**

**Revati and Krittika:** Krittika feel warm and friendly towards everyone, but cannot express it. They may keep you at arm's length. They expect you to make all the effort. You can be jealous of their many friends. You cannot always deal with the Krittika inability to talk about love. If you want to analyse your partnership, they do not want to know. **32% compatible**

**Revati and Rohini:** Idealistic Revati and Romantic Rohini – both of you are looking for something that is rare in this materialistic world. But you tend to weave your fantasies around Rohini and they are not able to live up to them. You may need a more realistic partner than Rohini; you can get too carried away by love. Reality can disappoint. **53% compatible**

**Revati and Mrigasira:** An attraction of opposites. Your idealism touches some deep emotion in the intellectual Mrigasira. You feel energized by their courage and mental strength. They love to analyse your relationship and together you find ways to improve its quality. You agree to disagree on fundamentals and that is why it works so beautifully. **74% compatible**

**Revati and Ardra:** Ardra are unconventional, a bit crazy and eccentric: they like to live life with super intensity. They bring excitement and fun. You love them for being so different. They engage you in hours of philosophical discussion and are happy to discuss your relationship in detail. They go from being in emotional denial to expressing love. **72% compatible**

**Revati and Punarvasu:** You are insecure and Punarvasu advise you and help you to be more confident. They will take over your problems and you feel comfortable leaning on them emotionally. Be careful you do not get into a pupil–teacher relationship and ignore the intimacy of love. The high compatibility suggests you won't. **69% compatible**

**Revati and Pushya:** Your rulers, Saturn and Mercury are good friends; you can adapt to Pushya's needs. You feel supported by the steadfastness of Pushya. They love you, care for you and they take their commitment to you seriously. You feel they will not let you down. You try to make their life easier and help them to open up emotionally. **72% compatible**

# REVATI

**Revati and Ashlesha:** You want your relationship to be special and your partner to concentrate on you but Ashlesha are unable to give you the unconditional love you seek. You feel that Ashlesha are holding back, keeping a part of their life private. How can love flourish under such circumstances? You feel insecure and unloved. **33% compatible**

**Revati and Magha:** You can love Magha too much, but you can also get disappointed when Magha do not live up to your expectations. Magha will increase your insecurity with their inability to control their sensual indulgences. A Magha and Revati relationship is a spiritually complex one. You can cause each other unhappiness and be self-destructive. **33% compatible**

**Revati and Purva Phalguni:** You are happy to be doing whatever it takes to make Purva Phalguni happy. You love their creativity and their ability to have fun, but mostly you fall for their commitment to love and family life. They also take your relationship seriously. Purva Phalguni never understand your spiritual needs but you are happy to compromise. **67% compatible**

**Revati and Uttara Phalguni:** Both of you believe that sexuality should be within committed relationships and are serious about love. You like the Uttara Phalguni dependability. They are realistic whereas your head can be in the clouds. Your relationship works so well because each one of you gives what the other does not have. **69% compatible**

**Revati and Hasta:** You love the way Hasta try to transcend their destiny, trying to improve the quality of their life. You can see the difficulties they face, as they need to mature spiritually. Hasta will look to you for support and you need theirs. You can guide them spiritually while they can make you more comfortable with your emotions. **66% compatible**

**Revati and Chitra:** You are attracted to the passionate, courageous and talented Chitra. But you find them to be lazy lovers. They do not always consider your needs. When you point it out, they become defensive and feel you are being unnecessarily critical. Chitra are not into commitment and you may feel they do not respect your wishes at all. **43% compatible**

**Revati and Swati:** You are an idealist: you look at life through rose-tinted glasses. Swati are pragmatists but you imagine them to be romantic and perfect. Swati can feed this illusion. When the veil lifts from your eyes, you get very disappointed. Hurtful arguments can follow. Try to be more realistic and avoid unnecessary heartache. **24% compatible**

**Revati and Vishakha:** Vishakha are very sexual and you can go from being earthy and passionate to being guilty about your sensuality. If you try to control Vishakha, they are not going to take to it kindly. Vishakha cannot be supportive and committed. You feel hurt by their lack of love and their detachment from you. **18% compatible**

**Revati and Anuradha:** Anuradha love you in a way that makes you feel special. You reciprocate their love. Both of you try to anticipate each other's needs and fulfil your desires. Their love will complete you. Anuradha support your more unrealistic flights of fancy while you help them to reconcile their outer world with their inner self. **72% compatible**

**Revati and Jyeshta:** Two Mercury-ruled Nakshatras, both at spiritual junctions in life. You seek idealism in love and Jyeshta want sensuality. Jyeshta can make you feel unsure by their ability to play fast and loose with your emotions. Both of you tend to analyse every aspect of your relationships which can sometimes create problems where there were none. **55% compatible**

**Revati and Mula:** You fall for the unconventional Mula. You know how to deal with their changing nature and tastes. You have no problem keeping up with the quick-thinking Mula. You offer friendship and unconditional love. Mula are learning to renounce worldly ties while you are already comfortable with giving them up. Sexual issues may emerge. **72% compatible**

**Revati and Purva Ashadha:** Creative, talented, bright and intelligent:

# REVATI

Purva Ashadha appear perfect. You fall for them quickly. This is a relationship where you do not get disappointed. Purva Ashadha have the capacity to surprise you with their wisdom and their ability to be creative. A great relationship where love flourishes. **83% compatible**

**Revati and Uttara Ashadha:** Complex, hard to understand and ascetic – Uttara Ashadha do not encourage you to get to know them, much less love them. You love their strength, their ability to face pain. You love them even though they keep pushing you away. You need to keep them aware of your love and not let them wallow in their loneliness. **55% compatible**

**Revati and Shravana:** Your sentimentality towards each other can create unrealistic expectations. You have deep psychic connections. You understand each other's insecurities and struggles. You will sacrifice all for the love of Shravana. You can live in an unreal world so be prepared to deal with life's struggles and not blame each other. **64% compatible**

**Revati and Dhanishta:** You worst sexual partner. Both of you are dominant personalities and should treat each other with respect. Your problem is that you never allow Dhanishta into your space. This relationship can be sexually frustrating and emotionally dry. You want them to revere you and they want you to worship them; both are sure to be disappointed. **36% compatible**

**Revati and Shatabhishak:** Shatabhishak can hurt you and they do not appreciate you or love you enough. You can never be sure of them. Their ability to be elusive and secretive is usually overlooked by you initially. You can love unwisely and they are not always right for you. They are too complex and their lack of commitment makes you insecure. **42% compatible**

**Revati and Purva Bhadra:** Your worst sexual partner but you will compromise. Sex is not the most important factor in your relationships. You have so much in common and you usually divide your responsibilities. But as the female elephant you are not as aggressive towards the lion Purva Bhadra as you feel towards the lioness Dhanishta. **68% compatible**

**Revati and Uttara Bhadra:** You revere Uttara Bhadra and treat your relationship as sacred. You want to create something everlasting from your love for each other. Peace, happiness and compatibility are all there. This doesn't mean you do not face problems but that you are strong together and your love transcends anything the world throws at you. **91% compatible**

**Revati and Revati:** The relationship between two idealists can have its difficulties. Both of you want such perfection that it is impossible to deliver. This can make you disappointed with life and disillusioned. You must learn to be realistic and keep your feet on the ground. Watch out for jealousy from other people as it can wreck your dream. **77% compatible**

# Cusps

Those born at the end or beginning of Revati should see pages 387–8.

# PART 3

# COMPATIBILITY GRIDS AND CUSP CHARTS

# Nakshatra Compatibility Grid

0–25% Below Average, 25%–50% Average,
50%–75% Good, 75%–100% Great

|     | Ash | Bha | Kri | Roh | Mri | Ard | Pun | Pus | Ash | Ma | PP | UP | Has |
|-----|-----|-----|-----|-----|-----|-----|-----|-----|-----|----|----|----|-----|
| Ash | 77  | 91  | 61  | 62  | 61  | 44  | 55  | 83  | 75  | 55 | 67 | 34 | 27  |
| Bha | 91  | 77  | 65  | 64  | 43  | 69  | 76  | 61  | 66  | 53 | 47 | 60 | 50  |
| Kri | 61  | 65  | 65  | 30  | 54  | 49  | 56  | 68  | 57  | 47 | 43 | 53 | 44  |
| Roh | 62  | 64  | 30  | 55  | 77  | 64  | 66  | 75  | 33  | 28 | 66 | 72 | 69  |
| Mri | 61  | 43  | 54  | 77  | 64  | 78  | 67  | 41  | 47  | 57 | 46 | 73 | 82  |
| Ard | 44  | 69  | 49  | 64  | 78  | 77  | 51  | 55  | 33  | 58 | 75 | 61 | 67  |
| Pun | 55  | 76  | 56  | 66  | 67  | 51  | 57  | 76  | 60  | 51 | 62 | 50 | 57  |
| Pus | 83  | 61  | 68  | 75  | 41  | 55  | 76  | 77  | 80  | 50 | 39 | 52 | 69  |
| Ash | 75  | 66  | 57  | 33  | 47  | 33  | 60  | 80  | 77  | 41 | 41 | 50 | 53  |
| Ma  | 55  | 53  | 47  | 28  | 57  | 58  | 51  | 50  | 41  | 77 | 83 | 55 | 39  |
| PP  | 67  | 47  | 43  | 66  | 46  | 75  | 62  | 39  | 41  | 83 | 77 | 80 | 55  |
| UP  | 34  | 60  | 53  | 72  | 73  | 61  | 50  | 52  | 50  | 55 | 80 | 61 | 58  |
| Has | 27  | 50  | 44  | 69  | 82  | 67  | 57  | 69  | 53  | 39 | 55 | 58 | 77  |
| Chi | 47  | 22  | 61  | 49  | 37  | 65  | 58  | 30  | 67  | 58 | 19 | 47 | 79  |
| Swa | 70  | 78  | 32  | 42  | 50  | 75  | 74  | 69  | 30  | 27 | 66 | 69 | 72  |
| Vis | 55  | 50  | 51  | 30  | 50  | 46  | 51  | 54  | 41  | 54 | 55 | 50 | 53  |
| An  | 66  | 47  | 60  | 80  | 47  | 53  | 62  | 47  | 53  | 66 | 61 | 80 | 72  |
| Jye | 36  | 53  | 76  | 67  | 53  | 14  | 22  | 55  | 69  | 88 | 66 | 39 | 36  |
| Mul | 33  | 53  | 65  | 36  | 51  | 42  | 29  | 47  | 61  | 66 | 53 | 32 | 42  |
| PA  | 66  | 47  | 47  | 53  | 40  | 77  | 65  | 33  | 42  | 53 | 50 | 75 | 75  |
| UA  | 66  | 72  | 30  | 37  | 55  | 67  | 58  | 63  | 27  | 15 | 60 | 68 | 64  |
| Shr | 72  | 77  | 32  | 50  | 39  | 61  | 68  | 75  | 36  | 11 | 50 | 61 | 66  |
| Dha | 53  | 26  | 70  | 53  | 35  | 50  | 46  | 24  | 60  | 55 | 19 | 40 | 51  |
| Sha | 38  | 53  | 75  | 76  | 65  | 33  | 25  | 36  | 50  | 66 | 50 | 37 | 27  |
| PB  | 42  | 62  | 54  | 60  | 69  | 48  | 41  | 60  | 39  | 47 | 64 | 39 | 38  |
| UB  | 64  | 11  | 50  | 75  | 49  | 72  | 70  | 50  | 55  | 50 | 44 | 75 | 72  |
| Rev | 72  | 69  | 32  | 53  | 74  | 72  | 69  | 72  | 33  | 33 | 67 | 69 | 66  |

**How to Study the Compatibility Chart**

Look in the vertical column for your Nakshatra and the horizontal column for your partner's Nakshatra. The number you arrive at is the % compatibility you have with your partner. E.g. if your Nakshatra is Chitra and your partner's is Shatabhishak, you find Chitra in the vertical column and Shatabhishak in the horizontal one, and you will see the number is 69. Therefore your compatibility with your partner is 69%.

# Nakshatra Compatibility Grid

|     | Chi | Swa | Vis | An | Jye | Mul | PA | UA | Shr | Dha | Sha | PB | UB | Rev |
|-----|-----|-----|-----|----|----|-----|----|----|-----|-----|-----|----|----|-----|
| Ash | 47 | 70 | 55 | 66 | 36 | 33 | 66 | 66 | 72 | 53 | 38 | 42 | 64 | 72 |
| Bha | 22 | 78 | 50 | 47 | 53 | 53 | 47 | 72 | 77 | 26 | 53 | 62 | 11 | 69 |
| Kri | 61 | 32 | 51 | 60 | 76 | 65 | 47 | 30 | 32 | 70 | 75 | 54 | 50 | 32 |
| Roh | 49 | 42 | 30 | 80 | 67 | 36 | 53 | 37 | 50 | 53 | 76 | 60 | 75 | 53 |
| Mri | 37 | 50 | 50 | 47 | 53 | 51 | 40 | 55 | 39 | 35 | 65 | 69 | 49 | 74 |
| Ard | 65 | 75 | 46 | 53 | 14 | 42 | 77 | 67 | 61 | 50 | 33 | 48 | 72 | 72 |
| Pun | 58 | 74 | 51 | 62 | 22 | 29 | 65 | 58 | 68 | 46 | 25 | 41 | 70 | 69 |
| Pus | 30 | 69 | 54 | 47 | 55 | 47 | 33 | 63 | 75 | 24 | 36 | 60 | 50 | 72 |
| Ash | 67 | 30 | 41 | 53 | 69 | 61 | 42 | 27 | 36 | 60 | 50 | 39 | 55 | 33 |
| Ma  | 58 | 27 | 54 | 66 | 88 | 66 | 53 | 15 | 11 | 55 | 66 | 47 | 50 | 33 |
| PP  | 19 | 66 | 55 | 61 | 66 | 53 | 50 | 60 | 50 | 19 | 50 | 64 | 44 | 67 |
| UP  | 47 | 69 | 50 | 80 | 39 | 32 | 75 | 68 | 61 | 40 | 37 | 39 | 75 | 69 |
| Has | 79 | 72 | 53 | 72 | 36 | 42 | 75 | 64 | 66 | 51 | 27 | 38 | 72 | 66 |
| Chi | 66 | 65 | 74 | 23 | 62 | 75 | 36 | 55 | 58 | 50 | 69 | 45 | 18 | 43 |
| Swa | 65 | 77 | 40 | 58 | 41 | 63 | 75 | 55 | 61 | 65 | 61 | 60 | 53 | 24 |
| Vis | 74 | 40 | 60 | 59 | 72 | 66 | 38 | 32 | 36 | 70 | 70 | 49 | 41 | 18 |
| An  | 23 | 58 | 59 | 77 | 86 | 41 | 36 | 64 | 72 | 32 | 61 | 66 | 47 | 72 |
| Jye | 62 | 41 | 72 | 86 | 77 | 39 | 44 | 50 | 55 | 68 | 47 | 26 | 55 | 55 |
| Mul | 75 | 63 | 66 | 41 | 39 | 77 | 77 | 36 | 39 | 65 | 58 | 41 | 66 | 72 |
| PA  | 36 | 75 | 38 | 36 | 44 | 77 | 77 | 77 | 61 | 26 | 64 | 66 | 61 | 83 |
| UA  | 55 | 55 | 32 | 64 | 50 | 36 | 77 | 68 | 58 | 52 | 63 | 66 | 83 | 55 |
| Shr | 58 | 61 | 36 | 72 | 55 | 39 | 61 | 58 | 77 | 61 | 47 | 66 | 80 | 64 |
| Dha | 50 | 65 | 70 | 32 | 68 | 65 | 26 | 52 | 61 | 63 | 77 | 58 | 17 | 36 |
| Sha | 69 | 61 | 70 | 61 | 47 | 58 | 64 | 63 | 47 | 77 | 77 | 51 | 66 | 42 |
| PB  | 45 | 60 | 49 | 66 | 26 | 41 | 66 | 66 | 66 | 58 | 51 | 60 | 76 | 68 |
| UB  | 18 | 53 | 41 | 47 | 55 | 66 | 61 | 83 | 80 | 17 | 66 | 76 | 77 | 91 |
| Rev | 43 | 24 | 18 | 72 | 55 | 72 | 83 | 55 | 64 | 36 | 42 | 68 | 91 | 77 |

# Sexual Compatibility Grid

0 = None, 25 = below average, 50 = average,
75 = good, 100 = perfect

|     | Ash | Bha | Kri | Roh | Mri | Ard | Pun | Pus | Ash | Ma  | PP  | UP  | Has |
|-----|-----|-----|-----|-----|-----|-----|-----|-----|-----|-----|-----|-----|-----|
| Ash | 100 | 50  | 50  | 75  | 75  | 50  | 50  | 50  | 50  | 50  | 50  | 25  | 00  |
| Bha | 50  | 100 | 75  | 75  | 75  | 50  | 50  | 75  | 50  | 50  | 50  | 25  | 75  |
| Kri | 50  | 75  | 100 | 50  | 50  | 25  | 50  | 100 | 50  | 25  | 25  | 75  | 75  |
| Roh | 75  | 75  | 50  | 100 | 100 | 50  | 25  | 50  | 25  | 25  | 25  | 25  | 25  |
| Mri | 75  | 75  | 50  | 100 | 100 | 50  | 25  | 50  | 25  | 25  | 25  | 25  | 25  |
| Ard | 50  | 50  | 25  | 50  | 50  | 100 | 50  | 25  | 50  | 25  | 25  | 50  | 50  |
| Pun | 50  | 50  | 50  | 25  | 25  | 50  | 100 | 50  | 100 | 00  | 00  | 50  | 50  |
| Pus | 50  | 75  | 100 | 50  | 50  | 25  | 50  | 100 | 50  | 25  | 25  | 75  | 75  |
| Ash | 50  | 50  | 50  | 25  | 25  | 50  | 100 | 50  | 100 | 00  | 00  | 50  | 50  |
| Ma  | 50  | 50  | 25  | 25  | 25  | 25  | 00  | 25  | 00  | 100 | 100 | 50  | 50  |
| PP  | 50  | 50  | 25  | 25  | 25  | 25  | 00  | 25  | 00  | 100 | 100 | 50  | 50  |
| UP  | 25  | 25  | 75  | 25  | 25  | 50  | 50  | 75  | 50  | 50  | 50  | 100 | 75  |
| Has | 00  | 75  | 75  | 25  | 25  | 50  | 50  | 75  | 50  | 50  | 50  | 75  | 100 |
| Chi | 25  | 25  | 25  | 50  | 50  | 25  | 25  | 25  | 25  | 50  | 50  | 00  | 25  |
| Swa | 00  | 75  | 75  | 25  | 25  | 50  | 50  | 75  | 50  | 50  | 50  | 75  | 100 |
| Vis | 25  | 25  | 25  | 50  | 50  | 25  | 25  | 25  | 25  | 50  | 50  | 00  | 25  |
| An  | 75  | 50  | 50  | 50  | 50  | 00  | 75  | 50  | 75  | 50  | 50  | 75  | 50  |
| Jye | 75  | 50  | 50  | 50  | 50  | 00  | 75  | 50  | 75  | 50  | 50  | 75  | 50  |
| Mul | 50  | 50  | 25  | 50  | 50  | 100 | 50  | 25  | 50  | 25  | 25  | 50  | 50  |
| PA  | 75  | 75  | 00  | 50  | 50  | 50  | 75  | 00  | 75  | 50  | 50  | 50  | 50  |
| UA  | 50  | 50  | 75  | 00  | 00  | 25  | 50  | 75  | 50  | 25  | 25  | 50  | 50  |
| Shr | 75  | 75  | 00  | 50  | 50  | 50  | 75  | 00  | 75  | 50  | 50  | 50  | 50  |
| Dha | 25  | 00  | 25  | 50  | 50  | 25  | 25  | 25  | 25  | 50  | 50  | 25  | 25  |
| Sha | 100 | 50  | 50  | 75  | 75  | 50  | 50  | 50  | 50  | 50  | 50  | 25  | 00  |
| PB  | 25  | 00  | 25  | 50  | 50  | 25  | 25  | 25  | 25  | 50  | 50  | 25  | 25  |
| UB  | 25  | 50  | 75  | 25  | 25  | 50  | 50  | 75  | 50  | 50  | 50  | 100 | 75  |
| Rev | 50  | 100 | 75  | 75  | 75  | 50  | 50  | 75  | 50  | 50  | 50  | 25  | 75  |

**How to Study the Sexual Compatibility Chart**

Look in the vertical column for your Nakshatra and the horizontal column for your partner's Nakshatra. The number you arrive at is the % sexual compatibility you have with your partner. E.g. if your Nakshatra is Magha and your partner's is Ashwini, you find Magha in the vertical column and Ashwini in the horizontal one, and you will see the number is 50. Therefore your sexual compatibility with your partner is 50%.

# Sexual Compatibility Grid

|     | Chi | Swa | Vis | An  | Jye | Mul | PA  | UA  | Shr | Dha | Sha | PB  | UB  | Rev |
|-----|-----|-----|-----|-----|-----|-----|-----|-----|-----|-----|-----|-----|-----|-----|
| Ash | 25  | 00  | 25  | 75  | 75  | 50  | 75  | 50  | 75  | 25  | 100 | 25  | 25  | 50  |
| Bha | 25  | 75  | 25  | 50  | 50  | 50  | 75  | 50  | 75  | 00  | 50  | 00  | 25  | 100 |
| Kri | 25  | 75  | 25  | 50  | 50  | 25  | 00  | 75  | 00  | 25  | 50  | 25  | 75  | 75  |
| Roh | 50  | 25  | 50  | 50  | 50  | 50  | 50  | 00  | 50  | 50  | 75  | 50  | 25  | 75  |
| Mri | 50  | 25  | 50  | 50  | 50  | 50  | 50  | 00  | 50  | 50  | 75  | 50  | 25  | 75  |
| Ard | 25  | 50  | 25  | 00  | 00  | 100 | 50  | 25  | 50  | 25  | 50  | 25  | 50  | 50  |
| Pun | 25  | 50  | 25  | 75  | 75  | 50  | 75  | 50  | 75  | 25  | 50  | 25  | 50  | 50  |
| Pus | 25  | 75  | 25  | 50  | 50  | 25  | 00  | 75  | 00  | 25  | 50  | 25  | 75  | 75  |
| Ash | 25  | 50  | 25  | 75  | 75  | 50  | 75  | 50  | 75  | 25  | 50  | 25  | 50  | 50  |
| Ma  | 50  | 50  | 50  | 50  | 50  | 25  | 50  | 25  | 50  | 50  | 50  | 50  | 50  | 50  |
| PP  | 50  | 50  | 50  | 50  | 50  | 25  | 50  | 25  | 50  | 50  | 50  | 50  | 50  | 50  |
| UP  | 00  | 75  | 00  | 75  | 75  | 50  | 50  | 50  | 50  | 25  | 25  | 25  | 100 | 25  |
| Has | 25  | 100 | 25  | 50  | 50  | 50  | 50  | 50  | 50  | 25  | 00  | 25  | 75  | 75  |
| Chi | 100 | 25  | 100 | 25  | 25  | 25  | 25  | 50  | 25  | 25  | 25  | 25  | 00  | 25  |
| Swa | 25  | 100 | 25  | 50  | 50  | 50  | 50  | 50  | 50  | 25  | 00  | 25  | 75  | 75  |
| Vis | 100 | 25  | 100 | 25  | 25  | 25  | 25  | 50  | 25  | 25  | 25  | 25  | 00  | 25  |
| An  | 25  | 50  | 25  | 100 | 100 | 00  | 50  | 50  | 50  | 25  | 75  | 25  | 75  | 50  |
| Jye | 25  | 50  | 25  | 100 | 100 | 00  | 50  | 50  | 50  | 25  | 75  | 25  | 75  | 50  |
| Mul | 25  | 50  | 25  | 00  | 00  | 100 | 50  | 25  | 50  | 25  | 50  | 25  | 50  | 50  |
| PA  | 25  | 50  | 25  | 50  | 50  | 50  | 100 | 75  | 100 | 50  | 75  | 50  | 50  | 75  |
| UA  | 50  | 50  | 50  | 50  | 50  | 25  | 75  | 100 | 75  | 50  | 50  | 50  | 50  | 50  |
| Shr | 25  | 50  | 25  | 50  | 50  | 50  | 100 | 50  | 100 | 50  | 75  | 50  | 50  | 75  |
| Dha | 25  | 25  | 25  | 25  | 25  | 25  | 50  | 50  | 50  | 100 | 25  | 100 | 25  | 00  |
| Sha | 25  | 00  | 25  | 75  | 75  | 50  | 75  | 50  | 75  | 25  | 100 | 25  | 25  | 50  |
| PB  | 25  | 25  | 25  | 25  | 25  | 25  | 50  | 50  | 50  | 100 | 25  | 100 | 25  | 00  |
| UB  | 00  | 75  | 00  | 75  | 75  | 50  | 50  | 50  | 50  | 25  | 25  | 25  | 100 | 50  |
| Rev | 25  | 75  | 25  | 50  | 50  | 50  | 75  | 50  | 75  | 00  | 50  | 00  | 25  | 100 |

# Spiritual Compatibility Grid

### o = None, Blank = 100%

|     | Ash | Bha | Kri | Roh | Mri | Ard | Pun | Pus | Ash | Ma | PP | UP | Has |
|-----|-----|-----|-----|-----|-----|-----|-----|-----|-----|-----|-----|-----|-----|
| Ash | 0   |     |     |     | 0   | 0   |     |     |     |    |    | 0  | 0   |
| Bha |     | 0   |     | 0   |     |     | 0   |     |     | 0  |    |    |     |
| Kri |     |     | 0   | 0   |     |     |     |     | 0   | 0  |    |    |     |
| Roh |     |     | 0   | 0   |     |     |     |     | 0   | 0  |    |    |     |
| Mri |     | 0   |     |     | 0   |     | 0   |     |     | 0  |    |    |     |
| Ard | 0   |     |     |     | 0   | 0   |     |     |     |    |    | 0  | 0   |
| Pun | 0   |     |     |     | 0   | 0   |     |     |     |    |    | 0  | 0   |
| Pus |     | 0   |     | 0   |     |     | 0   |     |     | 0  |    |    |     |
| Ash |     |     | 0   | 0   |     |     |     |     | 0   | 0  |    |    |     |
| Ma  |     |     | 0   | 0   |     |     |     |     | 0   | 0  |    |    |     |
| PP  |     | 0   |     | 0   |     |     | 0   |     |     | 0  |    |    |     |
| UP  | 0   |     |     |     | 0   | 0   |     |     |     |    |    | 0  | 0   |
| Has | 0   |     |     |     | 0   | 0   |     |     |     |    |    | 0  | 0   |
| Chi |     | 0   |     | 0   |     |     | 0   |     |     | 0  |    |    |     |
| Swa |     |     | 0   | 0   |     |     |     |     | 0   | 0  |    |    |     |
| Vis |     |     | 0   | 0   |     |     |     |     | 0   | 0  |    |    |     |
| An  |     | 0   |     |     | 0   |     | 0   |     |     | 0  |    |    |     |
| Jye | 0   |     |     |     | 0   | 0   |     |     |     |    |    | 0  | 0   |
| Mul | 0   |     |     |     | 0   | 0   |     |     |     |    |    | 0  | 0   |
| PA  |     | 0   |     | 0   |     |     | 0   |     |     | 0  |    |    |     |
| UA  |     |     | 0   | 0   |     |     |     |     | 0   | 0  |    |    |     |
| Shr |     |     | 0   | 0   |     |     |     |     | 0   | 0  |    |    |     |
| Dha |     | 0   |     | 0   |     |     | 0   |     |     | 0  |    |    |     |
| Sha | 0   |     |     |     | 0   | 0   |     |     |     |    |    | 0  | 0   |
| PB  | 0   |     |     |     | 0   | 0   |     |     |     |    |    | 0  | 0   |
| UB  |     | 0   |     | 0   |     |     | 0   |     |     | 0  |    |    |     |
| Rev |     |     | 0   | 0   |     |     |     |     | 0   | 0  |    |    |     |

## How to Study the Spiritual Compatibility Chart

Look in the vertical column for your Nakshatra and the horizontal column for your partner's Nakshatra. If there is 0, there is no spiritual compatibility, if the space is blank, this indicates 100% spiritual compatibility. E.g. if your Nakshatra is Ashlesha and your partner's is Uttara Bhadra, you find Ashlesha in the vertical column and Uttara Bhadra in the horizontal one, you will see there is nothing in that grid. Therefore your spiritual compatibility with your partner is 100%.

# Spiritual Compatibility Grid

|     | Chi | Swa | Vis | An | Jye | Mul | PA | UA | Shr | Dha | Sha | PB | UB | Rev |
|-----|-----|-----|-----|----|-----|-----|----|----|-----|-----|-----|----|----|-----|
| Ash |     |     |     |    | 0   | 0   |    |    |     |     | 0   | 0  |    |     |
| Bha | 0   |     |     | 0  |     |     | 0  |    |     | 0   |     |    | 0  |     |
| Kri |     | 0   | 0   |    |     |     |    | 0  | 0   |     |     |    |    | 0   |
| Roh |     | 0   | 0   |    |     |     |    | 0  | 0   |     |     |    |    | 0   |
| Mri | 0   |     |     | 0  |     | 0   |    |    |     | 0   |     |    | 0  |     |
| Ard |     |     |     |    | 0   | 0   |    |    |     |     | 0   | 0  |    |     |
| Pun |     |     |     |    | 0   | 0   |    |    |     |     | 0   | 0  |    |     |
| Pus | 0   |     |     | 0  |     | 0   |    |    |     | 0   |     |    | 0  |     |
| Ash |     | 0   | 0   |    |     |     |    | 0  | 0   |     |     |    |    | 0   |
| Ma  |     | 0   | 0   |    |     |     |    | 0  | 0   |     |     |    |    | 0   |
| PP  | 0   |     |     | 0  |     | 0   |    |    |     | 0   |     |    | 0  |     |
| UP  |     |     |     |    | 0   | 0   |    |    |     |     | 0   | 0  |    |     |
| Has |     |     |     |    | 0   | 0   |    |    |     |     | 0   | 0  |    |     |
| Chi | 0   |     |     | 0  |     | 0   |    |    |     | 0   |     |    | 0  |     |
| Swa |     | 0   | 0   |    |     |     |    | 0  | 0   |     |     |    |    | 0   |
| Vis |     | 0   | 0   |    |     |     |    | 0  | 0   |     |     |    |    | 0   |
| An  | 0   |     |     | 0  |     | 0   |    |    |     | 0   |     |    | 0  |     |
| Jye |     |     |     |    | 0   | 0   |    |    |     |     | 0   | 0  |    |     |
| Mul |     |     |     |    | 0   | 0   |    |    |     |     | 0   | 0  |    |     |
| PA  | 0   |     |     | 0  |     | 0   |    |    |     | 0   |     |    | 0  |     |
| UA  |     | 0   | 0   |    |     |     |    | 0  | 0   |     |     |    |    | 0   |
| Shr |     | 0   | 0   |    |     |     |    | 0  | 0   |     |     |    |    | 0   |
| Dha | 0   |     |     | 0  |     | 0   |    |    |     | 0   |     |    | 0  |     |
| Sha |     |     |     |    | 0   | 0   |    |    |     |     | 0   | 0  |    |     |
| PB  |     |     |     |    | 0   | 0   |    |    |     |     | 0   | 0  |    |     |
| UB  | 0   |     |     | 0  |     | 0   |    |    |     | 0   |     |    | 0  |     |
| Rev |     | 0   | 0   |    |     |     |    | 0  | 0   |     |     |    |    | 0   |

# Cusps

If you were born on a cusp date, first look up one of the two signs you could be. Then look up your year of birth in the left-hand column and read across to the time. This is the time (according to GMT) that the sun moved into the Nakshatra. To work out your sign you need to know whether you were born before or after this time. For example, if you were born on 23 October 1973 you could be either Chitra or Swati. The sun moved into Swati at 17.25 – if you were born at 09.30 then you are Chitra, if you were born at 18.00 you are Swati.

If you don't know your time of birth, work out your Nakshatra by assuming you were born at midday.

## Ashwini
### 13 to 27 April

| Year | Day | Time  | Year | Day | Time  |
|------|-----|-------|------|-----|-------|
| 1920 | 12  | 23.39 | 1937 | 13  | 08.09 |
| 1921 | 13  | 05.46 | 1938 | 13  | 14.22 |
| 1922 | 13  | 12.01 | 1939 | 13  | 20.27 |
| 1923 | 13  | 18.02 | 1940 | 13  | 02.37 |
| 1924 | 13  | 00.06 | 1941 | 13  | 08.54 |
| 1925 | 13  | 06.21 | 1942 | 13  | 15.06 |
| 1926 | 13  | 12.28 | 1943 | 13  | 21.11 |
| 1927 | 13  | 18.38 | 1944 | 13  | 03.19 |
| 1928 | 13  | 00.50 | 1945 | 13  | 09.30 |
| 1929 | 13  | 07.03 | 1946 | 13  | 15.40 |
| 1930 | 13  | 13.18 | 1947 | 13  | 21.44 |
| 1931 | 13  | 19.20 | 1948 | 13  | 03.49 |
| 1932 | 13  | 01.26 | 1949 | 13  | 10.01 |
| 1933 | 13  | 07.41 | 1950 | 13  | 16.13 |
| 1934 | 13  | 13.49 | 1951 | 13  | 22.19 |
| 1935 | 13  | 19.54 | 1952 | 13  | 04.32 |
| 1936 | 13  | 02.01 | 1953 | 13  | 10.47 |

## CUSPS

| Year | Day | Time | Year | Day | Time |
| --- | --- | --- | --- | --- | --- |
| 1954 | 13 | 16.56 | 1988 | 13 | 10.04 |
| 1955 | 13 | 23.00 | 1989 | 13 | 16.15 |
| 1956 | 13 | 05.06 | 1990 | 13 | 22.27 |
| 1957 | 13 | 11.18 | 1991 | 14 | 04.34 |
| 1958 | 13 | 17.30 | 1992 | 13 | 10.37 |
| 1959 | 13 | 23.33 | 1993 | 13 | 16.55 |
| 1960 | 13 | 05.40 | 1994 | 13 | 23.01 |
| 1961 | 13 | 11.52 | 1995 | 14 | 05.01 |
| 1962 | 13 | 18.01 | 1996 | 13 | 11.14 |
| 1963 | 14 | 00.10 | 1997 | 13 | 17.21 |
| 1964 | 13 | 06.22 | 1998 | 13 | 23.34 |
| 1965 | 13 | 12.36 | 1999 | 14 | 05.47 |
| 1966 | 13 | 18.49 | 2000 | 13 | 11.52 |
| 1967 | 14 | 00.53 | 2001 | 13 | 18.12 |
| 1968 | 13 | 06.58 | 2002 | 14 | 00.18 |
| 1969 | 13 | 13.13 | 2003 | 14 | 06.17 |
| 1970 | 13 | 19.19 | 2004 | 13 | 12.32 |
| 1971 | 14 | 01.22 | 2005 | 13 | 18.39 |
| 1972 | 13 | 07.31 | 2006 | 14 | 00.49 |
| 1973 | 13 | 13.38 | 2007 | 14 | 06.58 |
| 1974 | 13 | 19.54 | 2008 | 13 | 12.59 |
| 1975 | 14 | 02.02 | 2009 | 13 | 19.17 |
| 1976 | 13 | 08.12 | 2010 | 14 | 01.26 |
| 1977 | 13 | 14.31 | 2011 | 14 | 07.29 |
| 1978 | 13 | 20.37 | 2012 | 13 | 13.38 |
| 1979 | 14 | 02.41 | 2013 | 13 | 19.58 |
| 1980 | 13 | 08.51 | 2014 | 14 | 02.05 |
| 1981 | 13 | 14.59 | 2015 | 14 | 08.16 |
| 1982 | 13 | 21.12 | 2016 | 13 | 14.17 |
| 1983 | 14 | 03.17 | 2017 | 13 | 20.33 |
| 1984 | 13 | 09.19 | 2018 | 14 | 02.42 |
| 1985 | 13 | 15.35 | 2019 | 14 | 08.38 |
| 1986 | 13 | 21.42 | 2020 | 13 | 14.52 |
| 1987 | 14 | 03.48 | | | |

## Bharani
### 27 April to 10 May

| Year | Day | Time | Year | Day | Time |
| --- | --- | --- | --- | --- | --- |
| 1920 | 26 | 15.28 | 1952 | 26 | 20.21 |
| 1921 | 26 | 21.45 | 1953 | 27 | 02.37 |
| 1922 | 27 | 03.54 | 1954 | 27 | 08.53 |
| 1923 | 27 | 19.51 | 1955 | 27 | 14.47 |
| 1924 | 26 | 16.05 | 1956 | 26 | 21.00 |
| 1925 | 26 | 22.11 | 1957 | 27 | 03.13 |
| 1926 | 27 | 04.21 | 1958 | 27 | 09.16 |
| 1927 | 27 | 10.33 | 1959 | 27 | 15.29 |
| 1928 | 26 | 16.37 | 1960 | 26 | 21.31 |
| 1929 | 26 | 22.58 | 1961 | 27 | 03.42 |
| 1930 | 27 | 05.11 | 1962 | 27 | 09.57 |
| 1931 | 27 | 11.09 | 1963 | 27 | 15.56 |
| 1932 | 26 | 17.24 | 1964 | 26 | 22.13 |
| 1933 | 26 | 23.32 | 1965 | 27 | 04.31 |
| 1934 | 27 | 05.40 | 1966 | 27 | 10.34 |
| 1935 | 27 | 11.51 | 1967 | 27 | 16.47 |
| 1936 | 26 | 17.50 | 1968 | 26 | 22.51 |
| 1937 | 27 | 00.05 | 1969 | 27 | 05.01 |
| 1938 | 27 | 06.16 | 1970 | 27 | 11.15 |
| 1939 | 27 | 12.13 | 1971 | 27 | 17.10 |
| 1940 | 26 | 18.33 | 1972 | 26 | 23.21 |
| 1941 | 27 | 00.45 | 1973 | 27 | 05.35 |
| 1942 | 27 | 06.55 | 1974 | 27 | 11.38 |
| 1943 | 27 | 13.08 | 1975 | 27 | 17.53 |
| 1944 | 26 | 19.08 | 1976 | 27 | 00.04 |
| 1945 | 27 | 01.23 | 1977 | 27 | 06.17 |
| 1946 | 27 | 07.36 | 1978 | 27 | 12.33 |
| 1947 | 27 | 13.31 | 1979 | 27 | 18.30 |
| 1948 | 26 | 19.45 | 1980 | 27 | 00.40 |
| 1949 | 27 | 01.55 | 1981 | 27 | 06.56 |
| 1950 | 27 | 08.00 | 1982 | 27 | 13.20 |
| 1951 | 27 | 14.15 | 1983 | 27 | 19.08 |

## CUSPS

| Year | Day | Time  | Year | Day | Time  |
|------|-----|-------|------|-----|-------|
| 1984 | 27  | 01.16 | 2003 | 27  | 22.10 |
| 1985 | 27  | 07.21 | 2004 | 27  | 04.17 |
| 1986 | 27  | 13.36 | 2005 | 27  | 10.33 |
| 1987 | 27  | 19.38 | 2006 | 27  | 16.38 |
| 1988 | 27  | 01.50 | 2007 | 27  | 22.44 |
| 1989 | 27  | 08.11 | 2008 | 27  | 04.55 |
| 1990 | 27  | 14.14 | 2009 | 27  | 11.04 |
| 1991 | 27  | 20.23 | 2010 | 27  | 17.14 |
| 1992 | 27  | 02.33 | 2011 | 27  | 23.21 |
| 1993 | 27  | 08.40 | 2012 | 27  | 05.32 |
| 1994 | 27  | 14.54 | 2013 | 27  | 11.51 |
| 1995 | 27  | 20.53 | 2014 | 27  | 17.56 |
| 1996 | 27  | 03.00 | 2015 | 28  | 00.00 |
| 1997 | 27  | 09.17 | 2016 | 27  | 06.12 |
| 1998 | 27  | 15.21 | 2017 | 27  | 12.21 |
| 1999 | 27  | 21.32 | 2018 | 27  | 18.29 |
| 2000 | 27  | 03.47 | 2019 | 28  | 00.32 |
| 2001 | 27  | 09.58 | 2020 | 27  | 06.37 |
| 2002 | 27  | 16.09 |      |     |       |

### Krittika
### 11 to 25 May

| Year | Day | Time  | Year | Day | Time  |
|------|-----|-------|------|-----|-------|
| 1920 | 10  | 09.48 | 1931 | 11  | 05.26 |
| 1921 | 10  | 15.56 | 1932 | 10  | 11.33 |
| 1922 | 10  | 22.08 | 1933 | 10  | 17.40 |
| 1923 | 11  | 04.09 | 1934 | 10  | 23.55 |
| 1924 | 10  | 10.13 | 1935 | 11  | 05.59 |
| 1925 | 10  | 16.29 | 1936 | 10  | 12.08 |
| 1926 | 10  | 22.34 | 1937 | 10  | 18.18 |
| 1927 | 11  | 04.41 | 1938 | 11  | 00.25 |
| 1928 | 10  | 10.37 | 1939 | 11  | 06.30 |
| 1929 | 10  | 17.09 | 1940 | 10  | 12.40 |
| 1930 | 10  | 23.22 | 1941 | 10  | 18.58 |

## CUSPS

| Year | Day | Time  | Year | Day | Time  |
|------|-----|-------|------|-----|-------|
| 1942 | 11  | 01.10 | 1977 | 11  | 00.33 |
| 1943 | 11  | 07.14 | 1978 | 11  | 06.40 |
| 1944 | 10  | 13.24 | 1979 | 11  | 12.42 |
| 1945 | 10  | 19.37 | 1980 | 10  | 18.55 |
| 1946 | 11  | 01.44 | 1981 | 11  | 01.03 |
| 1947 | 11  | 07.48 | 1982 | 11  | 07.12 |
| 1948 | 10  | 13.56 | 1983 | 11  | 13.19 |
| 1949 | 10  | 20.08 | 1984 | 10  | 19.23 |
| 1950 | 11  | 02.17 | 1985 | 11  | 01.38 |
| 1951 | 11  | 08.21 | 1986 | 11  | 07.45 |
| 1952 | 10  | 14.34 | 1987 | 11  | 13.46 |
| 1953 | 10  | 20.51 | 1988 | 10  | 20.04 |
| 1954 | 11  | 02.59 | 1989 | 11  | 02.16 |
| 1955 | 11  | 09.04 | 1990 | 11  | 08.25 |
| 1956 | 10  | 15.12 | 1991 | 11  | 14.35 |
| 1957 | 10  | 21.23 | 1992 | 10  | 20.39 |
| 1958 | 11  | 03.32 | 1993 | 11  | 02.56 |
| 1959 | 11  | 09.36 | 1994 | 11  | 09.03 |
| 1960 | 10  | 15.44 | 1995 | 11  | 15.01 |
| 1961 | 10  | 21.59 | 1996 | 10  | 21.17 |
| 1962 | 11  | 04.04 | 1997 | 11  | 03.24 |
| 1963 | 11  | 10.10 | 1998 | 11  | 09.31 |
| 1964 | 10  | 16.25 | 1999 | 11  | 15.44 |
| 1965 | 10  | 22.38 | 2000 | 10  | 21.51 |
| 1966 | 11  | 04.50 | 2001 | 11  | 04.11 |
| 1967 | 11  | 10.56 | 2002 | 11  | 10.19 |
| 1968 | 10  | 17.02 | 2003 | 11  | 16.16 |
| 1969 | 10  | 23.17 | 2004 | 10  | 22.33 |
| 1970 | 11  | 05.21 | 2005 | 11  | 04.41 |
| 1971 | 11  | 11.24 | 2006 | 11  | 10.46 |
| 1972 | 10  | 17.35 | 2007 | 11  | 16.58 |
| 1973 | 10  | 23.42 | 2008 | 10  | 23.01 |
| 1974 | 11  | 05.53 | 2009 | 11  | 05.16 |
| 1975 | 11  | 12.02 | 2010 | 11  | 11.26 |
| 1976 | 10  | 18.12 | 2011 | 11  | 17.25 |

# CUSPS

| Year | Day | Time | Year | Day | Time |
|---|---|---|---|---|---|
| 2012 | 10 | 23.46 | 2017 | 11 | 06.31 |
| 2013 | 11 | 05.59 | 2018 | 11 | 12.41 |
| 2014 | 11 | 12.02 | 2019 | 11 | 18.37 |
| 2015 | 11 | 18.15 | 2020 | 11 | 00.51 |
| 2016 | 11 | 00.18 | | | |

## Rohini
### 24 May to 8 June

| Year | Day | Time | Year | Day | Time |
|---|---|---|---|---|---|
| 1920 | 24 | 06.00 | 1945 | 24 | 15.51 |
| 1921 | 24 | 12.16 | 1946 | 24 | 22.04 |
| 1922 | 24 | 18.26 | 1947 | 25 | 03.59 |
| 1923 | 25 | 00.20 | 1948 | 24 | 10.14 |
| 1924 | 24 | 06.35 | 1949 | 24 | 16.27 |
| 1925 | 24 | 12.44 | 1950 | 24 | 22.27 |
| 1926 | 24 | 18.48 | 1951 | 25 | 04.40 |
| 1927 | 25 | 01.01 | 1952 | 24 | 10.49 |
| 1928 | 24 | 07.05 | 1953 | 24 | 17.03 |
| 1929 | 24 | 13.25 | 1954 | 24 | 23.19 |
| 1930 | 24 | 19.40 | 1955 | 25 | 05.15 |
| 1931 | 25 | 01.37 | 1956 | 24 | 11.27 |
| 1932 | 24 | 07.53 | 1957 | 24 | 17.43 |
| 1933 | 24 | 14.04 | 1958 | 24 | 23.41 |
| 1934 | 24 | 20.07 | 1959 | 25 | 05.54 |
| 1935 | 25 | 02.19 | 1960 | 24 | 12.01 |
| 1936 | 24 | 08.21 | 1961 | 24 | 18.10 |
| 1937 | 24 | 14.35 | 1962 | 25 | 00.24 |
| 1938 | 24 | 20.46 | 1963 | 25 | 06.22 |
| 1939 | 25 | 02.41 | 1964 | 24 | 12.37 |
| 1940 | 24 | 08.58 | 1965 | 24 | 18.58 |
| 1941 | 24 | 15.14 | 1966 | 25 | 00.59 |
| 1942 | 24 | 21.19 | 1967 | 25 | 07.11 |
| 1943 | 25 | 03.33 | 1968 | 24 | 13.20 |
| 1944 | 24 | 09.38 | 1969 | 24 | 19.28 |

## CUSPS

| Year | Day | Time | Year | Day | Time |
|---|---|---|---|---|---|
| 1970 | 25 | 01.40 | 1996 | 24 | 17.26 |
| 1971 | 25 | 07.37 | 1997 | 24 | 23.43 |
| 1972 | 24 | 13.47 | 1998 | 25 | 05.44 |
| 1973 | 24 | 20.03 | 1999 | 25 | 11.52 |
| 1974 | 25 | 02.03 | 2000 | 24 | 18.10 |
| 1975 | 25 | 08.15 | 2001 | 25 | 00.21 |
| 1976 | 24 | 14.29 | 2002 | 25 | 06.31 |
| 1977 | 24 | 20.41 | 2003 | 25 | 12.34 |
| 1978 | 25 | 02.56 | 2004 | 24 | 18.42 |
| 1979 | 25 | 08.57 | 2005 | 25 | 00.57 |
| 1980 | 24 | 15.06 | 2006 | 25 | 07.01 |
| 1981 | 24 | 21.24 | 2007 | 25 | 13.05 |
| 1982 | 25 | 03.23 | 2008 | 24 | 19.20 |
| 1983 | 25 | 09.31 | 2009 | 25 | 01.28 |
| 1984 | 24 | 15.43 | 2010 | 25 | 07.35 |
| 1985 | 24 | 21.48 | 2011 | 25 | 13.43 |
| 1986 | 25 | 04.00 | 2012 | 24 | 19.55 |
| 1987 | 25 | 10.01 | 2013 | 25 | 02.13 |
| 1988 | 24 | 16.12 | 2014 | 25 | 08.18 |
| 1989 | 24 | 22.34 | 2015 | 25 | 14.22 |
| 1990 | 25 | 04.37 | 2016 | 24 | 20.36 |
| 1991 | 25 | 10.45 | 2017 | 25 | 02.45 |
| 1992 | 24 | 16.59 | 2018 | 25 | 08.50 |
| 1993 | 24 | 23.06 | 2019 | 25 | 14.55 |
| 1994 | 25 | 05.16 | 2020 | 24 | 21.02 |
| 1995 | 25 | 11.19 | | | |

### Mrigasira
### 7 to 22 June

| Year | Day | Time | Year | Day | Time |
|---|---|---|---|---|---|
| 1920 | 7 | 04.01 | 1924 | 7 | 04.26 |
| 1921 | 7 | 10.10 | 1925 | 7 | 10.41 |
| 1922 | 7 | 16.18 | 1926 | 7 | 16.45 |
| 1923 | 7 | 22.20 | 1927 | 7 | 22.49 |

## CUSPS

| Year | Day | Time | Year | Day | Time |
|------|-----|------|------|-----|------|
| 1928 | 7 | 05.04 | 1963 | 8 | 04.17 |
| 1929 | 7 | 11.18 | 1964 | 7 | 10.33 |
| 1930 | 7 | 17.30 | 1965 | 7 | 16.45 |
| 1931 | 7 | 23.36 | 1966 | 7 | 22.55 |
| 1932 | 7 | 05.45 | 1967 | 8 | 05.03 |
| 1933 | 7 | 11.59 | 1968 | 7 | 11.11 |
| 1934 | 7 | 18.05 | 1969 | 7 | 17.27 |
| 1935 | 8 | 00.08 | 1970 | 7 | 23.29 |
| 1936 | 7 | 06.19 | 1971 | 8 | 05.31 |
| 1937 | 7 | 12.31 | 1972 | 7 | 11.45 |
| 1938 | 7 | 18.36 | 1973 | 7 | 17.52 |
| 1939 | 8 | 00.40 | 1974 | 7 | 23.59 |
| 1940 | 7 | 06.50 | 1975 | 8 | 06.07 |
| 1941 | 7 | 13.06 | 1976 | 7 | 12.18 |
| 1942 | 7 | 19.17 | 1977 | 7 | 18.37 |
| 1943 | 8 | 01.21 | 1978 | 8 | 00.45 |
| 1944 | 7 | 07.34 | 1979 | 8 | 06.48 |
| 1945 | 7 | 13.48 | 1980 | 7 | 13.05 |
| 1946 | 7 | 19.53 | 1981 | 7 | 19.13 |
| 1947 | 8 | 01.57 | 1982 | 8 | 01.17 |
| 1948 | 7 | 08.08 | 1983 | 8 | 07.26 |
| 1949 | 7 | 14.19 | 1984 | 7 | 13.32 |
| 1950 | 7 | 20.26 | 1985 | 7 | 19.46 |
| 1951 | 8 | 02.30 | 1986 | 8 | 01.51 |
| 1952 | 7 | 08.42 | 1987 | 8 | 07.51 |
| 1953 | 7 | 14.59 | 1988 | 7 | 14.10 |
| 1954 | 7 | 21.06 | 1989 | 7 | 20.22 |
| 1955 | 8 | 03.11 | 1990 | 8 | 02.28 |
| 1956 | 7 | 09.23 | 1991 | 8 | 08.41 |
| 1957 | 7 | 15.33 | 1992 | 7 | 14.47 |
| 1958 | 7 | 21.39 | 1993 | 7 | 21.01 |
| 1959 | 8 | 03.44 | 1994 | 8 | 03.09 |
| 1960 | 7 | 09.53 | 1995 | 8 | 09.07 |
| 1961 | 7 | 16.09 | 1996 | 7 | 15.25 |
| 1962 | 7 | 22.12 | 1997 | 7 | 21.33 |

# CUSPS

| Year | Day | Time | Year | Day | Time |
|---|---|---|---|---|---|
| 1998 | 8 | 03.35 | 2010 | 8 | 05.30 |
| 1999 | 8 | 09.48 | 2011 | 8 | 11.29 |
| 2000 | 7 | 15.57 | 2012 | 7 | 17.50 |
| 2001 | 7 | 22.14 | 2013 | 8 | 00.04 |
| 2002 | 8 | 04.24 | 2014 | 8 | 06.05 |
| 2003 | 8 | 10.09 | 2015 | 8 | 12.19 |
| 2004 | 7 | 16.40 | 2016 | 7 | 18.26 |
| 2005 | 7 | 22.48 | 2017 | 8 | 00.35 |
| 2006 | 8 | 04.49 | 2018 | 8 | 06.45 |
| 2007 | 8 | 11.02 | 2019 | 8 | 12.42 |
| 2008 | 7 | 17.08 | 2020 | 7 | 18.57 |
| 2009 | 7 | 23.21 | | | |

## Ardra
### 21 June to 6 July

| Year | Day | Time | Year | Day | Time |
|---|---|---|---|---|---|
| 1920 | 21 | 03.00 | 1938 | 21 | 17.43 |
| 1921 | 21 | 09.14 | 1939 | 21 | 23.38 |
| 1922 | 21 | 15.24 | 1940 | 21 | 05.54 |
| 1923 | 21 | 21.19 | 1941 | 21 | 12.10 |
| 1924 | 21 | 03.34 | 1942 | 21 | 18.12 |
| 1925 | 21 | 09.44 | 1943 | 22 | 00.27 |
| 1926 | 21 | 15.44 | 1944 | 21 | 06.36 |
| 1927 | 21 | 21.57 | 1945 | 21 | 12.46 |
| 1928 | 21 | 04.03 | 1946 | 21 | 19.00 |
| 1929 | 21 | 10.19 | 1947 | 22 | 00.56 |
| 1930 | 21 | 16.35 | 1948 | 21 | 07.10 |
| 1931 | 21 | 22.33 | 1949 | 21 | 13.26 |
| 1932 | 21 | 04.51 | 1950 | 21 | 19.22 |
| 1933 | 21 | 11.04 | 1951 | 22 | 01.35 |
| 1934 | 21 | 17.03 | 1952 | 21 | 07.46 |
| 1935 | 21 | 23.15 | 1953 | 21 | 13.56 |
| 1936 | 21 | 05.21 | 1954 | 21 | 20.12 |
| 1937 | 21 | 11.32 | 1955 | 22 | 02.11 |

## CUSPS

| Year | Day | Time  | Year | Day | Time  |
|------|-----|-------|------|-----|-------|
| 1956 | 21  | 08.24 | 1989 | 21  | 19.26 |
| 1957 | 21  | 14.40 | 1990 | 22  | 01.28 |
| 1958 | 21  | 20.36 | 1991 | 22  | 07.36 |
| 1959 | 22  | 02.47 | 1992 | 21  | 13.53 |
| 1960 | 21  | 08.59 | 1993 | 21  | 19.59 |
| 1961 | 21  | 15.05 | 1994 | 22  | 02.07 |
| 1962 | 21  | 21.18 | 1995 | 22  | 08.13 |
| 1963 | 22  | 03.18 | 1996 | 21  | 14.21 |
| 1964 | 21  | 09.31 | 1997 | 21  | 20.37 |
| 1965 | 21  | 15.52 | 1998 | 22  | 02.38 |
| 1966 | 21  | 21.52 | 1999 | 22  | 08.44 |
| 1967 | 22  | 04.04 | 2000 | 21  | 15.02 |
| 1968 | 21  | 10.18 | 2001 | 21  | 21.12 |
| 1969 | 21  | 16.23 | 2002 | 22  | 03.20 |
| 1970 | 21  | 22.34 | 2003 | 22  | 09.28 |
| 1971 | 22  | 04.34 | 2004 | 21  | 15.37 |
| 1972 | 21  | 10.43 | 2005 | 21  | 21.50 |
| 1973 | 21  | 16.59 | 2006 | 22  | 03.52 |
| 1974 | 21  | 22.57 | 2007 | 22  | 09.57 |
| 1975 | 22  | 05.06 | 2008 | 21  | 16.13 |
| 1976 | 21  | 11.24 | 2009 | 21  | 22.21 |
| 1977 | 21  | 17.32 | 2010 | 22  | 04.26 |
| 1978 | 21  | 23.47 | 2011 | 22  | 10.35 |
| 1979 | 22  | 05.52 | 2012 | 21  | 16.47 |
| 1980 | 21  | 12.02 | 2013 | 21  | 23.03 |
| 1981 | 21  | 18.19 | 2014 | 22  | 05.08 |
| 1982 | 22  | 00.17 | 2015 | 22  | 11.14 |
| 1983 | 22  | 06.24 | 2016 | 21  | 17.29 |
| 1984 | 21  | 12.39 | 2017 | 21  | 23.37 |
| 1985 | 21  | 18.43 | 2018 | 22  | 05.40 |
| 1986 | 22  | 00.52 | 2019 | 22  | 11.47 |
| 1987 | 22  | 06.56 | 2020 | 21  | 17.57 |
| 1988 | 21  | 13.06 |      |     |       |

## Punarvasu
## 5 to 20 July

| Year | Day | Time | Year | Day | Time |
|---|---|---|---|---|---|
| 1920 | 5 | 02.40 | 1952 | 5 | 07.20 |
| 1921 | 5 | 08.50 | 1953 | 5 | 13.35 |
| 1922 | 5 | 14.57 | 1954 | 5 | 19.41 |
| 1923 | 5 | 21.01 | 1955 | 6 | 01.48 |
| 1924 | 5 | 03.08 | 1956 | 5 | 08.02 |
| 1925 | 5 | 09.21 | 1957 | 5 | 14.11 |
| 1926 | 5 | 15.24 | 1958 | 5 | 20.15 |
| 1927 | 5 | 21.28 | 1959 | 6 | 02.22 |
| 1928 | 5 | 03.43 | 1960 | 5 | 08.31 |
| 1929 | 5 | 09.55 | 1961 | 5 | 14.45 |
| 1930 | 5 | 16.04 | 1962 | 5 | 20.49 |
| 1931 | 5 | 22.14 | 1963 | 6 | 02.54 |
| 1932 | 5 | 04.25 | 1964 | 5 | 09.11 |
| 1933 | 5 | 10.38 | 1965 | 5 | 15.21 |
| 1934 | 5 | 16.43 | 1966 | 5 | 21.29 |
| 1935 | 5 | 22.46 | 1967 | 6 | 03.39 |
| 1936 | 5 | 04.59 | 1968 | 5 | 09.49 |
| 1937 | 5 | 11.10 | 1969 | 5 | 16.03 |
| 1938 | 5 | 17.14 | 1970 | 5 | 22.06 |
| 1939 | 5 | 23.20 | 1971 | 6 | 04.08 |
| 1940 | 5 | 05.30 | 1972 | 5 | 10.24 |
| 1941 | 5 | 11.42 | 1973 | 5 | 16.30 |
| 1942 | 5 | 17.51 | 1974 | 5 | 22.34 |
| 1943 | 5 | 23.57 | 1975 | 6 | 04.44 |
| 1944 | 5 | 06.12 | 1976 | 5 | 10.54 |
| 1945 | 5 | 12.25 | 1977 | 5 | 17.10 |
| 1946 | 5 | 18.30 | 1978 | 5 | 23.19 |
| 1947 | 6 | 00.36 | 1979 | 6 | 05.24 |
| 1948 | 5 | 06.48 | 1980 | 5 | 11.43 |
| 1949 | 5 | 12.57 | 1981 | 5 | 17.50 |
| 1950 | 5 | 19.03 | 1982 | 5 | 23.52 |
| 1951 | 6 | 01.08 | 1983 | 6 | 06.03 |

## CUSPS

| Year | Day | Time | Year | Day | Time |
|---|---|---|---|---|---|
| 1984 | 5 | 12.10 | 2003 | 6 | 08.58 |
| 1985 | 5 | 18.21 | 2004 | 5 | 15.16 |
| 1986 | 6 | 00.28 | 2005 | 5 | 21.25 |
| 1987 | 6 | 06.28 | 2006 | 6 | 03.23 |
| 1988 | 5 | 12.46 | 2007 | 6 | 09.37 |
| 1989 | 5 | 18.57 | 2008 | 5 | 15.46 |
| 1990 | 6 | 01.00 | 2009 | 5 | 21.54 |
| 1991 | 6 | 07.15 | 2010 | 6 | 04.04 |
| 1992 | 5 | 13.24 | 2011 | 6 | 10.05 |
| 1993 | 5 | 19.36 | 2012 | 5 | 16.24 |
| 1994 | 6 | 01.44 | 2013 | 5 | 22.38 |
| 1995 | 6 | 07.44 | 2014 | 6 | 04.37 |
| 1996 | 5 | 14.02 | 2015 | 6 | 10.53 |
| 1997 | 5 | 20.11 | 2016 | 5 | 17.03 |
| 1998 | 6 | 02.09 | 2017 | 5 | 23.08 |
| 1999 | 6 | 08.24 | 2018 | 6 | 05.19 |
| 2000 | 5 | 14.33 | 2019 | 6 | 11.18 |
| 2001 | 5 | 20.45 | 2020 | 5 | 17.32 |
| 2002 | 6 | 02.57 | | | |

## Pushya
### 19 July to 3 August

| Year | Day | Time | Year | Day | Time |
|---|---|---|---|---|---|
| 1920 | 19 | 02.10 | 1931 | 19 | 21.41 |
| 1921 | 19 | 08.22 | 1932 | 19 | 03.59 |
| 1922 | 19 | 14.34 | 1933 | 19 | 10.14 |
| 1923 | 19 | 20.20 | 1934 | 19 | 16.11 |
| 1924 | 19 | 02.45 | 1935 | 19 | 22.24 |
| 1925 | 19 | 08.56 | 1936 | 19 | 04.33 |
| 1926 | 19 | 14.52 | 1937 | 19 | 10.39 |
| 1927 | 19 | 21.06 | 1938 | 19 | 16.52 |
| 1928 | 19 | 03.14 | 1939 | 19 | 22.50 |
| 1929 | 19 | 09.25 | 1940 | 19 | 05.04 |
| 1930 | 19 | 15.40 | 1941 | 19 | 11.19 |

## CUSPS

| Year | Day | Time  | Year | Day | Time  |
|------|-----|-------|------|-----|-------|
| 1942 | 19  | 17.17 | 1977 | 19  | 16.37 |
| 1943 | 19  | 23.32 | 1978 | 19  | 22.49 |
| 1944 | 19  | 05.46 | 1979 | 20  | 04.59 |
| 1945 | 19  | 11.53 | 1980 | 19  | 11.10 |
| 1946 | 19  | 18.07 | 1981 | 19  | 17.26 |
| 1947 | 20  | 00.07 | 1982 | 19  | 23.25 |
| 1948 | 19  | 06.20 | 1983 | 20  | 05.31 |
| 1949 | 19  | 12.35 | 1984 | 19  | 11.48 |
| 1950 | 19  | 18.31 | 1985 | 19  | 17.51 |
| 1951 | 20  | 00.43 | 1986 | 19  | 23.59 |
| 1952 | 19  | 06.56 | 1987 | 20  | 06.06 |
| 1953 | 19  | 13.02 | 1988 | 19  | 12.14 |
| 1954 | 19  | 19.17 | 1989 | 19  | 18.30 |
| 1955 | 20  | 01.20 | 1990 | 20  | 00.33 |
| 1956 | 19  | 07.32 | 1991 | 20  | 06.42 |
| 1957 | 19  | 13.49 | 1992 | 19  | 13.01 |
| 1958 | 19  | 19.44 | 1993 | 19  | 19.06 |
| 1959 | 20  | 01.55 | 1994 | 20  | 01.13 |
| 1960 | 19  | 08.09 | 1995 | 20  | 07.22 |
| 1961 | 19  | 14.12 | 1996 | 19  | 13.30 |
| 1962 | 19  | 20.25 | 1997 | 19  | 19.43 |
| 1963 | 20  | 02.29 | 1998 | 20  | 01.45 |
| 1964 | 19  | 08.40 | 1999 | 20  | 07.51 |
| 1965 | 19  | 14.58 | 2000 | 19  | 14.09 |
| 1966 | 19  | 20.57 | 2001 | 19  | 20.16 |
| 1967 | 20  | 03.09 | 2002 | 20  | 02.23 |
| 1968 | 19  | 09.27 | 2003 | 20  | 08.35 |
| 1969 | 19  | 15.30 | 2004 | 19  | 14.45 |
| 1970 | 19  | 21.40 | 2005 | 19  | 20.56 |
| 1971 | 20  | 03.44 | 2006 | 20  | 02.59 |
| 1972 | 19  | 09.52 | 2007 | 20  | 09.04 |
| 1973 | 19  | 16.07 | 2008 | 19  | 15.20 |
| 1974 | 19  | 22.05 | 2009 | 19  | 21.27 |
| 1975 | 20  | 04.13 | 2010 | 20  | 03.31 |
| 1976 | 19  | 10.32 | 2011 | 20  | 09.43 |

## CUSPS

| Year | Day | Time  | Year | Day | Time  |
|------|-----|-------|------|-----|-------|
| 2012 | 19  | 15.54 | 2017 | 19  | 22.43 |
| 2013 | 19  | 22.06 | 2018 | 20  | 04.46 |
| 2014 | 20  | 04.13 | 2019 | 20  | 10.55 |
| 2015 | 20  | 10.20 | 2020 | 19  | 17.05 |
| 2016 | 19  | 16.36 |      |     |       |

### Ashlesha
### 2 to 17 August

| Year | Day | Time  | Year | Day | Time  |
|------|-----|-------|------|-----|-------|
| 1920 | 2   | 01.06 | 1945 | 2   | 10.50 |
| 1921 | 2   | 07.15 | 1946 | 2   | 16.54 |
| 1922 | 2   | 13.22 | 1947 | 2   | 23.02 |
| 1923 | 2   | 19.30 | 1948 | 2   | 05.16 |
| 1924 | 2   | 01.37 | 1949 | 2   | 11.23 |
| 1925 | 2   | 07.47 | 1950 | 2   | 17.28 |
| 1926 | 2   | 13.50 | 1951 | 2   | 23.36 |
| 1927 | 2   | 19.55 | 1952 | 2   | 05.47 |
| 1928 | 2   | 02.10 | 1953 | 2   | 11.59 |
| 1929 | 2   | 08.20 | 1954 | 2   | 18.05 |
| 1930 | 2   | 14.26 | 1955 | 3   | 00.13 |
| 1931 | 2   | 20.38 | 1956 | 2   | 06.29 |
| 1932 | 2   | 02.52 | 1957 | 2   | 12.37 |
| 1933 | 2   | 09.03 | 1958 | 2   | 18.40 |
| 1934 | 2   | 15.09 | 1959 | 3   | 00.49 |
| 1935 | 2   | 21.14 | 1960 | 2   | 06.58 |
| 1936 | 2   | 03.27 | 1961 | 2   | 13.10 |
| 1937 | 2   | 09.36 | 1962 | 2   | 19.15 |
| 1938 | 2   | 15.39 | 1963 | 3   | 01.21 |
| 1939 | 2   | 21.48 | 1964 | 2   | 07.38 |
| 1940 | 2   | 03.59 | 1965 | 2   | 13.46 |
| 1941 | 2   | 10.07 | 1966 | 2   | 19.51 |
| 1942 | 2   | 16.14 | 1967 | 3   | 02.04 |
| 1943 | 2   | 22.22 | 1968 | 2   | 08.15 |
| 1944 | 2   | 04.37 | 1969 | 2   | 14.27 |

# CUSPS

| Year | Day | Time | Year | Day | Time |
|---|---|---|---|---|---|
| 1970 | 2 | 20.32 | 1996 | 2 | 12.27 |
| 1971 | 3 | 02.36 | 1997 | 2 | 18.37 |
| 1972 | 2 | 08.51 | 1998 | 3 | 00.35 |
| 1973 | 2 | 14.56 | 1999 | 3 | 06.50 |
| 1974 | 2 | 20.58 | 2000 | 2 | 13.00 |
| 1975 | 3 | 03.11 | 2001 | 2 | 19.07 |
| 1976 | 2 | 09.20 | 2002 | 3 | 01.19 |
| 1977 | 2 | 15.32 | 2003 | 3 | 07.23 |
| 1978 | 2 | 21.41 | 2004 | 2 | 13.40 |
| 1979 | 3 | 03.48 | 2005 | 2 | 19.51 |
| 1980 | 2 | 10.08 | 2006 | 3 | 01.48 |
| 1981 | 2 | 16.16 | 2007 | 3 | 08.02 |
| 1982 | 2 | 22.17 | 2008 | 2 | 14.13 |
| 1983 | 3 | 04.30 | 2009 | 2 | 20.17 |
| 1984 | 2 | 10.38 | 2010 | 3 | 02.29 |
| 1985 | 2 | 16.45 | 2011 | 3 | 08.33 |
| 1986 | 2 | 22.54 | 2012 | 2 | 14.48 |
| 1987 | 3 | 04.56 | 2013 | 2 | 21.02 |
| 1988 | 2 | 11.12 | 2014 | 3 | 03.00 |
| 1989 | 2 | 17.21 | 2015 | 3 | 09.17 |
| 1990 | 2 | 23.22 | 2016 | 2 | 15.30 |
| 1991 | 3 | 05.39 | 2017 | 2 | 21.32 |
| 1992 | 2 | 11.50 | 2018 | 3 | 03.44 |
| 1993 | 2 | 17.58 | 2019 | 3 | 09.47 |
| 1994 | 3 | 00.09 | 2020 | 2 | 15.57 |
| 1995 | 3 | 06.10 |  |  |  |

## Magha
### 15 to 31 August

| Year | Day | Time | Year | Day | Time |
|---|---|---|---|---|---|
| 1920 | 15 | 22.43 | 1924 | 15 | 23.20 |
| 1921 | 16 | 04.51 | 1925 | 16 | 05.30 |
| 1922 | 16 | 11.05 | 1926 | 16 | 11.24 |
| 1923 | 16 | 17.06 | 1927 | 16 | 17.39 |

## CUSPS

| Year | Day | Time | Year | Day | Time |
| --- | --- | --- | --- | --- | --- |
| 1928 | 15 | 23.50 | 1963 | 16 | 23.05 |
| 1929 | 16 | 05.55 | 1964 | 16 | 05.14 |
| 1930 | 16 | 12.10 | 1965 | 16 | 11.30 |
| 1931 | 16 | 18.14 | 1966 | 16 | 17.29 |
| 1932 | 16 | 00.30 | 1967 | 16 | 23.40 |
| 1933 | 16 | 06.46 | 1968 | 16 | 06.00 |
| 1934 | 16 | 12.43 | 1969 | 16 | 12.02 |
| 1935 | 16 | 18.57 | 1970 | 16 | 18.12 |
| 1936 | 16 | 01.09 | 1971 | 16 | 00.21 |
| 1937 | 16 | 07.11 | 1972 | 16 | 06.27 |
| 1938 | 16 | 13.23 | 1973 | 16 | 12.40 |
| 1939 | 16 | 19.27 | 1974 | 16 | 18.39 |
| 1940 | 16 | 01.38 | 1975 | 17 | 00.48 |
| 1941 | 16 | 07.52 | 1976 | 16 | 07.06 |
| 1942 | 16 | 13.48 | 1977 | 16 | 13.08 |
| 1943 | 16 | 20.02 | 1978 | 16 | 19.18 |
| 1944 | 16 | 02.19 | 1979 | 17 | 01.32 |
| 1945 | 16 | 08.23 | 1980 | 16 | 07.42 |
| 1946 | 16 | 14.37 | 1981 | 16 | 13.57 |
| 1947 | 16 | 20.43 | 1982 | 16 | 19.59 |
| 1948 | 16 | 02.53 | 1983 | 17 | 02.06 |
| 1949 | 16 | 09.08 | 1984 | 16 | 08.23 |
| 1950 | 16 | 15.04 | 1985 | 16 | 14.24 |
| 1951 | 16 | 21.16 | 1986 | 16 | 20.31 |
| 1952 | 16 | 03.32 | 1987 | 17 | 02.43 |
| 1953 | 16 | 09.33 | 1988 | 16 | 08.49 |
| 1954 | 16 | 15.46 | 1989 | 16 | 15.01 |
| 1955 | 16 | 21.54 | 1990 | 16 | 21.05 |
| 1956 | 16 | 04.04 | 1991 | 17 | 03.14 |
| 1957 | 16 | 10.21 | 1992 | 16 | 09.33 |
| 1958 | 16 | 16.18 | 1993 | 16 | 15.38 |
| 1959 | 16 | 22.28 | 1994 | 16 | 21.44 |
| 1960 | 16 | 04.44 | 1995 | 17 | 03.58 |
| 1961 | 16 | 10.44 | 1996 | 16 | 10.05 |
| 1962 | 16 | 16.56 | 1997 | 16 | 16.15 |

# CUSPS

| Year | Day | Time | Year | Day | Time |
|---|---|---|---|---|---|
| 1998 | 16 | 22.20 | 2010 | 17 | 00.03 |
| 1999 | 17 | 04.27 | 2011 | 17 | 06.18 |
| 2000 | 16 | 10.43 | 2012 | 16 | 12.28 |
| 2001 | 16 | 16.48 | 2013 | 16 | 18.37 |
| 2002 | 16 | 22.53 | 2014 | 17 | 00.44 |
| 2003 | 17 | 05.08 | 2015 | 17 | 06.54 |
| 2004 | 16 | 11.18 | 2016 | 16 | 13.09 |
| 2005 | 16 | 17.28 | 2017 | 16 | 19.16 |
| 2006 | 16 | 23.34 | 2018 | 17 | 01.19 |
| 2007 | 17 | 05.40 | 2019 | 17 | 07.31 |
| 2008 | 16 | 11.54 | 2020 | 16 | 13.40 |
| 2009 | 16 | 17.59 | | | |

## Purva Phalguni
### 29 August to 13 September

| Year | Day | Time | Year | Day | Time |
|---|---|---|---|---|---|
| 1920 | 29 | 18.40 | 1938 | 30 | 09.15 |
| 1921 | 30 | 00.48 | 1939 | 30 | 15.26 |
| 1922 | 30 | 06.55 | 1940 | 29 | 21.38 |
| 1923 | 30 | 13.07 | 1941 | 30 | 03.44 |
| 1924 | 29 | 19.16 | 1942 | 30 | 09.49 |
| 1925 | 30 | 01.23 | 1943 | 30 | 15.58 |
| 1926 | 30 | 07.26 | 1944 | 29 | 22.12 |
| 1927 | 30 | 13.33 | 1945 | 30 | 04.23 |
| 1928 | 29 | 19.47 | 1946 | 30 | 10.29 |
| 1929 | 30 | 01.56 | 1947 | 30 | 16.40 |
| 1930 | 30 | 08.00 | 1948 | 29 | 22.54 |
| 1931 | 30 | 14.14 | 1949 | 30 | 04.59 |
| 1932 | 29 | 20.27 | 1950 | 30 | 11.04 |
| 1933 | 30 | 02.37 | 1951 | 30 | 17.15 |
| 1934 | 30 | 08.44 | 1952 | 29 | 23.25 |
| 1935 | 30 | 14.52 | 1953 | 30 | 05.34 |
| 1936 | 29 | 21.04 | 1954 | 30 | 11.40 |
| 1937 | 30 | 03.12 | 1955 | 30 | 17.49 |

# CUSPS

| Year | Day | Time  | Year | Day | Time  |
|------|-----|-------|------|-----|-------|
| 1956 | 30  | 00.05 | 1989 | 30  | 10.59 |
| 1957 | 30  | 06.12 | 1990 | 30  | 16.58 |
| 1958 | 30  | 12.16 | 1991 | 30  | 23.16 |
| 1959 | 30  | 18.29 | 1992 | 30  | 05.27 |
| 1960 | 30  | 00.37 | 1993 | 30  | 11.32 |
| 1961 | 30  | 06.45 | 1994 | 30  | 17.46 |
| 1962 | 30  | 12.51 | 1995 | 30  | 23.52 |
| 1963 | 30  | 19.00 | 1996 | 30  | 06.05 |
| 1964 | 30  | 01.16 | 1997 | 30  | 12.15 |
| 1965 | 30  | 07.22 | 1998 | 30  | 18.13 |
| 1966 | 30  | 13.25 | 1999 | 31  | 00.31 |
| 1967 | 30  | 19.41 | 2000 | 30  | 06.40 |
| 1968 | 30  | 01.51 | 2001 | 30  | 12.42 |
| 1969 | 30  | 08.01 | 2002 | 30  | 18.55 |
| 1970 | 30  | 14.09 | 2003 | 31  | 01.02 |
| 1971 | 30  | 20.16 | 2004 | 30  | 07.15 |
| 1972 | 30  | 02.30 | 2005 | 30  | 13.28 |
| 1973 | 30  | 08.34 | 2006 | 30  | 19.26 |
| 1974 | 30  | 14.35 | 2007 | 31  | 01.42 |
| 1975 | 30  | 20.51 | 2008 | 30  | 07.53 |
| 1976 | 30  | 02.59 | 2009 | 30  | 13.52 |
| 1977 | 30  | 09.06 | 2010 | 30  | 20.06 |
| 1978 | 30  | 15.17 | 2011 | 31  | 02.14 |
| 1979 | 30  | 21.24 | 2012 | 30  | 08.25 |
| 1980 | 30  | 03.42 | 2013 | 30  | 14.38 |
| 1981 | 30  | 09.52 | 2014 | 30  | 20.37 |
| 1982 | 30  | 15.54 | 2015 | 31  | 02.53 |
| 1983 | 30  | 22.09 | 2016 | 30  | 09.08 |
| 1984 | 30  | 04.17 | 2017 | 30  | 15.08 |
| 1985 | 30  | 10.21 | 2018 | 30  | 21.22 |
| 1986 | 30  | 16.32 | 2019 | 31  | 03.29 |
| 1987 | 30  | 22.37 | 2020 | 30  | 09.35 |
| 1988 | 30  | 04.50 |      |     |       |

# CUSPS

## Uttara Phalguni
### 12 to 27 September

| Year | Day | Time | Year | Day | Time |
|------|-----|------|------|-----|------|
| 1920 | 12 | 12.29 | 1952 | 12 | 17.22 |
| 1921 | 12 | 18.33 | 1953 | 12 | 23.20 |
| 1922 | 13 | 00.49 | 1954 | 13 | 05.31 |
| 1923 | 13 | 06.55 | 1955 | 13 | 11.42 |
| 1924 | 12 | 13.06 | 1956 | 12 | 17.49 |
| 1925 | 12 | 19.18 | 1957 | 13 | 00.06 |
| 1926 | 13 | 01.12 | 1958 | 13 | 06.06 |
| 1927 | 13 | 07.36 | 1959 | 13 | 12.17 |
| 1928 | 12 | 13.39 | 1960 | 12 | 18.34 |
| 1929 | 12 | 19.40 | 1961 | 13 | 00.32 |
| 1930 | 13 | 01.54 | 1962 | 13 | 06.41 |
| 1931 | 13 | 08.02 | 1963 | 13 | 12.56 |
| 1932 | 12 | 14.14 | 1964 | 12 | 19.02 |
| 1933 | 12 | 20.30 | 1965 | 13 | 01.16 |
| 1934 | 13 | 02.29 | 1966 | 13 | 07.17 |
| 1935 | 13 | 08.44 | 1967 | 13 | 13.27 |
| 1936 | 12 | 14.58 | 1968 | 12 | 19.46 |
| 1937 | 12 | 20.57 | 1969 | 13 | 01.48 |
| 1938 | 13 | 03.09 | 1970 | 13 | 07.58 |
| 1939 | 13 | 09.17 | 1971 | 13 | 14.13 |
| 1940 | 12 | 15.25 | 1972 | 12 | 20.17 |
| 1941 | 12 | 21.39 | 1973 | 13 | 02.27 |
| 1942 | 13 | 03.36 | 1974 | 13 | 08.29 |
| 1943 | 13 | 09.48 | 1975 | 13 | 14.37 |
| 1944 | 12 | 16.05 | 1976 | 12 | 20.55 |
| 1945 | 12 | 22.06 | 1977 | 13 | 02.56 |
| 1946 | 13 | 04.21 | 1978 | 13 | 09.03 |
| 1947 | 13 | 10.32 | 1979 | 13 | 15.21 |
| 1948 | 12 | 16.40 | 1980 | 12 | 21.28 |
| 1949 | 12 | 22.55 | 1981 | 13 | 03.42 |
| 1950 | 13 | 04.53 | 1982 | 13 | 09.49 |
| 1951 | 13 | 11.04 | 1983 | 13 | 15.56 |

# CUSPS

| Year | Day | Time  | Year | Day | Time  |
|------|-----|-------|------|-----|-------|
| 1984 | 12  | 22.12 | 2003 | 13  | 18.57 |
| 1985 | 13  | 04.13 | 2004 | 13  | 01.07 |
| 1986 | 13  | 10.18 | 2005 | 13  | 07.14 |
| 1987 | 13  | 16.34 | 2006 | 13  | 13.24 |
| 1988 | 12  | 22.40 | 2007 | 13  | 19.32 |
| 1989 | 13  | 04.48 | 2008 | 13  | 01.44 |
| 1990 | 13  | 10.54 | 2009 | 13  | 07.48 |
| 1991 | 13  | 17.02 | 2010 | 13  | 13.52 |
| 1992 | 12  | 23.19 | 2011 | 13  | 20.09 |
| 1993 | 13  | 05.25 | 2012 | 13  | 02.19 |
| 1994 | 13  | 11.32 | 2013 | 13  | 08.25 |
| 1995 | 13  | 17.49 | 2014 | 13  | 14.34 |
| 1996 | 12  | 23.55 | 2015 | 13  | 20.44 |
| 1997 | 13  | 06.03 | 2016 | 13  | 02.57 |
| 1998 | 13  | 12.10 | 2017 | 13  | 09.04 |
| 1999 | 13  | 18.19 | 2018 | 13  | 15.10 |
| 2000 | 13  | 00.32 | 2019 | 13  | 21.23 |
| 2001 | 13  | 06.37 | 2020 | 13  | 03.31 |
| 2002 | 13  | 12.41 |      |     |       |

## Hasta
### 26 September to 11 October

| Year | Day | Time  | Year | Day | Time  |
|------|-----|-------|------|-----|-------|
| 1920 | 26  | 03.54 | 1931 | 26  | 23.31 |
| 1921 | 26  | 10.02 | 1932 | 26  | 05.43 |
| 1922 | 26  | 16.10 | 1933 | 26  | 11.51 |
| 1923 | 26  | 22.25 | 1934 | 26  | 18.00 |
| 1924 | 26  | 04.35 | 1935 | 27  | 00.12 |
| 1925 | 26  | 10.40 | 1936 | 26  | 06.22 |
| 1926 | 26  | 16.45 | 1937 | 26  | 12.30 |
| 1927 | 26  | 22.53 | 1938 | 26  | 18.33 |
| 1928 | 26  | 05.05 | 1939 | 27  | 00.45 |
| 1929 | 26  | 11.13 | 1940 | 26  | 06.58 |
| 1930 | 26  | 17.17 | 1941 | 26  | 13.02 |

## CUSPS

| Year | Day | Time | Year | Day | Time |
| --- | --- | --- | --- | --- | --- |
| 1942 | 26 | 19.07 | 1977 | 26 | 18.24 |
| 1943 | 27 | 01.18 | 1978 | 27 | 00.36 |
| 1944 | 26 | 07.28 | 1979 | 27 | 06.45 |
| 1945 | 26 | 13.37 | 1980 | 26 | 12.59 |
| 1946 | 26 | 19.46 | 1981 | 26 | 19.10 |
| 1947 | 27 | 01.59 | 1982 | 27 | 01.13 |
| 1948 | 26 | 08.13 | 1983 | 27 | 07.31 |
| 1949 | 26 | 14.18 | 1984 | 26 | 13.40 |
| 1950 | 26 | 20.22 | 1985 | 26 | 19.40 |
| 1951 | 27 | 02.36 | 1986 | 27 | 01.53 |
| 1952 | 26 | 08.45 | 1987 | 27 | 08.00 |
| 1953 | 26 | 14.52 | 1988 | 26 | 14.10 |
| 1954 | 26 | 20.59 | 1989 | 26 | 20.21 |
| 1955 | 27 | 03.07 | 1990 | 27 | 02.19 |
| 1956 | 26 | 09.22 | 1991 | 27 | 08.36 |
| 1957 | 26 | 15.29 | 1992 | 26 | 14.47 |
| 1958 | 26 | 21.34 | 1993 | 26 | 20.49 |
| 1959 | 27 | 03.50 | 1994 | 27 | 03.06 |
| 1960 | 26 | 09.58 | 1995 | 27 | 09.16 |
| 1961 | 26 | 16.03 | 1996 | 26 | 15.25 |
| 1962 | 26 | 22.11 | 1997 | 26 | 21.36 |
| 1963 | 27 | 04.10 | 1998 | 27 | 03.35 |
| 1964 | 26 | 10.35 | 1999 | 27 | 09.52 |
| 1965 | 26 | 16.42 | 2000 | 26 | 16.03 |
| 1966 | 26 | 22.44 | 2001 | 26 | 22.02 |
| 1967 | 27 | 05.00 | 2002 | 27 | 04.15 |
| 1968 | 26 | 11.09 | 2003 | 27 | 10.25 |
| 1969 | 26 | 17.17 | 2004 | 26 | 16.33 |
| 1970 | 26 | 23.29 | 2005 | 26 | 22.48 |
| 1971 | 27 | 05.37 | 2006 | 27 | 04.50 |
| 1972 | 26 | 11.50 | 2007 | 27 | 11.04 |
| 1973 | 26 | 17.55 | 2008 | 26 | 17.17 |
| 1974 | 26 | 23.56 | 2009 | 26 | 23.13 |
| 1975 | 27 | 06.12 | 2010 | 27 | 05.27 |
| 1976 | 26 | 12.21 | 2011 | 27 | 11.39 |

# CUSPS

| Year | Day | Time  | Year | Day | Time  |
|------|-----|-------|------|-----|-------|
| 2012 | 26  | 17.45 | 2017 | 27  | 00.28 |
| 2013 | 26  | 23.59 | 2018 | 27  | 06.43 |
| 2014 | 27  | 06.00 | 2019 | 27  | 12.55 |
| 2015 | 27  | 12.14 | 2020 | 26  | 18.57 |
| 2016 | 26  | 18.30 |      |     |       |

## Chitra
### 9 October to 24 October

| Year | Day | Time  | Year | Day | Time  |
|------|-----|-------|------|-----|-------|
| 1920 | 9   | 16.52 | 1945 | 10  | 02.30 |
| 1921 | 9   | 22.52 | 1946 | 10  | 08.43 |
| 1922 | 10  | 05.10 | 1947 | 10  | 15.00 |
| 1923 | 10  | 11.21 | 1948 | 9   | 21.05 |
| 1924 | 9   | 17.29 | 1949 | 10  | 03.19 |
| 1925 | 9   | 23.43 | 1950 | 10  | 09.21 |
| 1926 | 10  | 05.39 | 1951 | 10  | 15.30 |
| 1927 | 10  | 11.51 | 1952 | 9   | 21.48 |
| 1928 | 9   | 18.06 | 1953 | 10  | 03.47 |
| 1929 | 10  | 00.05 | 1954 | 10  | 09.56 |
| 1930 | 10  | 06.18 | 1955 | 10  | 16.11 |
| 1931 | 10  | 12.29 | 1956 | 9   | 22.14 |
| 1932 | 9   | 18.35 | 1957 | 10  | 04.38 |
| 1933 | 10  | 00.52 | 1958 | 10  | 10.34 |
| 1934 | 10  | 06.54 | 1959 | 10  | 16.43 |
| 1935 | 10  | 13.08 | 1960 | 9   | 23.01 |
| 1936 | 9   | 19.24 | 1961 | 10  | 05.00 |
| 1937 | 10  | 01.22 | 1962 | 10  | 11.07 |
| 1938 | 10  | 07.33 | 1963 | 10  | 17.24 |
| 1939 | 10  | 13.46 | 1964 | 9   | 23.29 |
| 1940 | 9   | 19.50 | 1965 | 10  | 05.41 |
| 1941 | 10  | 02.04 | 1966 | 10  | 11.47 |
| 1942 | 10  | 08.05 | 1967 | 10  | 17.54 |
| 1943 | 10  | 14.13 | 1968 | 9   | 00.10 |
| 1944 | 9   | 20.30 | 1969 | 10  | 06.14 |

## CUSPS

| Year | Day | Time | Year | Day | Time |
|---|---|---|---|---|---|
| 1970 | 10 | 12.23 | 1996 | 10 | 04.26 |
| 1971 | 10 | 18.42 | 1997 | 10 | 10.31 |
| 1972 | 10 | 00.45 | 1998 | 10 | 16.41 |
| 1973 | 10 | 06.53 | 1999 | 10 | 22.50 |
| 1974 | 10 | 13.00 | 2000 | 10 | 05.01 |
| 1975 | 10 | 19.06 | 2001 | 10 | 11.07 |
| 1976 | 10 | 01.22 | 2002 | 10 | 17.11 |
| 1977 | 10 | 07.25 | 2003 | 10 | 23.26 |
| 1978 | 10 | 13.31 | 2004 | 10 | 05.35 |
| 1979 | 10 | 19.48 | 2005 | 10 | 11.41 |
| 1980 | 10 | 01.54 | 2006 | 10 | 17.54 |
| 1981 | 10 | 08.05 | 2007 | 11 | 00.04 |
| 1982 | 10 | 14.17 | 2008 | 10 | 06.13 |
| 1983 | 10 | 20.25 | 2009 | 10 | 12.19 |
| 1984 | 10 | 02.40 | 2010 | 10 | 18.23 |
| 1985 | 10 | 08.42 | 2011 | 11 | 00.38 |
| 1986 | 10 | 14.47 | 2012 | 10 | 06.49 |
| 1987 | 10 | 21.04 | 2013 | 10 | 12.54 |
| 1988 | 10 | 03.10 | 2014 | 10 | 19.04 |
| 1989 | 10 | 09.16 | 2015 | 11 | 01.15 |
| 1990 | 10 | 15.25 | 2016 | 10 | 07.24 |
| 1991 | 10 | 21.32 | 2017 | 10 | 13.32 |
| 1992 | 10 | 03.45 | 2018 | 10 | 19.41 |
| 1993 | 10 | 09.52 | 2019 | 11 | 01.54 |
| 1994 | 10 | 15.59 | 2020 | 10 | 08.03 |
| 1995 | 10 | 22.18 | | | |

### Swati
#### 23 October to 6 November

| Year | Day | Time | Year | Day | Time |
|---|---|---|---|---|---|
| 1920 | 23 | 03.15 | 1924 | 23 | 03.59 |
| 1921 | 23 | 09.23 | 1925 | 23 | 10.05 |
| 1922 | 23 | 15.32 | 1926 | 23 | 16.11 |
| 1923 | 23 | 21.47 | 1927 | 23 | 22.20 |

## CUSPS

| Year | Day | Time | Year | Day | Time |
|---|---|---|---|---|---|
| 1928 | 23 | 04.28 | 1963 | 24 | 03.48 |
| 1929 | 23 | 10.37 | 1964 | 23 | 10.00 |
| 1930 | 23 | 16.44 | 1965 | 23 | 16.10 |
| 1931 | 23 | 22.55 | 1966 | 23 | 22.12 |
| 1932 | 23 | 05.06 | 1967 | 24 | 04.27 |
| 1933 | 23 | 11.13 | 1968 | 23 | 10.35 |
| 1934 | 23 | 17.22 | 1969 | 23 | 16.40 |
| 1935 | 23 | 23.37 | 1970 | 23 | 22.55 |
| 1936 | 23 | 05.46 | 1971 | 24 | 05.06 |
| 1937 | 23 | 11.54 | 1972 | 23 | 11.16 |
| 1938 | 23 | 18.01 | 1973 | 23 | 17.25 |
| 1939 | 24 | 00.11 | 1974 | 23 | 23.25 |
| 1940 | 23 | 06.22 | 1975 | 24 | 05.40 |
| 1941 | 23 | 12.28 | 1976 | 23 | 11.50 |
| 1942 | 23 | 18.34 | 1977 | 23 | 17.51 |
| 1943 | 24 | 00.46 | 1978 | 24 | 00.06 |
| 1944 | 23 | 06.52 | 1979 | 24 | 06.14 |
| 1945 | 23 | 12.59 | 1980 | 23 | 12.22 |
| 1946 | 23 | 19.11 | 1981 | 23 | 18.36 |
| 1947 | 24 | 01.23 | 1982 | 24 | 00.41 |
| 1948 | 23 | 07.37 | 1983 | 24 | 06.57 |
| 1949 | 23 | 13.45 | 1984 | 23 | 13.10 |
| 1950 | 23 | 19.49 | 1985 | 23 | 19.08 |
| 1951 | 24 | 02.03 | 1986 | 24 | 01.22 |
| 1952 | 23 | 08.11 | 1987 | 24 | 07.31 |
| 1953 | 23 | 14.16 | 1988 | 23 | 13.37 |
| 1954 | 23 | 20.28 | 1989 | 23 | 19.50 |
| 1955 | 24 | 02.34 | 1990 | 24 | 01.51 |
| 1956 | 23 | 08.45 | 1991 | 24 | 08.03 |
| 1957 | 23 | 14.54 | 1992 | 23 | 14.15 |
| 1958 | 23 | 20.59 | 1993 | 23 | 20.15 |
| 1959 | 24 | 03.17 | 1994 | 24 | 02.33 |
| 1960 | 23 | 09.25 | 1995 | 24 | 08.46 |
| 1961 | 23 | 15.29 | 1996 | 23 | 14.52 |
| 1962 | 23 | 21.40 | 1997 | 23 | 21.06 |

# CUSPS

| Year | Day | Time | Year | Day | Time |
|---|---|---|---|---|---|
| 1998 | 24 | 03.08 | 2010 | 24 | 04.56 |
| 1999 | 24 | 09.20 | 2011 | 24 | 11.11 |
| 2000 | 23 | 15.24 | 2012 | 23 | 17.14 |
| 2001 | 23 | 21.32 | 2013 | 23 | 23.29 |
| 2002 | 24 | 03.45 | 2014 | 24 | 05.34 |
| 2003 | 24 | 09.57 | 2015 | 24 | 11.42 |
| 2004 | 23 | 15.59 | 2016 | 23 | 17.58 |
| 2005 | 23 | 22.15 | 2017 | 23 | 23.57 |
| 2006 | 24 | 04.21 | 2018 | 24 | 06.12 |
| 2007 | 24 | 10.33 | 2019 | 24 | 12.28 |
| 2008 | 23 | 16.48 | 2020 | 23 | 18.28 |
| 2009 | 23 | 22.44 | | | |

## Vishakha
### 5 to 20 November

| Year | Day | Time | Year | Day | Time |
|---|---|---|---|---|---|
| 1920 | 5 | 11.24 | 1938 | 6 | 02.07 |
| 1921 | 5 | 17.22 | 1939 | 6 | 08.22 |
| 1922 | 5 | 23.38 | 1940 | 5 | 14.23 |
| 1923 | 6 | 05.53 | 1941 | 5 | 20.37 |
| 1924 | 5 | 11.59 | 1942 | 6 | 02.43 |
| 1925 | 5 | 18.14 | 1943 | 6 | 08.48 |
| 1926 | 6 | 00.16 | 1944 | 5 | 15.03 |
| 1927 | 6 | 06.23 | 1945 | 5 | 21.03 |
| 1928 | 5 | 12.38 | 1946 | 6 | 03.14 |
| 1929 | 5 | 18.38 | 1947 | 6 | 09.34 |
| 1930 | 6 | 00.51 | 1948 | 5 | 15.38 |
| 1931 | 6 | 07.05 | 1949 | 5 | 21.52 |
| 1932 | 5 | 13.06 | 1950 | 6 | 03.59 |
| 1933 | 5 | 19.21 | 1951 | 6 | 10.04 |
| 1934 | 6 | 01.28 | 1952 | 5 | 16.21 |
| 1935 | 6 | 07.38 | 1953 | 5 | 22.23 |
| 1936 | 5 | 13.56 | 1954 | 6 | 04.31 |
| 1937 | 5 | 19.57 | 1955 | 6 | 10.47 |

## CUSPS

| Year | Day | Time | Year | Day | Time |
|---|---|---|---|---|---|
| 1956 | 5 | 16.48 | 1989 | 6 | 03.53 |
| 1957 | 5 | 22.59 | 1990 | 6 | 10.05 |
| 1958 | 6 | 05.10 | 1991 | 6 | 16.11 |
| 1959 | 6 | 11.17 | 1992 | 5 | 22.19 |
| 1960 | 5 | 17.34 | 1993 | 6 | 04.27 |
| 1961 | 5 | 23.38 | 1994 | 6 | 10.37 |
| 1962 | 6 | 05.44 | 1995 | 6 | 16.54 |
| 1963 | 6 | 12.00 | 1996 | 5 | 23.04 |
| 1964 | 5 | 18.04 | 1997 | 6 | 05.09 |
| 1965 | 6 | 00.14 | 1998 | 6 | 11.20 |
| 1966 | 6 | 06.26 | 1999 | 6 | 17.29 |
| 1967 | 6 | 12.30 | 2000 | 5 | 23.37 |
| 1968 | 5 | 18.43 | 2001 | 6 | 05.46 |
| 1969 | 6 | 00.49 | 2002 | 6 | 11.52 |
| 1970 | 6 | 06.56 | 2003 | 6 | 18.03 |
| 1971 | 6 | 13.17 | 2004 | 6 | 00.11 |
| 1972 | 5 | 19.22 | 2005 | 6 | 06.18 |
| 1973 | 6 | 01.29 | 2006 | 6 | 12.31 |
| 1974 | 6 | 07.40 | 2007 | 6 | 18.44 |
| 1975 | 6 | 13.44 | 2008 | 6 | 00.52 |
| 1976 | 5 | 19.57 | 2009 | 6 | 06.58 |
| 1977 | 6 | 02.03 | 2010 | 6 | 13.05 |
| 1978 | 6 | 08.09 | 2011 | 6 | 19.16 |
| 1979 | 6 | 14.25 | 2012 | 6 | 01.27 |
| 1980 | 5 | 20.30 | 2013 | 6 | 07.34 |
| 1981 | 6 | 02.38 | 2014 | 6 | 13.44 |
| 1982 | 6 | 08.53 | 2015 | 6 | 19.54 |
| 1983 | 6 | 15.02 | 2016 | 6 | 02.01 |
| 1984 | 5 | 21.15 | 2017 | 6 | 08.08 |
| 1985 | 6 | 03.21 | 2018 | 6 | 14.22 |
| 1986 | 6 | 09.26 | 2019 | 6 | 20.33 |
| 1987 | 6 | 15.41 | 2020 | 6 | 02.42 |
| 1988 | 5 | 21.47 | | | |

## Anuradha
### 18 November to 3 December

| Year | Day | Time | Year | Day | Time |
|------|-----|-------|------|-----|-------|
| 1920 | 18 | 17.18 | 1952 | 18 | 22.18 |
| 1921 | 18 | 23.25 | 1953 | 19 | 04.22 |
| 1922 | 19 | 05.36 | 1954 | 19 | 10.37 |
| 1923 | 19 | 11.49 | 1955 | 19 | 16.43 |
| 1924 | 18 | 18.02 | 1956 | 18 | 22.49 |
| 1925 | 19 | 00.10 | 1957 | 19 | 05.00 |
| 1926 | 19 | 06.17 | 1958 | 19 | 11.05 |
| 1927 | 19 | 12.27 | 1959 | 19 | 17.21 |
| 1928 | 18 | 18.33 | 1960 | 18 | 23.33 |
| 1929 | 19 | 00.41 | 1961 | 19 | 05.36 |
| 1930 | 19 | 06.52 | 1962 | 19 | 11.51 |
| 1931 | 19 | 13.01 | 1963 | 19 | 17.58 |
| 1932 | 18 | 19.10 | 1964 | 19 | 00.05 |
| 1933 | 19 | 01.17 | 1965 | 19 | 06.19 |
| 1934 | 19 | 07.26 | 1966 | 19 | 12.23 |
| 1935 | 19 | 13.41 | 1967 | 19 | 18.34 |
| 1936 | 18 | 19.50 | 1968 | 19 | 00.44 |
| 1937 | 19 | 01.58 | 1969 | 19 | 06.45 |
| 1938 | 19 | 08.10 | 1970 | 19 | 13.02 |
| 1939 | 19 | 14.17 | 1971 | 19 | 19.14 |
| 1940 | 18 | 20.26 | 1972 | 19 | 01.21 |
| 1941 | 19 | 02.35 | 1973 | 19 | 07.35 |
| 1942 | 19 | 08.42 | 1974 | 19 | 13.38 |
| 1943 | 19 | 14.53 | 1975 | 19 | 19.48 |
| 1944 | 18 | 20.59 | 1976 | 19 | 02.00 |
| 1945 | 19 | 03.03 | 1977 | 19 | 08.00 |
| 1946 | 19 | 09.18 | 1978 | 19 | 14.16 |
| 1947 | 19 | 15.28 | 1979 | 19 | 20.25 |
| 1948 | 18 | 21.40 | 1980 | 19 | 02.28 |
| 1949 | 19 | 03.52 | 1981 | 19 | 08.43 |
| 1950 | 19 | 09.57 | 1982 | 19 | 14.50 |
| 1951 | 19 | 16.09 | 1983 | 19 | 21.03 |

# CUSPS

| Year | Day | Time | Year | Day | Time |
|------|-----|-------|------|-----|-------|
| 1984 | 19 | 03.19 | 2003 | 20 | 00.09 |
| 1985 | 19 | 09.18 | 2004 | 19 | 06.08 |
| 1986 | 19 | 15.33 | 2005 | 19 | 12.23 |
| 1987 | 19 | 21.43 | 2006 | 19 | 18.34 |
| 1988 | 19 | 03.45 | 2007 | 20 | 00.42 |
| 1989 | 19 | 10.01 | 2008 | 19 | 06.59 |
| 1990 | 19 | 16.05 | 2009 | 19 | 12.59 |
| 1991 | 19 | 22.12 | 2010 | 19 | 19.08 |
| 1992 | 19 | 04.25 | 2011 | 19 | 01.23 |
| 1993 | 19 | 10.24 | 2012 | 19 | 07.24 |
| 1994 | 19 | 16.41 | 2013 | 19 | 13.39 |
| 1995 | 19 | 22.57 | 2014 | 19 | 19.49 |
| 1996 | 19 | 05.00 | 2015 | 20 | 01.52 |
| 1997 | 19 | 11.16 | 2016 | 19 | 08.07 |
| 1998 | 19 | 17.22 | 2017 | 19 | 14.09 |
| 1999 | 19 | 23.29 | 2018 | 19 | 20.21 |
| 2000 | 19 | 05.44 | 2019 | 20 | 02.40 |
| 2001 | 19 | 11.44 | 2020 | 19 | 08.41 |
| 2002 | 19 | 17.56 | | | |

## Jyeshta
### 1 to 16 December

| Year | Day | Time | Year | Day | Time |
|------|-----|-------|------|-----|-------|
| 1920 | 1 | 21.38 | 1931 | 2 | 17.22 |
| 1921 | 2 | 03.37 | 1932 | 1 | 23.21 |
| 1922 | 2 | 09.50 | 1933 | 2 | 05.33 |
| 1923 | 2 | 16.07 | 1934 | 2 | 11.44 |
| 1924 | 1 | 22.10 | 1935 | 2 | 17.50 |
| 1925 | 2 | 04.27 | 1936 | 2 | 00.08 |
| 1926 | 2 | 10.36 | 1937 | 2 | 06.14 |
| 1927 | 2 | 16.38 | 1938 | 2 | 12.23 |
| 1928 | 1 | 22.53 | 1939 | 2 | 18.39 |
| 1929 | 2 | 04.55 | 1940 | 2 | 00.38 |
| 1930 | 2 | 11.06 | 1941 | 2 | 06.50 |

## CUSPS

| Year | Day | Time | Year | Day | Time |
|---|---|---|---|---|---|
| 1942 | 2 | 13.03 | 1977 | 2 | 12.23 |
| 1943 | 2 | 19.05 | 1978 | 2 | 18.30 |
| 1944 | 2 | 01.17 | 1979 | 3 | 00.42 |
| 1945 | 2 | 07.21 | 1980 | 2 | 06.48 |
| 1946 | 2 | 13.29 | 1981 | 2 | 12.54 |
| 1947 | 2 | 19.48 | 1982 | 2 | 19.09 |
| 1948 | 2 | 01.53 | 1983 | 3 | 01.19 |
| 1949 | 2 | 08.06 | 1984 | 2 | 07.30 |
| 1950 | 2 | 14.19 | 1985 | 2 | 13.41 |
| 1951 | 2 | 20.21 | 1986 | 2 | 19.49 |
| 1952 | 2 | 02.34 | 1987 | 3 | 01.59 |
| 1953 | 2 | 08.41 | 1988 | 2 | 08.07 |
| 1954 | 2 | 14.49 | 1989 | 2 | 14.14 |
| 1955 | 2 | 21.04 | 1990 | 2 | 20.25 |
| 1956 | 2 | 03.05 | 1991 | 3 | 02.33 |
| 1957 | 2 | 09.13 | 1992 | 2 | 08.37 |
| 1958 | 2 | 15.27 | 1993 | 2 | 14.46 |
| 1959 | 2 | 21.33 | 1994 | 2 | 20.57 |
| 1960 | 2 | 03.48 | 1995 | 3 | 03.10 |
| 1961 | 2 | 09.57 | 1996 | 2 | 09.22 |
| 1962 | 2 | 16.03 | 1997 | 2 | 15.31 |
| 1963 | 2 | 22.18 | 1998 | 2 | 21.41 |
| 1964 | 2 | 04.22 | 1999 | 3 | 03.50 |
| 1965 | 2 | 10.30 | 2000 | 2 | 09.56 |
| 1966 | 2 | 16.45 | 2001 | 2 | 16.06 |
| 1967 | 2 | 22.49 | 2002 | 2 | 22.16 |
| 1968 | 2 | 04.58 | 2003 | 3 | 04.23 |
| 1969 | 2 | 11.06 | 2004 | 2 | 10.30 |
| 1970 | 2 | 17.14 | 2005 | 2 | 16.38 |
| 1971 | 2 | 23.31 | 2006 | 2 | 22.50 |
| 1972 | 2 | 05.40 | 2007 | 3 | 05.03 |
| 1973 | 2 | 11.47 | 2008 | 2 | 11.12 |
| 1974 | 2 | 18.01 | 2009 | 2 | 17.21 |
| 1975 | 3 | 00.05 | 2010 | 2 | 23.30 |
| 1976 | 2 | 06.13 | 2011 | 3 | 05.37 |

CUSPS

| Year | Day | Time  | Year | Day | Time  |
|------|-----|-------|------|-----|-------|
| 2012 | 2   | 11.46 | 2017 | 2   | 18.27 |
| 2013 | 2   | 17.57 | 2018 | 3   | 00.43 |
| 2014 | 3   | 00.05 | 2019 | 3   | 06.52 |
| 2015 | 3   | 06.15 | 2020 | 2   | 13.02 |
| 2016 | 2   | 12.21 |      |     |       |

## Mula
### 15 to 29 December

| Year | Day | Time  | Year | Day | Time  |
|------|-----|-------|------|-----|-------|
| 1920 | 15  | 00.31 | 1945 | 15  | 10.17 |
| 1921 | 15  | 06.37 | 1946 | 15  | 16.33 |
| 1922 | 15  | 12.50 | 1947 | 15  | 22.42 |
| 1923 | 15  | 18.59 | 1948 | 15  | 04.51 |
| 1924 | 15  | 01.11 | 1949 | 15  | 11.08 |
| 1925 | 15  | 07.23 | 1950 | 15  | 17.14 |
| 1926 | 15  | 13.32 | 1951 | 15  | 23.24 |
| 1927 | 15  | 19.42 | 1952 | 15  | 05.34 |
| 1928 | 15  | 01.47 | 1953 | 15  | 11.36 |
| 1929 | 15  | 07.53 | 1954 | 15  | 17.53 |
| 1930 | 15  | 14.08 | 1955 | 16  | 00.00 |
| 1931 | 15  | 20.16 | 1956 | 15  | 06.03 |
| 1932 | 15  | 02.22 | 1957 | 15  | 12.16 |
| 1933 | 15  | 08.32 | 1958 | 15  | 18.21 |
| 1934 | 15  | 14.39 | 1959 | 16  | 00.33 |
| 1935 | 15  | 20.52 | 1960 | 15  | 06.48 |
| 1936 | 15  | 03.02 | 1961 | 15  | 12.52 |
| 1937 | 15  | 09.11 | 1962 | 15  | 19.08 |
| 1938 | 15  | 15.27 | 1963 | 16  | 01.17 |
| 1939 | 15  | 21.33 | 1964 | 15  | 07.18 |
| 1940 | 15  | 03.38 | 1965 | 15  | 13.35 |
| 1941 | 15  | 09.51 | 1966 | 15  | 19.42 |
| 1942 | 15  | 15.58 | 1967 | 16  | 01.49 |
| 1943 | 15  | 22.08 | 1968 | 15  | 08.00 |
| 1944 | 15  | 04.15 | 1969 | 15  | 14.01 |

## CUSPS

| Year | Day | Time  | Year | Day | Time  |
|------|-----|-------|------|-----|-------|
| 1970 | 15  | 20.16 | 1996 | 15  | 12.16 |
| 1971 | 16  | 02.30 | 1997 | 15  | 18.33 |
| 1972 | 15  | 08.34 | 1998 | 16  | 00.45 |
| 1973 | 15  | 14.52 | 1999 | 16  | 06.45 |
| 1974 | 15  | 20.59 | 2000 | 15  | 13.00 |
| 1975 | 16  | 03.03 | 2001 | 15  | 19.05 |
| 1976 | 15  | 09.17 | 2002 | 16  | 01.14 |
| 1977 | 15  | 15.18 | 2003 | 16  | 07.29 |
| 1978 | 15  | 21.33 | 2004 | 15  | 13.26 |
| 1979 | 16  | 03.45 | 2005 | 15  | 19.39 |
| 1980 | 15  | 09.43 | 2006 | 16  | 01.54 |
| 1981 | 15  | 15.58 | 2007 | 16  | 07.57 |
| 1982 | 15  | 22.08 | 2008 | 15  | 14.15 |
| 1983 | 16  | 04.15 | 2009 | 15  | 20.22 |
| 1984 | 15  | 10.33 | 2010 | 16  | 02.28 |
| 1985 | 15  | 16.37 | 2011 | 16  | 08.42 |
| 1986 | 15  | 22.50 | 2012 | 15  | 14.43 |
| 1987 | 16  | 05.02 | 2013 | 15  | 20.57 |
| 1988 | 15  | 11.01 | 2014 | 16  | 03.11 |
| 1989 | 15  | 17.17 | 2015 | 16  | 09.11 |
| 1990 | 15  | 23.27 | 2016 | 15  | 15.24 |
| 1991 | 16  | 05.29 | 2017 | 15  | 21.30 |
| 1992 | 15  | 11.42 | 2018 | 16  | 03.38 |
| 1993 | 15  | 17.44 | 2019 | 16  | 09.56 |
| 1994 | 15  | 23.55 | 2020 | 15  | 16.01 |
| 1995 | 16  | 06.13 |      |     |       |

### Purva Ashadha
### 28 December to 11 January

| Year | Day | Time  | Year | Day | Time  |
|------|-----|-------|------|-----|-------|
| 1920 | 28  | 02.46 | 1924 | 28  | 03.18 |
| 1921 | 28  | 08.50 | 1925 | 28  | 09.33 |
| 1922 | 28  | 14.58 | 1926 | 28  | 15.49 |
| 1923 | 28  | 21.14 | 1927 | 28  | 21.50 |

## CUSPS

| Year | Day | Time | Year | Day | Time |
|---|---|---|---|---|---|
| 1928 | 28 | 04.01 | 1963 | 29 | 03.29 |
| 1929 | 28 | 10.08 | 1964 | 28 | 09.35 |
| 1930 | 28 | 16.16 | 1965 | 28 | 15.43 |
| 1931 | 28 | 22.32 | 1966 | 28 | 21.57 |
| 1932 | 28 | 04.33 | 1967 | 29 | 04.03 |
| 1933 | 28 | 10.42 | 1968 | 28 | 10.08 |
| 1934 | 28 | 16.56 | 1969 | 28 | 16.19 |
| 1935 | 28 | 22.58 | 1970 | 28 | 22.26 |
| 1936 | 28 | 05.13 | 1971 | 29 | 04.39 |
| 1937 | 28 | 11.25 | 1972 | 28 | 10.50 |
| 1938 | 28 | 17.34 | 1973 | 28 | 17.00 |
| 1939 | 28 | 23.49 | 1974 | 28 | 23.14 |
| 1940 | 28 | 05.51 | 1975 | 29 | 05.19 |
| 1941 | 28 | 12.00 | 1976 | 28 | 11.25 |
| 1942 | 28 | 18.16 | 1977 | 28 | 17.36 |
| 1943 | 29 | 00.17 | 1978 | 28 | 23.46 |
| 1944 | 28 | 06.27 | 1979 | 29 | 05.54 |
| 1945 | 28 | 12.34 | 1980 | 28 | 12.01 |
| 1946 | 28 | 18.40 | 1981 | 28 | 18.08 |
| 1947 | 29 | 00.55 | 1982 | 29 | 00.20 |
| 1948 | 28 | 07.03 | 1983 | 29 | 06.30 |
| 1949 | 28 | 13.15 | 1984 | 28 | 12.40 |
| 1950 | 28 | 19.32 | 1985 | 28 | 18.53 |
| 1951 | 29 | 01.35 | 1986 | 29 | 01.05 |
| 1952 | 28 | 07.43 | 1987 | 29 | 07.10 |
| 1953 | 28 | 13.54 | 1988 | 28 | 13.19 |
| 1954 | 28 | 20.01 | 1989 | 28 | 19.29 |
| 1955 | 29 | 02.13 | 1990 | 29 | 01.39 |
| 1956 | 28 | 08.18 | 1991 | 29 | 07.47 |
| 1957 | 28 | 14.24 | 1992 | 28 | 13.51 |
| 1958 | 28 | 20.38 | 1993 | 28 | 19.59 |
| 1959 | 29 | 02.44 | 1994 | 29 | 02.11 |
| 1960 | 28 | 08.55 | 1995 | 29 | 08.20 |
| 1961 | 28 | 15.10 | 1996 | 28 | 14.32 |
| 1962 | 28 | 21.18 | 1997 | 28 | 20.46 |

# CUSPS

| Year | Day | Time | Year | Day | Time |
|---|---|---|---|---|---|
| 1998 | 29 | 02.56 | 2010 | 29 | 04.47 |
| 1999 | 29 | 09.04 | 2011 | 29 | 10.51 |
| 2000 | 28 | 15.10 | 2012 | 28 | 16.58 |
| 2001 | 28 | 21.19 | 2013 | 28 | 23.13 |
| 2002 | 29 | 03.31 | 2014 | 29 | 05.20 |
| 2003 | 29 | 09.37 | 2015 | 29 | 11.28 |
| 2004 | 28 | 15.43 | 2016 | 28 | 17.36 |
| 2005 | 28 | 21.54 | 2017 | 28 | 23.40 |
| 2006 | 29 | 04.03 | 2018 | 29 | 05.56 |
| 2007 | 29 | 10.14 | 2019 | 29 | 12.04 |
| 2008 | 28 | 16.26 | 2020 | 28 | 18.13 |
| 2009 | 28 | 22.35 | | | |

## Uttara Ashadha
### 10 to 24 January

| Year | Day | Time | Year | Day | Time |
|---|---|---|---|---|---|
| 1920 | 10 | 22.35 | 1938 | 10 | 13.19 |
| 1921 | 10 | 04.42 | 1939 | 10 | 19.36 |
| 1922 | 10 | 10.46 | 1940 | 11 | 01.45 |
| 1923 | 10 | 17.00 | 1941 | 10 | 07.47 |
| 1924 | 10 | 23.06 | 1942 | 10 | 14.03 |
| 1925 | 10 | 05.16 | 1943 | 10 | 20.10 |
| 1926 | 10 | 11.33 | 1944 | 11 | 02.16 |
| 1927 | 10 | 17.42 | 1945 | 10 | 08.28 |
| 1928 | 10 | 23.52 | 1946 | 10 | 14.29 |
| 1929 | 10 | 05.59 | 1947 | 10 | 20.42 |
| 1930 | 10 | 12.03 | 1948 | 11 | 02.52 |
| 1931 | 10 | 18.19 | 1949 | 10 | 08.57 |
| 1932 | 11 | 00.26 | 1950 | 10 | 15.18 |
| 1933 | 10 | 06.31 | 1951 | 10 | 21.27 |
| 1934 | 10 | 12.44 | 1952 | 11 | 03.33 |
| 1935 | 10 | 18.49 | 1953 | 10 | 09.45 |
| 1936 | 11 | 00.58 | 1954 | 10 | 15.48 |
| 1937 | 10 | 07.11 | 1955 | 10 | 22.02 |

## CUSPS

| Year | Day | Time  | Year | Day | Time  |
|------|-----|-------|------|-----|-------|
| 1956 | 11  | 04.12 | 1989 | 10  | 15.14 |
| 1957 | 10  | 10.13 | 1990 | 10  | 21.28 |
| 1958 | 10  | 16.28 | 1991 | 11  | 03.42 |
| 1959 | 10  | 22.34 | 1992 | 11  | 09.41 |
| 1960 | 11  | 04.39 | 1993 | 10  | 15.53 |
| 1961 | 10  | 10.56 | 1994 | 10  | 21.59 |
| 1962 | 10  | 17.04 | 1995 | 11  | 04.05 |
| 1963 | 10  | 23.18 | 1996 | 11  | 10.22 |
| 1964 | 11  | 05.30 | 1997 | 10  | 16.28 |
| 1965 | 10  | 11.29 | 1998 | 10  | 22.44 |
| 1966 | 10  | 17.46 | 1999 | 11  | 05.00 |
| 1967 | 10  | 23.56 | 2000 | 11  | 10.58 |
| 1968 | 11  | 05.58 | 2001 | 10  | 17.10 |
| 1969 | 10  | 12.12 | 2002 | 10  | 23.31 |
| 1970 | 10  | 18.14 | 2003 | 11  | 05.25 |
| 1971 | 11  | 00.24 | 2004 | 11  | 11.40 |
| 1972 | 11  | 06.40 | 2005 | 10  | 17.41 |
| 1973 | 10  | 12.42 | 2006 | 10  | 23.51 |
| 1974 | 10  | 19.02 | 2007 | 11  | 06.07 |
| 1975 | 11  | 01.14 | 2008 | 11  | 12.08 |
| 1976 | 11  | 07.14 | 2009 | 10  | 18.24 |
| 1977 | 10  | 13.28 | 2010 | 11  | 00.37 |
| 1978 | 10  | 19.33 | 2011 | 11  | 06.41 |
| 1979 | 11  | 01.43 | 2012 | 11  | 12.54 |
| 1980 | 11  | 07.57 | 2013 | 10  | 18.58 |
| 1981 | 10  | 13.56 | 2014 | 11  | 01.09 |
| 1982 | 10  | 20.09 | 2015 | 11  | 07.25 |
| 1983 | 11  | 02.21 | 2016 | 11  | 13.25 |
| 1984 | 11  | 08.22 | 2017 | 10  | 19.34 |
| 1985 | 10  | 14.41 | 2018 | 11  | 01.45 |
| 1986 | 10  | 20.51 | 2019 | 11  | 07.49 |
| 1987 | 11  | 03.01 | 2020 | 11  | 14.04 |
| 1988 | 11  | 09.14 |      |     |       |

## Shravana
### 23 January to 6 February

| Year | Day | Time  | Year | Day | Time  |
|------|-----|-------|------|-----|-------|
| 1920 | 24  | 00.48 | 1952 | 24  | 05.53 |
| 1921 | 23  | 06.59 | 1953 | 23  | 11.58 |
| 1922 | 23  | 13.09 | 1954 | 23  | 18.11 |
| 1923 | 23  | 19.13 | 1955 | 24  | 00.18 |
| 1924 | 24  | 01.26 | 1956 | 24  | 06.27 |
| 1925 | 23  | 07.32 | 1957 | 23  | 12.36 |
| 1926 | 23  | 13.45 | 1958 | 23  | 18.42 |
| 1927 | 23  | 20.04 | 1959 | 24  | 00.53 |
| 1928 | 24  | 02.06 | 1960 | 24  | 06.59 |
| 1929 | 23  | 08.15 | 1961 | 23  | 13.08 |
| 1930 | 23  | 14.27 | 1962 | 23  | 19.25 |
| 1931 | 23  | 20.32 | 1963 | 24  | 01.36 |
| 1932 | 24  | 02.45 | 1964 | 24  | 07.44 |
| 1933 | 23  | 08.51 | 1965 | 23  | 13.53 |
| 1934 | 23  | 14.58 | 1966 | 23  | 20.01 |
| 1935 | 23  | 21.12 | 1967 | 24  | 02.13 |
| 1936 | 24  | 03.13 | 1968 | 24  | 08.20 |
| 1937 | 23  | 09.24 | 1969 | 23  | 14.25 |
| 1938 | 23  | 15.41 | 1970 | 23  | 20.35 |
| 1939 | 23  | 21.49 | 1971 | 24  | 02.43 |
| 1940 | 24  | 04.03 | 1972 | 24  | 08.51 |
| 1941 | 23  | 10.09 | 1973 | 23  | 15.03 |
| 1942 | 23  | 16.16 | 1974 | 23  | 21.17 |
| 1943 | 23  | 22.31 | 1975 | 24  | 03.30 |
| 1944 | 24  | 04.34 | 1976 | 24  | 09.37 |
| 1945 | 23  | 10.41 | 1977 | 23  | 15.42 |
| 1946 | 23  | 16.53 | 1978 | 23  | 21.53 |
| 1947 | 23  | 22.57 | 1979 | 24  | 04.04 |
| 1948 | 24  | 05.07 | 1980 | 24  | 10.10 |
| 1949 | 23  | 11.18 | 1981 | 23  | 16.18 |
| 1950 | 23  | 17.30 | 1982 | 23  | 22.28 |
| 1951 | 23  | 23.47 | 1983 | 24  | 04.35 |

## CUSPS

| Year | Day | Time | Year | Day | Time |
|---|---|---|---|---|---|
| 1984 | 24 | 10.44 | 2003 | 24 | 07.48 |
| 1985 | 23 | 16.54 | 2004 | 24 | 13.55 |
| 1986 | 23 | 23.07 | 2005 | 23 | 19.59 |
| 1987 | 24 | 05.22 | 2006 | 24 | 02.14 |
| 1988 | 24 | 11.27 | 2007 | 24 | 08.19 |
| 1989 | 23 | 17.35 | 2008 | 24 | 14.27 |
| 1990 | 23 | 23.48 | 2009 | 23 | 20.42 |
| 1991 | 24 | 05.55 | 2010 | 24 | 02.51 |
| 1992 | 24 | 12.03 | 2011 | 24 | 09.04 |
| 1993 | 23 | 18.10 | 2012 | 24 | 15.11 |
| 1994 | 24 | 00.16 | 2013 | 23 | 21.15 |
| 1995 | 24 | 06.27 | 2014 | 24 | 03.32 |
| 1996 | 24 | 12.34 | 2015 | 24 | 09.39 |
| 1997 | 23 | 18.45 | 2016 | 24 | 15.44 |
| 1998 | 24 | 01.04 | 2017 | 23 | 21.55 |
| 1999 | 24 | 07.13 | 2018 | 24 | 03.59 |
| 2000 | 24 | 13.20 | 2019 | 24 | 10.10 |
| 2001 | 23 | 19.28 | 2020 | 24 | 16.20 |
| 2002 | 24 | 01.36 | | | |

### Dhanishta
#### 5 February to 19 February

| Year | Day | Time | Year | Day | Time |
|---|---|---|---|---|---|
| 1920 | 6 | 04.00 | 1931 | 5 | 23.45 |
| 1921 | 5 | 10.10 | 1932 | 6 | 05.54 |
| 1922 | 5 | 16.15 | 1933 | 5 | 11.57 |
| 1923 | 5 | 22.27 | 1934 | 5 | 18.13 |
| 1924 | 6 | 04.33 | 1935 | 6 | 00.19 |
| 1925 | 5 | 10.39 | 1936 | 6 | 06.21 |
| 1926 | 5 | 16.58 | 1937 | 5 | 12.36 |
| 1927 | 5 | 23.09 | 1938 | 5 | 18.45 |
| 1928 | 6 | 05.16 | 1939 | 6 | 01.00 |
| 1929 | 5 | 11.28 | 1940 | 6 | 07.13 |
| 1930 | 5 | 17.33 | 1941 | 5 | 13.14 |

# CUSPS

| Year | Day | Time | Year | Day | Time |
|---|---|---|---|---|---|
| 1942 | 5 | 19.31 | 1977 | 5 | 18.55 |
| 1943 | 6 | 01.39 | 1978 | 6 | 01.05 |
| 1944 | 6 | 07.41 | 1979 | 6 | 07.08 |
| 1945 | 5 | 13.56 | 1980 | 6 | 13.24 |
| 1946 | 5 | 20.00 | 1981 | 5 | 19.26 |
| 1947 | 6 | 02.08 | 1982 | 6 | 01.37 |
| 1948 | 6 | 08.19 | 1983 | 6 | 07.50 |
| 1949 | 5 | 14.22 | 1984 | 6 | 13.48 |
| 1950 | 5 | 20.42 | 1985 | 5 | 20.03 |
| 1951 | 6 | 02.56 | 1986 | 6 | 02.19 |
| 1952 | 6 | 08.58 | 1987 | 6 | 08.26 |
| 1953 | 5 | 15.13 | 1988 | 6 | 14.40 |
| 1954 | 5 | 21.18 | 1989 | 5 | 20.44 |
| 1955 | 6 | 03.27 | 1990 | 6 | 02.55 |
| 1956 | 6 | 09.39 | 1991 | 6 | 09.10 |
| 1957 | 5 | 15.41 | 1992 | 6 | 15.09 |
| 1958 | 5 | 21.55 | 1993 | 5 | 21.20 |
| 1959 | 6 | 04.04 | 1994 | 6 | 03.31 |
| 1960 | 6 | 10.03 | 1995 | 6 | 09.31 |
| 1961 | 5 | 16.21 | 1996 | 6 | 15.46 |
| 1962 | 5 | 22.32 | 1997 | 5 | 21.55 |
| 1963 | 6 | 04.42 | 1998 | 6 | 04.09 |
| 1964 | 6 | 10.58 | 1999 | 6 | 10.27 |
| 1965 | 5 | 16.58 | 2000 | 6 | 16.27 |
| 1966 | 5 | 23.12 | 2001 | 5 | 22.37 |
| 1967 | 6 | 05.25 | 2002 | 6 | 04.51 |
| 1968 | 6 | 11.24 | 2003 | 6 | 10.52 |
| 1969 | 5 | 17.38 | 2004 | 6 | 17.05 |
| 1970 | 5 | 23.46 | 2005 | 5 | 23.12 |
| 1971 | 6 | 05.48 | 2006 | 6 | 05.19 |
| 1972 | 6 | 12.04 | 2007 | 6 | 11.33 |
| 1973 | 5 | 18.08 | 2008 | 6 | 17.35 |
| 1974 | 6 | 00.26 | 2009 | 5 | 23.47 |
| 1975 | 6 | 06.43 | 2010 | 6 | 06.05 |
| 1976 | 6 | 12.42 | 2011 | 6 | 12.09 |

# CUSPS

| Year | Day | Time  | Year | Day | Time  |
|------|-----|-------|------|-----|-------|
| 2012 | 6   | 18.20 | 2017 | 6   | 01.01 |
| 2013 | 6   | 00.29 | 2018 | 6   | 07.14 |
| 2014 | 6   | 06.36 | 2019 | 6   | 13.16 |
| 2015 | 6   | 12.51 | 2020 | 6   | 19.26 |
| 2016 | 6   | 18.54 |      |     |       |

## Shatabhishak
### 19 February to 5 March

| Year | Day | Time  | Year | Day | Time  |
|------|-----|-------|------|-----|-------|
| 1920 | 19  | 08.30 | 1945 | 18  | 18.23 |
| 1921 | 18  | 14.39 | 1946 | 19  | 00.36 |
| 1922 | 18  | 20.53 | 1947 | 19  | 06.40 |
| 1923 | 19  | 02.55 | 1948 | 19  | 12.46 |
| 1924 | 19  | 09.04 | 1949 | 18  | 18.58 |
| 1925 | 18  | 15.14 | 1950 | 19  | 01.10 |
| 1926 | 18  | 21.24 | 1951 | 19  | 07.25 |
| 1927 | 19  | 03.43 | 1952 | 19  | 13.34 |
| 1928 | 19  | 09.48 | 1953 | 18  | 19.40 |
| 1929 | 18  | 15.56 | 1954 | 19  | 01.52 |
| 1930 | 18  | 22.11 | 1955 | 19  | 07.59 |
| 1931 | 19  | 04.14 | 1956 | 19  | 14.05 |
| 1932 | 19  | 10.23 | 1957 | 18  | 20.17 |
| 1933 | 18  | 16.34 | 1958 | 19  | 02.26 |
| 1934 | 18  | 22.41 | 1959 | 19  | 08.33 |
| 1935 | 19  | 04.52 | 1960 | 19  | 14.39 |
| 1936 | 19  | 10.55 | 1961 | 18  | 20.47 |
| 1937 | 18  | 17.02 | 1962 | 19  | 03.03 |
| 1938 | 18  | 23.20 | 1963 | 19  | 09.16 |
| 1939 | 19  | 05.29 | 1964 | 19  | 15.24 |
| 1940 | 19  | 11.41 | 1965 | 18  | 21.34 |
| 1941 | 18  | 17.51 | 1966 | 19  | 03.45 |
| 1942 | 18  | 23.59 | 1967 | 19  | 09.52 |
| 1943 | 19  | 06.11 | 1968 | 19  | 16.00 |
| 1944 | 19  | 12.16 | 1969 | 18  | 22.07 |

## CUSPS

| Year | Day | Time | Year | Day | Time |
|------|-----|------|------|-----|------|
| 1970 | 19 | 04.17 | 1996 | 19 | 20.14 |
| 1971 | 19 | 10.24 | 1997 | 19 | 02.23 |
| 1972 | 19 | 16.30 | 1998 | 19 | 08.44 |
| 1973 | 18 | 22.40 | 1999 | 19 | 14.53 |
| 1974 | 19 | 04.58 | 2000 | 19 | 20.59 |
| 1975 | 19 | 11.08 | 2001 | 19 | 03.11 |
| 1976 | 19 | 17.17 | 2002 | 19 | 09.17 |
| 1977 | 18 | 23.26 | 2003 | 19 | 15.25 |
| 1978 | 19 | 05.34 | 2004 | 19 | 21.36 |
| 1979 | 19 | 11.44 | 2005 | 19 | 03.40 |
| 1980 | 19 | 17.50 | 2006 | 19 | 09.55 |
| 1981 | 18 | 23.59 | 2007 | 19 | 16.01 |
| 1982 | 19 | 06.12 | 2008 | 19 | 22.04 |
| 1983 | 19 | 12.16 | 2009 | 19 | 04.22 |
| 1984 | 19 | 18.22 | 2010 | 19 | 10.31 |
| 1985 | 19 | 00.34 | 2011 | 19 | 16.42 |
| 1986 | 19 | 06.46 | 2012 | 19 | 22.53 |
| 1987 | 19 | 13.00 | 2013 | 19 | 04.56 |
| 1988 | 19 | 19.07 | 2014 | 19 | 11.12 |
| 1989 | 19 | 01.15 | 2015 | 19 | 17.20 |
| 1990 | 19 | 07.30 | 2016 | 19 | 23.22 |
| 1991 | 19 | 13.36 | 2017 | 19 | 05.37 |
| 1992 | 19 | 19.42 | 2018 | 19 | 11.41 |
| 1993 | 19 | 01.53 | 2019 | 19 | 17.47 |
| 1994 | 19 | 07.59 | 2020 | 19 | 23.58 |
| 1995 | 19 | 14.06 | | | |

### Purva Bhadra
### 3 to 18 March

| Year | Day | Time | Year | Day | Time |
|------|-----|------|------|-----|------|
| 1920 | 3 | 14.49 | 1924 | 3 | 15.25 |
| 1921 | 3 | 21.03 | 1925 | 3 | 21.29 |
| 1922 | 4 | 03.10 | 1926 | 4 | 03.48 |
| 1923 | 4 | 09.17 | 1927 | 4 | 09.59 |

## CUSPS

| Year | Day | Time | Year | Day | Time |
| --- | --- | --- | --- | --- | --- |
| 1928 | 3 | 16.05 | 1963 | 4 | 15.29 |
| 1929 | 3 | 22.22 | 1964 | 3 | 21.47 |
| 1930 | 4 | 04.28 | 1965 | 4 | 03.53 |
| 1931 | 4 | 10.34 | 1966 | 4 | 10.03 |
| 1932 | 3 | 16.46 | 1967 | 4 | 16.16 |
| 1933 | 3 | 22.49 | 1968 | 3 | 22.14 |
| 1934 | 4 | 05.05 | 1969 | 4 | 04.28 |
| 1935 | 4 | 11.13 | 1970 | 4 | 10.40 |
| 1936 | 3 | 17.11 | 1971 | 4 | 16.37 |
| 1937 | 3 | 23.27 | 1972 | 3 | 22.52 |
| 1938 | 4 | 05.36 | 1973 | 4 | 04.59 |
| 1939 | 4 | 11.46 | 1974 | 4 | 11.12 |
| 1940 | 3 | 18.03 | 1975 | 4 | 17.31 |
| 1941 | 4 | 00.07 | 1976 | 3 | 23.33 |
| 1942 | 4 | 06.22 | 1977 | 4 | 05.45 |
| 1943 | 4 | 12.32 | 1978 | 4 | 11.59 |
| 1944 | 3 | 18.31 | 1979 | 4 | 17.58 |
| 1945 | 4 | 00.47 | 1980 | 4 | 00.12 |
| 1946 | 4 | 06.55 | 1981 | 4 | 06.20 |
| 1947 | 4 | 12.57 | 1982 | 4 | 12.27 |
| 1948 | 3 | 19.10 | 1983 | 4 | 18.40 |
| 1949 | 4 | 01.13 | 1984 | 4 | 00.38 |
| 1950 | 4 | 07.30 | 1985 | 4 | 06.50 |
| 1951 | 4 | 13.46 | 1986 | 4 | 13.09 |
| 1952 | 3 | 19.48 | 1987 | 4 | 19.13 |
| 1953 | 4 | 02.04 | 1988 | 4 | 01.27 |
| 1954 | 4 | 08.13 | 1989 | 4 | 07.38 |
| 1955 | 4 | 14.15 | 1990 | 4 | 13.44 |
| 1956 | 3 | 20.29 | 1991 | 4 | 19.58 |
| 1957 | 4 | 02.34 | 1992 | 4 | 02.00 |
| 1958 | 4 | 08.45 | 1993 | 4 | 08.09 |
| 1959 | 4 | 14.56 | 1994 | 4 | 14.24 |
| 1960 | 3 | 20.53 | 1995 | 4 | 20.21 |
| 1961 | 4 | 03.09 | 1996 | 4 | 02.32 |
| 1962 | 4 | 09.23 | 1997 | 4 | 08.45 |

# CUSPS

| Year | Day | Time | Year | Day | Time |
|---|---|---|---|---|---|
| 1998 | 4 | 14.56 | 2010 | 4 | 16.53 |
| 1999 | 4 | 21.14 | 2011 | 4 | 22.58 |
| 2000 | 4 | 03.18 | 2012 | 4 | 05.08 |
| 2001 | 4 | 09.27 | 2013 | 4 | 11.21 |
| 2002 | 4 | 15.42 | 2014 | 4 | 17.27 |
| 2003 | 4 | 21.41 | 2015 | 4 | 23.37 |
| 2004 | 4 | 03.52 | 2016 | 4 | 05.44 |
| 2005 | 4 | 10.04 | 2017 | 4 | 11.51 |
| 2006 | 4 | 16.10 | 2018 | 4 | 18.04 |
| 2007 | 4 | 22.20 | 2019 | 5 | 00.05 |
| 2008 | 4 | 04.25 | 2020 | 4 | 06.11 |
| 2009 | 4 | 10.35 |  |  |  |

## Uttara Bhadra
### 16 to 31 March

| Year | Day | Time | Year | Day | Time |
|---|---|---|---|---|---|
| 1920 | 16 | 23.21 | 1938 | 17 | 14.07 |
| 1921 | 17 | 05.28 | 1939 | 17 | 20.15 |
| 1922 | 17 | 11.44 | 1940 | 17 | 02.26 |
| 1923 | 17 | 17.45 | 1941 | 17 | 08.40 |
| 1924 | 16 | 23.51 | 1942 | 17 | 14.50 |
| 1925 | 17 | 06.04 | 1943 | 17 | 20.57 |
| 1926 | 17 | 12.12 | 1944 | 17 | 03.04 |
| 1927 | 17 | 18.27 | 1945 | 17 | 09.12 |
| 1928 | 17 | 00.36 | 1946 | 17 | 15.25 |
| 1929 | 17 | 06.46 | 1947 | 17 | 21.29 |
| 1930 | 17 | 13.02 | 1948 | 17 | 03.33 |
| 1931 | 17 | 19.04 | 1949 | 17 | 09.46 |
| 1932 | 17 | 01.10 | 1950 | 17 | 15.58 |
| 1933 | 17 | 07.24 | 1951 | 17 | 22.09 |
| 1934 | 17 | 13.32 | 1952 | 17 | 04.20 |
| 1935 | 17 | 19.40 | 1953 | 17 | 10.30 |
| 1936 | 17 | 01.44 | 1954 | 17 | 16.41 |
| 1937 | 17 | 07.51 | 1955 | 17 | 22.47 |

## CUSPS

| Year | Day | Time  | Year | Day | Time  |
|------|-----|-------|------|-----|-------|
| 1956 | 17  | 04.52 | 1989 | 17  | 16.02 |
| 1957 | 17  | 11.04 | 1990 | 17  | 22.17 |
| 1958 | 17  | 17.16 | 1991 | 18  | 04.22 |
| 1959 | 17  | 23.20 | 1992 | 17  | 10.26 |
| 1960 | 17  | 05.26 | 1993 | 17  | 16.42 |
| 1961 | 17  | 11.36 | 1994 | 17  | 22.47 |
| 1962 | 17  | 17.48 | 1995 | 18  | 04.51 |
| 1963 | 18  | 00.00 | 1996 | 17  | 11.01 |
| 1964 | 17  | 06.10 | 1997 | 17  | 17.08 |
| 1965 | 17  | 12.22 | 1998 | 17  | 23.26 |
| 1966 | 17  | 18.35 | 1999 | 18  | 05.38 |
| 1967 | 18  | 00.39 | 2000 | 17  | 11.43 |
| 1968 | 17  | 06.46 | 2001 | 17  | 18.00 |
| 1969 | 17  | 12.57 | 2002 | 18  | 00.05 |
| 1970 | 17  | 19.05 | 2003 | 18  | 06.08 |
| 1971 | 18  | 01.10 | 2004 | 17  | 12.21 |
| 1972 | 17  | 07.17 | 2005 | 17  | 18.26 |
| 1973 | 17  | 12.25 | 2006 | 18  | 00.40 |
| 1974 | 17  | 19.43 | 2007 | 18  | 06.47 |
| 1975 | 18  | 01.52 | 2008 | 17  | 12.48 |
| 1976 | 17  | 08.02 | 2009 | 17  | 19.07 |
| 1977 | 17  | 14.16 | 2010 | 18  | 01.16 |
| 1978 | 17  | 20.23 | 2011 | 18  | 07.23 |
| 1979 | 18  | 02.30 | 2012 | 17  | 13.39 |
| 1980 | 17  | 08.38 | 2013 | 17  | 19.44 |
| 1981 | 17  | 14.46 | 2014 | 18  | 01.56 |
| 1982 | 17  | 21.00 | 2015 | 18  | 08.05 |
| 1983 | 18  | 03.03 | 2016 | 17  | 14.06 |
| 1984 | 17  | 09.07 | 2017 | 17  | 20.23 |
| 1985 | 17  | 15.21 | 2018 | 18  | 02.30 |
| 1986 | 17  | 21.31 | 2019 | 18  | 08.29 |
| 1987 | 18  | 03.42 | 2020 | 17  | 14.42 |
| 1988 | 17  | 09.53 |      |     |       |

## CUSPS

### Revati
### 30 March to 13 April

| Year | Day | Time | Year | Day | Time |
|------|-----|------|------|-----|------|
| 1920 | 30 | 10.10 | 1952 | 30 | 15.07 |
| 1921 | 30 | 16.27 | 1953 | 30 | 21.24 |
| 1922 | 30 | 22.35 | 1954 | 31 | 03.37 |
| 1923 | 31 | 04.37 | 1955 | 31 | 09.33 |
| 1924 | 30 | 10.48 | 1956 | 30 | 15.47 |
| 1925 | 30 | 16.52 | 1957 | 30 | 21.56 |
| 1926 | 30 | 23.07 | 1958 | 31 | 04.04 |
| 1927 | 31 | 05.19 | 1959 | 31 | 10.17 |
| 1928 | 30 | 11.23 | 1960 | 30 | 16.15 |
| 1929 | 30 | 17.44 | 1961 | 30 | 22.28 |
| 1930 | 30 | 23.53 | 1962 | 31 | 04.44 |
| 1931 | 31 | 05.54 | 1963 | 31 | 10.45 |
| 1932 | 30 | 12.08 | 1964 | 30 | 17.03 |
| 1933 | 30 | 18.13 | 1965 | 30 | 23.16 |
| 1934 | 31 | 00.26 | 1966 | 31 | 05.22 |
| 1935 | 31 | 06.36 | 1967 | 31 | 11.35 |
| 1936 | 30 | 12.32 | 1968 | 30 | 17.35 |
| 1937 | 30 | 18.48 | 1969 | 30 | 23.47 |
| 1938 | 31 | 00.59 | 1970 | 31 | 06.01 |
| 1939 | 31 | 07.01 | 1971 | 31 | 11.57 |
| 1940 | 30 | 13.21 | 1972 | 30 | 18.09 |
| 1941 | 30 | 19.29 | 1973 | 31 | 00.20 |
| 1942 | 31 | 01.42 | 1974 | 31 | 06.28 |
| 1943 | 31 | 07.53 | 1975 | 31 | 12.46 |
| 1944 | 30 | 13.51 | 1976 | 30 | 18.52 |
| 1945 | 30 | 20.08 | 1977 | 31 | 01.05 |
| 1946 | 31 | 02.19 | 1978 | 31 | 07.20 |
| 1947 | 31 | 08.17 | 1979 | 31 | 13.17 |
| 1948 | 30 | 14.31 | 1980 | 30 | 19.28 |
| 1949 | 30 | 20.37 | 1981 | 31 | 01.42 |
| 1950 | 31 | 02.48 | 1982 | 31 | 07.46 |
| 1951 | 31 | 09.04 | 1983 | 31 | 13.57 |

# CUSPS

| Year | Day | Time  | Year | Day | Time  |
|------|-----|-------|------|-----|-------|
| 1984 | 30  | 19.59 | 2003 | 31  | 16.58 |
| 1985 | 31  | 02.08 | 2004 | 30  | 23.07 |
| 1986 | 31  | 08.26 | 2005 | 31  | 05.22 |
| 1987 | 31  | 14.28 | 2006 | 31  | 11.28 |
| 1988 | 30  | 20.41 | 2007 | 31  | 17.36 |
| 1989 | 31  | 02.58 | 2008 | 30  | 23.43 |
| 1990 | 31  | 09.03 | 2009 | 31  | 05.52 |
| 1991 | 31  | 15.14 | 2010 | 31  | 12.07 |
| 1992 | 30  | 21.19 | 2011 | 31  | 18.13 |
| 1993 | 31  | 03.28 | 2012 | 31  | 00.23 |
| 1994 | 31  | 09.43 | 2013 | 31  | 06.40 |
| 1995 | 31  | 15.41 | 2014 | 31  | 12.45 |
| 1996 | 30  | 21.48 | 2015 | 31  | 18.52 |
| 1997 | 31  | 04.04 | 2016 | 31  | 01.01 |
| 1998 | 31  | 10.12 | 2017 | 31  | 07.09 |
| 1999 | 31  | 16.27 | 2018 | 31  | 13.20 |
| 2000 | 30  | 22.37 | 2019 | 31  | 19.22 |
| 2001 | 31  | 04.46 | 2020 | 31  | 01.26 |
| 2002 | 31  | 11.00 |      |     |       |